A Garland Series

OUTSTANDING THESES
IN THE FINE ARTS
from

British
Universities

Graphic Journalism in England During the 1830s and 1840s

Celina Fox

Garland Publishing, Inc., New York & London

1988

Copyright © 1988
by Celina Fox
All rights reserved

All volumes in this series are printed
on acid-free, 250-year-life paper.

Library of Congress Cataloging-in-Publication Data
Fox, Celina.
Graphic journalism in England during the 1830s and 1840s / Celina Fox.
p. cm.—(Outstanding theses in the fine arts from British universities)
Originally presented as the author's thesis (doctoral)—University of Oxford, 1974.
Bibliography: p.
ISBN 0-8240-0098-6
1. English newspapers—Illustrations—History—19th century.
2. Magazine illustration—19th century—England. 3. Illustrated periodicals—England—History—19th century. 4. Press—England—History—19th century. I. Title. II. Series.
NC970.F68 1988
741.65'0942—dc19   87-28416

Printed in the United States of America

GRAPHIC JOURNALISM IN ENGLAND DURING THE 1830s AND 1840s

BY

CELINA FOX
ST. ANTONY'S COLLEGE, OXFORD

THESIS SUBMITTED TO THE FACULTY OF MODERN HISTORY IN THE
UNIVERSITY OF OXFORD FOR THE DEGREE OF DOCTOR OF PHILOSOPHY
TRINITY TERM 1974

CONTENTS

I	Introduction: The Status of Graphic Art	1
II	The Condition of Wood Engraving 1830 - 1850	26
III	The Development of Political Caricature 1830 - 1836	73
IV	The Freedom of the Press 1830 - 1836	120
V	From Cheap Politics to Cheap Fiction 1836 - 1846	172
VI	Punch and its Rivals 1841 - 1850	214
VII	The Illustration of News 1840 - 1850	266
VIII	Conclusion	314
	Bibliography	322
	Illustrations	345

INTRODUCTION

THE STATUS OF GRAPHIC ART

I

The status of art during the early nineteenth century in England emerged from a tradition whose principal features had been established by academic theory. In order to comprehend the status of graphic journalism during the period 1830 to 1850, it is necessary first to examine this wider context. Sir Joshua Reynolds' Discourses on Art (1769-90), which provided the most illustrious example of the English interpretation of Franco-Italian seventeenth century theory, rested on a belief in the moral benefits bestowed through the cultivation of art; the painter 'instead of endeavouring to amuse mankind with the minute neatness of his imitations, ... must endeavour to improve them by the grandeur of his ideas'.[1] Reynolds used the auspicious occasion of the opening of the Royal Academy at Somerset House in 1780, when he was at the height of his career, to deliver his inspiring ninth Discourse and promote the status of his profession: 'Whatever abstracts the thoughts from sensual gratifications, whatever teaches us to look for happiness within ourselves, must advance in some measure the dignity of our nature'. Furthermore, the artist had an even more glorious mission than the salvation of individual souls:-

> The estimation in which we stand in respect to our neighbours, will be in proportion to the degree in which we excel or are inferior to them in the acquisition of intellectual excellence, of which trade and its consequential riches must be acknowledged to give the means; but a people whose whole attention is absorbed in those means, and who forget the end, can aspire but little above the rank of a barbarous nation.[2]

This then was the ideal relationship between artist and society. Patronage of the highest type of art would lead the people through

---

1. Reynolds, Discourse III (1770).
2. Reynolds, Discourse IX (1780).

'contemplation of universal rectitude and harmony' to virtue. Furthermore, prestige would accrue to the country in the eyes of other countries. Reynolds, having toyed with mercantilist theories which recognized the intimate connection between the nation's art, wealth and trade, assigned the latter to a lower shelf: 'If it has an origin no higher, no taste can ever be formed in manufactures; but if the higher arts of design flourish, these inferior ends will be answered of course'.[1]

Reynolds' Discourses were in part a reply to those critics who sought to devalue the position of painting compared with that of poetry, who believed that poetry and rhetoric alone had the power to express ideas, stimulate the imagination and raise powerful emotions. Edmund Burke, in his Philosophical Enquiry into the Origin of Our Ideas of the Sublime and Beautiful (1757) distinguished between clearness and obscurity, attributing the latter characteristic not only to despotic governments and religions founded on fear, but also to some verbal descriptions. In contrast, clarity was the characteristic of painting:-

> In reality, poetry and rhetoric do not succeed in exact description so well as painting does; their business is to affect rather by sympathy than imitation; to display rather the effect of things on the mind of the speaker, or of others, than to present a clear idea of the things themselves.[2]

Reynolds rebutted Burke's implication that art was merely mechanical imitation appealing to the eye rather than the mind by insisting that both poet and painter could work upon the passions and affectations of the mind; they differed only as to the means.[3] And some of Reynolds'

---

1. Reynolds, Discourse I (1769).

2. Burke, Philosophical Enquiry, ed. and introd. J. T. Boulton (1958), p.172.

3. Reynolds, Discourse VIII (1778). Burke later showed more sympathy with Reynolds' view of painting as a literate and liberal profession, an art working rather by sympathy than by exact description, in his Letter to a Noble Lord (1795).

followers took his argument to even greater lengths. The Reverend Robert Anthony Bromley, author of A Philosophical and Critical History of the Fine Arts (1793) argued in favour of the advantages of painting, 'in an improved state, over all other modes of writing', in scope, force, dignity and universality of instruction. Compared with writing, which could only be appreciated in progressive stages, the fine arts could be taken in at once, thus gaining in force and dignity. Painting was 'intelligible to all in every country, and in every period of time', because Nature had given us a common sensibility, passions and feelings which all could recognize.[1]

The terms of the debate - instruction or amusement, elevation or narrow imitation, the ideal or the mechanical, universality through unadorned exactitude of description or through recognition of our common humanity - were bequeathed to the nineteenth century and were tossed around as verbal tags among the leading participants at every level of artistic involvement. Unfortunately, the principal object to which these sentiments were attached, namely history painting, was in a sorry state in England during the first half of the century. Sir Martin Archer Shee bemoaned the fate of English history painting in his Rhymes on Art (1805). All patriotic interest in the cultivation of British genius appeared to be at an end. He came to the conclusion that only the state could retrieve it from the doldrums, as the civilisations of Greece and Rome had done, France under Louis XIV and as even Russia was doing now. It was a mistake to conceive that the arts:

> left to the influence of ordinary events, turned loose upon society, to fight and scramble, in the rude and revolting contest of coarser occupations, can ever arrive at that perfection which contributes so materially to the permanent glory of a state.[2]

---

1. Bromley, Philosophical and Critical Inquiry, i. 21-23.
2. Shee, Rhymes on Art, p.xx-xxi.

Shee reiterated Reynolds' arguments, though without the latter's confidence in their inevitable victory. Shee argued at a time of war, when he felt beleaguered by what he termed 'a commercial as well as a political jacobinism.' He countered the laissez-faire attitudes and principles of free trade propagated by Adam Smith, which argued against any special consideration being made by the state to look after the arts and thus interfere with the market forces of supply and demand, with the view that the principles of art and those of trade were incompatible:

> With those who would leave the arts, unassisted, to find their level in society; who consult Adam Smith for their theory of taste as well as of trade; and would regulate the operation of virtù on the principles of the pin manufactory; with all those, in short, to whom this world is but one vast market - a saleshop of sordid interests and selfish gratifications, arguments drawn from the importance of the arts as objects of taste and refinement, will have little weight.[1]

Shee was fighting for the position of art to be seen on the summit of civilisation not dependent on the low wants and caprices of millions, and for the reservation of, what he admitted to be, ' a few old fashioned sentiments in this general sale of our faculties and understandings; let us, if possible, keep some few spots dry in this commercial deluge, upon which wit, and taste, and genius, may repose'.[2]

However, the awakening of government concern in the fine arts owed as much to commerce as to old fashioned sentiment. The relationship between art and industry, the necessity of encouraging both the 'highest branches of poetical design' and the 'lowest connexion between design and manufactures' was first brought to public notice in the Select Committee on Arts and Manufactures of 1835-1836. It was appointed to inquire into 'the best means of extending a knowledge of the ARTS and of the PRINCIPLES of DESIGN among the People (especially the Manufacturing Population) of the Country', as

---

1. Shee, <u>Rhymes on Art</u>, p.xx-xxi.
2. <u>Ibid</u>.

well as to examine the existing institutions connected with the Arts, namely the National Gallery and the Royal Academy. The committee exposed a lack of faith in the products and designs of British manufacturers compared with those of the French, and a low standard of taste in the community at large, which needed to be remedied. What was required was art education for the whole country 'from the prince to the mechanic'. The rot began at the highest level with indiscriminate private patronage, and the neglect of art by the ' aristocracy' in their public schools and universities. This was seen to be matched by an equal want of study and education in the arts amongst manufacturers who produced fabrics and goods requiring applied design. Finally, there existed a total lack of discrimination throughout the general public. Thus the designs in demand would, 'in the nature of things, always be of the least tasteful description; that is to say, till the bulk of mankind are much more cultivated than they now are, or are likely soon to be'.[1]

The remedy for this absence of art and design from the supply-demand cycle was seen by the committee to take the shape of a general diffusion process. Education of a specifically practical nature would increase the means of applying art to the manufactures of the country and extend the scope of employment, while elementary art education would increase the demand for goods which exhibited a high level of quality in design. Exhibitions would, through good practice and emulation, lead to 'improved taste in the public and an improved capability on the part of the working man', stimulating invention. Casts, paintings, works of proportion and beauty - for scientific improvements in machinery depended, it was thought, on the perfection of form in construction - 'everything in short which exhibits in combination the efforts of the artist and workman' - should be shown in free

---

1. Parl. Papers 1835, v (598), pp.46, 120, 130: minutes of evidence qus. 670, 1598, 1721. Parl. Papers 1836, ix (568), pp.24-26: minutes of evidence qus. 245, 270.

galleries, or perhaps in rooms connected with factories. One class of mechanics always knew others and improvements would spread swiftly from one department to another. Thus, the supply of art would in its turn create a demand for art, and the demand for art would in its turn create a supply of art. Finally, to seal the contract with the academic blessing, this creation of a new taste would greatly improve the morals of the country.[1]

Despite the predictably pessimistic view of manufacture taken before the committee by Shee, (whose family later condemned the whole proceedings, detecting 'a strong bias in favour of the Benthamite heresy combined to develop the most offensive form of utilitarian dogmatism, in all matters of political or administrative discussion'),[2] it was clear, the committee believed, that the government should intervene on every level that would encourage the 'development and extension of art', though neither control its action nor force its cultivation. State patronage would serve the end of national status, under pressure from economic necessity:

> Our national greatness rests on the skilled industry of our people; it must be a part of sound domestic policy to foster, by every means within our reach, the talent which gives currency and importance to our indigenous products, and draws within the vortex of British manufacture the raw material of other climes, to be spread again over the world, enhanced in value by the labour, skill and taste of British artisans.[3]

The committee report recommended the establishment of a Normal School of Design, the formation of open public galleries or museums of art, and that the principles of design should be part of any permanent system of elementary education.

It is within this context that we must understand the growth of illustrated journalism during the period 1830 to 1850. The role of the

1. Parl. Papers 1835, v (598), p.130: minutes of evidence, qus. 1724-7.
   Parl. Papers 1836, ix (568), p.31: minutes of evidence, qu. 330.
2. Parl. Papers 1836, ix (568), p.162: minutes of evidence qus. 1973-4.
   M.A. Shee, Life of Sir Martin Archer Shee (1860), ii. 47.
3. Parl. Papers 1835, v (598), p.116: minutes of evidence qu.1566.

print as the popularizer of art had long been recognized; as John Pye, the engraver, pointed out, its very essence was 'expansion and diffusion'.[1] How much this quality had been enhanced by the development of wood engraving in the 1830's, which could be printed by machine in large quantities, was stressed in the 1836 select committee. One manufacturer of machine presses declared that the diffusion of works by the old masters, of painting and sculpture by means of wood engravings in papers like the Penny Magazine, extended a knowledge of art, 'of science and taste and good feeling, without one sentence of an immoral tendency in the whole'.[2] Similarly, Henry Cole when writing on wood engraving in 1838 expressed the belief:

> The great end of the whole art of engraving is to render the spirit and genius of a great artist accessible to the thousands, or the millions, by embodying them in cheap and portable forms. Wood engraving, professedly the cheapest and most portable of all the representations of great pictures, excels equally in fulfilling the highest mission of its art, by the superior accuracy and fidelity with which it represents the spirit and genius of the picture.

Cole used his subject as the taking-off point for a flight into the realms of traditional academic theory. The cheapness and commercial success of wood engraving would, by bringing copies of beautiful pictures to the cottages of poor men, 'help to lessen the rudeness which is not necessarily, but is too usually associated with poverty':

> There is a deep morality in the love of the beautiful. The Spartan blessing, "the Beautiful to the Good", had its fulfilment in itself, for beauty is only one of the qualities of goodness. The character or action which is right, is of necessity also beautiful, or noble, and he must be prepared to overlook everything great in the civilization of the ancient Greeks who does not see that great things may come of creating a love of art among all ranks, since all the inner life of that wonderful people was derived from their reverence of beauty, - their religion was the religion of the beautiful. Serene and harmonious objects, by the very emotions which those words express, make the soul into which they sink, like themselves by doing

---

1. J. Pye, Patronage of British Art (1845), p.296.

2. Parl. Papers 1836, ix (568), pp.50-51: minutes of evidence, qus.590-9.

so; the beauty which the eye drinks re-appears in the affection which the heart feels; the moral qualities which the beautiful has in itself are brought out variously and sweetly in the lives of the lovers of it: the white light falls on the flowers and re-appears in iris hues.

Cole went on to praise Charles Knight, the founder of the Penny Magazine for using wood engraving for the moral good of the poor of the whole civilized world, multiplying and extending the pleasures of the beautiful where they were scarcely known before.[1] More specifically, Charles Smith, the sculptor and one of the Commissioners concerned with the decoration of the Palace of Westminster, in declaring his support for free access to cathedrals before the Select Committee on Public Monuments in 1841, as a means of improving the general conduct and morals of the people, added that he thought the people, after reading such publications as the Penny Magazine in which frequent reference was made with plates to cathedrals, abbeys and the like, 'have a great desire to see them, and thus, somewhat comprehending their merit and interest, they have a great desire to protect and take care of them'.[2]

The Penny Magazine itself was happy to participate in what might be described as the Victorian propagation of the gospel of academic virtù for all. It was aware that some of its unexampled success was to be ascribed to the liberal use of wood-cuts and to make its success permanent intended only to use the best artists as draughtsmen and engravers, 'to gratify a proper curiosity, and cultivate an increasing taste, by giving representations of the finest Works of Art, of Monuments of Antiquity, and of subjects of Natural History, in a style that had been previously considered to belong only to expensive books'.[3] It produced a guide to the National Gallery, and

---

1. (H. Cole), 'Modern Wood Engraving', London and Westminster Review, xxix (1838), 268-9.

2. Parl. Papers 1841, vi (416), p.77: minutes of evidence, qus.1558-64.

3. 'Preface', Penny Magazine, 18 December 1832.

favoured more liberal admission to museums and exhibitions, in order to win 'a love and taste of the higher efforts of art, and a relish for the beautiful wherever it exists'.[1] It believed in the cultivation of popular taste, for 'By diffusing a love of nature and of art amongst the people, the higher faculties of the mind will be awakened, and the impulses under which men seek for excitement in vicious indulgences, will be more easily overcome'. The peculiar direction of labour in this country, large masses working in factories and workshops, was far from being unfavourable to the development of the faculties once aroused. As Adam Smith had observed, in a civilized state, the variety of occupations in a community at large enhanced the opportunity for making comparisons and quickening observation.[2] And it actively identified itself with the Schools of Design in this country, as well as in France, even the productions of the Wedgwood potteries, all of which helped towards the cultivation of art and the formation of popular taste.[3]

The Penny Magazine was not the only illustrated periodical of the 1830s to take over the language used by Reynolds to justify high art and use it to suit its own purposes. The Art-Union journal applied the theory to the whole of illustrated literature:-

> Our leading artists may bear in mind, that the great object and end of art is to improve mankind, by refining the taste and strengthening the mind; and that this object and this end will be certainly accomplished by a union of art with literature - a combination which is more readily made by means of wood-engraving than by any other mode with which we are at present acquainted.[4]

1. Penny Magazine, i (1832), 13-15, iv (1835), 491-2.

2. Penny Magazine v (1836), 479-80.

3. Penny Magazine, v (1836), 516.

4. Art-Union, i (1839), 32. Also, Art-Union, viii (1846), 11: 'engraving on wood is destined to do far more for "the million" than it had yet done; if our artists will aid our wood engravers, they will effect great things for the mass'.

More specifically, although it acknowledged the lack of permanence in the illustrations of periodicals and newspapers, nevertheless, 'some of the finest efforts of genius have made their entrances and exits with the ephemera they were created to illustrate'. Even in Punch, where much of the satire was 'personal' that should only be 'universal', the Art-Union was able to find, 'some "little bit" that merits immortality for the lesson it inculcates - of integrity, or sympathy, or duties even higher'.[1]

As for the illustrated newspapers, they were not behindhand in latching onto the prevailing trend in their prefaces and parade of principles. The Illustrated London News declared:-

> We perceived that a love of art, not merely for its own sake, but from a deep and dearly-cherished consciousness of those high aims which its cultivation will promote and perpetuate, was growing up in the national soul of our beloved country; we determined, at all hazards, to lend our aid towards the work of directing this love of art to those high and noble purposes which we believed it best qualified to subserve - to plunge into the great ocean of human affairs, and to employ the pencil and burin in the work of illustrating not only the occurrences of the day, but the affections, the passions, the desires of men, and the faculties of the immortal soul.[2]

The Pictorial Times was no less conscious of its moral role, believing that 'the amount of intelligence and good feeling which may be acquired through the medium of the eye alone, from works of art, in truthfulness, entireness, and in its immediate effect upon the sensibilities and the mind, had never yet been sufficiently estimated'. Again, it declared, 'The brush is as great a moral teacher as the pen, and capable of exercising its influence independently of the sister instructress'.[3] And in case anyone should pause

---

1. Art-Union, vii (1845), 165-7.

2. Illustrated London News, 27 May 1843.

3. 'Preface', Pictorial Times, ii (1844). Also, Pictorial Times, 4 September 1847.

to think what any of these permanent qualities of high art had to do with the transient record of passing events, the Illustrated London News had an answer. Such illustrations provided 'stores to History'; they were the 'pictured register of the world's history'; they aided 'Art and Literature, as well as the Christian Policy, and Concentrated General Intelligence, and Universal History'.[1] In other words, the Illustrated London News felt it had been bequeathed the honours reserved for history painting in the academic hierarchy.

A cluster of lesser beatitudes gathered round to enjoy the reflected glory. Beauty, delicacy, taste, judgement all ensured that the higher sort of illustrated literature, news magazine or even humorous journal could be left out on the drawing room table and no blush would rise to any maiden's cheek. In contrast, woodcuts of a rude, crude, low, vulgar, demoralising, or scurrilous nature were rejected, almost as an academic painter might reject the work of a primitive. Thus, Charles Knight recalled the lesson-books, 'with blotches called pictures, that puzzled the schoolboy mind half a century ago, to distinguish what some daub was meant to delineate', compared with his own fine efforts.[2] The Penny Magazine contrasted its own contribution to the advance of public taste with 'the old manufacture of the red and blue prints which are still scattered by travelling Jews amongst the cottages of the agricultural population, and of the green and yellow parrots which are still sometimes seen upon the Italian boy's head, in ill-assorted company with Canova's Graces'.[3] While Henry Cole anticipated the argument that the higher levels of art were wasted on the masses by

---

1. Illustrated London News, 'Preface', to vols.i (1842), iv (1844), vi (1845).
2. C. Knight, Passages of a Working Life (1864), ii. 115-6.
3. Penny Magazine, v (1836), 516.

expressing a firm, if patronizing, belief in the improvements which had already taken place:-

> The mind which has fresh upon it the disgust excited by the affectations of those whose talk is of tone, of chiar'oscuro, of Claudes and Guidos, may be disposed to think any approach to such talk a degradation of a bold peasantry, - and we sympathise in the thought, - but a single conception of what our peasants really are, a reminiscence of red-faced, bare-necked men in smock frocks, sitting at the ale-house door with their pipes and porter pots, will more than suffice to exhibit the improvement which would be evinced by them even in conceited criticisms on cross-hatchings and deep tones, stipplings and good taste.[1]

Furthermore, such writers paid at least lip service to the idea that their art was accurate and universally comprehensible. Taking a more Burke-inspired than Reynolds-inspired line, the Illustrated London News expressed the belief that, 'The public will have henceforth under their glance, and within their grasp, the very form and presence of events as they transpire, in all their substantial reality, and with evidence visible as well as circumstantial'.[2] And when a new Chancellor was installed at Cambridge in 1842, it congratulated itself on being able to illustrate events 'uncontaminated by party spirit - in a word, with truth, and without bias - to present to its readers pictorial records of all the high festivals of the nation'.[3] Throughout the early decades, in the descriptions attached to the news illustrations, there was a constant stress on authenticity - 'an accurate and most faithful sketch', 'a spirited and authentic sketch', 'a faithful delineation' - as if to convince themselves and others of their rather shaky claims to fulfil the artistic virtue of 'exact description'.

The moral and universal effects of art, and those of education generally

---

1. Cole, 'Modern Wood Engraving', 268-9.
2. Illustrated London News, 14 May 1842.
3. Illustrated London News, 9 July 1842.

could readily be welded together to form a new utility for art. This opportunity was not missed by leading spirits in the popular education movement, and it is they, more than anyone, who provided the motive and the energy behind the progress of wood engraving. Charles Knight was the first to exploit the 'legitimate purpose of wood-engraving' by harnessing it to the power of cheap and rapid printing, to produce illustrated publications for the Society for the Diffusion of Useful Knowledge.[1] Henry Cole's very life can be said to personify the interaction of art and education. He was one of the first to realise the relevance of wood engraving and to exploit it for propaganda purposes. He went on to organize the Great Exhibition, take over the Schools of Design and was responsible for much of the history of art education during the third quarter of the century, including the creation of elementary art education and the founding of the Victoria and Albert Museum. It was only after Cole had been placed in charge of the Schools of Design in 1851, The Times believed, that Adam Smith's suggestion in his Wealth of Nations was taken seriously:-

> "There is scarce a common trade, which does not afford some opportunities of applying to it the principles of geometry and mechanics, and which would not therefore gradually exercise and improve the common people in those principles, the necessary introduction to the most sublime as well as the most useful sciences."[2]

Cole's own method of teaching, which used formal and symmetrical geometry as its base, seems remarkably close to Smith's idea. Armed with training in the principles of design and the elements of drawing, the student, the public and the manufacturer would no longer be bound by the 'thraldom of fashionable caprice'. Art education was not a luxury but a necessity.

1. Knight, op.cit., ii. 115-6.
2. The Times, 7 October 1876, quoted in Sir H. Cole, Fifty Years of Public Work (1884), i. 280-1.

Drawing was the power of expressing things correctly, while writing merely dealt in ideas. And with a peculiar extension of Burke's theory until it almost, in a paradoxical way, met Reynolds', he believed that 'this power will also assist them to obtain increasing accuracy in all other ways, and therefore become all the more truthful and sensible of God's wisdom'.[1] Richard Redgrave, Cole's assistant as head of the London School of Design, enlarged on the benefits to be accrued. It would give all a knowledge of form as a means of expressing their thoughts and an improvement among all classes in the perception of what was really excellent in design applied to the things and uses of daily life. Art acted as a universal language, a condensed shorthand. Because of the correctness of eye it encouraged, the perceptive faculties generally were improved, opening up the pleasurable perception of beauty, order and symmetry in man-made and 'Great Creator-made' things. Furthermore:-

> nourishing as it does, the love of beauty, order and perfection, it is so far the enemy of vice that he who would succeed in it must cultivate his mind, and strive to improve his general intelligence and information, making him a better workman, a better artist, a better member of society, and a better man.[2]

In Cole's system, utility and pragmatism, backed by a debased notion of the moral efficacy of such teaching affected every level of art education and made the Gradgrind image of the results not so much a caricature as has generally been supposed.[3] It also provides the context for much of the opposition against education through wood engraving, through pictorial facts. For some people, it was as if, to paraphrase Shee, the principles of art and

---

1. Parl. Papers 1852-53, liv (1615), pp.54-59: Address by H. Cole at the Opening of an Elementary Drawing School at Westminster, Appendix II (A) to the First Report of the Department of Practical Art.

2. Parl. Papers 1852-53, liv (1615), pp.59-63: Address by Richard Redgrave, Appendix II (B) to the First Report of the Department of Practical Art.

3. See K. J. Fielding, 'Charles Dickens and the Department of Practical Art,' Modern Language Review, xlviii (1953), 270-7. Also, S. Macdonald, The History and Philosophy of Art Education (1970), pp.228-33.

those of trade had been confused, to the detriment of the higher aspirations of both art and education, and to the gain only of commercial men. As early as 1800, a Professor Christian querulously remarked, 'we do not grow wiser than our forefathers; the fury for prints proves the frivolity of the times, and our books, I fear, will shrink from a comparison with those of the age of Queen Anne, which were not adorned with superfluous and meretricious decorations'. 'How would the professor lament over the "Illustrations" of the present day!' the Quarterly Review commented forty years later.[1] The Morning Chronicle of 1836, having criticised in crushing terms the quality and accuracy of one of Knight's 'Library of Entertaining Knowledge' volumes, went on to make a larger point and question the feasibility of '"diffusing a taste for the fine arts"'. It asserted, 'As there is no royal road to mathematics, so we say, once for all, there is no Penny Magazine road to the fine arts'. Every ingredient in the cultivation of the arts, and in their practice was expensive: great length of time 'which all political economists know to be the dearest ingredients in production', materials and models, 'and lastly, genius and invention, which are not to be purchased'.[2] The Quarterly Review of 1844 extended the jibe against political economists and the bandying about of Adam Smith in connection with art. Such illustrated literature was 'a partial return to baby literature', to 'a second childhood of learning', in which the eye was appealed to rather than the understanding. It stemmed not 'from an acute and accurate perception of

1. 'Illustrated Books', Quarterly Review, lxxiv (1844), 168.
2. Morning Chronicle, 19 October 1836.

beauty of design, as from a low utilitarian wish to give and receive the greatest possible amount of knowledge at the least possible expense of time, trouble, money, and, we may add, of intellect.[1] Even Wordsworth, picking up a copy of the Illustrated London News in 1846, was provoked to compose an extremely bad sonnet:

> Discourse was deemed Man's noblest attribute,
> And written words the glory of his hand;
> Then followed Printing with enlarged command
> For thought - dominion vast and absolute
> For spreading truth, and making love expand.
> Now prose and verse, sunk into disrepute,
> Must lacquey a dumb Art that best can suit
> The taste of this once-intellectual land.
> A backward movement surely have we here,
> From manhood, - back to childhood; for the age -
> Back towards caverned life's first rude career.
> Avaunt this vile abuse of pictured page!
> Must eye be all-in-all, the tongue and ear
> Nothing? Heaven keep us from a lower stage.[2]

The conservatives wished to reserve education and art for the few, believing it to be an expensive and difficult goal. The popular educators, on the contrary, believed it to be a cheap shorthand for the many. But the many failed to appreciate the gesture. They too saw it as 'namby pamby stuff', and a substitute for thought. However, rather than believing it to be a substitution for the more esoteric realms of academic speculation, they proclaimed it was 'published expressly to stultify the minds of the working people and make them spiritless and unresisting victims of oppression'.[3] The whole philosophy behind such illustrated publications was attacked not only because their high art ideas were irrelevant, but also because of the suspicion that they were a conscious diversion from other more important matters, a suspicion that was enhanced by the politics of the people involved.

---

1. 'Illustrated Books', p.171.
2. Quoted by C.K. Shorter, 'Illustrated Journalism: its Past and its Future', Contemporary Review, lxxv (1899), 494.
3. Poor Man's Guardian, 14 April 1832.

Douglas Jerrold, who firmly believed in the democratic mission of art, attacked the Art-Union's ideas on illustration which purported to elevate and refine, devoid of politics and personality:

> The Art-Union is established as a twelve-penny temple, whereto men are invited that they may therein ponder on the beautiful; where there are no politics, no social iniquity, no want, no human suffering to ruffle and distress the prejudices and sympathies of the reader.[1]

In contrast, Jerrold believed in an illustrated paper that would fill its natural place in society; painting and more especially, engraving now appealed:

> to other classes than kings and senators, generals and admirals; and to other feelings than those of admiration for factitious heroes, and of superstitious reverence for mystical or supernatural events. By her vivid representations of rags and roofless cabins - of the daring violations of custom-house regulations - of the victims of game-laws - of criminals, the offspring of legal injustice - by her bold satires of the foolish eccentricities of men armed with power, or endowed with wealth, she has become a great teacher on the side of Nature, and the auxiliary of honest labour. Her claims are prized accordingly. Her fearless exposures have been a great help to liberty. Now that she seeks rewards from administering to the enjoyments of the multitude, she too has become generous and truthful, and is scoffed at when she yet lends her pallet to gild and hide the chains of superstition, or consecrate the deeds of the despot and man-slayer ... The natural office of the Fine Arts is not merely to add to the pleasures of the opulent, but to diffuse enjoyment amidst the workers.[2]

Thus Jerrold spoke on behalf of those illustrated publications which did not clothe themselves in the humbug of high art, which were passionate, political and partisan, not glibly elevating, smoothly progressive and blandly universally acceptable. He lifted the illustration of periodicals out of an academic debate about the value of high art into the more realistic world of politics. That which had been rated low on the academic hierarchy of subject matter, namely 'low' and 'vulgar' subject matter, was now seen to be an intrinsic part of the function of art as communication.

1. Punch, viii (1845), 256.
2. 'The Place of the Fine Arts in the Natural System of Society', Douglas Jerrold's Shilling Magazine, vi (1847), 79-81.

In considering the status of art in the nineteenth century in England it is necessary to discuss its social context. In France during the same period, the interaction of art with society has always seemed to be much more prominent, owing to the occasion of specific moments - the revolutions of 1830, 1848 and 1870 - which, to some extent, crystallized attitudes and provided focal points for the study of a defined range of artistic reactions. However, even in France in 1848, as well as the postures, or lack of postures adopted by the individual artistic prima-donnas, Charles Blanc as head of the Bureau des Beaux-Arts conceived of his role to encourage public art both in terms of frescoed mural paintings in public buildings and the less spectacular encouragement of lithographs and engravings for the countryside.[1] Thus, he followed the pattern set by the English government in its much publicized decoration schemes for the Palace of Westminster, and more surreptitious support for the Penny Magazine. The educational function of art, who controlled the different off-shoots and for what purpose, who opposed this control and for what reasons, was a political issue. The background to the problem lay in the 1820s with the founding of the Mechanics' Institutes, University College London and the efforts made to free primary education from religious domination. However, the 1830s and 1840s were two of the most politically unstable decades of the century in England. They encompassed the reform agitation, violent opposition to the whole fabric of 'old corruption' as well as to the more recent manifestations of industrial exploitation and Whig reprisals, the birth - and death - of Chartism and the Anti-Corn Law League. In this context, given a new ideological and technological urgency in the 1830s, graphic art was not merely the passive onlooker of political events, adding a little light relief or contingent verification to pages of written evidence. It had its own role to play, conditioned by its own history, provenance and relation to its audience; it fought its own battles for art, for education, for politics.

1. T.J. Clark, The Absolute Bourgeois (1973), p.57.

Yet, at the same time, graphic art was part of the whole context of journalism and depended upon it increasingly as a vehicle to carry its products from source to audience. This context helped to establish its pedigree and labelled its destination. It is not surprising that the Penny Magazine compared itself to a stage coach; the image carried with it overtones of speed and technological progress which were now made available to all classes through the steam press, graphic art, as it were, hitching a lift inside.[1] It carried information to the whole country at a time when it was becoming increasingly important to communicate knowledge of events and individuals, policies or ideas to an audience beyond a closed circle of cognoscenti. Before 1800, public ignorance had been largely matched by official aloofness, an embargo of political information. This vicious circle began to break down in the late eighteenth century. Newspapers were allowed to report the daily debates in parliament from 1771, and juries were able to pronounce their verdict in matters of libel, formerly reserved to the judge.[2] Significantly, around this period the flood gates of English political caricature in the metropolis were opened wide.[3] The growth in the size, wealth and 'consciousness' of the middle classes during the Napoleonic wars and after forced concessions from the government which included, eventually, political reform.[4] Politicians of an older generation and conservative stamp hated the change. For Wharncliff, a seat in the House of Commons

1. Penny Magazine, i (1832), 1.
2. P. Fraser, 'The British Government's Use of Parliamentary Publicity in the Past',Gazette, xi (1965), 192.
3. M. D. George, English Political Caricature to 1792 (Oxford, 1959), pp.145-9.
4. A. Briggs, 'Middle-Class Consciousness in English Politics 1780-1846', Past & Present, No.9 (1956), pp.65-74.

would cease to be an object of ambition to honourable and independent men, 'if it can only be obtained by cringing and servility to the rabble of great towns, and when it shall be established that the Member is to be a Slave, bound hand and foot by pledges, and responsible for every vote he gives to masters who are equally tyrannical and unreasonable'.[1] Wellington had to have it gently pointed out to him by Greville that the appointment of Lord Londonderry to be ambassador in St. Petersburg was bound to be unpopular, despite the fact that Wellington knew he wrote good dispatches, 'I said this might be all true, but that though he knew it, the generality of people did not, and the public could only judge of him by what they heard or read of his speeches; that on that account he was very obnoxious'.[2] The change of view-point did not come suddenly. Londonderry went to Russia. The composition of the House of Commons barely altered in 1832.[3] Nevertheless, by the middle of the century Bagehot had diagnozed the emergence of a new type of politician - the constitutional statesman - and implied he was the product of political communication over a much wider expanse of people than ever before, identifying himself with their needs.[4]

A comparison of conditions for newspaper reporters in parliament is revealing. In the old House of Commons, they were squashed in the back seats of the Strangers' Gallery, unable to hear properly and often lacking the skill in shorthand necessary to take down what could be heard; in the House of Lords, it was a serious breach of privilege to be seen taking notes.[5] In contrast, Greville thought the Reporters' Gallery in the new

---

1. The Greville Memoirs, ed. L. Strachey and R. Fulford (1938), iii. 9.

2. Ibid., iii. 173.

3. S. F. Woolley, 'The Personnel of Parliament of 1833', English Historical Review, liii (1938), 240-62.

4. (W. Bagehot), 'The Character of Sir Robert Peel', National Review, iii (1856), 146-50.

5. S. C. Hall, Retrospect of a Long Life (1883), i. 112-5.

House of Commons, 'a sort of public and avowed homage to opinion, and a recognition of the right of the people to know through the medium of the press all that passes within those walls'.[1] However, such reports from the political microcosm of the nation only reached, initially, a very limited audience. Before 1815, a newspaper had to be printed by hand, stamped, taxed and distributed via a rudimentary Post Office and a primitive road system.[2] Its price, despite make-shift arrangements in the form of reading rooms, coffee and ale-houses, prohibited the growth of what could really be described as a popular, respectable press until the middle of the century.[3] Journalism was not generally considered to be an honourable profession.[4] However, a highly organized, illegal unstamped press undercut the established newspapers and circulated its own view of affairs to large audiences during the early decades of the century, as has recently been shown.[5] Similarly, there was a range of graphic responses, which can be cross-compared given an understanding of the technical facilities and artistic forms available.

The 1830s and 1840s are crucial decades for the study of the developing means of political communication in the nineteenth century. This is especially so in the field of graphic journalism. In 1830, such a generic term is almost too portentous to describe what amounted to an unpredictable flow of political and personal satirical prints in London, sporadic outbursts

---

1. The Greville Memoirs, iii. 153.

2. A. Aspinall, Politics and the Press 1780-1850 (1949), pp.7-24.

3. J. Vincent, The Formation of the British Liberal Party 1857-1868 (1966), pp.58-65.

4. A. Aspinall, 'The Social Status of Journalists at the Beginning of the Nineteenth Century', Review of English Studies, xxi (1945), 216-32.

5. W. H. Wickwar, The Struggle for the Freedom of the Press (1928), which covers the post-Napoleonic war period; J. H. Wiener, The War of the Unstamped (1969) and P. Hollis, The Pauper Press (Oxford, 1970), which both study the illegal press to 1836.

of visual propaganda in the provinces and an irregular supply of topical illustrations in newspapers and broadsides. By 1850, the vehicles for such material had been developed and streamlined into a continuous, large scale production of illustrated newspapers and magazines, distributed throughout the country, some of which are still in business today. Firstly, therefore, it is necessary to examine the technological basis for this change, which can largely be accounted for in the development of wood engraving. This growth not only influenced the nature of graphic journalism, the styles of illustration and the methods of production, but also helps to explain the intricate and changing character of the social alignments involved in the process. Unfortunately for the popular educators and their optimistic dreams of a straightforward path to artistic and moral perfection, many of the old methods still lingered on. The decade of the 1830s was a period of flux between technical expansion and the decline of old traditions, and further, between middle and working class ideas on the presentation of politics, instruction and amusement. There were tensions within the trade of wood engraving. The ambivalent status of the engravers, stranded between the traditional creative pride assigned to an individual artist and the rather less appealing results of the mass production process, reinforced with a vengeance that of the journalistic world in general. It is not to be supposed then that the output of such an industry in a state of complex change can be fitted into a single pattern. The stylistic differences, on a scale from the most primitive to the most progressive, were reinforced by differences in artistic and editorial personnel, in production and distribution methods as well as in the imagery and the subject matter of the illustrations.

The 1830s and the 1840s was a period of equipoise between the virulent anarchy of the individual prints and the comparative anonymity of the large-scale journalistic concerns. There existed an intimate pattern of connection between artist, wood engraver, writer and printer who depended upon one another for their survival. As a result, there had to be at least some continuity of editorial and artistic policy, some rapport between editorial line and audience response for a journal to be an economic proposition. The gradual consolidation of such attempts enables an illustrated periodical for the first time to be examined over some years and to be cross-compared with other periodicals of the same type. The significance of such a study is that it not only adds to the historical evidence on the range of political views of the period, but is symptomatic of the growing importance of the communication process itself in the face of an enlarging political audience. I examine this process during the first half of the 1830s in the field of political caricature and cover a range of reactions to traditional issues and to the new controversies provoked by the actions of the Whig government. This leads into a study of the responses arising from the 'March of Mind' and the 'War of the Unstamped', which heightened the awareness of the press generally and political caricature in particular of their own role in politics, and their importance in the battle to maintain the independence of communications from government interference. This chapter can be seen as the pivot of my argument. On the one hand, there are the responses of a partisan popular press, as expressed through the unstamped newspapers and the liberty afforded to political caricatures. On the other, there is the government's active concern to suppress such works through the law, and more insidiously by flooding the market with cheap, copiously illustrated publications from the Society for the Diffusion of Useful Knowledge, in particular the Penny Magazine with its blockbusting mission to unite all behind its crusade in search of technical perfectability and moral and educational progress.

The fact that the government maintained the initiative in 1836 through the new stamp act effectively held up the development of penny political newspapers for twenty years.[1] This seems in retrospect also to have been the turning point for illustrated journalism which ensured that its future would lie with the relentless power of the steam press, large-scale engraving concerns, high capital turnover, profits and investment. The small, independent efforts had had their day. Even such a traditional vehicle as the illustrated police gazette, which exploited the age-old emotional fascination of crime,[2] was adapted and expanded to embrace the widening expectations of an audience not content with static styles of depiction, but who sought novelty in the presentation of news, politics and satire, literature and amusement. The individual response was squeezed out beneath the steam-roller pressure of the common denominator. Of course, this process was neither sudden nor all-embracing. As I point out in the chapter on Punch, which largely depended for its success on the mobilization of a steady flow of capital to support its weekly issue, some writers and artists jibbed at acknowledging the inevitableness of the connection between business solvency and a steady, safe editorial line designed to offend the fewest readers. Furthermore, they also chafed under the burden of carrying the whole moral and educational package onwards and upwards. However, by the 1840s, beneath them lay the depths of the scurrilous and licentious press: through such papers as the Town and the Satirist, satire had become, quite literally, a dirty word. Similar considerations constrained the development of illustrated newspapers during the 1840s. The Illustrated London News' pretensions to impartiality, its lip-service

1. For a detailed account of the motives behind the passage of Spring Rice's bill in 1836, and the results, see P. Hollis, The Pauper Press (Oxford, 1970), pp.84-92 and J.H. Wiener, The War of the Unstamped (1969), pp.260-77.

2. See E. Wind, 'The Revolution of History Painting', Journal of the Warburg Institute, ii (1938), 121.

to the cause of moral elevation forbade it to venture so far as the Blue Books, The Times' special correspondent reports or the small-scale campaigning journals put out as propaganda by private charities in exhibiting disturbing material. By 1850, the mainstream of graphic journalism catered for a family audience with good clean fun, adventures abroad not troubles at home, agreeable enough in its technical and artistic facility to ensure commercial success.

The study of any aspect of press history in England inevitably faces problems over source material, in particular, destruction through the bombing of central London or the less calculated, but often more devastating, destruction in successive moves. In addition, the more ephemeral, light weight or short term the paper, the less likely the chances of finding it. For these reasons, this survey can in no way pretend to be definitive. I have made use of as many of the collections in the public libraries, museums and art galleries in London and provincial cities as I found useful, as well as some private collections, gathered by individuals who had the foresight to collect such material.[1] However, I hope this study will help to reveal new sources of evidence and encourage more detailed work in this area.

---

1. For a fuller bibliographical note on the print sources used see below p. 322.

THE CONDITION OF WOOD ENGRAVING

1830 - 1850

II

The development of wood engraving during the first half of the nineteenth century provided the basic technical conditions from which graphic journalism could grow. This chapter indicates three characteristics of wood engraving in this period, later to be reinforced by an examination of its products. First, there was a natural sympathy, a close – almost family – connection among those involved in wood engraving in particular, and graphic journalism in general in the metropolis. Secondly, nevertheless, distinctions were created in terms of personnel and groupings, which arose from skill or reputation. Thirdly, the growth of a technology of wood engraving, the beginnings of a mechanized industry, though it was neither sudden nor comprehensive, changed the character of graphic journalism and altered the social framework of the people involved in its production. Therefore, a study of the expanding technology of wood engraving gives some insight into the sort of graphic journalism which was likely to develop.

The trade of wood engraving was inextricably a part of the printing and publishing world. It stood where artistic and journalistic 'bohemias' met. Its revival in the late eighteenth century, which had depended mainly on the genius of one artist, Thomas Bewick, in Newcastle, had developed by the 1830s into a metropolitan craft, half way towards a mechanized industry. Bewick himself, in a letter to George Lawford of 1828, wrote:-

> Little did I think, while I was sitting whistling at my workbench, that wood engraving would be brought so conspicuously forward, and that I should have pupils to take the lead, in that branch of art, in the great Metropolis; but old as I am, and tottering on the downhill of life, my ardour is not a bit abated, and I hope those who have succeeded me will pursue that department of engraving still further towards perfection.[1]

The metropolitan world in which the wood engravers found their business was closely knit and mutually dependent, yet competitive and highly risky. Superficially at least, there was not too much change in the pattern of connection and the atmosphere among those who were involved in producing copy for growing audiences during the first half of the nineteenth century. In retrospect, a convivial glow blurred memories, and more than one journalist, looking back to his youth from a respectable old age, found himself at a loss to recall it satisfactorily. London's bohemia in the early nineteenth century witnessed the last round of the manners and customs of the eighteenth century taverns and coffee houses. Its clientele was not loyal; it had largely vanished by the middle of the

---

1. A. Dobson, Thomas Bewick and his Pupils (1884), p.171. Also, K. Lindley, The Woodblock Engravers (Newton Abbot, 1970), p.28, who quotes Bewick as having said:-
> The more I have since thought upon the subject, the more I am confirmed in the opinions I have entertained, that the use of woodcuts will know no end, or, so long as the importance of printing is duly appreciated and the liberty of the press held sacred.

century.[1] However, a few discernible features help to explain its attractions and also to outline the mechanics of journalistic production in general, those of illustrated journalism in particular.

Firstly, all parties concerned were centred on the same area of London, straddling the cities of London and Westminster, bound by Ludgate Hill to the East, Charing Cross to the West, Holborn to the North and the Strand to the South.[2] It included the parishes of St. Giles and St. Clement Danes, the neighbourhoods to Seven Dials and Fleet Street, the latter being variously dubbed the 'cradle of printing', 'the hot bed, the forcing house' of the Fourth Estate.[3] Of course, the variety was infinite. Nevertheless, there were certain common meeting places which, in a trade far from fully industrialized by mechanization, ensured a cross-fertilization of personnel and ideas, a coming together in the face of common problems, which transcend any simplified notion of class.

These included the engraving premises themselves, which were far from being closed factories. Most frequently, like the printing offices of

---

1. F. Greenwood, 'The Newspaper Press. Half a Century's Survey', Blackwood's Edinburgh Magazine, clxi (1897), 704-6, who pointed out that even W. M. Thackeray's Pendennis (1848-50) afforded 'but faint uncertain glimpses of an underworld which has never been well described to this day', largely because Thackeray's own experience of it was so equivocal. See below p.225 . Also, J. Hatton, Journalistic London (1882), pp.41-42, who like Greenwood believed it was a 'vanished land' by the second half of the century. For more recent attempts to describe this world see J. C. Reid, Bucks and Bruisers (1971) on the early decades of the century. For the 1830s and 1840s, the introduction by J. C. Bradley to Selections from London Labour and the London Poor (1965). Also, E. P. Thompson, 'Mayhew and the "Morning Chronicle"', The Unknown Mayhew, ed. and introd. E. P. Thompson and E. Yeo (1971), pp.12-20.

2. For the history of the area see P. Cunningham, A Handbook for London, Past and Present (1849). Knight's Cyclopaedia of London (1851).

3. J. Britton, Autobiography (1849-50), i. 287-98. Also, J. Diprose, Some Account of the Parish of St. Clement Danes (Westminster) Past and Present (1868), i.238-46. According to the 1841 Census, referring to Middlesex, Holborn heads the list for the largest number of printers and engravers, and is second for print-sellers and colourers in the metropolitan area. Parl. Papers 1844, xxvii (587), pp.108-25: Great Britain. Occupation abstract. County of Middlesex.

the area,[1] they were poky and squalid, overcrowded and insalubrious, to be found in converted houses up narrow yards and courts off the Strand or Drury Lane, crammed with a back-log of blocks and presses. For Joseph Hatton, Crane Court seemed to be 'the most prolific of journalistic nurseries', and included among its progeny the early editions both of Punch and the Illustrated London News.[2] Edward Evans' first premises were next door to the Cheshire Cheese in Wine-Office Court, although he soon received notice to quit, 'for my pressmen had to work early and late and utterly disturbed a quiet lawyer who had his rooms below me'. He then moved to 4 Racquet Court, Fleet Street and shortly afterwards, acquired a whole house and two or three more hand-presses.[3] George Augustus Sala's business as a wood engraver was carried on in a house in Upper Wellington

1. For descriptions of typical printing offices see T. Frost, Forty Years Recollections (1880), pp.229-30. (J.F. Wilson), A Few Personal Recollections by an Old Printer (1896), pp.16-19. A compositors' memorial to the master printers, dated 16 January 1866, stated that a recent Royal Commission had recorded 'the death-rate of printers is 47 per cent higher than that of the whole community, and that 70 per cent of the deaths occurring are ascribable to some form of chest disease'. E. Howe, The London Compositor (1947), p.270. See also, G. Rosen, 'Disease, Debility, and Death,' The Victorian City, ed. H.J. Dyos and M. Wolff (1973), ii. 645. In addition, the drainage of the Drury Lane area was notoriously bad. See the Builder, xi (1853), 257-8, 465-6, 601-2, 626-7.
   Luke Hansard virtually had to gut his premises before converting them in the 1820's. James Moyes' old premises were gutted by accident in 1824 and were replaced by the first building specifically erected as a printing office in London, the following year. Unfortunately, he went bankrupt. I. Bain, 'James Moyes and his Temple Printing Office of 1825', Journal of the Printing Historical Society, iv (1968), 1-10. Charles Manby Smith records a well organized printing office, that of William Clowes & Sons, in which he worked during 1835-36; it was the first to print woodcuts by steam press and specialized in government work for the Stationer's Office. C. Manby Smith, The Working Man's Way in the World (1853), pp.223-5. This, however, was the exception. Indeed, it has been suggested that government work, which protected a few firms who made large enough profits to mechanize, proved a drag chain on the development of the printing industry in the middle decades of the nineteenth century. B.W.E. Alford, 'Government Expenditure and the Growth of the Printing Industry in the Nineteenth Century', Economic History Review, xvii. 2nd Ser., (1964-65), 96-112.

2. Hatton, op.cit., p.8. For the Court's somewhat more illustrious past see Cunningham, op.cit., i. 244.

3. The Reminiscences of Edward Evans, ed. and introd. R. McLean (1967) pp. 24-26.

Street, Strand on which he had taken the lease. His workshop was on the ground floor; the first floor was let to a friend, and his own bedroom was on the second floor. The rest of the house was unfurnished and unoccupied as he could not afford to buy more furniture and he did not want lodgers.[1] Such men frequently acted as outworkers for master engravers, as the Dalziel brothers evidently did for Landells when they first came to London.[2] Even at the end of the century, Charles Booth was able to speak of wood engraving readily adapting itself to home work, while other engravers combined two or three together to hire a work-room, though each man retained his own clients and earnings.[3] William James Linton's business was on a larger scale, yet his premises in Hatton Garden do not appear to have been any more streamlined:

> It consisted of rather a ramshackle old workshop of two storeys, across a yard, with low ceilings and rough floors, and windows extending the whole length of one side each room, of the old workshop or factory type with small frames of blown glass, showing bull's eyes here and there ... There was a long room off the yard, and nearer the street the office proper. The view of the roofs (mostly pantiled and haunted by cats), brick chimneys, and back-yards occasionally gained a certain unusual distinction by the presence of a peacock and hen belonging to some neighbours.

For a few years, Linton did have more spacious premises at No.33 Essex Street, Strand, but again these were in an old eighteenth century house, which was entirely turned over to offices, of which he had the third floor and top garrets.[4]

As a result, there was a good deal of encounter among the trades. Junior apprentices acted as messengers and ran errands. Linton, as an

---

1. G.A. Sala, Things I have Seen (1894), i. 64-65.

2. The Brothers' Dalziel, A Record of Work 1840-1890 (1901), pp.4-6. See also Wilkie Collins, The Woman in White (1860), in which the artist, Walter Hartright, lived in the East End and earned a living by drawing and engraving on wood for the cheap periodicals at home, first on his own account and later for a large practice.

3. C. Booth, Life and Labour of the People in London (2nd Ser., 1903), iv. 110.

4. W. Crane, An Artist's Reminiscences (1907), pp.47, 57.

apprentice to George Willmot Bonner, was sent to get drawings from Thomas Hood in his chambers in the Adelphi for his Comic Annual.[1] Similarly, Evans, who was apprenticed to Ebenezer Landells, took drawings to the Dalziels and to Dickens, and remembers answering the door at Bidborough Street for many of the staff of Punch.[2] When Linton became a partner of John Orrin Smith, he got to know most of the personnel of the Illustrated London News and Punch. Henry Vizetelly, as a junior apprentice in the same firm, remembers the frequent visits of Kenny Meadows, who lived near by, and also John Leech in his youth, when he came to live with the Smith family. It was quite customary to take in impecunious boarders, as well as to give meals to fellow workers down on their luck.[3] And even in the large wood engraving work-rooms, artists and writers used to wander in for a chat and a smoke.[4]

An apprenticeship was the recognized form of learning the trade. Evans paid a premium of £30 for his to Landells, Linton one of £50 to Bonner.[5] This varied in length also, usually taking from five to seven years, during which time the apprentice was not allowed to undertake private commissions.[6] Instead, he could 'slaughter' odd drawings on wood with his graver, would learn to prepare the boxwood block with a little zinc-white powder

---

1. W.J. Linton, Memories (1895), p.11.

2. Evans, op.cit., pp.9-12.

3. H. Vizetelly, Glances Back Through Seventy Years (1893), i. 134-5. Also, Linton, op.cit., pp.55-60.

4. J.B. Groves, Rambling Recollections and Modern Thoughts by an Old Engraver (MS. in Punch library. c.1900), p.16. Also Crane, op.cit., p.51.

5. Evans, op.cit., p.8. Indenture of Apprenticeship of William James Linton to Mr. George Willmot Bonner, 3 July 1828. Feltrinelli Institute, Milan. W.J. Linton Papers. Booth said that a premium of £30-£80 was usually paid. Op.cit., iv. 113.

6. Booth, op.cit., iv. 113. Linton's Indenture of Apprenticeship was for six years. Crane, op.cit., p.63.

(generally oxide of bismuth) mixed with water, on to which the design was traced, and eventually he was trusted with engraving parts of blocks in which he was known to be competent.[1] In the 1830's, his day was apparently ten hours long, a seventy-two hour week; in the middle of the century, nine hours; by the end, a forty-two to forty-eight hour week.[2] In addition, keen pupils took it upon themselves to have drawing lessons and practise from plaster casts. For the majority, however, either the long working hours discouraged pupils from attending the school established by the Dalziels, or the small fee prevented them from going to lessons at the Working Men's College.[3] A few exceptionally gifted boys were taken on by master engravers to train exclusively in the art of drawing on wood. The length of their apprenticeship was only three years and they kept government office hours, from ten to four, with a half holiday on Saturdays.[4] The Whympers even encouraged leave of absence to enable their pupils to work in public galleries.[5]

What leisure time there was seems to have been spent wandering round the Fleet Street area, attending meetings or frequenting the taverns of the district. Not surprisingly in these surroundings, the result would seem to have been a high degree of political awareness and in general, a radical political attitude. Linton, of course, is an outstanding example of one whose 'first perversion' from a fellow engraver led him to read and meet Thomas Wade and Richard Henry Horne, visit James Watson's shop and become a

1. Vizetelly, op.cit., i. 120. Crane, op.cit., pp.48-49. Booth wrote that it took two years for an apprentice to become really useful; in his time, only small establishments thought it worth while to take boys on. Op.cit., iv. 113.

2. Vizetelly, op.cit., i. 120. The Brothers' Dalziel, op.cit., p.343. Booth, op.cit., iv. 112.

3. The Brothers' Dalziel, op.cit., pp.343-4. Groves, op.cit., p.19.

4. For example, Walter Crane, who was apprenticed to Linton from 1858 to 1862, without having to pay the usual premium. Crane, op.cit., pp.45-65.

5. H. Hartley, Eighty-Eight Not Out (1939), p.228.

close friend, a leading Chartist and later, an ally of Mazzini.[1] Less dramatically, Vizetelly recalls from his youth Richard Carlile's shop, meeting him in Fleet Street, and seeing Burdett, O'Connell and W.J. Fox at political and religious meetings. Later, during his apprenticeship, he recounts that the most democratic opinions were current in Bonner's shop, where Linton had trained eight years before, and the forbidden books read outside working hours were freely discussed while work was going on.[2] Even Sala, whose memoirs do not betray much sense of political affiliation, writes that, 'When I had any politics at all ... I was one of the people called Radicals, and a very bitter and perhaps blatant Radical to boot'.[3]

Yet despite this background, only the upper ranks of the trade were in any way organized during this period. Some of its leading practitioners, who could produce satisfactory specimens of their work, and three nominees from amongst the existing membership, were elected to the Artists' Annuity Fund. This was the joint stock branch of the Artists' Fund, established in 1810 and incorporated in 1827, to protect its members - who included painters, sculptors, architects, metal engravers and draughtsmen - against sickness and superannuation. Its money came entirely from the investments made on the annual subscription of members, and during the course of a somewhat chequered early financial career, this seems to have been two guineas for those under the age of thirty, and rising on an ascending scale for the rest up to the age of forty-five.[4] In return, the member was promised thirty

---

1. Linton, op.cit., p.77. His Chartist activities apparently damaged his trade, keeping him away from his business and customers away from him. For a full account of Linton's political activities see F.B. Smith, Radical Artisan. William James Linton 1812-97 (Manchester, 1973).

2. Vizetelly, op.cit., i. 121.

3. G.A. Sala, Life and Adventures (1894), i. 27-28.

4. For an account of the early workings of the Artists' Annuity Fund see Pye, Patronage of British Art pp.309-400.

shillings a week during sickness and forty pounds a year for protracted illness or superannuation. In addition, the 'Benevolent' branch of the Artists' Fund provided by voluntary subscription to protect the widows and children of members of the Annuity Fund, by contributing on average twenty pounds per annum and five pounds for each child below the age of sixteen.[1] However, owing to the personal nature of the occupation, organization along trade union lines for the average worker was non-existent until the 1880's.[2]

Piece work was the usual method of remuneration, the price being fixed per square inch or for the block, and it varied according to the character of the work. Thus, it is difficult to assess the average income of a wood engraver or ascertain with any accuracy his standard of living, especially as many would work for several different masters as well as on their own account. A few rather unintelligible bills of Landells and some vague pages of accounts drawn up by Linton when he proposed to wind up his business in 1846 give some idea of the prices paid to established engravers. Landells charged in 1842 between four and five shillings for engraving the tiny silhouette visual puns called 'blackies', created by William Newman on Punch, eight to fifteen shillings for the small (one by two inches to two by four inches) black and white cuts, and twelve guineas for the large frontispiece

---

1. Mrs. Sophia Bonner, widow of George Willmot Bonner, received this gratuity for herself and her three children from 1837, as did Mrs. Mary Elizabeth Gray, widow of the wood engraver Charles Gray, from 1845. Minutes of the Artists' Benevolent Fund, No. 5 (1836-42), No. 6 (1842-47).

2. Booth mentions the International Society of Wood Engravers, established in 1887, the subscription for which was sixpence a week with an entrance fee of two shillings. During sickness, the members were entitled to ten shillings a week for thirteen weeks, and seven and sixpence for thirteen more. The Society held occasional exhibitions of wood engravings and had about eighty members in London. The National Society of Lithographic Artists, Designers and Writers, and Copper-plate and Wood Engravers was formed earlier, in 1886, but had few wood engravers once their own Society was established. Booth, op.cit., ii.224, iv. 117-8.

designed by 'Phiz', Hablôt K. Browne.[1] However, the cash received was eaten into by other expenses like premises, tools and blocks, the price of which was increasing in the 1830s because of the growing demand,[2] besides that of wages. The Penny Magazine proudly stated that its wood cuts cost about £2,000 per annum; when Swain headed the engraving establishment of Punch, its supply of engravings cost on average £1,500 a year; Linton completed £1,764 15s 6d worth of work for the Illustrated London News between January and October 1846, which was the largest of his many accounts.[3] Yet out of the gross receipts of around £2,400 for the same period, he reckoned that £1,600 was taken by expenses of wood, drawing, engraving, the house and discounts, leaving £800 net profit for nine months or £1,060 per annum. He thought that 'with moderate application', the income of each partner ought never to be less than £300.[4] The ordinary

1. M. H. Spielmann, The History of Punch (1893), pp.34, 413. Orlando Jewitt received £1 13s 6d, in 1841, for the device of Oxford University arms, which was used for many years on the Gazette. H. Carter, Orlando Jewitt (1962), p.42. A wood cut for a penny-issue novel apparently cost ten shillings. L. James, Fiction for the Working Man (1963), p.32.

2. 'Wood-cutting and Type Founding', Penny Magazine, ii (1833), 421. In the 1840s, a block four inches square cost around one shilling and sixpence. 'Wood Engraving', Chambers' Miscellany, ix. No.85 (1846), 3.

3. Penny Magazine, ii (1833), 421. Spielmann, op.cit., p.249. Feltrinelli: Linton.

4. Ibid. Linton proposed to continue to be actively engaged in the business for a further two years, taking half the profits, and then to retire from all commercial part in it:
    and only doing such things as may be required to keep up the character of the work (that is to say such parts of work which you are unable to do yourselves) and also helping in emergencies. Being except so far as this a sleeping partner with one fourth of the profits of the concern.
His business commitments were complicated by a sum of £285, payable annually to Orrin Smith's widow until January 1849, and the fact that the lease of the house in Hatton Garden, on which more than £200 had been spent in the previous three years, was about to end. However, Linton's partners (Smith's sons, Harvey and Horace) seem to have accepted the arrangement, for Linton went off to the Lake District in September, 1848.

wood engraver, who lacked both the responsibility of running a business and the pretensions to artistry of a master, probably received something closer to the wage of an average copper-plate engraver of the period, a guinea a week, or thirty shillings a week upwards for a better workman.[1]

Indeed, more than a hint of impecuniosity held together much of the journalistic world of this period, a fact which was often forgotten later in the wake of fame and success. Evans was apparently considered unusual for paying his ink bill on time.[2] That Linton was sometimes over-sanguine is evident from a letter sent to him by the printer with whom he often dealt, Robert Palmer, dated 23 February 1848:-

> I am much pressed for money; and must really beg of you to see seriously about doing some thing for me - I am being baited every day, and much wish to be getting into smoother water.
>
> I am aware you will have some drawback and paper, cuts & other portion of our joint affair, but it is nothing, I imagine, to anything like the amount of our a/c against you...

Palmer then added a short account of the money owed since August of the preceding year, which added up to £417 19s 11d. He concluded, 'Do pray let something be done in the affair and that with dispatch'.[3] The

---

1. I. Bain, 'Thomas Ross & Son. Copper and Steel-plate Printers since 1833', Journal of the Printing Historical Society, ii (1966), 8-10. Also Sala, Life and Adventures, i. 210, who speaks of Calvert, his master, being unable to pay his assistant a sufficient sum for really artistic work. See below p.43 . By contrast in the 1820s, Charles Knight states that the few wood engravers in London at the time were real artists, paid at artists' prices. C. Knight, The Old Printer and the Modern Press (1854), p.244. Booth distinguishes between the pictorial engravers who could earn between £3 and £5 a week if they worked regularly, and an ordinary piece worker, who made thirty shillings to £2. Home workers made less. However, not too much confidence should be placed in these figures since it was so much later in the century and economic conditions had changed. There was a serious loss of trade within the trade to 'process' methods of reproduction, leading to a general demoralization. Some firms, formerly employing twenty engravers, were now down to half a dozen and even these were on half time. Op.cit., iv. 109, 112-3.

2. Evans, op.cit., p.26.

3. Feltrinelli, Linton.

unemployment and bankcruptcy of printers was far from uncommon, the results of over-expansion in the early nineteenth century being aggravated by economic fluctuations and by the seasonal nature of government work.[1] Editors and authors were notorious for the amount of time they spent in and out of the bankcruptcy courts and debtors prisons.[2] Of the Punch staff, Gilbert à Beckett, later a Police Magistrate, had been declared bankrupt in 1834; Henry Mayhew was in 1846; Frederick Fox Cooper, who likewise dabbled in theatricals and short-lived journals, was in gaol for debt in 1831, 1836 and 1839.[3] Herbert Ingram's difficulties in organizing a team to produce the Illustrated London News were considerably enhanced by the fact that his editor, F.W.N. Bayley, was liable at any moment to be arrested for debt.[4] 'Whips round' in the familiar taverns of the area emphasize the clannishness of this bohemia, which was prolonged more artificially in the penchant for clubs which many of its members displayed later in life. The whole area was combed with taverns patronized

1. E. Howe, 'Preface', The Working Man's Way in the World (1967 edn.), pp.vii-ix. The number of printing offices doubled between 1785 and 1835 and too many apprentices were taken on.

2. According to James Grant, in his description of the five London debtors' prisons:
   > of all classes of men to be found in the Queen's Bench, that of authors, in proportion to their relative numbers to society generally, is by far the most numerous. On some occasions they are to be seen in crowds, in that locality... It is, beyond all comparison, the worst trade going. For one man that succeeds in it, thousands fail.
   J. Grant, Sketches in London (1838), pp.79-80. Also, R. Nicholson, An Autobiography (1860), p.136. For the difficulties and vicissitudes of literary bohemia in the first half of the century see. C. Scott and C. Howard, Edward Leman Blanchard (1891), i. 44-46, 68-70. Sala, Things I have Seen, ii. 40-41, 57-69. Vizetelly remembers collecting copy for his father, a printer, from the prisons. Op.cit., i. 110.

3. Thompson and Yeo, op.cit., pp.14-15. F. R. Cooper, Nothing Extenuate, the Life of Frederick Fox Cooper (1964).

4. Vizetelly, op.cit., i. 228-31.

by the writers, printers and publishers from the small offices in the neighbourhood, all 'living more or less from hand to mouth'.[1] Despite some evidence as to the advancing respectability of journalists,[2] it is clear that among lesser lights than Perry, Barnes or Leigh Hunt, their reputation for uncertain social and political morals, their cliquishness compensating for lack of real identification with any one class, continued. Those involved in wood engraving were part of this world, an important link in the chain of journalistic production. United by slender means, dependent upon each other for getting work, and getting paid, they could not afford to be too choosy about their acquaintances. If one link broke, then the whole system temporarily collapsed into insolvency, only to be patched up again and regrouped with fresh optimism around a new publication a few months later.

1. Wilson, op.cit., pp.34-37. Greenwood wrote, in justifying the late hours and heavy drinking of this world, 'As the rough and tumble of football is good for the muscles and the temper, so the rough and tumble of such encountering talk was good for the wit and the temper'. 'The Newspaper Press', 706.
For glimpses of this ambiance, see G. Hodder, Memories of my Times (1870), pp.363-4. J. N. Leno, The Aftermath (1892), pp.74-75. Sala, Things I Have Seen, ii. 177-85. A. Mayhew, A Jorum of Punch (1895), pp.27-36. Taverns, drinking clubs and gin palaces provided the social setting necessary to lubricate smoothly the teams which produced both Punch and the Illustrated London News. See below, chapters six and seven. On the later clubs founded and patronized by Jerrold and his friends, see J. Timbs, Club Life in London (1866), i. 308-13. D. Masson, Memories of London in the Forties (1908), pp.211-56.

2. Aspinall, 'The Social Status of Journalists at the Beginning of the Nineteenth Century', 227-32. Greenwood, 'The Newspaper Press', 704-9. Hatton, op.cit., pp.41-42.

II

A closer examination of the development of wood engraving during the early nineteenth century does not bear out the assumption of a rapid, untroubled growth. For a start, some of Bewick's pupils died before him; others retired or changed profession; only a handful went to London.[1] In the 1820s, there were perhaps one or two dozen engravers whose skill as craftsmen and artists could be relied upon. They took their time and cost money, as this example of the state of wood engraving in 1825 reveals:-

> Illustrations were so seldom used that the preparation of even a small woodcut was of much moment to all concerned. I have heard the late William Harvey relate that when Whittingham, the well-known printer, wanted a new cut for his "Chiswick Press" series, he would write to Harvey and John Thompson, the engraver, appointing a meeting at Chiswick, when printer, designer and engraver talked over the matter with as much deliberation as if they were about to produce a costly national monument, and, after they had settled all points over a snug supper, the result of their labours was the production, months afterwards, of a small woodcut measuring perhaps two inches by three. At this time only about a dozen persons, besides Bewick's pupils, were practising the art of wood-engraving in England.[2]

With such work, personal connection still counted for much. William Harvey (1796-1866), Bewick's favourite pupil, was by this time principally

---

1. Dobson, op.cit., p.172. Linton counted sixteen apprentices of Bewick. Of these, by Bewick's death in 1828, Robert Johnson and John Bewick, his brother, were also dead; Charlton Nesbit, the most distinguished of his elder pupils, had retired to his native village; Luke Clennell was mad by 1817 and before this occurred, had become principally a painter; Harvey was exclusively a designer by 1824. Armstrong, Willis and White, Landells and Jackson are the only ones who seem to have worked in London. W. J. Linton, Masters of Wood Engraving (1889), pp.154-72. J. Jackson (and W. A. Chatto), Treatise on Wood Engraving (1839), pp.605-27. Pye, op.cit., p.386.

2. M. Jackson, The Pictorial Press: its Origins and Progress (1885), p.359. Dobson quotes one writer who said that there were not more than three masters in London who had sufficient business to employ, even occasionally, an assistant, and to keep an apprentice or two. Op.cit., pp.172-3. J. Johnson, Typographica (1824), ii. 652, lists nineteen. Together with those mentioned in Pigot and Co.'s London and Provincial Directory for the same year, there would appear to have been twenty four.

a draughtsman and designer, but another of the older followers, Henry White, engraved many of George Cruikshank's squibs for William Hone.[1] Ebenezer Landells (1808-1860) served his apprenticeship chiefly with Isaac Nicholson (1789-1848), an old pupil of Bewick's in Newcastle, and went to the Dalziels' father for drawing lessons. He came to London, helped to found Punch, engraved for the Illustrated London News and Douglas Jerrold's Illuminated Magazine, and founded the first Lady's Newspaper. Edward Evans (1826-1905), recommended by the overseer at the printing firm of Samuel Bentley, became Landells' apprentice, and Birket Foster (1825-1899) also trained with him, mainly in a designing capacity, for Foster's father had known Landells in Newcastle. Landells' eldest son, Robert (1833-1877) continued the tradition by becoming an art war correspondent on the Illustrated London News.[2] Similarly, John Jackson (1801-1848), a pupil of Armstrong, Bewick and Harvey, was largely employed on the Penny Magazine and other publications of the Society for the Diffusion of Useful Knowledge. He initiated and contributed much of the information for the most comprehensive nineteenth century English treatise on wood engraving, first published in 1839, while his brother, Mason Jackson (1819-1903), wrote the first history of illustrated journalism almost half a century later, when

---

1. Jackson and Chatto, op.cit., pp.622-6. Linton, Masters of Wood Engraving, pp.185-7. Between 1830 and 1840, Harvey was probably the sole person to whom engravers could apply for an original design with security, and who devoted himself entirely to the production of such designs. Dobson, op.cit., p.206. His only predecessor was Thurston, a pupil of James Heath, the copper-plate engraver, whose designs had been engraved by Clennell, Nesbit, Hole, Branston, White, Byfield, John Thompson and W. H. Hughes. He died in 1821.
Henry White first worked for John Lee in London. See below, p.46.

2. Evans, op.cit., pp.8-20. Dobson, op.cit., pp.220-1. The Brothers Dalziel, op.cit., pp.4-12. Cole, 'Modern Wood Engraving', 277.

picture editor of the Illustrated London News.[1] However, although the father of the most successful team hailing from Newcastle, the Dalziel Brothers, was an artist, the fourth son George (1815-1902) went to London in 1835 for his training as a wood engraver under Charles Gray (1809-1845), to be joined at the end of the decade by his brother, Edward (1817-1905), and later by John (1822-1869), in 1852, and Thomas (1823-1906), in 1860, who had been trained as a copper-plate engraver.[2]

Another 'school' was founded by Robert Branston (1778-1827) in London, who was the son of a copper-plate engraver from Norfolk.[3] His pupils included his nephew, George Willmot Bonner (1796-1836), and the brothers Charles (1791-1843) and John Thompson (1796-1866), whose son Charles Thurston (1816-1868) followed them and also became official photographer at the South Kensington Museum.[4] Bonner, in turn, taught the short-lived but gifted William Henry Powis (1808-1836), William James Linton (1812-1898) and later, Henry Vizetelly (1820-1894), who went into partnership with his elder brother, a printer, engraved for

---

1. Linton, Masters of Wood Engraving, p.192. Dobson, op.cit., pp.216-20. Cole, 'Modern Wood Engraving', 277. T. Gilks, A Sketch of the Origin and Progress of the Art of Wood-Engraving (1868), pp.70-71. For the division of labour between Chatto and Jackson in their Treatise on Wood Engraving see Art-Union, i (1839), 91, 123-4. Dobson, op.cit., pp.217-9. Mason Jackson wrote The Pictorial Press: its Origins and Progress (1885).

2. The Brothers Dalziel, op.cit., pp.1-4.

3. Linton, Masters of Wood Engraving, pp.173-84. Jackson and Chatto, op.cit., pp.627-33. Cole, 'Modern Wood Engraving', 275-6. Gilks, op.cit., pp.71-72.

4. There is an undated letter from Richard Doyle to Mark Lemon referring to their joint project The Enchanted Doll (1849), a fairy tale by Lemon with illustrations by Doyle. Doyle suggested that as Swain could not cut all the drawings in the time that remained, he should take the cover drawing to the 'young Thompson', who was quite as good as his father, but cheaper. Punch library. See also, Cole, Fifty Years of Public Work, i. 290. Thurston Thompson accompanied Cole to Toulouse in 1855 to inspect and record the Soulages collection.

the <u>Illustrated London News</u>, and started its rival, the <u>Pictorial Times</u> in 1843.[1] Linton's pupils included William Luson Thomas (1830-1900), who founded the <u>Graphic</u>, the main rival of the <u>Illustrated London News</u> in the second half of the century.[2] The self-taught Samuel Williams (1788-1853) founded another group with his younger brother, Thomas, and their sister, Mary Ann. The elder Williams engraved William Hone's <u>Everyday Book</u>, while his pupil John Orrin Smith (1799-1843) became Linton's partner, as did Smith's two sons, Harvey and Horace, when their father died.[3] Another pupil, Joseph Swain (1820-1909) took over the engravings for <u>Punch</u> after Landells' departure, with his brother John acting as shop-foreman.[4] A further large scale wood engraving concern was established by Josiah Wood Whymper (1813-1903), who was self-taught and came from Ipswich. With his son, Edward (1840-1911) he specialized in engraving for the Christian Knowledge Society publications, and, requiring a high standard of work, took on many artists to learn to design on wood, including Robert Barnes, Charles Green, Charles Keene, J. W. North and Frederick Walker.[5] Thus, the pattern would seem to follow a two-stage development from the master engravers to the metropolis, from working on Hone's publications in the 1820s, through the <u>Penny Magazine</u> in the 1830s, to <u>Punch</u> and the <u>Illustrated London News</u> in the 1840s. By 1850, there existed the large engraving establishments of the Dalziel, Swain

1. Linton, <u>Memories</u>, pp.8-9. Vizetelly, <u>op.cit</u>, i. 119-21.

2. W. L. Thomas, 'The Making of the Graphic', <u>Universal Review</u>, ii (1888), 80-93. Shorter, 'Illustrated Journalism - its past and its future', 487-9.

3. Linton, <u>Masters of Wood Engraving</u>, pp.194-6. Cole, 'Modern Wood Engraving', 275-7. Draft accounts, Feltrinelli: Linton. Crane, <u>op.cit</u>., p.47.

4. Spielmann, <u>op.cit</u>., pp.247-53. Groves. <u>op.cit</u>., pp.719. As the business increased, John wanted to be taken into partnership but his brother refused. John left, brought out the <u>Penny Mechanic</u>, went bankrupt, but later took up 'process' work successfully.

5. Hartley, <u>op.cit</u>., pp.228-30. Groves, <u>op.cit</u>., pp.5-6. The Brothers Dalziel, <u>op.cit</u>., pp.193, 230.

and Whymper families, and that which had been set up by the <u>Illustrated London News</u> itself.[1]

Even within this dominant group of master engravers there were differences in skill and reputation. Joseph Swain, though a good businessman, was thought to have no artistic capability and to be but a poor engraver, unlike the elder Dalziel brothers, who were clever artists too.[2] Vizetelly sneered at his master, Bonner as 'a second-rate wood-engraver', though he was a family friend and then at the end of his life.[3] Likewise, Sala reveals that even engravers who had received the best training did not always keep their reputations intact. He started his career with a man named Calvert in Lambeth, who was 'exclusively employed in preparing the blocks for the illustration of a number of cheap, and it must be admitted, vulgar weekly publications'. These included Lloyd's penny dreadfuls, the designs for which, by outside draughtsmen, were 'engraved, or rather chopped', by Calvert, or his ageing assistant, Armstrong. Armstrong had once been a pupil of Bewick. Of a particularly delicate artist's work Sala wrote:-

---

1. See below, pp.306-07. Linton describes how, in 1849, the newspaper proprietors decided to undertake their own engraving, drew off his workmen and forced him out of business. <u>Memories</u>, pp.77-78.

2. Groves, op.cit., p.8. Linton, <u>Masters of Wood Engraving</u>, p.205.

3. Linton was apprenticed to Bonner from 1828 to 1834 and seems to have been quite happy with him; 'Bonner was a clever artist, and a good master, making his pupils learn and do everything connected with their work, even to sawing up a box-wood log and planing and smoothing the rounds of wood to fit them to receive the drawings'. <u>Memories</u>, p.8. However, there was some delay before Bonner was elected to the Artists' Annuity Fund in 1826, owing to his inability to produce enough specimens of work. <u>Minutes of the Artists' Annuity Fund</u>, No.2 (1825-28), 3 January, 4 July 1826. Vizetelly lived with the Bonner family during his apprenticeship (Bonner's teacher and uncle, Branston, had a son who was a partner of Vizetelly's father, in a printing business), but Bonner died, after a brief illness, the year after Vizetelly's apprenticeship began. <u>Op.cit.</u>, i. 119.

it was lamentable to see his beautiful cross hatching ruthlessly slashed by Calvert's graver and shading tools; while poor old Mr. Armstrong, who in his day had executed work of the highest kind, was fain to be also a "scauper" and a slasher, because the engraver could not afford to pay him a sufficient sum for really artistic work.[1]

For every well-known master mentioned by Henry Cole in his 1838 article on 'Modern Wood Engraving', in the 1838 Westminster Review, or in Chatto and Jackson's Treatise, published the following year,[2] or who were able to satisfy the standards of the Artists' Annuity Fund,[3] an underworld of hacks plodded on. In the range of talent it would appear, for example, that George Dorrington, who worked on John Cleave's and William Carpenter's A Slap at the Church, engraving the drawings of George Cruikshank and Robert Seymour, was considered less respectable than Landells.[4] Engravers like W. C. Walker or Joseph Welch, who worked for Figaro in London, or J. Meadows, who engraved the cuts of Giovanni in London, and James March on Punch in London rarely appear outside the trades' directories.[5] The lower the level in the engraving hierarchy the more short-lived and under-financed the work to be engraved, and the closer one comes to the anonymous woodcut blocks of the chapbook and broadside tradition. This was virtually the monopoly of John Pitts

---

1. Sala, Life and Adventures, i. 208-10. Armstrong worked on the engravings for Giovanni in London and at one point had his own establishment.

2. See above p.41 , ft.1, and below, section III, p. 66 , ft.2.

3. Those wood engravers elected to the Fund during this period were: Bonner, Branston, Gray, Hart, Harvey, John Jackson, Mason Jackson, Landells, Linton, Powis, Sargent, John Thompson, Samuel Williams and Wheeler. Minutes of the Artists' Annuity Fund, Nos.2-6 (1825-47).

4. Evans, op.cit., p.8. Dorrington advertised for an apprentice, but the overseer at Bentley's, who had never heard of him, recommended that Evans should go to Ebenezer Landells instead.

5. See Robson's and Pigot's London Directories for these years.

and James Catnach during the first half of the nineteenth century.[1]
It was a static mode, uninfluenced by Bewick's innovations, by which
blocks were handed from printer to printer over generations. Cluer Dicey
and John Marshall, who had expanded the eighteenth century trade from
Bow Church Yard and Aldermary Church Yard, were succeeded by Pitts and
Catnach; and they in their turn were followed by Anne Ryle and
W. S. Fortey, who took over the stocks of both men.[2] Not surprisingly,
'Conservatism of thought and expression, impermeability and repugnance
to change', were the main features distinguishing this popular art.[3]
Often, they were scarcely relevant to the broadside text; only occasionally
were they reworked. As the blocks used were of less hard-wearing quality
than boxwood, cut on the plank not engraved on the end grain, they wore
out quickly with constant use and were discarded by their former owners,
lost in stock-piled heaps, or thrown out when the shop became too full.[4]
The prints, similarly, failed to survive beneath the more weighty volumes
of respectable examples of the engraver's craft. They fell into children's
hands, were pinned up on walls, and being printed on flimsy paper, they

1. See C. Hindley, The Life and Times of James Catnach (1878) and
   The Catnach Press (1886). L. Shepard, John Pitts. Ballad Printer of
   Seven Dials, London (1969).

2. See J. and R. M. Wood's Typographical Advertiser, i (1863), 73 for a
   description of the Catnach shop when Fortey ran it. Hindley recalls
   Catnach's collection of woodblocks 'of the oddest and most ludicrous
   character'. History of the Catnach Press, pp.257-8. See also, L. Shepard,
   The History of Street Literature (Newton Abbot, 1973). V. E. Neuburg,
   'The Literature of the Streets, 'The Victorian City, i. 191-209.

3. D. P. Bliss, A History of Wood-Engraving (1928), p.164.

4. Ibid., p.167. He mentions that Rabier at Orleans and the Garniers at Chartres
   burnt their stock of ancient blocks, which were occupying too much space.
   Part of Fortey's collection came into the hands of G.F. Wilson of Advance
   Foundry Ltd., and is now on loan to the St. Bride Printing Library, London.
   The Angus Collection, Victoria and Albert Museum, gives some idea of a
   typical collection of broadside blocks.

swiftly disintegrated.[1]

Nevertheless, this tradition was far from moribund in the first half of the century. Hannah More knew members of both the Dicey and Marshall families, and it was to Marshall she turned for help in adapting the broadside format to her Cheap Repository Tracts. 'Mr. M. has never belied my first opinion of him, selfish, tricking and disobliging from first to last', she wrote to Zachary Macaulay in September 1797.[2] John Lee engraved the cuts for her, being the best of the London engravers before Branston. He died in 1804 and his pupil, Henry White, went to Newcastle and served out the rest of his time under Bewick. Lee's son, James Lee, was also a wood engraver and executed the portraits in T.C. Hansard's Typographica (1825).[3]

Catnach himself introduced dramatic layout and typographical styles, treated topical events, especially murders, with sensational headlines and even new blocks. Sometimes he was his own engraver:

> and while the compositors were setting up the types, he would carve out the illustration on the back of an old pewter music plate, and by nailing it on to a piece of wood made it into an improvised stereotype off-hand, for he was very handy at this sort of work, at which also his sister, with his instruction, could assist; so they soon managed to rough out a figure or two, and when things were dull and slack they generally got one or two subjects ready in stock.[4]

Finally, they were covered with flashy water colours 'gorgeous to the uneducated eye', and sold in the streets accompanied by the patterers' cant, which emphasized the sensational matter of the contents.[5] As Punch snidely

---

1. According to Charles Manby Smith, the paper used by the Seven Dials printers weighed four to five pounds a ream, compared with the sixteen or seventeen pounds of normal paper. It was 'in quality so vile that no decent shopkeeper would condescend to use it to wrap up copper change'. The Little World of London (1857), pp.261-5.

2. G.H. Spinney, 'Cheap Repository Tracts: Hazard and Marshall Edition', Library, xx. 4th Ser., (1939), 305.

3. Jackson and Chatto, op.cit., pp.627-8.

4. Hindley, Life and Times of James Catnach, p.392.

5. Manby Smith, The Little World of London, pp.261-3. H. Mayhew, London Labour and the London Poor (1861-62. Dover edn., 1968), i. 222, 234, 301-2.

observed in its guide to the 'Geography of Seven Dials': 'The balladography daily issuing from Messrs. Pitt and Catnach's toy and marble warehouses finds an immediate circulation throughout the neighbourhood, and also forms a considerable article of export to St. Giles's, and other colonies.'[1]

It is to this tradition that the woodcuts of the most radical engraver bear most resemblance. Charles Jameson Grant was responsible for most of the serial woodcuts of the early 1830's, for the front page cartoons of Cleave's Penny Gazette and Cousins' Penny Satirist through to the mid 1840's, and for many single prints throughout the twenty years of the period. For better publishers he used the lithographic stone, and it is as a lithographic printer that he appears for the only time in the trade directories of the period.[2] Apparently, however, he quarrelled with Tregear, one of his most regular publishers, and it is for his woodcuts in the stock block manner - simple and crude, with little or no cross hatching, eliminating middle tones, more cut than engraved - that his style is at its most distinctive.[3]

A further adaptation was made for the promotion of penny literature and the cheap theatre. Calvert's business obviously specialized in this kind of work and a letter from Edward Lloyd to Sala suggests that the exaggerated, crude style of the firm was not solely the result of the lack of cash or competence of its owner. 'The eyes', Lloyd wrote, 'must be larger; and there must be more blood - much more blood!'[4] Such effects could only be

---

1. Punch, ii (1842), 86-87, 171-2. For a send-up of 'The Literary Gentleman' - the composer of such broadside sentiments - see Punch, ii (1842), 68.

2. Grant. Charles James. Lithographic Printer, 12 St. Chad's Row, Gray's Inn Road. Robson's London Directory for 1839, pp.140, 516.

3. For the development of the stock block in the nineteenth century see Lindley, op.cit., pp.90-102. For Grant's quarrel with Tregear see J.J. Lamb, '"Gallery of Comicalities",' Notes and Queries, 4th Ser., v. (1870), 209-10. He also mentions a note of Grant's, dated 1840, in which he writes of 'such an obscure object in the background as myself'. See below p.182.

4. Sala, Life and Adventures, i. 209.

gained by using the bold, clear cut style, not with the fine lines of a graver. Nor is it surprising that some of the leading designers for this type of literature appear to have been scene painters.[1] They knew how to attract the interest of a large audience within the theatre in the same way as their posters achieved this effect in the street.

Linton, while working with Bonner, describes how he:

> worked occasionally in the fifteenth century mode of wood-work, with a knife instead of a graver, on cuts for placards for Ducrow, the manager of Astley's Ampitheatre, the one horse-circus in London, in Westminster Bridge Road.[2]

Such aesthetic interest was rare, however. The only real exception until the late nineteenth century was Joseph Crawhall (1821-1896). He came from Newcastle and although influenced by Bewick, was more inspired by the broadsides and chapbooks of the eighteenth century and earlier. He made no attempt to convey the half-tones of a wash by means of finickity cross hatching, but returned instead to a broad line cut. His work, A Collection of Right Merrie Garlands for North Country Anglers, published in 1864, was received with veiled condescension or outright incomprehension. The Athenaeum complained of the 'sheer foppery' and the 'uncouthness' of the woodcuts.[3] The trouble was that such art was no longer the norm, as it had been a hundred years before. This same mockery and hostility was directed against Catnach's sheets, and, as will be seen, against Grant's caricatures and the

---

1. According to George Hodder, Sala was himself a scene-painter at one time. Op.cit., pp.363-4. E.L. Blanchard's biographers say of Cleave's Gazette of Variety in the 1840's, that it was 'adorned with coarse caricatures, designed by an artist named Jack Wright, scene-painter subsequently to Brading, of the Albert Saloon'. Scott and Howard, op.cit., i. 30. For the posters painted by standing patterers to illustrate their murder sheets see Mayhew, op.cit., i. 301-2.

2. Linton, Memories, pp.8-9.

3. Athenaeum, No.1926 (24 September 1864), p.398, quoted in C.S. Felver, Joseph Crawhall (Newcastle, 1973), p.22.

penny news and fiction cuts, which lingered on into the middle of the century.[1] Often, this reaction was voiced in the most progressive vehicles for wood engraving. The last part of this chapter examines in detail the expansion of the medium. It was a phenomenon so overwhelming that it dwarfed all others and has led to a bias in favour of the success stories of graphic journalism, and an ignorance about the old patterns of the trade which still lingered on. Yet the difference between the two extremes, which superficially might appear to be only one of style, in fact was an instantly recognizable line of demarcation between technological expansion and the decline of old traditions, between middle and lower class ideas on the presentation of politics, instruction and amusement.

---

1. See above p.47 and below pp.174, 181-3.

III

> By showing what engraving on wood could effect in a popular way, and exciting a taste for art in the more humble ranks of life, they created a new era in the history of publication. They are the parents of the present cheap literature, which extends to the sale of at least four hundred thousand written copies every week, and gives large and constant employment to talent in that particular branch of engraving which I selected as the best adapted to enforce, and give circulation to my own thoughts.[1]

This was written by William Hone in 1824, a trifle prematurely perhaps, puffing his own collaboration with George Cruikshank, half a dozen years or less previously. The claim could be, and was made with more justification about Charles Knight's Penny Magazine, for it was only then that wood engraving's main advantage - that it could be printed by machine in the same sheet as letterpress - was successfully exploited for periodical publications.

Knight himself describes the first attempt to print wood engravings with a cylinder press, for the Society for the Diffusion of Useful Knowledge publication of his Menageries in 1828. The patentee of the machine and the whole committee of the Society stood around to see the first copies roll off the press, to produce:-

> an illustrated volume not despicable as a work of art, and yet cheap - something very different from the lesson books with blotches called pictures, that puzzled the school-boy mind half a century ago, to distinguish what some daub was meant to delineate.[2]

In 1820, Knight had failed with a journal called the Plain Englishman, and he assigned the blame partly to the fact that he could not render it more attractive by means of pictures in the then condition of wood engraving.[3]

---

1. W. Hone, Aspersions Answered (1824), p.49.
2. Knight, Passages of a Working Life ii. 115-6.
3. Ibid., i. 244.

By 1833, the Penny Magazine, in its four-part commercial history, stated that the price of box had increased owing to the demand and that the wood engravings for the Magazine cost about £2,000 per annum. The encouragement to the trade had been such that there were now more than a hundred wood engravers in London. The impulse had even spread abroad. Not only were English engravers employed on French publications, but the Penny Magazine supplied metal stereotype casts to France, Germany and Russia to help these countries, who had scarcely any wood engravers of their own, produce works similar to the Penny Magazine at a cheap rate.[1] By 1836, the list had extended to include Holland, Livonia, Bohemia, Italy, the Ionian Islands, Sweden, Norway, Spanish America and the Brazils. In addition, the entire work was reprinted in the United States from plates sent from this country.[2] The Magazine was not slow to identify its progress with the high state of civilization in England. This was not only manifest in the technology and mechanical skill it employed, especially stereotyping and machine printing,[3] but also in the general elevation of the taste of the public. It begged the question as to whether the popular taste would have been as much advanced 'by the encouragement of the old manufacture of the red and blue prints which are still scattered by travelling Jews amongst the cottages of the agricultural population'.[4] It sought reassurance from the evidence of Mr. Edward Cowper, the printing machine maker, who asserted before the Select Committee on Arts and the Principles of Design in 1836:-

1. 'Wood cutting and type founding', Penny Magazine, ii (1833), 421. This fact should not be confused with the acknowledged superiority of French artists during the same period. However, the leading wood engraver in France at the time was an Englishman, Charles Thompson (see above p.41), who trained a later generation of French wood engravers as well as assisting on many joint Anglo-French publishing ventures. See below p.66, ft.2.
2. 'Address', Penny Magazine, v. (1836), 516.
3. 'Preface', Penny Magazine, i. (1832), iii-iv.
4. Penny Magazine, v. (1836), 516.

> it is indeed the paper currency of art, and always represents
> sterling value. I should say, whatever means may be derived,
> either by public lectures, museums, &c., for the circulation
> of art, that those means may be rendered effective by means
> of the printing-machine.

Confident in the power wrought by the machine press in collaboration with wood engraving, he stated:-

> every Saturday I have the satisfaction of reflecting that
> 360,000 copies of these useful publications are issued to
> the public, diffusing science and taste and good feeling,
> without one sentence of an immoral tendency in the whole.

He maintained that the wood engraver, instead of working only with his hands, had been obliged to take five or six pupils to get through the work.[1]

It is rather difficult to confirm or deny Cowper's estimate. The trade directories of the period only list the wood engraving firms and their increase was not spectacular: from twenty four in 1824, to twenty six in 1832, thirty in 1840-41, thirty three in 1844, forty two in 1851.[2] Nor are the census figures much help. In 1841, there were sixty five male wood engravers over the age of twenty in Middlesex, thirty seven under twenty, as well as four women over twenty and eleven under twenty.[3] About this time, Vizetelly reports that all known members of the profession in London including assistants and apprentices, signed a petition to support Rowland Hill's penny postage. They numbered about two hundred.[4] Neither the census for 1831 nor for 1851, unfortunately,

---

1. Ibid., 515, quoting from Parl. Papers 1836, ix (568), pp.50-51: minutes of evidence, qus.590-9.
2. Compiled from Robson's London Directory and Classification of Trades, Pigot & Co.'s London and Provincial New Commercial Directory and the Post Office London Directory for these years. Also, Johnson, op.cit.ii. 652.
3. Parl. Papers 1844, xxvii (587), pp.112-3: Great Britain, Occupation abstract
4. Vizetelly, op.cit., i. 179.

give a separate estimate for wood engravers in the metropolis.[1] In any case, the numbers would fluctuate owing to the demand and skilled men, as in printing, often would find themselves out of a job in the slack season.[2] It is fairly safe to assume, however, that the more respectable the firm, the larger the staff. Thus, Calvert only had one assistant and one apprentice and employed outside draughtsmen. Bonner also employed outside draughtsmen, had several assistants and two apprentices when Vizetelly was there.[3] Landells supervised a team

1. For 1831, in England the suspiciously low figure of 3 print cutters in wood is given for the Metropolis, and 7 engravers. By 1841, the latter had apparently risen to 4,209; in 1851, it stood at 3,936. These figures are all adapted to the 1831 criteria of being only concerned with males over the age of twenty one. However, it is not so easy to establish a norm for other aspects of the census. One reason for startling discrepancies was that the criteria differed every ten years. The 1841 census introduction stated:-
> instead of circulating lists to contain by anticipation every existing trade or calling, the enumerator was directed to insert each man's description of himself opposite his name, so that when the enumerator's schedules were returned to us we might arrange the whole upon such form as should be most easy of reference. The result was, that many occupations were returned that will not be found on the list of 1831.

Another probable result was that any wood engraver, asked to describe himself in 1841, might say lithographer or copper-plate engraver, which he might also be, or simply the all-engulfing term, engraver. This confusion also arises in the trade directories, where Robson's, for example, warns the reader that for 'Engravers - wood', he should also consult 'Engravers' and 'Wood Type cutters'. Similarly, Booth went to great lengths to list over fifteen subdivisions of engraving and still ended up with the category, 'artisans undefined'. Op.cit., iv. 108. In the 1851 census, the categories had changed again, with no special wood engraving section at all, but two sections of Class XI - Persons engaged in Art and Mechanical Productions - (publishers, printers, booksellers and actors were in the same class), one simply termed 'Engravers' and another, 'Others employed about Pictures and Engravings'. Parl. Papers 1852/3, lxxxviii pt.1 (1691-i), pp.ccxx-ccxxiii: Census of Great Britain, 1851. Also, Parl. Papers 1844, xxvii (587), p.7, pp.27-30, pp.46-47: Great Britain. Occupation abstract.

2. For printers, see above p.37. Also, Bain, 'Thomas Ross & Son', 9-10.

3. Sala, op.cit., i. 209. Vizetelly, op.cit., i. 120.

of eighteen engravers, 'all eminent in their particular departments', to complete the panorama of London for the Illustrated London News, though it is probable that some of these were outworkers.[1] Punch's engraving arrangements, managed by Joseph Swain, functioned in the early days with eight assistants, but the number gradually increased when Swain began to take on work on his own account.[2] By 1850, his establishment, that of the Dalziels, Whympers and Linton's, before he abandoned it, could be compared to small factories. Linton says he sometimes had 'as many as twenty journeymen and pupils in my employ, whose work I superintended and with whom I worked'.[3] Walter Crane gave a vivid picture of the business in Essex Street in the middle of the century:-

> His office was a typical wood-engraver's office of that time, a row of engravers at work at a fixed bench covered with green baize running the whole length of the room under the windows with the eyeglass stands and rows of gravers. And for night work, a round table with a gas lamp in the centre, surrounded with a circle of large clear glass globes filled with water to magnify the light and concentrate it on the blocks upon which the engravers... worked, resting them upon small circular leather bags or cushions filled with sand, upon which they could easily be held and turned about by the left hand while being worked upon with the tool in the right. There were, I think, three or four windows, and I suppose room for about half a dozen engravers; the experienced hands, of course, in the best light, and the prentice hands between them. There were four or five of these latter....[4]

1. Illustrated London News, i (1842), 545. See above p.30.

2. Spielmann, op.cit., p.249.

3. Linton, Memories, p.77.

4. Crane, op.cit., p.48. In fact, the description was so typical, that Groves lifted most of it in order to describe Swain's establishment, only adding:
   > His workshop consisted of two rooms on the second floor, but he rented the whole house, so that as business increased, he could add to suit its requirements which he eventually did. The rooms were bare without any pretence of adornment, plain coloured walls without pictures, no matting or oilcloth on the floor and the only artistic ornament in the rooms was a plaster cast that stood on the mantelpiece, an old worn-out horse, that would have served for Don Quixote's Rosinante.

   Op.cit., pp.7-8. For Swain's later changes see below p.70.

Multiplying its impact, the trump card it held over every other branch of graphic art was the cheap rate at which wood engraving could be disseminated in conjunction with types, by means of the press. As Knight explained, if the old system had continued, probably only 20,000 copies of the Penny Magazine could have been produced, at a thousand copies a day at one press worked by two men. By machine, 16,000 could be produced and in ten days with two presses, 160,000. This number could never have been reached even with sixteen hand presses, for hand labour added at least forty per cent. to the cost of production. Furthermore, improvements in stereotype founding for duplicates ensured a limitless supply of prints, while the cost of re-engraving woodcuts, and of re-composing the types, would have put a 'natural commercial limit' on the operation.[1]

In comparison, copper engravings could not be printed with letterpress, and besides, the final results were not very lasting. It was pointed out that a metal plate was useless after a few thousand impressions, while a woodblock was good for some two or three hundred thousand. Thus, the expenses - and it cost much less to produce a first-rate wood engraving than a first-rate copper plate - were divided among nearly a hundred times as many purchasers.[2] Admittedly, the steel engraving for which England was famous in the 1830s could be produced in much larger editions

---

1. Knight, The Old Printer and the Modern Press, pp.253-6. For the stereotyping process see Jackson and Chatto, op.cit., pp.637-8. Also Cole, 'Modern Wood Engraving', 273. Cole, Fifty Years of Public Work, ii. 171. Penny Magazine, ii (1833), 471-2. T. H. Fielding, The Art of Engraving (1841), p.74.

2. Cole, 'Modern Wood Engraving', 268.

- estimates varied from five to twenty times as many as the copper plate[1] - but also took three times as long to complete owing to the hardness of the metal, and was disliked by many engravers.[2] It was chiefly used for the small vignette plates in annuals, which enjoyed the luxury of long deadlines unknown in journalistic circles. By the 1840s, even this market had been glutted by mediocre work and was on the decline.[3]   Lithography, although cheaper and faster than engraving as far as the initial draughtsmanship stage, was slower in printing because it was necessary to damp the stone beforehand, and the pulling through the press under pressure took time. Therefore, it was at a disadvantage already at the hand press level. By 1848, when the output of the steam driven letterpress machine had reached as many as 12,000 impressions an hour, the lithographic printer struggled to produce a hundred prints an hour for the simplest ink-drawn work, and even less for chalk drawings. The first successful powered lithography machine was made by Sigl as late as 1851. It was first used in England three years later, by the firm of Maclure, Macdonald and Macgregor, who claimed, probably with some exaggeration, that it produced 3,000 impressions an hour.[4] Not surprisingly, Chatto ended his Treatise

---

1. Parl. Papers 1845, vii (612), pp.xiv, 228, 239: Select Committee on Art Unions. Report. Minutes of evidence, qus.3740, 3963.

2. Ibid., p.239: qus.3957, 3962.

3. Fielding, op.cit., pp.29-31.

4. M. Twyman, 'The Lithographic Hand Press 1796-1850', Journal of the Printing Historical Society, iii (1967), 41-50. Also, M. Twyman, Lithography 1800-1850 (1970), pp.112-3, in which he refers to Senefelder's prophetic judgement that one of the greatest imperfections of lithography was that the quality of the printing depended to a large extent on the skill of the printer, and that, 'Till the voluntary action of the human hand is no longer necessary, and till the impression can be produced wholly by good machinery', he would not believe that the art of lithography had reached its highest perfection. A. Senefelder, Complete Course of Lithography (1819), p.180.

on Wood Engraving exultant in the knowledge of his subject's unmatchability:-

> a good thing is valuable in proportion as many can enjoy it .... the productions of no other kindred art have been more generally disseminated nor with greater advantage to those for whom they were intended... As at least one hundred thousand good impressions can be obtained from a wood-cut, if properly engraved and carefully printed; and as the additional cost of printing wood-cuts with letter-press is inconsiderable when compared with the cost of printing steel or copper plates separately, the art will never want encouragement, nor sink again into neglect, so long as there are artists of talent to furnish designs, and good engravers to execute them.[1]

Nevertheless, it was not without encountering some snags that the art of wood engraving pressed forward. There were other aspects to be considered besides mere quantity, as Thackeray complained in the Westminster Review of 1839:-

> With ourselves, among whom money is plenty, enterprize so great, and everything matter of commercial speculation, Lithography has not been so much practised as wood or steel-engraving, which, by the aid of great original capital and spread of sale, are able more than to compete with the art of drawing on stone.

The article went on to dub the former as art done by machinery, and confessed to a prejudice in favour of the honest work of hand, in matters of art, preferring the rough workmanship of the painter to smooth copies produced on the wood-block or the steel-plate.[2] The greatest advantage of lithography was that the artist could retain the freedom and spirit of his drawing on the stone throughout the process of multiplying it. Whether the wood engraving could, or indeed should retain these was increasingly called into question by the commercial demands made upon it.

Bewick was unequivocally in control, had engraved his own designs and was free to interpret them, at the same time remaining faithful to the tech-

1. Jackson and Chatto, op.cit., pp.737-8.
2. (W. M. Thackeray), 'Parisian Caricatures', London and Westminster Review, xxxii (1839), 283.

nical nature of the wood engraving process. Its main characteristic is that, in direct contrast to copper engraving, every cutting by the graver prints white, every untouched space black. Simple black lines, therefore, are the result of cutting two white lines, one on either side, while crossed black lines are obtained by laboriously cutting out all the white lozenges between them. In Bewick's cuts, there are many white lines, both crossed and uncrossed, but his black lines never cross, for he ingeniously contrived to make as much use as possible of the black background. Such was the secret of his natural and comparatively rapid wood engraving technique.[1]

However, immediately there was a division between draughtsman and engraver, the problem of interpretational priority arose, and an ambivalence over status. Was the engraver to follow precisely the 'black line' of a draughtsman's pencil, with a mechanical 'facsimile' style, or was he to have the freedom to interpret it according to his own artistic inclinations and knowledge of the medium? Naturally enough, many master engravers favoured the latter. Linton believed that the rot had started even with some of Bewick's most gifted pupils, especially those who had relied upon the draughtsman Thurston, who had started out as a copper-plate engraver and led his wood engravers astray along the 'black line' path. Branston too, being trained as a copper-plate engraver was part of this school. Even Linton's partner, John Orrin Smith, produced 'the best of an essentially false style'. Having to rely upon draughtsmen,

---

1. P. G. Hamerton's article on 'Wood Engraving', <u>Encyclopaedia Britannica</u> (Edinburgh, 9th edn. 1878), viii. 436-9 uses the example of a fishing net in which he managed to place the net 'in the light' against a space or black shade under some bushes. Therefore, every string of the net could be cut in white line.

the engravers ceased to draw, ceased to rely upon themselves: 'Wanting the wider power, the inevitable course was only, in the following years, through mediocrity to mechanism'. By the time the *Illustrated London News* had set up its own engraving department, and the Dalziels and Swains were firmly established, 'Manufacture was everywhere displacing art'.[1] Linton summed up the prevailing current in the middle of the century:-

> there was in England only combed smoothness of tints, formless and void of expression, or an imbecile niggling at fac-simile, mere rat-like gnawing between the line of Leech and Gilbert: as Thompson himself said to me, "not engraving at all".[2]

The highest achievement in the 'black line' style, which tried to achieve the effect of a copper-plate engraving without that medium's freedom, was displayed in the expensive single art prints, commissioned in a similar way to work by line engravers, or the fine art series run in the illustrated newspapers. The Art Union of London decided to produce a book with illustrations on wood, designed by many leading British artists, and engraved by 'our best wood engravers', in 1847, choosing as its subject, Milton's 'L'Allegro and Il Penseroso'.[3] Linton made several agreements, one with the Art Union, to select, draw, engrave and supervise the printing of thirty pictures by deceased British artists, for £1,000 in instalments over a seventeen month period; another, with the publisher, Thomas Longman, to engrave four drawings of pictures by Perugino, at £50 each.[4] In this 'pictorial' department of wood engraving, the wood engraver,

---

1. Linton, *Masters of Wood Engraving,* pp.176-205.
2. Ibid., p.204.
3. 'Art-Union of London', *Art-Union*, ix (1847), 74, 109.
4. Feltrinelli, Linton. The Art Union agreement was dated 31 July 1855, that with Longman, 20 June 1859.

through using his tinting and shading tools and techniques, had to interpret the artist's wash and brush work, his tone and texture. However, as was frequently pointed out, the result could not compete with the copper-plate print in point of delicacy and fineness of line and tone. Such prints, it was thought, would only be purchased for their curiosity value, but not as a serious rival to copper-plate prints, nor for their own qualities.[1] One line engraver wrote to the Art-Union in 1840 to deprecate one such attempt to supersede the work of the under-employed line engravers, attacking the 'vile trash' palmed off as 'works of art'. He added:-

> No one appreciates wood-engraving more than I do, when legitimately applied, as the French apply it, for sketches, or small subjects, with the advantage of cheapness, being printed with type; but when they are made to supersede line engraving it becomes a miserable failure, as in the present instance it undoubtedly is.[2]

Fortunately, the 'facsimile' or 'mechanical' type of wood engraving made up the bulk of production.[3] It required little artistic skill and was easily learnt and executed even by apprentices, the chief thing being careful attention to the drawing to retain the artist's line. For Henry Cole, this was the positive advantage the wood engraver possessed over copper:-

> there neither need be, nor is, any intermediate person or process between the designer and the engraver. In almost all cases of engraving on copper, the picture has first of all to be reduced from its original size to the intended size of the engraving; in all cases it has to be drawn reversed on the plate.

1. J. Landseer, Lectures on the Art of Engraving, (1807), pp.114-5, 118. Jackson and Chatto, op.cit., p.737. T. Gilks, The Art of Wood Engraving (1866), p.56. Linton, Masters of Wood Engraving, p.205. Hamerton, 'Wood Engraving', 438: 'The wood cut is like a polyglot who has learnt to speak many languages at the risk of forgetting his own'.

2. 'Misapplication of Wood-Engraving', Art-Union, ii (1840), 23-24.

3. Crane, op.cit., p.60: 'All seemed fish to the engraver's net then - diagrams of all sorts, medical dissections, tale cuts, Bible pictures, book illustrations'. The least enjoyable work he can remember was the drawing of an incredible number of iron bed-steads for a Heal's catalogue, which was being engraved in the office: 'It was distinctly tiring, to say the least'.

Thus, the drawing was twice translated, usually by two different translators, and then a third translation was made by the engraver. In wood engraving, the drawing was made by the draughtsman straight onto the wood block: his black line was not cut away but the engraver left it untouched and cut round it.[1] This was the type of engraving Linton most despised, especially as applied in the periodicals, in particular, the small drawings of Gilbert and Leech, or Cruikshank and Seymour before them. Under the false appearance of liberty, it chained the engravers to subservience, misled them back to mechanism:-

> That such drawing well suited the hasty sketches needed in Hone's Political Tracts and Punch, that as sketches they satisfied the special occasion, that there is a charm in this loose free handling, that they were quickly drawn and easily - only too easily engraved, that they were satisfactorily cheap to publishers, - is true; yet no less were they detrimental to the art of engraving.[2]

The need for haste was the essential reason why the mass of wood engraving in the illustrated periodicals followed this latter course. In the factories of the Dalziels and the Swains, blocks were the products of numerous hands and there were many engravers who were entrusted with only a part of the engraving. Figures were assigned to one, landscape to another, sky to a third and the harmony of the whole adjusted by the master, who 'must possess all the talents of an artist to direct skilfully the mechanism of a manufacturer'.[3] A cursory glance at most of the

---

1. Cole, 'Modern Wood Engraving', 267-8. Also, (H. Cole), 'Wood Engraving among Female Artists', London and Westminster Review, xxxviii (1842), 215.

2. Linton, Masters of Wood Engraving, p.205.

3. Cole, 'Modern Wood Engraving', 270. This rather spoilt his earlier argument about the 'superior accuracy and fidelity' of transmission in wood engraving compared with the copper-plate. There would thus seem, on his own admission, to be more, not less people involved in producing a wood engraving. Also, Groves, op.cit., p.16:
    > It was usual in a block containing figures and faces for the heads to be cut by the master's hand, and what was called the less important "facsimile" work by the apprentices. For many years, I, having become very skilful, was entrusted with this more important work, and for a long period the heads and hands, in the Punch pictures, were the work of my hands.

work of the period shows that such men were few and far between. The practice which began in order to make use of the best available talent developed into a method for speeding up production. On Punch, the small humorous cuts, usually devoid of topical reference, need not be hurried, and if they were not ready for one week, were held over to the next. In contrast, a single block was used for the weekly political 'big cut'; it was therefore often roughly drawn and hastily cut.[1] This reached its depressing nadir on the news magazines, for whom time was an 'imperative necessity'. To compensate for the narrow girth of the box tree, large blocks were made up of pieces glued together, or fastened by means of a bolt passing through the entire block.[2] When in a hurry, the block was engraved piece by piece as parts of the drawing were completed, so as to enable the engravers and draughtsmen to work on the same subject at the same time. In some cases, the draughtsman never saw the whole of his drawing completed: John Gilbert often worked in this way. When the drawing was completed, the master engraver 'set' the lines across the joints of the block to try to achieve a harmonious whole ready for the printing process.[3] The result of these exertions was often deplorable. The engravers were sometimes working from the 'merest memoranda', jottings in the pictorial shorthand of an artist abroad, too rushed to fill

1. Spielmann, op.cit., pp.249-53.

2. The Times, 29 February 1844, congratulated Vizetelly's firm for their production of a wood engraving from Wilkie's 'Blind Fiddler'. The print, the article said, was as good as a copper-plate impression and yet was fresh after 5,000 impressions. The novelty of the process used was that it was printed by steam from four separate blocks compressed together. According to Spielmann, around 1860, Charles Wells, a cabinet maker and boxwood importer of Bouverie Street, invented the jointed block. The six or more pieces were taken apart after the drawing or photograph had been placed on the surface; then it was distributed among the engravers and finally, screwed together again. Op.cit., p.249.

3. Jackson, op.cit., pp.315-24.

in the details.[1] As one art critic commented, the wood engraver was not <u>merely</u> a translator, but an 'elaborating, labour-saving secretary':-

> Just as a man whose time is very precious marks in pencil on the back of letters a word or two indicating the nature of the reply to be delivered, but leaves the work of arranging the form of it to his secretary, so the designer on wood washes in a shade with his camel-hair brush, but leaves the labour of making the lines which are to represent that shade to the cutter who comes after him. The economy of time which is effected by this is enough to settle the question from the pecuniary point of view.[2]

The engravers over-compensated with their uniform training in the conventional system of linear structure, their predetermined 'nets of rationality', and reduced all work to a 'flat dull plain of reasonability', bearing little relation to the individuality of the original.[3] The final dimension added to this unsatisfactory division of labour was that which existed between the engraver and the printer. Ellic Howe has suggested that the iron press, with its more exact techniques of press work, had been developed largely to obtain the best results for 'white line' wood engraving, with their delicate incisions and variations in tone.[4] With the advent of the steam press, such care could not be taken with the printing, paper or ink. The cuts could not be aided with overlays; they had to be lowered to a greater depth as the blanket on the cylinder penetrated further down between the lines, and finished perfectly before leaving the engraver, to avoid expensive reworking by the printer.[5] Often,

---

1. C. G. Harper, <u>English Pen Artists of Today</u> (1892), pp.257-60. Jackson, <u>op.cit.</u>, pp.317-20.

2. P. G. Hamerton, <u>Thoughts about Art</u> (1873 edn.), pp.377-8.

3. W. M. Ivins, <u>Prints and Visual Communication</u> (1953), pp.60-61, 99.

4. Howe, <u>The London Compositor</u>, p. 295.

5. Jackson and Chatto, <u>op.cit.</u>, p.705.

therefore, complaints by artists directed at the engraver could be more properly aimed at the printing process itself, on the black printer's ink and slight thickening of lines, compared with their own fine pencillings.[1]

Besides changing the quality and nature of wood engraving, these divisions also had important social consequences. In the 1830s, as Henry Cole noted, few of the best artists condescended to design on wood.[2] The situation in England was frequently compared unfavorably with that in France, and placed in the context of a greater awareness of design generally in France.[3] The Art-Union, which included in its first volume an article on the rise and progress of wood engraving and frequently printed specimens of the art, made a point of drawing attention to the opportunity missed by leading English artists thereby 'to improve mankind, by refining the taste and strengthening the mind!'.[4] In 1846 it commented, 'For a long period, drawing on wood was considered by our English artists as a mode of professional occupation by which he lost caste'. Fortunately, 'a liberal and a wealthy publisher', Thomas Longman, had come to the rescue with enough capital to commission Cope, Creswick, Redgrave, Horsley and Taylor to produce designs for an edition of The

---

1. Ibid., pp.724-5. For unfavorable comparisons to hand press work see W. Savage, A Dictionary of the Art of Printing (1841), pp.215, 465-7. For the necessity of adapting designs and engraving to the conditions of rapid machine printing see Chambers Miscellany, ix.No.85 (1846), 14-15. Hamerton, Thoughts about Art, p.382. Spielmann, op.cit., pp.252-3.

2. Cole, 'Modern Wood Engraving', 277-8.

3. Thackeray, 'Parisian Caricatures', 283-8. Also, Gilks, op.cit., p.56. 'Speaking to the Eye', Economist, ix (1851), 533.

4. 'Wood Engraving', Art-Union, i (1839), 25-32. For specimens of wood engravings, Art-Union, iv (1842), 49-56; v (1843), 113-20.

Poetical Works of Oliver Goldsmith (1846).[1] However, it was not until a decade later that the initiative of a few publishers, the increasing fame and status of designers on wood like Leech and Gilbert, and the prospect of good pay and wide circulation attracted sufficient numbers of distinguished artists to replace the stigma attached to such work with anything like an aesthetic interest.[2] Those who had to make a living by it frequently expressed exasperation at their interpreters. Dean Hole reports that John Leech used to groan when Punch arrived at his breakfast table on Tuesday morning and he saw some small aberration had detracted from his design and achievement.[3] George du Maurier wrote of one of his early designs, 'the wretches have completely spoilt it in the engraving and I intend to make a great fuss'.[4] Similarly, Hubert von Herkomer, later in the century, wrote that when the original drawing was cut away, the only satisfaction left was to 'growl' at the engraver; 'In only too many cases the creed of the latter was "cut through that shower of lines, never mind what the artist drew", with the result that we could barely recognize our own work'.[5] Some of the novices asked for trouble. Dante Gabriel Rossetti's highly wrought design for 'The Maids of Elfen-Mere', in The Music Master volume of William Allingham's Day and Night Songs (1855) employed several types of media and produced 'a very nice effect'. But as the Dalziel brothers observed, 'the engraved reproduction of this many tinted drawing, reduced to the stern

1. 'English Artists on Wood', Art-Union, viii (1846), 11.
2. For the so-called 'golden age' of English illustration see G. White, English Illustration 'The Sixties': 1855-70 (1897). F. Reid, Illustrators of the Sixties (1928).
3. F. Reynolds Hole, Memories (1892), pp.28-29.
4. The Young George du Maurier, ed. D. du Maurier (1951), p.17.
5. H. von Herkomer, The Herkomers (1910), pp.82-83. Also, A.S. Hartrick, A Painter's Pilgrimage through Fifty Years (Cambridge, 1939), pp.68-69.

realities of black and white by printer's ink, failed to satisfy him'.[1]

Such complaints by artistic prima-donnas distract from less conspicuous social developments within the trade. Henry Cole suggested in his Westminster Review article of 1838 that wood engraving could become a suitable occupation for 'educated gentlewomen of the middle classes, who now earn a subsistence chiefly as governesses'. It was seen as 'an honourable, elegant, and lucrative employment, easily acquired, and in every way becoming their sex and habits'.[2] Already in 1839, the Art-Union cast doubt on the assertion that wood engraving was '"easily acquired"' by amateurs, so as to become '"honourable, elegant and lucrative"', finding it 'misleading to advise a pursuit very difficult of achievement, and in

---

1. The Brothers Dalziel, op.cit., pp.86-87. For Rossetti's reactions to this and to the Dalziels' engraving of his illustrations for the Moxon edition of Tennyson in 1857 see Reid, op.cit., pp.30-43.

2. Cole, 'Modern Wood Engraving', 278. Cole's Diary for 1838 gives a clear idea of how he prepared the article. It was evidently originally inspired by the publication of a number of illustrated works, some in French, of which the most important was the L. Curmer edition of Bernardin de Saint-Pierre's Paul et Virginie et La Chaumière Indienne, published both in Paris and London, with wood engravings by many leading English artists, including Bonner, Branston, Gray, Powis, Orrin Smith and the Williams family. During April and May, Cole visited the publishers and printers most involved in providing illustrated literature - Bentley, Knight and Clowes - as well as talking to and getting to know a number of the more important wood engravers. John Jackson he found 'to be a most intelligent man and most willing to afford every assistance for the article, by means of blocks &c.' In contrast, one Sunday afternoon he walked to Chiswick 'to solicit loan of blocks from Mr. Whittingham, who, notwithstanding I took an introduction from Mr. Thompson was very grumpy'. Cole also went into the history of the art, examining Bewick's Quadrupeds, reading Jackson's Treatise on Wood Engraving (presumably in proof form) and learning much from the Thompson family, who became friends, and brought him prints by Durer, as well as examples of their own work, to study. He wrote and revised his article over June and early July, and despite some evidence of his dissatisfaction over the state in which it was inserted, the article saw the light of day in the August number of the Westminster Review, signed with the initial 'X'. Cole's autobiography rather misleadingly disclaims the actual writing of the article, as opposed to collecting the information and the illustrations for it, and misdates its publication as 1840. Fifty Years of Public Work, i. 102.

which mediocrity is miserable - more so than in any other class of art'.[1]
However, by 1842, Cole had produced his Handbook for Architecture, Sculpture, Tombs and Decorations of Westminster Abbey, 'with fifty six embellishments on wood, engraved by ladies', issued under his nom de plume of Felix Summerly. With characteristic false modesty he reviewed the work anonymously in the Westminster Review:

> Without taking more credit to our suggestions than they deserve, we believe it may fairly be said that all the engravers of these specimens became such after the 'Westminster Review' (No. LXI) first pointed out the suitableness of wood-engraving as an employment for ladies; and, either directly or indirectly, in consequence of that suggestion.[2]

The decision to set up a wood engraving class in the new Female School of Design the same year provoked more controversy. In 1843, a meeting was held by the wood engravers of London, chaired by John Thompson, to prepare a memorial for presentation to the Council of the School of Design, persuading them to drop the scheme. The Council declined to be moved. The Art-Union appeared to sympathize with the wood engravers' case, especially at such a time, when prices for good work were so wretchedly low as to render the occupation of a clever and skilful artist scarcely more profitable than that of a bricklayer:

> It is notorious that scores of "lads" are employed to produce cheap cuts for the two illustrated papers; and it is certain that ere long, the "supply" of hands will so far exceed the "demand" that it would seem likely for every woodcut to be executed, there will be half a dozen applicants - these illustrated newspapers not being destined to have a very prolonged existence.

Despite such a gloomy forecast, however, the Art-Union did not believe that the wood engravers' 'unreasonable' behaviour would solve the problems of the trade. Furthermore, 'we must bear in mind that engraving on wood is one

---

1. 'Wood Engraving', Art-Union, i (1839), 25.
2. Cole, 'Wood Engraving among Female Artists', 215. Also Cole Diary for 1842: 13 April. Wm Hickson called and said he wd have a short paper on Ladies Wood Engraving ... 4 May. In the Evg napping and writing a notice for Westminster Review. 11 May ... called on W. Hickson & gave him notice of W. Abb.
See also, Cole, Fifty Years of Public Work, i. 99-101; ii. 197-207.

of the few employments that ladies may undertake without losing "caste".'
In England they had few outlets of a non-menial character. The governess
or teacher was worse paid than a domestic servant, 'and the poor plain or
fancy worker, if she labours at home, and so "keeps up her respectability",
may earn ninepence per diem, to be doubled if she braves licentious stares
twice a day, alone and unprotected in public streets'.[1] The Athenaeum also
supported the ladies, stressing that wood engraving was cheap, clean and
could be respectably performed in the quiet of the home, while at the same
time pointing out the difficulties involved, especially in acquiring skill
in drawing. Without such skill, without a feeling for art:

> The utmost that could be hoped for is, that after a hard practice
> of about two years, she might become sufficiently skilful to cut
> well enough for the cheap illustrated periodicals. In another two
> years, if kept in sufficient employment, she may be qualified to
> take rank among the average professional engravers of the day, which,
> indeed, is no great position to take as an artist; but sufficient,
> with connexions, to obtain employment.[2]

On reading this, John Thompson, who was not prepared to stand for a snub
directed against wood engraving in general, no matter what he thought of
lady wood engravers in particular, wrote off to his friend Cole to protest:

> I cannot help thinking that their general tone is very prejudicial
> to the Profession and in some of the details most assuredly unjust and
> that if the Art is at all worth cultivating, degrading its professors
> in the eyes of the public, is a very bad course, as it will naturally
> deter young men of talent from persevering in a pursuit from which a
> very limited profit is, and no reputation will then be obtained.[3]

The following year, the wood engravers again memorialized the School of
Design to abolish the ladies' class of drawing and engraving on wood and were
again turned down. The Art-Union felt their memorial to be 'discourteous',
and regretted that 'so numerous and so respected a class of artists should

---

1. 'The Wood-Engravers', Art-Union, v (1843), 271.
2. 'Our Weekly Gossip', Athenaeum, No. 839 (25 November 1843), pp.1048-9.
3. Victoria and Albert Museum, Cole Papers, Box 12: Thompson to Cole, 29 November 1843.

have taken so injudicious and so illiberal a step'. What made it so particularly 'odious' was that it was directed against ladies, whose earnings might be 'miserable pittances', but they would not lose their position in society by so doing, and their pay was better than for bazaar work, 'to which, we know, many young ladies well born, delicately nurtured, and expensively educated have been compelled to submit, toiling for bare life from sunrise till long after the sun has set'.[1] And when in 1845 Mrs. S.C. Hall, wife of the editor, visited the Female School of Design, she again reinforced the message of helping to provide ladies of '"the middle rank of life"', yet without independence, in other words, money, with the means and the training to gain it.[2] In 1849, Linton was asked to take on a female pupil by one of his lady friends:

> Would you like to have Miss Annette Winnaid for one year or two, and if so what must be the premium? She would wish to board and live altogether with your family, to help you with your work if she could (& Miss Waterhouse at the School of Design says that Miss Annette could be of great use to any Engraver, & asks why she does not seek work on her own account) and receive your instruction. They think & justly that there may be many reasons why anyone may object to receiving an inmate into their house. I know her well, & thoroughly respect her for her love of independence, her perseverance and sound principle. She is also amiable and thoroughly well read ...[3]

Mrs. McIan, the Head Mistress of the Female School, defended the adoption of a course on wood engraving before the Select Committee on the Schools of Design in 1849 on the grounds that it enabled her students to understand the sort of drawing necessary for wood blocks, and that wood engraving was one of the means of giving employment to the women in the country. She could not avoid admitting, however, that there were already

---

1. 'The Wood-Engravers', Art-Union, vi (1844), 123.
2. Mrs. S.C. Hall, 'A Visit to the Female School of Design', Art-Union, vii (1845), 231.
3. Feltrinelli, Linton. Ellen Randell to Linton, 3 June 1849.

too many wood engravers in the country.[1] Nevertheless, the 1853 Report of the Department of Practical Art testifies to the continued existence of the class, now reorganized, rather surprisingly, under John Thompson, who must have been won over by Cole, with the emphasis laid on both drawing on wood and engraving:-

> for it is a remarkable fact that a very small proportion of the present wood engravers are able to draw at all; and it is evident that an engraver cannot thoroughly understand how to render lines correctly with his graver who cannot make them first with his pencil.[2]

The trade, however, could offer shelter from degradation for even worthier causes than ladies' self-respect. Crane reports that some of Linton's apprentices were deaf, 'It was, indeed, very usual to apprentice deaf and sometimes even dumb youths to wood-engravers. They went by the name of "Dummies" in the office', and communicated by sign language.[3]

It can thus be seen that the 'wood peckers' or 'peckers' as they were commonly called, had greatly declined in status since Bewick's time, their uncertain footing not made more sure by the ambivalence of their journalistic surroundings. As the trade expanded, their increasing social isolation from the free and easy world of the creative artist and writer was accentuated by physical divisions. On Punch, for example, Swain's department was removed from the premises of the printing works to one of the old residential houses in Bouverie Street. Gradually, Groves, one of their engravers, witnessed the loss of contact between the engravers and staff:-

> as the business increased and with it the Competition, the Masters, fearing that this intimacy might prove injurious to themselves, refused to allow any visitors whatever inside the engraving-rooms. They had their Offices on a lower floor, and above that there was "No admittance". Mr. Swain removed to the first floor, had his room papered; put matting on the floor, and pictures on the walls, and was thus quite up to date.[4]

---

1. Parl. Papers 1849, xviii (576), p.117:- minutes of evidence, qus.1370-9.
2. Parl. Papers 1852-53, liv (1615), pp.20-21:- First Report of the Department of Practical Art.
3. Crane, op.cit., p.48.
4. Groves, op.cit., p.17.

In contrast to their staff, the master engravers became men of prestige and importance, akin to factory owners. The Dalziels, with their office and workshops in High Street, Camden Town, were far more speculative than any other engraving firm, becoming, in addition, both printers and publishers. George du Maurier, as a young man, revealed in his letters the power of their position. He confessed that sooner than continue meeting important people in 'society', he would far rather 'be invited to the gin and whisky parties of the brothers Dalziel ... when the Queen's English is solemnly murdered every other Saturday, I believe'. A year later, he was worrying because the 'Dalziels have snubbed me awfully, I really cannot think why, perhaps because I shewed myself too anxious to work for them'.[1] Such were the extremes of status that division of labour had brought to the one time art of wood engraving.

---

1. Du Maurier, op.cit., pp.150, 215.

> The great end of the whole art of engraving is to render the
> spirit and genius of a great artist accessible to the thousands,
> or the millions, by embodying them in cheap and portable forms.
> Wood engraving, professedly the cheapest and most portable of all
> the representations of great pictures, excels equally in fulfilling
> the highest mission of its art, by the superior accuracy and fidelity
> with which it represents the spirit and genius of the picture.[1]

Henry Cole, when surveying the state of wood engraving in 1838 could afford to be optimistic. Its cheapness offered the possibility, he believed, of lessening the rudeness in the cottages of poor men, of creating a love of art and beauty, and hence of moral good. However, as we have seen, despite this progress, there were tensions within the industry which complicate, and sometimes almost negate the process of a smooth path towards perfection. First, of course, there was still a prominent body of engravers who employed traditional techniques and were not part of any growth towards universal mechanical facility. Furthermore, sneers at their stylistic backwardness were symptomatic of deeper - economic and social, ultimately political - divisions. Secondly, the conditions in which many engravers worked and lived in central London did not exactly conform to the highest ideals and expectations placed in the art by some of its supporters. Finally, even within the large-scale expansion, the chequered character of much of the work, mirrored in the ambivalent status of the wood engraver, was not calculated to further artistic standards and aesthetic harmony. That Henry Cole's article, Edward Cowper's hopes of diffusing 'science and taste and good feeling, without one sentence of an immoral feeling in the whole', or the Art-Union's 'to improve mankind, by refining the taste and strengthening the mind', were over-optimistic and never found general acceptance is one of the major themes of this study.

---

1. Cole, 'Modern Wood Engraving', 268.

THE DEVELOPMENT OF POLITICAL CARICATURE

1830 - 1836

III

The development in complexity and sophistication of graphic journalism during the 1830s and 1840s is, as has been shown, due partly to the technical means available, but also to the use made of these by the leading personnel involved, on both artistic and editorial sides, and the audiences to whom the results were directed. Political caricature, however, has so far resisted efforts to set up a theoretical framework based on hypotheses about historical context, motive and impact.[1] It is true that the single caricature print, the normal mode of issue until the third decade of the nineteenth century, has been described as an instantaneous reaction to a political event and forms, as such, a temperature chart of popular opinion, evoking counter-prints in its wake if sufficiently controversial.[2] But it does not indicate how typical this largely metropolitan response was, nor the size of the response. Few facts are known about the sales of these prints, the marketing techniques adopted, the level of readership or the climate of views represented.

Fortunately, during the 1830s, certain improvements in the state of the evidence can be discerned and examined. First, much more is known about the personnel involved, largely owing to the indefatigable propensity of the period's metropolitan bohemia to write memoirs. Furthermore, certain advantages came with regularity of issue in the field of political caricature. It was a period of equipoise between the anarchy of individual prints and the large journalistic concerns, in which the political cartoon was subordinated to a minor role, calculated not to offend the proprietor nor the widest

---

1. See W. A. Coupe, 'Observations on a Theory of Political Caricature', Comparative Studies in Society and History, xi (1969), 79-95 in answer to L. H. Streicher, 'On a Theory of Political Caricature', Comparative Studies in Society and History, ix (1966-7), 427-45.

2. M. D. George, English Political Caricature 1792-1832 (Oxford, 1959), p.259.

possible audience.[1] This is not to say that there is one formula alone which can summarize the relationship between journalistic output and its impact on audiences. In some cases, the prints would seem to have been fairly personal statements by the artist, such as those of John Doyle - "H.B." - or C.J. Grant. The cuts in the humorous magazines, on the other hand, depended to a greater extent on editorial control. However, the majority of artists and journalists were part of a common context and depended on each other, as well as on the printers and engravers, for survival. As a result, a certain continuity of editorial and artistic policy had to be built up in order to secure some relationship between editorial opinion and market response and establish a regular readership. On this basis, the leading vehicles for political caricature during the 1830's - Figaro in London, with cuts by Robert Seymour, Grant's Political Drama and H.B.'s Political Sketches were able to keep alive for several years. A caricature, instead of representing the views of some scurrilous pamphleteer or wayward genius, now had some rapport with its audience in presentation style and content, against which that of another caricature from a series or journal can be measured. This chapter examines the range of such examples during the first part of the decade, and how the format, personnel and imagery of each type reinforced some of the stylistic differences already noted in the last chapter.

---

1. See D. Low, 'Forward', to H.R. Westwood, Modern Caricaturists (1932), p.xii: In the efforts to attract the last reader, the final subscriber, the attraction tends to take the form of amusement rather than instruction. Let our cartoons, say the newspaper proprietors, be amusing ... The rotary press and cheap paper have made it possible to produce more caricatures to-day than ever before, but they have also had the effect of making the modern newspaper cartoonist more restrained than his ancestors. His function within the framework of the modern newspaper has come to be recognised as that of entertainer-moralist in pictures - primarily entertainer, secondarily moralist.

I

A process of systematization took place in the 1830s by which order and continuity were lent to caricature through a variety of journalistic means. One line of development was followed by the quarto-size weekly humorous magazines. The most famous and long-lived of these was Figaro in London (1831-1839), but this was joined at various times by Giovanni in London (1832), the Devil or Asmodeus in London (1832), Punchinello (1832) and Punch in London (1832), as well as a host of provincial imitators.[1] All sported small emblematic cuts and included short editorials, jokes, puns and dramatic reviews which anticipated in style, as well as in overall format, the early editions of Punch. Secondly, political woodcuts of approximately folio size were issued in weekly or fortnightly series, for example, the Political Drama (1833-1835), the Political Play Bill (1835), and Lloyd's Political Jokes (1836). Some were more closely linked to a periodical format by being printed on both sides, in quarto or octavo sections on folio size paper, as was the case with the later issues of the Political Stage (1835). Others, following William Hone's example in producing A Slap at Slop (1821), were issued both as broadsheet and periodical,

---

1. For example, Figaro in Birmingham (1832), Figaro in Chesterfield (1832), Figaro in Liverpool (1833), Figaro in Sheffield (1832-8), Figaro in Wales (1835-6). Compiled from J. H. Wiener, A Descriptive Finding List of Unstamped British Periodicals 1830-1836 (Bibliographical Society, 1970). D. J. Gray, 'A List of Periodicals Published in Great Britain, 1800-1900', Victorian Periodicals Newsletter, No.15 (1972), p.17. There is one copy of Figaro in Bristol (? 1832) in Bristol City Library, Reference department. A Beckett kept a score of his rivals who went under in the "Notices to Correspondents" column of Figaro in London.

for instance John Bull's Picture Gallery (1832), the first twelve numbers of which were reissued in cardboard cover. The Weekly Show-Up (1832) and the Satirical Puppet Show (1833), both of which feature large woodcuts, can be more strictly defined as periodicals for they included at least three pages of text. The final stage in this development was the appearance of satirical woodcuts in the large broadsheet newspapers which started about 1836: Figaro (1836), Figaro's Life in London (1836), and more important, Cleave's Weekly Police Gazette (1834-1836). The satirical print had become the newspaper cartoon. Thirdly, there were the folio size lithographic magazines. These ranged from Everybody's Album and Caricature Magazine (1834-1835), illustrated by Grant and published by J. Kendrick, to McLean's Monthly Sheet of Caricatures, first called the Looking Glass, (1830-1836), published by Thomas McLean with illustrations by William Heath and Robert Seymour. The most famous of this type were the serial lithographs drawn by John Doyle, H.B.'s Political Sketches (1829-1851), which were published irregularly by McLean, several at a time during the parliamentary session.[1] Many modes had their imitators; few strictly adhered to their most usual format.[2]

1. The British Museum, Prints and Drawings department has the largest collection of serial woodcuts, bound in a volume entitled Penny Political Caricatures. Everybody's Album and Caricature Magazine ran for at least thirty two numbers between 1834 and 1835, but I have found only four in existence, in the John Johnson Collection, Bodleian Library. McLean's Monthly Sheet of Caricatures and H.B.'s Political Sketches are more commonly available, the Brit. Mus. Prints and Drawings also possessing Doyle's original drawings.

2. See M.D. George, Catalogue of Political and Personal Satires (1954), xi.p.xlvii for H.B.'s imitators. Grant's woodcuts for the Political Drama were also issued in lithographic form by G. Tregear. Victoria and Albert Museum, Prints and Drawings department. James Klugman collection. Seymour's cuts for Figaro in London were later issued together on large sheets, entitled Figaro's Comic Almanack and Caricature Gallery, as were Grant's for Cleave's Police Gazette, as Cleave's Picture Gallery of Grant's Comicalities. Brit. Mus. Prints and Drawings and Library.

However, in general there is consistency about the personnel who produced them and their content which may be categorized.

A dividing line can be established in terms of price, which indicates the level of readership aspired to and presumably acquired. At a time when, according to John Cleave, the difference between twopence and sevenpence represented the difference of a man's meal,[1] it is easy to see that H.B.'s Political Sketches, selling at two shillings each, or McLean's Monthly Sheet of Caricatures, whose plain editions, printed on both sides of two leaves, cost three shillings, while the four page gilt-edged coloured edition cost six, would reach the hands of very few of the lower classes. Everybody's Album and Caricature Magazine only cost sixpence plain or a shilling coloured, while Figaro in London, together with most of the other humorous magazines and serial cuts cost a penny. Its reputed sale was 70,000 copies; it had to be reprinted and after a year, the old parts were reissued in sixpenny monthly instalments.[2] Similarly, the popularity of John Bull's Picture Gallery was such, that of its first four numbers, issued in the last stages of the Reform Bill crisis, it claimed to have sold altogether about 100,000 copies.[3]

1. John Cleave, 'To the Readers of Cleave's Weekly Police Gazette', Cleave's Weekly Police Gazette, 3 September 1836.
2. W. Jerrold, Douglas Jerrold and 'Punch' (1910), p.4.
3. Wiener, Descriptive Finding List, p.23.

Distinctions can also be made along the lines of the personnel associated with a particular periodical. The publisher who saw the greatest number of caricatures through the presses during the period was Thomas McLean. He issued both H.B.'s Political Sketches and the Looking Glass, which he renamed McLean's Monthly Sheet of Caricatures, thereby stressing his own importance. Little else is known about him, but he seems to have been a man more pragmatic than idealistic: he placed faith in a large but select clientele, rather than in the political cause of a minority. In a signed preface to the 1832 volume of McLean's Monthly Sheet of Caricatures, he stated a desire 'to shake hands with all parties ... You may laugh with the Whigs at Toryism (I beg pardon Conservation) with the Tories at the Whigs, with the Radicals at both, and with both at the Radicals'. He prided himself upon the patronage of the nobility and gentry, 'the very highest classes of society'.[1]

In contrast, a new class of publisher-cum-printer catered for the lowest end of the market. William Chubb and George Drake were part of a group which included more illustrious promoters of cheap reading matter for the masses, Benjamin Cousins, Henry Hetherington and Edward Lloyd. In general, however, their movements are hard to trace through the back streets of journalistic London.[2]

---

1. T. McLean, An Illustrative Key to the Political Sketches of H.B. (1844) ii. p.iii and advertisement.

2. The most recent and comprehensive guide to printers in this period, giving their addresses and some idea of the length of time they remained in business, is W. B. Todd, A Directory of Printers and Others in Allied Trades, London and Vicinity 1800-1840 (Printing Historical Society, 1972).

On 8 November 1830, Francis Place wrote to John Hobhouse of 'a fellow named Chubb, a vagabond pamphlet seller in Holywell Street', who 'knows as well as any man can know how the vulgarity feel; he is acquainted with a multitude of vagabonds who are fit for any mischief'.[1] Unlike McLean, with his smart address at 26 Haymarket, Chubb's premises were in a street which had declined by this time into 'a narrow dirty lane', between St. Clement Danes and St. Mary-le-Strand, parallel to the Strand, and notorious for its 'old clothesmen and the vendors of low publications'.[2] One of their products was undoubtedly John Bull's Picture Gallery, illustrated by C. J. Grant, which Chubb printed and published in 1832. George Drake, who lived nearby at 12 Houghton Street, Clare Market, also used Grant to illustrate the Weekly Show-Up, the Satirical Puppet Show and the most successful of all the serial wood-cuts, the Political Drama, which continued for 131 numbers. Benjamin Cousins acted as witness for Drake in 1832 when the latter registered his press under the Seditious Societies Act (39 George III, cap. 79).[3] Cousins himself produced a second edition of the Political Drama in the 1840s for which Grant did the illustrations,[4] and he also provided the front page cartoon for Cousins' Penny Satirist (1837-1846). His shop at 18 Duke Street, Lincoln's Inn Fields, was reckoned to be, with James Watson's and Henry Hetherington's, one of the 'chief depots of the literature of unbelief'.[5]

1. Brit. Mus., Addit. MSS. 27,789 (Place Papers), f.193.
2. Cunningham, op.cit., i. 388-9. Knight's Cyclopaedia, p.764.
3. Todd, op.cit., p.60.
4. I have found only one number of this second edition of the Political Drama, No.15 entitled 'GRAND PROCESSION IN HONOUR OF THE ARRIVAL OF THE PRINCE OF WALES' (1841-2), in the Johnson collection.
5. Frost, op.cit., p.84.

During the 1830s, he was fined several times for selling unstamped literature, once in 1831 over cotton almanacs, in 1835 for his own Political Register.[1] From his own publications, it would seem that Cousins favoured Owenism, Co-operation and the free thought ideals of the Rev. James E. ('Shepherd') Smith, who left him the money he had made as editor of the Family Herald when he died.[2] The careers of John Cleave (c.1790-c.1847) and Henry Hetherington (1792-1849) in promoting unstamped journalism and radical politics are much better documented.[3] For the purpose of this discussion, however, it is enough to note that Hetherington printed and published the last four numbers of the Political Play Bill from his premises at 126 Strand, while Cleave put out his Weekly Police Gazette, with cartoons by Grant, from 1 Shoe Lane, Fetter Lane, Fleet Street. Edward Lloyd (1815-1890) also emerges from the shadows of anonymity because of his later success as the leading promoter of cheap fiction in the 1840s. He was born at Thornton Heath, Surrey, but left school early to come to London, enrol in the Chancery Lane Mechanics' Institute and open a small shop to sell publications.[4] His first registered address was at 44 Wych Street, a continuation of Drury Lane which joined Holywell Street at St. Clement Danes, much favoured by cheap prostitutes.[5]

1. Hollis, op.cit., p.310.
2. G. J. Holyoake, History of Co-operation (1875), i. 202.
3. For brief but comprehensive summaries of their careers see Hollis, op.cit., pp.309-11.
4. 'Death of Mr. Edward Lloyd', Lloyd's Weekly Newspaper, 13 April 1890.
5. Todd, op.cit., p.120.

From here, he produced Lloyd's Political Jokes in 1836, which was the last of the folio size serial woodcuts of the decade to be illustrated by Grant.

Evidence suggests that most of the serial woodcuts and the penny humorous magazines were sold on the streets by vendors.[1] However, the production arrangements of the humorous magazines do appear to have been the more sophisticated. Their printers were still mainly concentrated in the environs of the Strand and Fleet Street, Fetter Lane and Drury Lane, but all of the magazines except Punch in London arranged for separate publishing outlets with the better-known printers. William Strange, for instance, acted as publisher for Figaro in London before taking over the printing side for the last three years of its existence. His next door neighbour, Benjamin Steill, in Paternoster Row, the traditional book-selling street, put out five numbers of Punchinello and the whole of Giovanni in London.[2] In 1822, Strange had been a partner to George Cowie and subsequently, their careers intertwined through a variety of address changes and joint ventures. In 1834, they both became members of the Society for the Protection of Booksellers, a friendly society formed to give legal or monetary aid to those prosecuted for selling unstamped newspapers; in 1836, Strange acted as witness for Cowie when he registered his press.[3]

---

1. See below pp. 126-8.
2. Wiener, Descriptive Finding List, Nos.148, 163, 414. For a history and description of Paternoster Row, see Cunningham, op.cit., ii. 626-7.
3. Hollis, op.cit., pp.200-1, 310, 314. Todd, op.cit., p.48.

They collaborated to produce A Slap at the Times (1832), illustrated by Robert Cruikshank, Strange acting as publisher, Cowie as printer. Cowie printed and published twenty six numbers of the Devil or Asmodeus in London; Strange produced A Slap at the Church (1832), which was edited by John Cleave and William Carpenter, had illustrations by George Cruikshank and Robert Seymour, and was engraved partly by George Dorrington.[1]

As on other levels of political caricature, there is very little information about the financial arrangements of these publications. Profits were probably divided on a percentage basis among the parties involved in their production, but rather more typical are the frequent changes in publisher, printer and editorial staff, the short runs and sudden closures which point to unpaid debts and losses.[2] Any party was welcome to put up the initial capital; however, an outside backer was rarely found.[3] Thomas Lyttleton Holt (c.1794-1879) apparently owned Figaro in London and came from a genteel background, being educated at St. Paul's and Cambridge.[4] The fathers of both

---

1. Wiener, Descriptive Finding List, Nos.115, 468, 469.

2. Giovanni in London went through two printers; Figaro in London, three; Punchinello had two printers and two publishers; the Devil in London, four printers and two publishers. Wiener, Descriptive Finding List, Nos.115, 148, 163, 414.

3. Vizetelly, op.cit., i. 166.

4. An analysis of fifty six metropolitan newspaper editors in the early nineteenth century reveals that all but five came from 'comfortable middle-class homes', F. D. Roberts, 'More Early Victorian Newspaper Editors', Victorian Periodicals Newsletter, No.16 (1972), pp.15-28.

Gilbert à Beckett (1811-1856) and Henry Mayhew (1812-1887) were lawyers and could afford to send their sons to Westminster. But such an aura of respectability can be taken too far. Mayhew dropped out from Westminster, à Beckett from reading law and Holt from Cambridge. A Beckett's first youthful excursion into comic journalism, Cerberus, is said to have contained forty-three libels in four columns.[1] Holt's enthusiasm for founding ephemeral publications led both à Beckett and Mayhew to the insolvent's court;[2] à Beckett had to be 'locked up with a deal table, pen and ink and a gin bottle, when Figaro was short of "copy"'.[3] The motive behind their editorship of Figaro in London was more likely to be a means of venting youthful high spirits and hopes of a quick profit than any deep seated political purpose.

The professed aims of Figaro in London, its attitudes towards other publications as well as the reaction of other publications to it, confirm this view. It said it wanted 'to improve many and to amuse all by a little harmless satire'. It distinguished itself carefully from the 'pennyworth of blasphemy, and obscenity', which it felt ought to be prosecuted. Certainly, no harm was seen in it

---

1. Spielmann, op.cit., p.272.

2. Thompson, 'Mayhew and the "Morning Chronicle". pp.14-15. See below p.223. According to Alfred Bunn, A Word with Punch (11 November 1847), p.6, who extracted the information from the books of the Insolvents' Court, à Beckett's debts amounted to £3,748 1s 11d., his credit £20.

3. Punch library, Henry Silver diary, 9 December 1858.

by the magistrate who dismissed its only prosecution in 1832.[1] Furthermore, the paper attacked the Catnach press and the growth of 'scaffold literature', which particularly appealed to the populace, and poured scorn on its pretensions to accuracy.[2] Both Figaro in London and Punchinello emphasized their self-esteem by making entries in the Copyright Registers, which neither Catnach nor the printers of the serial woodcuts bothered with.[3] However, Figaro in London did advertise on several occasions in Hetherington's Poor Man's Guardian, possibly because Mayhew's eldest brother helped to run it.[4] In the Poor Man's Guardian it described itself as a weekly satirical paper, 'written in the spirit of the times', and including political pasquinades and notices of the drama. It quoted the Literary Gazette of December 1831, which called it 'a smart pennyworth of politics on the Whig side', and a copy of the United Kingdom which believed, 'So rich and sparkling is it, that we recommend it as a dinner companion to all those who cannot afford champagne'.[5]

1. Figaro in London, No.17, 31 March 1832, pp.65-66. See below p 128.

2. Figaro in London, No.157, 6 December 1834, p.194.

3. Stationers Hall, Copyright Registers; Punchinello, 146, 12 November 1831. Figaro in London, 190, 18 February 1832. See also, Hindley, Life and Times of James Catnach, p.392.

4. Hollis, op.cit., p.313.

5. Poor Man's Guardian, No.29, 31 December 1831, p.232.

That those beneath such luxuries were not particularly grateful for the offering is revealed in the following extract from the Poor Man's Guardian, when they reran a piece from Douglas Jerrold's Punch in London:

> It is far superior to the Figaro, and the people would do as well to withhold their support from every work that employs its wits against their rights and liberties. The Figaro in London is too much addicted to sneer at its humble supporters, and though the Punch in London is not much better in this respect, in the following article the Editor has done his duty by exposing the malignant and dastardly paltroons who govern this country.[1]

Similarly, Cleave's and Carpenter's A Slap at the Church, which professed as its aim the 'utter annihilation' of the Church, tossed back in Figaro in London's face its modest purpose, when it made the distinction between those periodicals who wanted only 'to amuse by a little harmless satire' and its own, more ambitious goals.[2] Therefore, even from this external evidence, it is clear that Figaro in London was not part of the radical politics represented in the leading unstamped papers: it neither considered itself to be, nor was considered by them as of the same mould.

Figaro in London was fortunate to have Robert Seymour (1798-1836) as artist for most of the time until he died. Seymour, like many others who descended into the world of journalism, came from a genteel but declassé background. He was apprenticed to a pattern-maker, Vaughan in Spitalfields, and then through his own exertions developed first into a painter and later, an illustrator on wood, in etching and lithography.[3]

---

1. Poor Man's Guardian, No.44, 14 April 1832, p.356. The cut and article from Punch in London, No.2, 7 March 1832, concerned the so-called Wooden Sword Conspiracy. Addit. MSS, 27,791,f, 395-8 described the incident and includes the Poor Man's Guardian page.

2. 'Exordium!', A Slap at the Church, No.1, 21 January 1832, p.1. 'To Our Readers', A Slap at the Church, No.17, 12 May 1832, p.68.

3. J.C. Hotten; 'Life' Sketches by Seymour (1867), pp.3-8. F.G. Roe, 'Seymour, the "Inventor" of "Pickwick"', 'Portrait Painter to "Pickwick"; or, Robert Seymour's Career', Connoisseur, lxxvii (1927), 67-71, 152-7.

He was paid half a guinea for each of the Figaro in London drawings, which seem largely to have been controlled by à Beckett and Mayhew, who used him to support their editorials. A Beckett once wanted a caricature on the subject of the collision between the two Houses of Parliament and suggested a number of ways that this might be done. On another occasion, Mayhew was more precise and told him:-

> Represent the Queen as a German Frow, as Cobbett calls her, making her coronet resemble those small caps the drovers wear, playing the hurdy-gurdy, and leading the King, who is to represent a monkey, about with a string, and a very capital one I think he will make. Make him looking up in the Queen's face as if afraid of her. You can form, I think, the head of the hurdy-gurdy into Wellington's face. You perhaps recollect there is generally a sort of scroll at the end of these instruments which I think admirably suited for that purpose.[1]

A Beckett's general condescension and extravagant puffing, erratic paying and bad printing eventually resulted in Seymour's break with the paper, but normal relations were resumed in January 1835, when Mayhew became editor.[2]

In complete contrast to this rather dubious level of metropolitan life, John Doyle (1797-1868) 'H.B.' came from a highly respectable Dublin family, received academic art training and from the start, was patronized by the gentry to delineate their families and horses, both in oils and later, using the lithographic stone.[3]

---

1. Hotten, 'Life' pp.5-7.

2. For a refutation that the quarrel had anything to do with Seymour's suicide, see A.W. à Beckett, The A Becketts of "Punch" (1903), pp.36-42. Also, Punch library: A.W. à Beckett to M. H. Spielmann, 3 June 1895. It was 'nothing more serious than an exchange of chaff'.

3. 'Obituary', Art Journal, new ser., vii (1868), 47. Also, Library of the Fine Arts, i (1831), 212 which mentions Doyle favourably, in his own name, as a well-known portrait lithographer.

He did not enter society, however, on the basis of his fame, nor was his work mentioned in his family circle.[1] His obituary stated that he was 'attached to the highest and purest ameliorative conservative principles of policy', yet never sought bribes or pensions from that party.[2] The publication of another batch of his Sketches was commented upon in The Times, noted in political diaries of the period and collected in the great houses of the land. The 'genteel' were the only people who could afford to buy them. Besides, as Thackeray remarked, they were not the sort of prints to provoke a roar from the 'grinning good-natured mechanics' who used to crowd round the windows of print sellers. They caused one to smile 'in a quiet, gentleman-like kind of way'.[3] For The Times, there was 'humour without coarseness, and satirical representation without any extravagant or offensive deviation from resemblance'.[4] For the Westminster Review, it was the 'utter absence of rancour and bitterness, and the delicacy and purity which almost uniformly characterises him'.[5]

1. In 1833, Thomas Moore met H.B., 'a very sensible and gentlemanlike person', when the anonyme was still kept up. Two years later, Moore witnessed an amusing incident in which H.B. was explained his own sketch, yet Moore still promised to respect the secret. Memoirs, Journal and Correspondence of Thomas Moore, ed. Lord John Russell (1853-6), vi. 334-5, vii.91. However, his identity seems to have been known generally by 1835. The Times, 27 December 1839, reprinted a paragraph from Cupid which revealed as news the identity of H.B., and commented scathingly, 'What this ninny whipper-snapper gives as news has, for the last four years at least, been as well known as the locality of St. Paul's'.
    For Doyle's relations with his family see A Journal kept by Richard Doyle in the year 1840, introd. J. Hungerford Pollen (1885), pp.vi-viii. Also see below p.222.

2. Art-Journal, new ser., vii (1868), 47.

3. (W. M. Thackeray), 'George Cruikshank', London and Westminster Review, xxxiv (1840), 6-7.

4. The Times, 14 February 1834, p.3.

5. 'The Caricatures of H.B. In 8 volumes from 1828 to 1837', London and Westminster Review, xxviii (1838), 290.

The Times viewed him as a 'sort of "chartered wag"' who 'sometimes aims a sly blow at his friends, but his object seems always a good one'. He would make the 'sternest Conservative smile'.[1]

Certainly, his admirers included Metternich and Wellington, the latter being reported to have enjoyed one of himself reading The Times to the king 'as much as any one cd'.[2] Grey had his own collection, as spotted by Macauley in 1831, while he was waiting to see him: 'I sat down and turned over two large portfolios of political caricatures. Earl Grey's face was in every print. I was very much diverted'.[3] Sir John Campbell was flattered to be depicted once,[4] while literary and artistic circles pondered on their merits. Benjamin Haydon noted in his diary for 29 October 1831:-

1. The Times, 12 April 1838, p.5.

2. Journal of Mrs. Arbuthnot (1950 edn.) ii. 305-6. Entry for 15 September 1829 about 'READING THE NEWS' (Political Sketches, No.5 George, Catalogue of Political and Personal Satires, xi. No. 15836 - hereafter referred to as B.M. No.15836). Greville suspected that Wellington specially mended his windows for the Waterloo dinner, after having seen H.B.'s caricature of him peering through the broken glass, 'A PORTRAIT FRAMED BUT NOT YET GLAZED' (Political Sketches, No.267). The Greville Memoirs, ii.382. Entry for 19 June 1833.

3. Quoted in G. M. Trevelyan, The Seven Years of William IV (1952), p.4. Macaulay continued, 'I had seen some of them before; but many were new to me and their merit is extraordinary. They were the caricatures of that remarkable artist who calls himself H.B.'

4. Life of John, Lord Campbell, ed. the Hon. Mrs. Hardcastle (1881), ii. 126. Campbell stated rashly in 1839 that Chartism had been put down by legal and constitutional means, before he heard of the Newport Rising:-
> There was much jocularity in the press on "the second-sight of Sir John Campbell", and H.B., the popular caricaturist, honoured me with a well-imagined print representing me addressing the electors of Edinburgh, with an extract of my speech coming out of my mouth, and, in the distance, Frost leading on his army to the assault on Newport.

> Exchanged several of H.B.'s admirable caricatures for my
> Napoleons. Whoever H.B. is, he is a man of great genius.
> He has an instinct for expression and power of drawing,
> without academical cant, I never saw before; but evidently
> an amateur from the delicacy of his touch, or timidity
> rather.[1]

Thomas Moore told Doyle in person what opinion Rogers, Wilkie and himself had of his caricatures compared with those of Gillray:-

> we all agreed that there was a quiet power about his
> caricatures, producing as they did their effect without
> either extravagance or ill-nature, which set them, in a
> very important respect, far above Gillray's.[2]

Wordsworth, however, was furious over H.B.'s caricature of Rogers in 'A BLOTTED LEAF FROM THE PLEASURES OF MEMORY' (Political Sketches, No.747) and thought him 'worthy of the tread-mill'.[3] And in addition to these luminaries, Grantley Berkeley recalls that there were portfolios of H.B.'s works in most country houses, 'as a provocative to cheerfulness'.[4]

---

1. Life of Benjamin Robert Haydon (1853 edn.) ii.292.

2. Moore, op.cit., vi. 334-5.

3. Reported in a letter to Crabb Robinson from Quillinan, 28 November 1842. Correspondence of Henry Crabb Robinson with the Wordsworth Circle, ed. E. J. Morley (Oxford, 1927), i.469-70. Earlier, however, Wordsworth had praised the caricature of Brougham as 'THE GHEBER WORSHIPPING THE RISING SUN' (Political Sketches, No.71), in a letter to Haydon of 12 June 1831. Haydon, op.cit., ii. 277.

4. The Hon. G. F. Berkeley, My Life and Recollections (1865), iv. 139-40, 'but the figures seem ghosts, and the wit of the design, if it ever has any, must have evaporated when the subject became obsolete'. Similarly, a desolate air hung over Coningsby Castle, in which there were no books, few flowers, no ornamental furniture or portfolios of fine drawings by English artists, 'not a print even, except portfolios of H.B.'s caricatures' B. Disraeli, Coningsby (1844, Bk.IV. ch.ix.) Also, Knight, Passages from a Working Life, iii.263.

Thus, from an examination of the personnel concerned in its production and its audience, it is very clear that the Political Sketches were catering for an upper class 'establishment' clientele; H.B. was their '"chartered"' jester. In contrast, Figaro in London and the humorous magazines were part of an amorphous metropolitan milieu, hawked about the streets rather than cosseted behind Haymarket windows. Their style of sale and low price ensured a more radical audience. Nevertheless, they were not catering for a working class audience in the sense that they represented and were at one with its grievance. The Poor Man's Guardian discerned that they sneered at their 'humble supporters'. The Guardian's printers and writers, leaders in the 'unstamped' agitation, were more involved in the production of the serial woodcuts. Therefore, the long runs of political caricature in the 1830s, already defined by format and style of reproduction, was also circumscribed by price and recognized by the company they kept. They were further characterized by their imagery and subject matter.

II

An important feature of these consolidating forms of political caricature was their London base: they were produced out of the metropolis, and were largely meant for a metropolitan audience. Other parts of the country did experience sporadic outbursts of print warfare, mainly during local political crises, but these died down through lack of subject matter, or technical and artistic momentum soon afterwards. In Newcastle in 1826, for instance, a particularly lawless election with a hard fought three-cornered contest triggered off a series of prints and broadsides, backing and attacking the various candidates. What is noteworthy is the air of provinciality and amateurishness about the campaign. All were locally printed in Newcastle; a couple were 'Designed and Etched by a Northumberland Freeholder'.[1] They reveal a primitive grasp of emblematic imagery, the stage coach being prominent, symbolizing as it did those used to convey the county electors to the polls. In another print, a woman representing 'Northumbria' weighed the claims of the candidates. The election was commemorated with songs and decorated mugs, and then faded into the background of provincial inertia.[2] At the turn of the decade, however, the reform agitation fanned the larger cities outside London back to life. The Birmingham Political Union, for example, put out posters and leaflets, songs and verses, addresses, declarations and reports. A large lithograph was printed of the gathering of

---

1. In fact the 'Northumberland Freeholder' appears to have been Mr. Joseph Crawhall (1793-1853), the father of the wood engraver (see above p.48), a rope-maker and prominent member of Newcastle industrial society who became Mayor in 1849. He was involved in politics and interested in the arts, using lithography to illustrate his own private jokes. Felver, op. cit., pp. 1-11. His 'NORTHUMBRIA weighing the Claims of her CANDIDATES 1826,' was produced in the workshop of Thomas Bewick, at a time when R. E. Bewick, his son, had almost taken over complete control. Bewick Workshop Day Book, June 1826. I am indebted for this information to M.A.V. Gill, Keeper of Applied Art, Laing Art Gallery and Museum, Newcastle upon Tyne.

2. From a collection in the Laing Art Gallery and Museum.

the Unions on New Hall Hill, Birmingham on 7 May 1832. Attwood was commemorated in highly emblematic prints, defending British liberty and independence.[1]

Nevertheless, it was London which presented, as has been shown, as many forms and style of political caricature as audiences to buy them. There is no single definition of political caricature for the period: it utilized broadside and emblem, caricature and quasi-representational styles and employed the woodcut, wood engraving and lithography as means. Sharing a common framework of political reference, it is not surprising that duplication of ideas over the presentation of a political event was frequent. Many notions originated with H.B. and were copied by less prominent artists. At the same time, however, the imagery employed, both in its style and iconography, marks the level from which it came and for whom it was intended. Robert Seymour, producing drawings on a small scale which were then engraved rather perfunctorily to foster the illusion of a thumb-nail sketch, on the front page of the humorous magazines, employed the emblematic tradition revived by Hone and Cruikshank a decade previously.[2] He made use of heraldry and burlesque heraldry, almanacks and mock prophecies, fables and inn signs.[3] For C.J. Grant also, this tradition provided a basic fund of traditional

3-6

---

1. See, for example, those in Birmingham Scrap Book, i and ii, Birmingham Public Library. Also, their collection of material on the Birmingham Political Union. For provincial representations of news events, particularly political disorder, see below pp. 274-5.

2. See R. Freeman, English Emblem Books (1948). M.D. George, English Political Caricature to 1792 (Oxford, 1959), pp.7-8, 111-2.

3. For example, in Figaro in London, 'ARMS OF THE BOROUGHMONGERS' (No. 15, 17 March 1832), 'THE ARMS OF THE CHURCH' (No. 32, 14 July 1832), 'FIGARO'S PROPHETIC ALMANACK' (No. 30, 30 June 1832), 'A BIT OF PROPHECY' (No. 156, 29 November 1834), 'A FABLE FOR IRELAND' (No. 66, 9 March 1833). In the Devil in London '"SIGNS" OF THE TIMES' (No. 36, 3 November 1832).

   Seymour was employed, at one point, on various kinds of heraldic work, including designing book-plates. Roe, 'Portrait Painter to "Pickwick"' p.152.

images into which more topical figures and references could be inserted and still be generally understood. Often, seasonal customs provided the unifying theme: fairs, street shows and wakes, pantomimes and Twelfth Night characters, valentines and April fools, May days and harvest homes.[1]   7-8
There was a whole range of popular historical and folk heroes to be employed: Robin Hood, Guy Fawkes, Don Quixote, Gulliver, Tam O'Shanter, as   9-10
well as characters from the Arabian Nights or Aesop's Fables, or bestiaries in general.[2] Common figures of speech, translated into graphic terms, could sum up a political situation. The most frequent to appear in this period were those which conveyed some impression of movement or change - reform mills or ladders, boats and balloons - as well as the   11-17
ancient metaphors of the balance of justice, the wheel of time, the temple of the constitution or the political plum pudding.[3] Perhaps the

---

1. In Figaro in London, 'THE POLITICAL VALENTINE WRITER' (No.11, 18 February 1832 and No.167, 14 February 1835), 'MAY DAY' (No.22, 5 May 1832). In McLean's Monthly Sheet of Caricatures, 'APRIL FOOLS' (No.40, 1 April 1833). The Political Drama provided 'TWELFTH NIGHT CHARACTERS' (No.31), 'BOXING DAY' (No.121) and 'ST VALENTINE'S DAY' (No. 127). In Lloyd's Political Jokes, 'SEPTEMBER SPORT' (No.10).

2. For example, in Figaro in London, 'GUY FAUX' (No.49, 10 November 1832 and No.153, 8 November 1834), using Wellington and Brougham respectively. Also, the Political Drama 'A BUNDLE OF GUY FAWKES' (No.113) and 'THE MODERN GUY FAWKES' (No.131), representing O'Connell. For political bestiaries and zoos, first devised by George Cruikshank for the Political Showman (B.M.Nos.14148-69) in 1821, see the Devil in London (Nos.11 and 18, May 12 and June 30 1832), John Bull's Picture Gallery (Nos.15 and 16), the Political Play Bill (No.12).

3. In Figaro in London, 'THE REFORM MILL FOR GRINDING THE OLD CONSTITUTION YOUNG' (No.28, 16 June 1832), 'THE BALANCE OF JUSTICE' (No.48, 3 November 1832), 'TIMES REVOLUTIONS' (No.56, 29 December 1832), 'THE PARLIAMENT PIE' (No.61, 2 February 1833), 'JOHN BULL'S CHRISTMAS PUDDING' (No.107, 21 December 1833). In the Devil in London, 'THE REFORM APPLE PIE' (No.12, 19 May 1832). In the Political Drama, 'CUTTING UP THE REFORM PUDDING' (No.67), 'THE ROYAL GERMAN SAUSAGE; OR, THE ADELAIDE AERIAL SHIP' (No.97), 'GRINDING THE OLD CORPORATORS YOUNG' (No.123). In the Political Play Bill, 'The Reform Boat, in Full Sail' (No.3), 'First Voyage of the Aerial Ship Sailing to H---L by Steam' (No.15). In Lloyd's Political Jokes, 'THE GREAT BALLOON' (No.9). For earlier treatments of these themes see George, English Political Caricature, i and ii.

most hackneyed theme employed, with the changes of government and party alliances in the early 1830s, was the rather unpredictable, somewhat fractious, coach of state.[1]

H.B.'s Political Sketches tended to rely for their inspiration more on the actual political scene of the time. Parliamentary speeches which contained some striking image or metaphor were eagerly seized upon and re-enacted in visual terms for his more sophisticated, newspaper-reading public. 'DAME PARTINGTON and the OCEAN (OF REFORM)' (Political Sketches, No. 163. B.M. No. 16801) referred to a speech made by Sidney Smith at a reform meeting in Taunton in October 1831, when he compared the attempts of the Lords to stop the Bill to a certain fictitious Dame Partington, who had tried to stop the Atlantic with her mop. 'A SELECT SPECIMEN OF THE BLACK STYLE' (Political Sketches, No.285), illustrating a black Lord Chancellor, fulfilled only too literally Lord Brougham's wish, as expressed during the debate on the Slavery Abolition Bill on 14 August 1833, to make the black man free in every respect, even to sit in the House of Lords. 'DR.SYNTAX ON HIS HUMBLE BUT FAITHFUL STEED, IN SEARCH OF THE PICTURESQUE' (Political Sketches, No. 465) mocked Sir Robert Peel's speech on his installation as Rector of Glasgow University in 1837. Peel was rash enough to reminisce over his early experiences of travelling around Scotland, having hired an 'humble and faithful steed', sometimes with no other companion to listen to than a Highland shepherd, with his 'simple annals and artless view of human life'.[2] Other features of H.B.'s imagery also betray

---

1. The coach of the Commonwealth enjoyed early popularity in prints, usually being driven by the Devil (B.M. Nos.1496 and 1497); it was revived in 1829 by Heath (B.M. Nos.15731-47), who depicted various politicians 'wot drives the sovereign'. In 1835, there appeared another spate of coaching prints to illustrate the change of government. In McLean's Monthly Sheet of Caricatures, 'WHIG COACH UPSET' (No.61, 1 January 1835), 'THE CONSERVATIVE OMNIBUS' (No.62, 1 February 1835), 'ANOTHER COACH NOW' (No.65, 1 May 1835), 'DRIVING THE SOVEREIGN IN QUITE A NEW WAY' (No.66, 1 June 1835). The Political Drama produced 'THE OLD TORY HACK COME TO A STAND' (No.73), 'THE UPSETTING OF THE TORY MUCK CART' (No.83) and 'THE RIVAL OMNIBUSES' (No.114).

2. For full descriptions of the first two-thirds of H.B.'s output, see McLean, op.cit.

expectations of rapport with an educated clientele. Almost a tenth of his nine hundred odd <u>Political Sketches</u> make use of classical allusions.[1] He produced sophisticated skits on paintings by Reynolds, West and David, as well as ones based on the work of Horace Vernet, Landseer, Leslie and Wilkie.[2]

However, occasionally H.B. left the lobbies of Westminster and the clubs and libraries of St. James' and partook in the current pleasures of the metropolis. 'FANCY BALL - JIM CROW DANCE & CHORUS' (<u>Political Sketches</u>, No.478) made use of the cant phrase to 'jump Jim Crow', signifying any kind of inconsistency, and applied it to politics. The phrase had originated in a dramatic piece put on at the Adelphi in 1837, in which the American actor, Rice, performed the part of a negro, singing a song which required him to act many parts, within a chorus refrain of a 'double shuffle' dance.[3] Indeed, in the metropolitan environment, with its swift means of verbal communication, there was a whole sub-language of gossip and slang which constantly changed and which often underscored the appeal of the prints. The <u>Westminster Review</u> in 1838 noted the presence of caricatures:

> which associate ideas of absurdity or of meanness with popular cant or slang expressions. London is a perpetual entertainment to the observer who does not confound what is common with what is vulgar, and who notices the varieties which are continually diversifying the phrases and terms of slang among the working people, and which salute the ears of every one in the streets and lanes of the metropolis.[4]

1. About half as many again made use of Aesop fables or popular sayings. Of literary sources, Don Quixote appeared at least half a dozen times, though Nicholas Nickleby and Barnaby Rudge also made the grade.

2. For example, 'MUSCIPULA' (No.629), 'A GREAT ACTOR BETWEEN TRAGEDY AND COMEDY' (No.843), 'SWEARING OF THE HORATII' (No.191), 'THE NEW PASHA OF EGYPT' (No.622), '<u>Not</u> by Horace Vernet'.

3. For 'musical epidemics' in London, particularly the 'jumping Jim Crow' phenomenon, see C. Mackay, <u>Through the Long Day</u> (1887), i. 127-42. Also, Vizetelly, <u>op.cit</u>., i. 101.

4. 'The Caricatures of H.B.' 274-5.

The treatment of 'ideas and words as shuttlecocks, to be bandied from one person to another as if with battledores,'[1] included 'Who are you,' 'All round my Hat' or 'What a shocking bad hat,' 'Flare up!' and 'The Man Wot...' during the period,[2] and recurred over and over again in the prints of the city.

If all of these literary and allegorical references, taken from classical scholarship to popular sayings and slang, provided a framework for all types of graphic artist, so too the prints of the 1830s present a spectrum of physiognomical depiction, ranging from the highest level of portraiture to stock types and gross caricature. It was all very well for H.B. to be complimented on the excellent vraisemblance of his Sketches, their unlabelled identities to be lightly pencilled in as a drawing room entertainment. Most people had never seen their rulers and needed a far from refined battery of devices in order to recognize them. This was what C. J. Grant was especially adept at providing.

There had always been certain stock characters to act as sign-posts pointing onto a changing scene. The oldest of these was the Devil, who gleefully dispatched the agents of corruption to hell. Grant used him frequently, 'THE INFERNAL MACHINE; OR, BLOWING ALL THE RUBBISH TO HELL, AT AN ANGLE OF FORTY-FIVE, a Devilish good Idea' (Political Drama, No.102), showing him in his most comprehensive role. The Devil, boldly shaded in white line on black, sits astride a tube labelled, 'PRO BONO PUBLICO.' This blows out a whole range of stock antipathies, the King and Queen, Wellington and Cumberland being clearly visible, together with representatives from the Church, parliament, judiciary, tax offices,

21-23

---

1. Balzac used this expression to describe the same process in Paris at the time, the meaningless remarks that passed for wit among certain classes of Parisians, always changing and never lasting longer than a month, 'A political event, a case being heard in the law-courts, a song of the streets or an actor's gag, anything and everything may provide material for this kind of drollery...' H. Balzac, Old Goriot, (1834) trans. M. A. Crawford (Penguin edn., 1951), p.74.

2. 'The Caricatures of H.B.', 274-5. Vizetelly, op.cit., i. 102-3.

and army. John Bull and a small group of fellow workers cheer him on.[1] The print is typical of many by Grant, all of which achieve a boldness of design through leaving large areas of the block to print black, cutting strongly round the figures to produce the white contrast and shading clearly where necessary to provide variety of tone or, as with the Devil's fur in this print, to suggest texture. The text is set into the block in an even column divided off from the print with hair lines. The caption is pithy, explanatory, frequently exclamatory.

Another stock character Grant often employed was John Bull, in a variety of guises. In John Bull's Picture Gallery, for example, he appeared both as bull and bull-dog, as well as the more typical corpulent rustic worthy.[2] He was shown overburdened, baited, butchered, or occasionally, dangerous. In the reform prints he was used as the champion of the rights of the free-born Englishman against all the forces of 'old corruption'. At first he looked optimistically into the future. 'THE STEPPING STONE; OR, JOHN BULL PEEPING INTO FUTURITY' (Weekly Show-Up, No.1, 30 June 1832. Compare with B.M.No.17143) depicts him with one foot on the stepping stone of 'REFORM', looking into the 'Land of promise', where cheap and plentiful food, unadulterated drink, free trade, no corn laws or window tax and a cornucopia of coins are to be found. The boroughmongers, according to the accompanying article, are only 'specks upon the distant horizon'. 'John Bull in the Character of Diogenes on the look out' (John Bull's Picture Gallery, No.17) is more cynical. Brougham asks, 'Johnny, are you looking for the Reform Bill?' to which John Bull replies, 'Na, meister,

---

1. Also, 'OLD NICK'S GATHERINGS' (John Bull's Picture Gallery, No.6). 'THE GENTLEMAN IN BLACK' - 'wots canvassing for the Tories' (Weekly Show-up, No.2, 7 July 1832). 'THE FIVE PLAGUES OF THE COUNTRY' (Political Drama, No.19), which made use of the common 'Five Alls' sequence. See George, English Political Satire to 1792, pp.9-10. 'A REGULAR FLARE UP!' (Political Drama, No.39).

2. In John Bull's Picture Gallery, 'POLITICAL WEATHER COCKS' (No.3, B.M. No.17080), 'THE RAT HUNT' (No.7, B.M.No.17156), 'Present State of John Bull' (No.12, B.M.No.17202), after Cruikshank's 'POOR BULL and his Burden' (B.M.No.13288). See below p.123. 'WORRYING THE BULL' (No.14, B.M.No.17256).

I ha gotten that, but I be looking for its benefits!' The tableau is set against various emblems from Cruikshank's pamphlets for Hone a dozen years before.

Other stock types which recurred during the 1830s were the bishops and the members of the corporation, to both of which a grossness of imagery in the Hogarth/Gillray tradition was employed by Grant, and to a lesser extent by Seymour. The bishops needed to be pumped of their worldly surfeit in order to be cured, their carbuncles bled to be made healthy once more, as in 'That old Irish Bunter, Mother Church, undergoing the operation of Purgation and Phlebotomy' (Political Drama, No.81). In Cleave's and Carpenters's A Slap at the Church, though infrequently illustrated, the masthead each week symbolised the Church as a wet-nurse spawning a progeny of pigs and clerics, surrounded by her tithe of the harvest. Its most prominent cut, possibly by George Dorrington, entitled 'THE PROMOTION OF PRIESTIANITY' (No.8, 10 March 1832) depicted cottagers, husbandmen, farmers and landlords dragging a cart laden with corn and bishops in the direction of Durham and Canterbury. The cart, labelled 'ACCORDING TO LAW' is protected by the army and police, although two demons have succeeded in making off with one bishop.[1] Similarly, in contrast to a starving population, the obesity of the corporations needed to be purged; bloated and degenerate, they fed on John Bull's body. Seymour produced 'APPLYING THE STOMACH PUMP TO THREE GREAT CORPORATE BODIES' (McLean's Monthly Sheet of Caricatures, No.46, 1 October 1833), which shows the corporations of London, Edinburgh and Dublin being pumped by three Whigs, including Grey and Brougham, of 'Unjust Exactions. Embezzled Charities. Cheating Monopolies, &c. &c. &c.'

28

29-31

32

---

1. Also, in the Political Drama, 'THE BENCH OF BISHOPS IN THE HOUSE OF LORDS DURING A DEBATE CONCERNING THE CHURCH' (No.16), 'THE UNNATURAL ALLIANCE OR, BILLY BLUBBER AND HIS BETTER HALF' (Nô.38). In Figaro in London, 'CASE OF SURFEIT IN A BISHOP' (No.6, 14 January, 1832), 'GREASING THE FAT SOW' (No.243, 30 July 1836).

Seymour often returns to this theme in his small cuts.[1] Among Grant's contributions to the same subject is 'Corporation Reform, or Lord John Russell's Specific for a System of corruption' (Political Play Bill, No.11), in which the central figure, a bloated many headed monster, coughs up and is bled of his wealth.[2] Primitive though this cut is compared with Seymour's efforts, the main figures bear some signs of individual character, William IV and Wellington, Brougham and perhaps, Althorp being discernible. A few weeks later, when the serial had been taken over by Hetherington, it printed 'Corporation Fed Witnesses being Examined by the Comic Sir Charles Wither-H-ell, before the Seraglio of Torys' (Political Play Bill, No.18). This image, for all its crudity, refers to the actual events of August 1835 when the Lords took evidence from local dignitaries, notably those from Coventry, as to the alleged partiality of the Municipal Corporations Commission.[3]

Some targets were of more recent origin and their character was emphasized by a whole range of nick-names or rhyming nonsense names.[4] Thus, Peel's new police were dubbed, 'THE BLUE DEVILS, ALIAS THE RAW LOBSTERS, ALIAS THE BLUDGEON MEN' (Political Drama, No.11), a verbal summary of their block-headed, yet treacherous visual image. Such verbal tags of equivalence combined with visual tags to conjure up Queen

1. For example, in Figaro in London, 'BLEEDING AN ALDERMAN' (No.103, 23 November 1833), 'CRUELTY TO AN ALDERMAN' (No.186, 27 June 1835), 'THE CORPORATION SURFEIT!' (No.196, 5 September 1835).

2. See also in the Political Drama, ' JACK AND THE BEANSTALK' (No.98), ' THE CORPORATION SAMPSON BEING SHORN OF HIS HAIR' (No.105), ' GRINDING THE OLD CORPORATORS YOUNG ' (No.123).

3. See G.B.A.M. Finlayson, ' The Municipal Corporation Commission and Report, 1833-35 ', Bulletin of the Institute of Historical Research, xxxvi (1963), 47.

4. The use of word puns in graphic satire was first noticed by E. Kris and E.H. Gombrich in their first article on caricature, 'The Principles of Caricature', British Journal of Medical Psychology, xvii (1938), 319-42, in which they speak of the infantile attitude towards words which is related to all wit, and discuss its psychological base. Ibid., p.338.

'Addlehead' and King 'Silly Billy' or 'Billy Blubber'. They aided the visual 'grammalogues'[1] attached to royalty, transforming the king into the epitome of infantile helplessness. He was rarely seen as the initiator of some abuse or corruption. He acted as a cat's-paw or mouth-piece for others. Seymour's most frequent device transformed him into a pump, worked by the government or Adelaide.[2] For Grant, he was also a toy or a baby and his most usual guardian, accompanied by her props of sauer-kraut and sausage, again was the Queen.[3] In 'BILLY'S BIRTHDAY' (Political Drama, No.36), she dandles her enormous baby on her lap while Cumberland and a group of German hangers-on bring their crude birthday gifts before him. Similarly, in 'SILLY BILLY's BIRTH-DAY' (Political Play Bill, No.8), she spoon-feeds William while Cumberland and Wellington give him some toy soldiers to play with. Often, it is the Queen herself who is seen to be furthering Germanic, militaristic government. In 'MEN AND MEASURES. Addle-head Reviewing her chosen Ministry a-la-German,' (Political Drama, No.65), she reviews an assortment of Tories, seated on her husband's shoulders. Peel, the 'rat-catcher' sits on a rat, has a trap over his shoulder and carries a spear ornamented with a banner which sums up the family fortune: 'MONEY IS STRENGTH. SPINNING JENNY IS POWER'. Wellington is also accompanied by symbols of his role, the weapons of militaristic authority and repressive government; Lyndhurst sits on the Woolsack; Palmerston on an elephant; Aberdeen on a barrel of gunpowder.

1. E. Kris and E. H. Gombrich, Caricature (1940), pp.18-19.

2. In Figaro in London, 'THE REAL KING'S SPEECH' (No.38, 25 August 1832), 'THE ROYAL PUPPET' (No.65, 2 March 1833), 'THE KING'S SPEECH' (No.91, 31 August 1833), to name but a few of its twice yearly attacks on the subject.

3. For example, 'THE ROYAL MOPSTICK PRO-ROGUE-ING THE HUMBUG PARLIAMENT; OR, CROSS READING THE SPEECH' (Political Drama, No.22). In Lloyd's Political Jokes , 'PROROGUING PARLIAMENT BY STEAM' (No.8), 'DOES ADELAIDE KNOW HE'S OUT?' (No.11), 'GETTING READY FOR OPENING PARLIAMENT' (No.15).

On a cannon is written, 'Machine to enforce all Tory Principles', and the cannon balls are labelled, 'Pills to Cure all RADICAL Diseases'. Again, a much more primitive version appeared in the last numbers of the Political Play Bill, printed by Hetherington, in which the troops are reviewed by Adelaide, this time sitting astride Cumberland.[1]

As for the politicians, just as those of Cruikshank's and Hone's era had nick-names in caricature,[2] so too did the leading lights of the 1830s. One of the most unfortunate victims was Alderman John Key, Lord Mayor of London from 1830 to 1832. When the King was advised to postpone his visit to the City on Lord Mayor's Day 1830, owing to fear of excessive reform agitation, even revolution, Key was involved in spreading the alarm and the banquet planned was cancelled. Key's bungled handling of the affair earned him criticism from every quarter and an outburst of prints spread across London. All made the same basic visual and verbal pun of 'Don-Key - the new Vicar of Bray', who was often accompanied by Sir Claudius Hunter, locum tenens for the retiring Lord Mayor, who was depicted on a hunting horse. There were at least forty seven varieties, issued over a fortnight, which followed the intricacies of relations between the Crown, the City and Westminster.[3] A similar use of puns helped to fix the identities of politicians in Parliament. Wellington, instantly recognizable by virtue of his nose and military uniform, was

---

1. 'The Royal Review at Woolwich, or Addle-head as General a-la-German' (No.16). See also, 'THE WINDSOR CAMP' (Figaro in London, No.37, 18 August, 1832).

2. See below p.124.

3. Sir John Key's personal collection of these is in the Guildhall Library, Print Room. That he was more amused than angered by such efforts is revealed by Vizetelly, who remembers the appearance of the prints during his school holidays in London:
   when his own (Sir John's) ward beadle, swollen with importance, brought some unfortunate fellow before him for hawking these caricatures about the streets, he at once discharged the man, amiably expressing a hope that he had found the trade profitable.
   Vizetelly, op.cit., i. 61. See also, The Greville Memoirs, ii.53.

variously dubbed in a Grant print, 'OLD SLAUGHTER ALIAS PADDY O'KILLUS ALIAS NOSEY, ALIAS THE DUKE OF BUTCHERLOO' (Political Drama, No.40)[1]. Daniel O'Connell sometimes received better treatment in the guize of 'THE MODERN SAINT PATRICK' (Political Drama, No.117) or 'DANIEL IN THE LION'S DEN' (Political Drama, No.108). Lord Brougham, equally distinct physiognomically, naturally was often accompanied by a broom (with the added implication that his services were for sale),[2] and was also known as Vaux(hall),[3] his title, or 'Jemmy Twitcher' from a nervous habit of twitching his nose.

This combination of nick-name and caricature moved as a snowball, enlarging as it went, taking a shape and a truth of its own, through constant repetition in the print series or publication numbers. It transformed politicians in popular eyes, burdening them with images which, in an age before photography, usually provided the most

1. Compare his official portraits in Lord G. Wellesley and J. Steegman, The Iconography of the First Duke of Wellington (1935), with the prints in J. Physick, The Duke of Wellington in Caricature (1965), principally by William Heath.

2. Timbs, op.cit., pp.525-6.

3. Life of Lord John Campbell, i. 494. 23 November 1830:
    I witnessed the august ceremony of Lord Brougham and Vaux being sworn in as a peer. Before, he was only Speaker of the House of Lords. He went through the ceremony with much gravity. He is laughed at about Vaux. It is an absurd piece of vanity. There are various jokes about him already. Vox et praeterea nihil. The Court of Chancery is to be called 'Vaux Hall'.
   For example, in H.B.'s Political Sketches, 'THE CELEBRATED VAUXHALL PERFORMER' (No.341), 'VAUX-HUNTING; OR, THE NEWEST VERSION OF TALLY-HO!' (No.346), 'FALL OF THE VAUX-HALL PERFORMER' (No.348), 'THE VAUX AND THE GRAPES' (No.364), and so on.

immediate means of recognition they would carry through life.[1] Thus, it was of considerable importance whether an audience received a view of, say, Wellington's election as Chancellor of the University of Oxford in 1834, in the form of a dignified lithographic portrait by Lady Salisbury, or H.B.'s double size, mildly ironic Political Sketch of the ceremony, from McLean's print shop; or whether it formed its impressions from any of the serial cuts, which made Wellington look foolish and the support he received attacked from the army and the clergy.[2] Similarly, H.B. pictured Brougham at home for Christmas with his mother, while Grant showed him breaking up families through the New Poor Law.[3] This is not to say audiences were entirely separate, and that an H.B. follower never saw a radical cut, or vice versa. Each type of serial print or magazine, however, was using a visual language whose style and content - ranging from mild-mannered

48
45
49
50

1. Kris and Gombrich have treated the process in psychological terms as 'image magic', the power to transform, to wound, to destroy: not only is the victim 'mocked at, or unmasked, but actually changed. He carries the caricature with him through his life and even through history'. 'The Principles of Caricature', 339-41. They frequently cite the Louis Philippe 'poire' example, of which Baudelaire wrote:
    An obliging analogy had discovered the symbol: from that time onwards the symbol was enough. With this kind of plastic slang, it was possible to say, and to make the people understand, anything one wanted. And so that tyrannical and accursed pear became the focus for the whole pack of patriotic blood-hounds.
   C. Baudelaire, 'Some French Caricaturists', The Painter of Modern Life and Other Essays, trans. and ed. J. Mayne (1964), p.172. For the power which Punch enjoyed in helping to mould the image of a politician, see below pp. 239-40, 265.

2. Compare 'THE CHANCELLOR OF THE UNIVERSITY OF OXFORD ATTENDED BY DOCTORS OF CIVIL LAW' (Political Sketches, No.350-1) with 'THE OXFORD INSTALLATION! OLD SLAUGHTER ALIAS PADDY O'KILLUS, ALIAS NOSEY, ALIAS THE DUKE OF BUTCHERLOO AS CHANCELLOR!!! READING HIS LATIN! SPEECH' (Political Drama, No.40). 'AUT CAESAR AUT NULLUS' (Passing Events, No.4, 20 February 1834), 'THE PILGRIMAGE TO OXFORD' and 'THE CONVOCATION AT OXFORD' (Political Stage, No.6), 'INSTALLATION HUMBUG' (Figaro in London, No.134, 28 June 1834).

3. Compare 'A CHRISTMAS FIRE-SIDE' (Political Sketches, No.236) with 'POOR LAWS IN ENGLAND' (Lloyd's Political Jokes, No.13). There is a collection of engraved portraits of Lord Brougham at University College, London. Brougham Papers.

portrayals to gross caricature, from classical allusion and parliamentary rhetoric to popular cant expressions and nick-names - could be most readily appreciated on certain levels of society. The significance of this range is not simply that it adds to historical evidence on the range of political views during the period, but that it is symptomatic of the growing importance of the communication process itself in the face of an enlarging political audience. The growth of consistent viewpoints in graphic journalism paralleled the growth of consistent political views in class and party, an increasingly important factor in determining the fate of politicians and their policies.

III

Through a framework of ancient allegory, through modern metropolitan slang, through stock types and caricature, Figaro in London and the serial cuts combined to attack the forces of old corruption: crown and aristocracy, church, corporations and Tories. The means were traditional, having been worked out in the eighteenth century and before.[1] However, it was more difficult to assimilate new events and experiences, more especially, those arising out of the growth of industrial society and the progress of Whig reforms in the 1830s. One solution was simply to ignore the problem, as in effect occurred in H.B.'s Political Sketches. The largest proportion of these were concerned with Parliament, where Doyle apparently 'became a quiet, silent, unsuspected frequenter of the lobby and gallery'.[2] He depicted prominent and not so prominent members at moments in the debates, even, in one print, Mr. Williams, the under-doorkeeper to the House of Commons.[3] He entered the inner sanctums of the cabinet, club-land and Holland House. 'SLEEPING PARTNERS IN A DOUBTFUL CONCERN' (Political Sketches, No.268) illustrates 'An interesting discovery upon the breaking up of a recent Council at Holland House (with variations)'. A note written by the third Lord Holland sheds

---

1. For a summary of the history of caricature, see 'Introduction', Caricature and its Role in Graphic Satire, exhib. catalogue of the Museum of Art, Rhode Island School of Design (Providence, 1971), pp.5-13.

2. 'Obituary', 47.

3. 'MARCH OF REFORM' (Political Sketches, No.252), which shows Cobbett, Gully and Pease entering the House, with the Tories looking on. See also, for example, 'DRAWING FOR TWELFTH CAKE – A HINT TO CABINET MAKERS' (Political Sketches, No.100) of the Whig Cabinet, and 'THE LAST OF THE BOROUGHBRIDGES' (Political Sketches, No.252) of many of the Tories surrounding Wetherall.

some light on the matter:

> The Cabinet dined at Holland House... After discussion was over, Melbourne on one couch and Ch. Grant on another went fast asleep. Grey said jokingly we should blow out the candles and leave them: and in about a week or ten days a caricature by H.B. was in all the shops, representing our two colleagues asleep at Holland House and the rest of us escaping with candles.[1]

For H.B., reform was seen, when at all, as a parliamentary not a social question, at least not one which concerned the mass of the people. Society for him meant the pleasures of intimate tête à têtes at Windsor, quiet card games, dining, dancing, duelling, racing and riding in the Row.[2] Perhaps the most serious affliction represented was gout.

In contrast, the small cuts of Seymour and the large prints by Grant attacked the results of reform, as they were progressively revealed during the decade. To depict them, the artists relied on the adaptation of old emblems or the introduction of figures like John Bull to act as a medium through which the topical point could be made. Furthermore, they tried their hand at imaginative reconstructions of the scenes of such events. On the whole, Seymour kept his means separate, adapting emblematic devices in Figaro in London, while expanding into larger scale, naturalistic scenes for his lithographs in McLean's Monthly Sheet of Caricatures. Often, Grant employed emblematic, caricature and representational methods together in the same cut, ingeniously to reinforce the point he wanted to make. The impression we thus gain is one of urgency, a desperate accumulation of abuse, harshly stated in contrasting woodcut tones, an effect which Seymour's softly shaded lithographic depictions rarely achieve.

In 'THE MARCH OF INTELLECT. POLITICAL' (B.M. No.15922. 1829)

---

1. Quoted in Trevelyan, op.cit., No.XXXIX. Another hint that H.B. did have some sort of informer from the inner sanctums is dropped in 'CONVERSATION AT WHITE'S (Political Sketches, No.101), of Burdett in conversation with Sefton, which one anonymous clubman, half hidden behind a newspaper, says he must report to H.B.
2. From his own drawings, now in the British Museum, Prints and Drawings department, it is apparent that Doyle did much of his sketching in the Park.

Seymour depicts a 'Malthusian', a butcher, who pours over calculations made from Malthus' Essay on Population. He says:

> Let's see! I've eight children, then if they each have 8 that's 64 they the same that's 512 again 4096 they the same 32768 again 262144 they 8 a piece that's 2097152 then if they should all have 8 that's 16617210 my Conscience!!! there won't be bread enough for the Scraggs family.

The answer in such circumstances seemed to be slavery either in the factories or in the work-house. The new Whig legislation proved to be severely inadequate in the case of the former, and appeared to worsen materially the plight of candidates for poor law provision. Both Figaro in London and the serial cuts were not slow to condemn the results. 'THE FACTORY FEROCITIES' (No.71, 13 April 1833) appeared in Figaro in London at the time of the setting up of the Royal Commission to look into the employment of children in factories. It combines the emblem of a primitive, open-jawed monster, surrounded with infernal flames, with a clock clutched between its claws, symbolizing thereby the new 'synchronization of labour' demanded by large-scale industry.[1] Grey, Brougham and Althorp feed it with children 'infant victims of the demon of Commercial interest'. Other images were occasioned by the comparison made in Richard Oastler's letter to the Leeds Mercury, of slavery in the factories and in the West Indies, where it had just been abolished.[2]

Again, contrast was used to attack the iniquities of the Poor Law

---

1. A phrase used by E. P. Thompson, 'Time, Work-Discipline, and Industrial Capitalism,' Past & Present, No.38 (December 1967), pp.56-97.
2. Reprinted in C. Driver, Tory Radical, The life of Richard Oastler (1946), pp.42-44. See, for example, 'THE HAPPY FREE LABOURERS OF ENGLAND', 'THE WRETCHED SLAVES IN THE WEST INDIES' (McLean's Monthly Sheet of Caricatures, No.43, 1 July 1833). 'WHITE NIGGERS', a print published by Richard Bentley in 1838, depicts the pauper children 'sold' to factory owners by parishes to relieve the rates. Klugman collection.

Amendment Act, the old system acquiring a positively rosy glow in retrospect.[1] Figaro in London saw the reform in every way worthy of Whig humbug. Furthermore, the paper came out very strongly against the theory on which it seemed to be based, especially its Malthusian aspects, as epitomized by 'old Mother Martineau'. 'A FEMALE PHILOSOPHER' [53] (Figaro in London, No.121, 29 March 1834), for example, depicts Brougham dressed as an old maid, surrounded by Malthusian statistics, Adam Smith, Cobbett's Register and useful knowledge tracts. The paper suggests that Miss Martineau is not the only 'sour old woman' to pour over preventive checks.[2] However, this attack takes on an air of flippancy when compared with the vehement expression of the psychological as well as the physical humiliation suffered in the work-house, which is to be found in Grant's serial cuts. The work-house had not escaped delineation previously. A publisher named Robert Wilkinson had issued a topographical series of the exteriors of London work-houses in the 1810s and 1820s.[3] Grant's interior views are rather different from these fine engravings. 'INTERIOR OF AN ENGLISH WORKHOUSE UNDER THE NEW POOR LAW [54] ACT' (Political Drama, No.57) 'Dedicated to those two ugly old women, Mothers Brougham and Martineau', provides an imaginative realisation of the fears and horrors of enclosed confinement. The overseers threaten shaven-headed paupers, who are employed to beat hemp while their children pick oakum. The mode of punishment is to be whipped, manacled or strung up.

1. See 'POOR LAWS AS THEY WERE' (McLean's Monthly Sheet of Caricatures, No.84, 1 December 1836), in which a pauper sits down to a meal and complains 'Wot only one Pound o' Roast Beef and half Pound o Pudding for a Man's Christmas Dinner?' 'AS THEY ARE' depicts a starving man looking gloomily at his ration of bread and water, while the overseer says, 'Vy I s'pose you'll be wanting a Fire next'.

2. See also, 'LAW FOR THE TORY PAUPERS' (Figaro in London, No.120, 22 March 1834), 'MORE AMENDMENT OF THE PAUPER LAWS' (McLean's Monthly Sheet of Caricatures, No.57, 1 September 1834).

3. Klugman collection.

According to one notice, the work hours are from four in the morning until ten at night, three hours being allotted for clearing away and sweeping the yard. In 'JOHN BULL TRYING ON HIS WORKHOUSE SUIT PROVIDED FOR HIM BY THE WHIG POOR LAWS AMENDMENT BILL' (Political Drama, No.41), John Bull wearing a shabby suit outside 'WORKHOUSE No 5000' seeks assurance from Althorp on how he looks. The latter's reply is flattering and he adds that his head is shaved because it is 'good for the health and uncommon pleasant in hot weather; as to all those foolish notions about National Pride you must endeavour to get over'. The New Poor Law provisions not only ensured a loss of self respect, but also, division of the family and brutal hardship in terms of human relations. 'POOR LAWS IN ENGLAND' (Lloyd's Political Jokes, No.13), issued two years later in 1836, shows Brougham and Bishop Blomfield spooning out pigs' gruel to feed the female ward. Brougham says, 'ye may thank a kind paternal government for these comforts - blessing me first as the original conceiver ... When you have half an hour or so to spare for reading, (those who can) you are indulged with a Bible!. Decent food and the presence of husbands are needless superfluities: 'besides, you see them every Sunday, for UPWARDS of 5 minutes, therefore think yourselves well off, considering how many DUMB ANIMALS are starving in the streets'. In 1836, Figaro in London renewed its attack, this time with more force. 'THE FRUITS OF THE NEW POOR LAW BILL' (No.249, 10 September 1836) depicts the Whig Commissioner exercising 'brute force' to separate parents from their children.[1]

---

1. See also in Figaro in London, 'THE NEW POOR LAWS' (No.220, 20 February 1836), 'THE POOR LAW MURDERERS' (No.258, 12 November 1836).

A further aspect of this human suffering was the effect of the 'sixty seventh' clause of the bill, much attacked in the radical woodcuts because of its cruel provisions for bastardy. 'EFFECTS OF THE NEW BASTARDY LAW' (Political Drama, No.60) depicts Brougham and Blomfield wheeling bastards to the workhouse. Brougham says, 'Awful fecundity - surely nothing is wanting to evince the march of knowledge among the young folks of the present day than this - Oh! Martineau and Malthus, what do you say to this! O Tempore! O Mores![1]

57

These examples of 'enclosed' coercion, in which factory and workhouse overseers governed labour in closely controlled areas, were matched by a parallel attack on the increasing regimentation of life outdoors. Peel's new policemen were identified with the military and with Tory coercion from their formation.[2] 'Innocent Pastime; or, the Blue Devils in their Glory' (Satirical Puppet Show, No.2, 23 May 1833) illustrating the police attacking women and children at Cold Bath Fields, is a print which owes much to the large broadside sheets of troops fighting and firing on civilians in the immediate post Napoleonic War period.[3] When, in 1833, the jury returned a verdict of justifiable homicide on the policeman killed, the Political Drama expressed its views

58

---

1. See also in the Political Drama, 'THE NEW BASTARDY LAW; OR THE SCHOOLMASTER AT HOME' (No.47), 'COERCION FOR THE FAIR SEX; OR, THE BASTARDY LAW IN FULL OPERATION' (No.48). 'THE POOR LAWS' AMENDMENT BILL, VIDE 67th CLAUSE (BASTARDY)' and 'THE WORKING OF THE NEW POOR ACT' (Popular Subjects, Nos.1 and 2, August 1834), Brit.Mus., Prints and Drawings.

2. For example, 'STATE WATCHMEN OF 1829' (B.M. No.15768), which depicts Wellington and Peel as sentries of the Grenadier Guards, keeping watch outside a prison, which supersedes the parish watch-house. Also, 'THE SELECT FEW ON THE POLICE' and 'THE RUDE MULTITUDE ON THE POLICE' (Looking Glass, No.12, 1 December 1830).

3. See for example, 'DREADFUL SCENE AT MANCHESTER MEETING OF REFORMERS Aug.16 1819' and similar large cuts of meetings in London. London Records Office, County Hall, Prints department.

in 'THE GLORIOUS VERDICT OF COLD BATH FIELDS; OR, A HARD PULL FOR JUSTICE' (No.7). It is the traditional image of a tug-of-war, here between the coroner, the government, helped by the Devil, and the jury. John Bull looks out from a window in the 'CALTHORP ARMS', being assured by the foreman of the jury, 'Never fear, John Bull, neither bribes nor threats shall subdue us, though they have got the Devil on their side - God and our country's on our's'. Between the two sides is a small gallows labelled 'JUSTIFIABLE HOMICIDE', on which hang 'PENSIONERS POLICEMEN BISHOPS AND OTHER VERMIN'. Grant thus employed, in one print, the emblem of the scales of justice, the stock figures of the Devil and John Bull, caricatures of Brougham and Peel, all contained in a semi-representational framework. Two years later, both Figaro in London and the Political Drama made use of the stock graphic formations to depict dragoons firing on an election crowd at Wolverhampton.[1] Nor did brutality within the army escape scrutiny with many particularly blood-thirsty depictions of flogging atrocities.[2]

One specific aspect of this coercion newly made topical in the 1830s was the government attitude towards the trades' unions. 'POPAY THE SPY, addressing a Political Meeting in the garb of a brother Mechanic' (Political Drama No.20) depicts the most notorious police spy inciting his audience to overthrow violently the government, church and crown in exchange for a republic. The parody of old-style revolutionary oratory he employed is   abruptly altered in the other

---

1. 'THE WOLVES LET LOOSE AT WOLVERHAMPTON' (Figaro in London, No.183, 6 June 1835). 'THE FREEDOM OF AN ENGLISH ELECTION; OR, THE DRUNKEN DRAGOONS SHOOTING OLD WOMEN AND CHILDREN AT WOLVERHAMPTON BY WAY OF KEEPING THEIR HAND IN' (Political Drama, No.91).

2. 'THE WHIG SECRETARY AT WAR'S IDEA OF MILITARY FLOGGING, BEFORE AND AFTER TAKING OFFICE' (Figaro in London, No.53, 8 December 1832 (p.210)) depicts Althorp against it in 1819 and in favour of its retention in 1832. The Weekly Show-Up attacked it in 'MILITARY PASTIME; OR, THE BASTARDS IN THEIR GLORY' (No.6, 4 August 1832), as did the Political Drama with 'THE LATE BLOODY AND BRUTAL EXHIBITION OF HORRID MILITARY TORTURE, OR, ARISTOCRATIC BASTARDS IN THEIR GLORY!!!' (No.46).

half of the cut, which depicts 'POPAY GIVING IN HIS REPORTS TO HIS EMPLOYERS', the Whigs, where he says, 'a few more such speeches, I have no doubt, my Lords, will be the means of bringing your wishes into full effect; viz. an open armed resistance to the authorities'. The government, in its turn, reveals that the Police Committee of Inquiry into Popay's behaviour had merely been a blind to the public, and in fact Popay will be promoted. The Political Drama went on to champion the cause of the trades' unions, attack the sentencing of the Dorchester Unionists and to support the strikes of both the builders and tailors.[1] The attitude of Figaro in London, however, was more ambivalent. Although it attacked Popay and the spy system warmly enough, a cut of 20th September 1834, entitled 'THE DAEMON OF MONOPOLY' (No. 146) reveals precisely where it parted from the serial cuts. The emblematic monster is shown being attacked by people carrying banners which read 'Vox Populi' and 'Unity is Strength'. Monopoly is, according to the editorial, 'at length happily doomed to destruction by the power of the Trades' Unions'. Nevertheless the paper summarizes its attitude thus:

> We are by no means advocates for the transfer of undue domination from the hands of the masters to those of the men, but it is quite evident that union among the latter is the only effectual means of counteracting the improper influence which the former have exercised for so long a period.

It goes on to warn that the only danger is that workmen should become tyrants in their turn, which would be 'even a more objectionable course than their submission to the tyranny of others'. Finally, 'We would warn them against this danger, and of the impropriety of allowing themselves to use with injustice the ascendancy they may acquire'. Compared then with the Political Drama, Figaro in London did not adopt a tone of natural identification with the interests of the lower classes. Hetherington's instincts

---

1. For example, THE DORCHESTER UNIONISTS IMPLORING MERCY!!! OF THEIR KING' (No. 32), 'THE MINISTERS AND THEIR CRONIES OFF TO BOTANY BAY, AND THE DORCHESTER MEN RETURNING' (No. 33), 'THE TAILORS' CAMPAIGN' (No.34), 'THE OPERATIVE BUILDERS AND THEIR WOULD-BE MASTERS' (No. 52).

were right. There is a hint of superiority, of paternalism, in the use of 'they' and a plea for moderation more in keeping with the old artisan radicalism than that of working class power.

An even greater contrast existed between the <u>Political Drama</u> and <u>McLean's Monthly Sheet of Caricatures</u> on the subject. In April 1834, the latter compared the landlords' and parsons' 'combinations' with that of the labourers (No. 52). The landlords are depicted being congratulated by Melbourne for helping to prolong a policy of protection through the Corn Laws, and their power is contrasted with the ruthless exaction of forced labour from parish paupers. The combination of bishops is seen to provoke, as a reaction, the swaying power of Methodism. The secret meeting of labourers simply resolves to obtain a fair price for labour and to abstain from all unlawful use of force. For this, the consequence is shown to be imprisonment and trial before Brougham, who denounces them and sentences them to transportation. This sympathetic reference to the fate of the Dorchester Unionists, however, did not extend to trades' unions generally. In 'MUTUAL LABOUR COMMITTEE' and 'COMBINATION AND EQUALITY' (No. 11, 1 November 1830), the former depicts, ironically, a man being mocked for having been brought up a gentleman. In the latter, the officers of the ship of state have been hanged, and it sinks with the rabble weighing it down. Owenism is defined as 'The poor may do without the rich, combine to supply each other with the necessarys of life, live in perfect equality and leisure to improve their minds'. Four years later, in May 1834, the Sheet renewed its attack. Seymour produced four representational views of scenes involving unionists. 'A MEETING OF THE TRADES' UNIONS' (No. 53, 1 May 1834) shows an agitator addressing a bedraggled street crowd with the words, 'Yes Gentlemen, these <u>is</u> my principles, - no K--g, - no L--ds, - no Parsons, - no Police, - no Taxes, - no Transportation, - no Nothing'. 'A SUNDAY "<u>TURN OUT</u>" OF THE TRADES' UNIONS' is of a respectable group of church-goers watching a procession of roughs emerging from three gin-palaces. 'A TRADES' UNION

COMMITTEE' represents the leader embezzling funds from the subscription box. The final print in the series, 'PUTTING DOWN THE TRADES' UNIONS' uses Wellington as front-man to box the unions into submission. Melbourne and Brougham remain in the background, the latter reassuring the former with the words, 'Don't be alarmed Gaffer, he's the only man to give these fellows an answer'. Although this extreme position of putting down the unions by force does not seem to have coincided quite with the Sheet's own views, nevertheless, the paper did express in more vitriolic fashion, the doubts and lack of identification with the cause, which we have observed in Figaro in London. Basically, sympathy was felt for 'brotherly combinations' which were, as Francis Place put it, open, continuous, respectable and limited to purely economic and educational purposes. But trades' unions 'composed of portions of several trades working through delegates, subject to momentary enthusiasms, possessed of a kind of German mystique', were condemned.[1] Seymour's cuts for McLean's Monthly Sheet of Caricatures and Figaro in London deplored the Whig government's actions - the police spying and harsh sentences against the Dorchester labourers - but condemned equally anarchists, agitators and organizations which could threaten the political order. They attacked the behaviour of unionists on marches and in meetings. This moral condemnation was entirely absent from Grant's cuts in the serial prints.

Furthermore, McLean's Monthly Sheet of Caricatures came out in favour of various types of moral reform more strongly than any other category of graphic journalism in the period. It vigorously supported the temperance campaign with a print entitled 'A DEDICATION TO THE TEMPERANCE SOCIETY - O'ER ALL THE ILLS OF LIFE VICTORIOUS' (No. 49, 1 January 1834), in which Seymour enlarged his typical worker figure, with his indiarubber features, spikey hair and

---

1. R.K. Webb, The British Working Class Reader (1955), p.145, referring to the manuscripts of four papers which Place wrote for Joseph Parkes on trades' unions. Brit. Mus., Addit. MSS. 27,834 (Place Papers), f.4-145.

shabby clothes, and stretched him out stupified on a barrel of gin. A plague of devils, demons and nightmares attack various parts of his body. 'THE TWO FISHERMEN, A DEDICATION TO THE TEMPERANCE SOCIETY' (No.53, 1 May 1834) expresses the personal catastrophe and ruin, both spiritual and physical, which follows in the wake of the bottle. In the first picture, a man fishes for monsters in the stormy waters of gin. The monsters are labelled famine, starvation, beggary, enormous taxation, discontent, hatred, malice, murder, squalidness, seduction, adultery, atheism, sickness, horrors and death. Behind him stands a hovel where his wife embraces her lover and the children fight each other. In contrast, the picture of the man fishing in pure water depicts him catching fish labelled cheap bread, civil and religious liberty, peace and quietness, health, wealth, chastity, happiness and content. Instead of a storm, the weather is fair and he is surrounded by an adoring wife and children with a pleasant home. Here it would seem all the ambitions of the respectable man find their fulfilment.[1]

'THE DRUNKEN PARLIAMENT DISCUSSING THE PREVENTION OF DRUNKENNESS BILL' is the only comment made by the Political Drama (No.49), on the subject, and in general the serial cuts confirm the judgement that the lower classes exhibited a marked dislike of attempts to legislate over morals. The suggestion made by Spencer Perceval in 1832 for a General Fast to be proclaimed for divine intercession on account of the cholera epidemic provided an opportunity to underline the contrast between a feasting clergy and a starving people. 'GENERAL FAST DAY, REPLETION v. STARVATION', which appeared in A Slap at the Church,

---

1. George Cruikshank had, around the same time, started to depict the dangers of gin. See, for example, 'THE GIN SHOP,' (1829) from Scraps and Sketches, and 'The Pillars of a GIN SHOP', (1833), 'The GIN JUGGARNATH (1835) from My Sketch Book.

(No.6, 25 February 1832) includes the caption, 'You fast - I'll pray: I'll feast - you pay'.[1] A year later, resentment at this aggressive, quasi-pastoral interference with the way people ran their lives was intensified by Sir Andrew Agnew's Sunday Observance Bill. Indeed, it is the subject which initiates the Political Drama. 'JOHN BULL; or, an Englishman's Fireside!' (No.4) shows John Bull sitting in a cold bare room with a policeman patrolling the street outside. He sums up the iniquities of the Bill thus:

> This is Observing the Sabbath with a vengeance! Didn't get my week's wages last night till all the shops were shut up ... an armed blue Devil parading about the street. So here I must sit, a free born Briton, and listening to the Chapel Bell over the way, Praying next door, and Psalm singing in the cellar.

The traditional image of John Bull, the free-born Englishman, was adapted for the purpose of attacking the more recent evils of the Metropolitan police and Sunday observance.[2] Agnew's bill was seen also by both Figaro in London and McLean's Monthly Sheet of Caricatures as a web, to entangle the poor and to be broken through by the rich, for they had enough money to buy food in advance and to eat it in private. Most virulently, the Satirical Puppet Show produced a crude woodcut entitled 'Church Fanaticism and the Gentlemen in Black' (No.1, 16 May 1833), in which the Church, the Agnewites and the Temperance brigade seem to want to keep hold of the Devil when he tries to scamper away. The cut is adorned with monuments carrying the cross of St. Andrew; a notice proclaims there is no sun-light on the

---

1. Also, 'THE GENERAL FAST' (Figaro in London, No.14, 10 March 1832). 'SAINT PRAISE GOD P...S..VAL', lithograph by C.J. Grant. Picton Library, Liverpool, William Thelwall Thomas collection.

2. Also in the Political Drama, 'PROTECTING THE SABBATH!!! OR COERCION FOR ENGLAND' (No.1), 'THE MODERN PURITAN' (No.2), 'THE SABBATH BREAKERS' (No.3), 'THINGS NOT TO BE DONE ON THE SABBATH' (No.5), 'THE SINNERS BEFORE ST. ANDREW' (No.6), 'THE AGONY BILL', a small coloured etching; 'GOING TO CHURCH. COMING OUT OF CHURCH. JOHN BULL'S SUNDAY ACCORDING TO SIR ANDREW AGNEW'S NEW ACT OF PARLIAMENT', folio woodcut by C.J. Grant. Brit.Mus., Prints and Drawings.

sabbath. The accompanying leader stated:

> They have commenced with us upon the seventh day, but if we submit to that day's slavery, we may very soon expect the restrictions to extend to the other six, and then farewell to the few remaining privileges and liberties which fall to the share of the WORKING CLASSES!

Neither the Whigs nor the Tories, it believed, were friends of the people. It concluded with the slogan 'Unanimity, Resolution and Perseverance'.

To what extent did these various forms of political caricature represent coherent class views? What patchy evidence we have concerning their varied sales and production techniques, the level of readership and the personnel associated with the series is further stratified by the style of depiction, the subject matter and the attitudes conveyed in the caricatures. The serial cuts, backed by working class leaders like Cleave and Hetherington, produced the most root and branch reactions and reform demands. They upheld trade unionism. That they saw themselves as representing organized and coherent men is clear from Grant's 'THE FOUR FACTIONS, WHICH DISTRACT THE COUNTRY' 76 (Political Drama, No.12). The Tory, Wellington, is depicted as a butcher; the Whig, Grey, is shown carrying the pickings of wealth and place; the Liberal is a 'rank coward', hiding down a chimney; while the Ultra-Radical is a grotesque dwarfed figure, 'not a true and honest Radical, but a scum of the rabble; a ragamuffin ruffian, everything to gain, and nothing to lose'. Yet the 'true and honest Radical', presumably representing the ideal reader, was not the same as the man catered for by Figaro in London. Certainly, the humorous magazines did attack suffering and injustice, humbug and officialdom and all aspects of 'old corruption'. These targets, this hostility to aristocratic lackeys and church dignitaries, this disillusionment with party politics, were common to all levels of metropolitan society since the days of 'Wilkes and Liberty'. Like the targets, so the slogans and the imagery had not been killed. Furthermore, in the 1830s, they were joined by a hatred of political economy, of the New Poor Law, its manifestation and the new Police, its guardian. Yet, if Figaro in London was not in sympathy with the goals of middle-class businessmen and politicians, neither was it a part of the working-class journalism being shaped by Cleave, Hetherington and Bronterre O'Brien. The solutions it offered were not based on the organization of the working classes for political ends, but sometimes tended more towards hope in moral reform. They represented the radicalism of young journalists and writers, reporters on rather than participants in the battle. These divisions can be drawn even more clearly during the period by examining two themes - the 'March of Mind' and the 'War of the Unstamped' - which made the press generally, and political caricature in particular, peculiarly aware of its role and its rapport with its audience. They underline the importance of the medium of communication, through the fight for its freedom in the face of not only legal, but also technological constraints.

THE FREEDOM OF THE PRESS

1830 - 1836

IV

Political caricature enjoyed in England a freedom from legal restraint which was not available to other forms of communication. It used this gift not only, as has been shown, to attack the persistent power of 'old corruption', but also to defend the freedom of the press generally to express its views, in the face of the 'gagging acts' of 1819. During the 1830s, the fruits of the 'March of Intellect' became increasingly apparent, and hence the necessity of directing new audiences away from dangerous political knowledge towards 'useful knowledge' of a harmless nature. Positive means were adopted through the Society for the Diffusion of Useful Knowledge, in particular, their illustrated Penny Magazine; the negative government defence consisted of prosecution of all illegal publications during the campaign which became known as the 'War of the Unstamped'. The radical cuts were active in their identification with and defence of the unstamped press, against the technical and political alienation of the Penny Magazine. By 1836, they had merged into the mainstream of radical journalism by becoming 'cartoons' on the front page of broadsheet-size, unstamped police gazettes. This chapter underlines the importance which was seen to exist in controlling all forms of public communication by those in authority. It also furthers the process of amalgamation between political caricature and journalism, and thus the strengthening of divisions in format and audience. It spotlights the conflict which was precipitated between what purported to be a country-wide and classless, unifying and universal, progressive and elevating style of engraving and that which we have already seen was metropolitan and sectional, divisive, partial and traditional.

I

Part of the time-honoured function of allegory has been to serve as an 'Aesop-language' to avoid censorship of dissident thought.[1] Dr. George has traced the long tradition of embodying the more risky allegations of a newspaper or pamphlet in a caricature without comment in the text.[2] If the injured parties did not have the sense to adopt the pose that such an attack was a joke and not meant to be taken seriously, then the defence would readily do so in court. Legally speaking, it was very difficult to prove 'malicious intention' in a case of parody and cases, the most notorious in this period being that brought against William Hone for blasphemous libel, were virtually laughed out of court.[3] This defence deflated the case of libel brought by the parish of St. Luke's against a print by George Cruikshank, although Lord Ellenborough, the judge, thought that such publications were 'highly unwarrantable'.[4] During the 1820s, Brougham noticed the increase in attacks on the royal family downwards, but wrote in retrospect, they had become as harmless as the Court Circular, 'and prosecution was never

---

1. A. Fletcher, Allegory, the Theory of a Symbolic Mode (Ithaca, 1964) p.22.
2. M. D. George, Catalogue of Political and Personal Satires, (1949-54), ix. x. xi. Introductions.
3. See N. St. John-Stevas, Obscenity and the Law (1956), p.149. Since Fox's Libel Act, a criminal intention has always been required in cases of blasphemy and sedition. For Hone's case, see W. Hone, The Three Trials of William Hone (1817-18). Also, F. W. Hackwood, The Life and Times of William Hone (1912), pp.118-88. G. D. Nokes, A History of the Crime of Blasphemy (1928).
4. George, Catalogue of Political and Personal Satires, ix. pp.xix-xx, for B.M. No.11951. See also, B.M. Nos.13493-5, for Cruikshank's comment on an 1815 case brought by a Margate attorney, Boys, against a young woman who had been circulating caricature drawings accusing him of dishonesty. Ellenborough tried the case and Boys, who had claimed £1,000 damages, received £10.

thought of for a moment'.[1] It is more likely, however, that the discouraging results of action for pictorial libel made the government cautious. Certainly, the King felt such prints to be harmful enough to go to the lengths of buying up the plate, copyright and any impressions which had already been printed, in an effort to suppress the most scurrilous. When he complained in 1823, writing to Peel, of caricatures and 'trash' alleging his madness, the Law Officers advised against prosecution, for a London jury would probably throw out the indictment.[2] The Constitutional Association had unsuccessfully tried to prosecute Benbow in 1821 for two caricatures, but the indictments were rejected by the Grand Jury. So was the case brought against The Queen's Matrimonial Ladder (B.M. No.13790-805) and Non Mi Ricordo! (B.M. Nos. 13844-6) both fruits of the collaboration between two old hands at exploiting the libel loopholes, Hone and Cruikshank.[3]

Furthermore, Hone and Cruikshank unswervingly defended the freedom of the press. This was symbolized most explicitly by the Stanhope hand-printing press, which acted as a rallying point for all the forces fighting the 'old corruption'. In the wake of the Liverpool administration's coercive and anti-press legislation after the Napoleonic Wars, it took on a new importance. In March 1817, a print by George Cruikshank

---

1. (Lord Brougham), 'Abuses of the Press', Edinburgh Review, lxvii (1838), 51.
2. C. S. Parker, Sir Robert Peel from his Private Papers (1891), i. 336-8. State Trials, new series ii. 1823-1831, ed. J. Macdonell (1889), 1-68.
3. The King wrote to Eldon, 9 January 1821, to ask what steps the Attorney-General intended to take 'upon the mode in which all the vendors of treason, and libellers such as Benbow, &c.&c.&c., are to be prosecuted'. H. Twiss, The Public and Private Life of Lord Chancellor Eldon (1844), ii.413. For the Hone Cruikshank collaboration and the Constitutional Association's attack see Wickwar, The Struggle for the Freedom of the Press pp.131-4, 163-5, 192-3.

was issued, 'LIBERTY SUSPENDED! with the Bulwark of the Constitution!' 77
(B.M. No.12871), which reflects the anger felt at the suspension of
Habeas Corpus and the temporary Seditious Meetings Act. The base of a
dismantled printing press, labelled 'BRITISH PRESS', serves as a scaffold for the Corpse of Liberty, gagged, bound and hanging from a gibbet.
Her gag is the 'Gagging Bill', and she holds a document labelled 'Magna
Charta, Bill of Rights, Habeas Corpus'. In 1819, the government passed
the Libels Act (60 Geo.III, c.9), which made cheap periodicals liable to
Pitt's newspaper act and the stamp duties. 'A FREE BORN ENGLISHMAN! THE 78
ADMIRATION of the WORLD!!! AND THE ENVY OF SURROUNDING NATIONS!!!!!'
(B.M. No.13287, 15 December 1819) was reissued, being adapted from a plate
of 1813 (B.M. No.12037), which was itself derived from prints of 1795.
John Bull is emaciated and derelict, shackled and with a padlocked mouth
labelled 'No GRUMBLING'. In his hands, tied behind his back, are pen and
paper on which he has written, 'Freedom of the Press' and 'Transportation'.
He stands on the 'MAGNA CHARTA' and the 'Bill of RIGHTS', with an axe
labelled, 'LAW of LIBEL' near his feet. In the background, his wife and
children are abandoned, while John Bull is apparently inside a debtors'
prison. This print appeared again in A Slap at Slop.[1] In 'Poor BULL & 79
his Burden - or the Political MURRAION!!!'(B.M. No.13288), John Bull, with
the full weight of 'old corruption' on his back, also wears a muzzle
labelled 'GAGGING BILL'. Thus, in these three prints the same points
are made. Liberty of the press is associated with the Magna Charta and
Bill of Rights, as what the free-born Englishman is entitled to expect.
In opposition to this stands the crown, church, government, magistrates,
standing army and a whole range of taxes.

1.. See below p.125.

This tradition was epitomized in William Hone's verse pamphlets, illustrated by Cruikshank, which started to appear during the latter part of 1819. They owed much in origin to the seventeenth century Emblem Book, which comprised of a series of small engravings, ranging from illustrated metaphors to more elaborate scenes, each with a motto and a moral exposition, usually in verse. Hone's adaptation of this to the field of politics produced, 'an entertaining and instructive admixture of notorious matter-of-fact with emblematic allusion'.[1] It enjoyed a licence not accorded to political libels in prose. Furthermore, unlike Cruikshank's earlier etchings, which could not have been produced in editions larger than a couple of thousand, this alliance between wood engraving and letter-press was technically almost limitless.[2] One of its most recurrent emblems was the printing press, which stood for freedom of speech and an Englishman's rights and liberties generally. In The Political House that Jack Built (B.M. Nos.13292-13304), said to have sold over 100,000 copies, it was 'THE THING' which would conquer despite the new Acts, the 'Vermin' of the Church, the standing army, pensioners, taxmen and lawyers. As in the 1830s, the leading politicians were dubbed with appropriate nick-names: 'The Doctor' (Sidmouth), 'Derry Down Triangle' (Castlereagh), and 'The Spouter of Froth by the Hour' (Canning).[3] Nearly all of the subsequent pamphlets contained some allusion to and image of the press.[4] Finally, there appeared A Slap at Slop and the Bridge Street

1. Hackwood, op.cit., p.219. See also, Radical Squibs and Loyal Ripostes, ed. E. Rickword (Bath, 1971).

2. See above p.55.

3. See above p.101.

4. They were The Man in the Moon (B.M. Nos.13508-21), A Political Christmas Carol (B.M.Nos.13518-9), The Queen's Matrimonial Ladder (B.M. Nos.13790-807), The Political Showman - At Home! (B.M.No.14148-69) and A Slap at Slop and the Bridge Street Gang (B.M. Nos14207-32). The only exception was Non Mi Ricordo (B.M. Nos.13844-6).

Gang (B.M. Nos.14207-14232), which mounted an attack on Stoddart, the
Constitutional Association and the New Times, in the format of a mock
folio size newspaper. By parodying newspaper paragraphs and advertise-
ments, it condemned prominent members of the Association like Sewell and
Wellington, as well as the crown, the church and the violence of Peterloo.
'THE "DAMNABLE ASSOCIATION"; OR, THE INFERNAL INQUISITION OF BLACK FRIARS'
(B.M. No.14221) anticipated the prosecutions of the 1830s,[1] but here
presented the Constitutional Association in their 'DEN' in Bridge Street.
Aided by bishops, they tie 'Truth' to a beam, demolish the printing press
with fire and axes, and burn pamphlets and caricatures before an imbecile
inquisitor, under a crown suspended from the ceiling. This 'newspaper'
even carried a mock stamp. It was in fact a paw (B.M. No.14231) attached
to a crown, which was inscribed 'Dieu et mon Droit' and 'On Every Thing
He Claps His Claw'.

The Hone-Cruikshank collaboration broke up soon afterwards.[2] It
survived prosecutions for libel and had consistently championed the
freedom of the press. Its influence lasted through the 1820's and the
1830 s, both in the style and iconography of its cuts in England and in

---

1. See below p.155.

2. Cruikshank's receipt of £100 from Carlton House may well have
contributed to his renunciation of political caricature. See
George, Catalogue of Political and Personal Satires, x. pp.xl-xlii.
According to Hone, he 'manifested what I have long suspected, that
he is by no means friendly to Reform!' A.M. Cohn, George Cruikshank,
a Catalogue Raisonné of the work executed ... 1806-1877 (1924)
p.xiii. See also, (W.M. Thackeray), 'George Cruikshank, 'London and
Westminster Review, xxxiv (1840), 10-11, who asserted that he never
took bribes. W. Bates, George Cruikshank (Birmingham, 1878), p.15:
'But the fact is George was no politician, and would make a design
with rigid impartiality for anyone that paid him'. For Cruikshank's
whole career, see B. Jerrold, The Life of George Cruikshank (1882).

France[1] and in its freedom from restraint. 'THE MAN WOTS GOT THE WHIP 84
HAND OF 'EM ALL' (B.M. No.15776, 30 May 1829), by Heath, for example,
revived the imagery of Cruikshank's Political Showman, with an animated
Stanhope press, surmounted by a cap of liberty. With one lever, it
holds a print of Wellington (B.M. No.15731), threatened with destruction
by fire. In the other, it holds a quill pen, bound by serpents which
spit at a departing Wellington. Brougham flies off in the other direction,
together with Eldon. The message of the print would seem to be that not
only Wellington, Eldon and the Tories, but also Brougham and the Whigs
had reason to fear the power of caricature in particular and the freedom of the press in general. Again, during the early 1830s, C. J. Grant
produced two cuts of self-reference, which recognized and revelled in
the freedom afforded to caricature. In 'MAGISTERIAL JUSTICE - A FACT' 85
(Political Drama, No.14), a policeman is shown bringing a vendor of
cheap publications, with his wife and six children, before a magistrate.
He reveals he was not in uniform when he made the arrest and gave a
forged sixpence to receive fivepence change. The arrest has been made
for selling the Political Drama, in fact, the number caricaturing the

---

1. Seymour adapted Cruikshank's series of political bestiaries and May Day characters for Figaro in London and Asmodeus; or the Devil in London, as did Grant in the serial cuts. See above p.93.'A NEW VERSION OF THE HOUSE THAT JACK BUILT', by Seymour, appeared ten years later; another version was engraved by Grant for Cleave's Gazette of Variety, 9 September 1843. William Carpenter revived the emblems of the printing press, the cap of liberty and so on for the mastheads of his Political and Historical Essays pamphlets in 1831. The whole of the Emblem Book format of illustrated verse was used by Punch for 'The Water that John Drinks', xvii (1849), 144-5.
   There is also a possibility that Charles Philipon was aware of Cruikshank's work when he started La Caricature in 1830. Certainly, many of its lithographs, especially those by Grandville (Jean Ignace Gérard) make use of the Stanhope press, the cap of liberty and the female figure personifying the freedom of the press. See below p.155.

police as a bunch of ne'er-do-wells (No.11). However, strictly speaking, such a print cannot be liable for prosecution as news, under the Stamp Act. The magistrate decides to convict him under the Hawker's Act instead, for selling them without a licence.[1] He adds, 'It is really a shame that there is no Act of Parliament to put all Caricatures down, and to imprison the artists, publishers, printers and purchasers'. Similar sentiments are voiced by Brougham in 'A TETE A TETE. A COUPLE OF GOOD JUDGES AT ALL EVENTS' (Political Drama, No.41), when he discusses the recent unsuccessful prosecution of Hetherington with Lyndhurst. Lyndhurst is pleased with the way the verdict has gone and says, 'I admire him (Hetherington) for his implacable hatred of the Whigs... In facto we decided for the Defendant relating to The Poor Man's Guardian, purely from those motives I assure ye'. Brougham, who holds a copy of the Political Drama bearing a caricature of himself, replies that the victory is really with the unstamped press, for the Law has been brought into disrepute, by making it a 'foot-ball' between parties. If the cheap press does defeat the government, however, he hopes, 'they will fix the Stamp (and make it a half-crown one) too upon those abominable Political Caricatures, for 'tis really attrocious that they should be allow'd to libel one in this way because there's no Law in being to prevent it'.

Such bravado was less appropriate when caricatures were sold in the company of, or included within, something more like an unstamped newspaper. One vendor, who was selling both the Poor Man's Guardian and John Bull's Picture Gallery, was sent to prison for a month, the Alderman at Bow Street saying of the latter, he was surprised that people would buy such inflammatory trash when they might see the journals of the day for

---

1. See J. H. Wiener, The War of the Unstamped (1969), pp.197-201 for prosecution of the unstamped under the Hawkers' Act of 1743.

the same amount.[1] John Cleave was fined, imprisoned and had his presses seized for producing Cleave's Weekly Police Gazette, which included Grant's cartoons. On the other hand, when a vendor of Figaro in London was arrested, the Commissioners of Stamps declined to prosecute. The Magistrate at Bow Street, Mr. Minshull added, however, 'he thought the caricatures in which something like ridicule was cast upon certain individuals in the State, ought to have been omitted'.

> The Editor (A Beckett):- The only object, Sir, was to create a laugh.
>
> Mr. Minshull:- Perhaps not; but Lord Bacon says that persons holding high offices in the State should never be made the subject of a joke.[2]

These differences in treatment will be placed in the larger context of the 'war of the unstamped' and the freedom of the press during the 1830s. However, before leaving aside the question of the status of caricature, it is significant to see the whole matter revived in 1850 in relation to Punch. Collet Dobson Collet, Secretary of the Newspaper Stamp Abolition Committee, took up the definition of a newspaper to be found in the 1836 Stamp Act (6 & 7 Will.IV, c.76) and accused Punch of being a newspaper in the legal rather than the popular sense, both as to giving news and commenting upon it. This was discounted by the Commissioners of Inland Revenue in replying to a letter Collet had got a friend of his to write, making the charge.[3] However,

---

1. Poor Man's Guardian, 7 July 1832, quoting from the Dispatch, 1 July 1832. See also, the case of Patrick Donovan, 'a poor emaciated Irishman', who was sent to prison for a month by the Bow Street court for selling the Poor Man's Guardian and John Bull's Picture Gallery. Poor Man's Guardian, 23 June 1832.

2. True Sun, 27 March 1832. Figaro in London, No.17, 31 March 1832. See below p.154.

3. Parl. Papers 1851, xvii (558), pp.119-24, pp.149-50, pp.486-7: minutes of evidence C. D. Collet, qus.758-75, 913. Appendix I.

Collet reiterated his view before the Select Committee on Newspaper Stamps in 1851 and both the Solicitor to the Board of Inland Revenue, John Timm, and the Assistant Secretary, Thomas Keogh, were forced to comment. They managed to repeat every judgement made on the subject during the previous half century. For a start, *Punch* did not give news and as for its comments, they were much too light-hearted to be taken seriously. As Timm said:-

> His only object is to make a pun or a piece of witticism, or something of that kind; not for the purpose of giving news. It is rather assumed in those cases, I think, that everybody is aware of the news or other matter which he puns or jests upon.

Similarly, Keogh felt that *Punch* referred to public events to make them the vehicle or the subject of some 'jest or humorous sally', and the point would be lost if the event were not previously known:

> The comments I consider to be not serious comments nor anything more than a joke, which it would be ridiculous to notice, I should say.[1]

Furthermore, there were practical objections. Keogh admitted that the discretion of the Board in instituting a prosecution was governed by their estimate of the opinion a jury was likely to form of the publication; Timm thought that if he were to attempt to prosecute that paper for being a newspaper unstamped, he would be laughed out of court.[2] The suggestion from the Chairman, Milner Gibson, that the object of the statesmen of 1820 was to prevent persons in small publications sold at a low price, from turning public institutions into ridicule, and treating with contempt the laws and public arrangements, was not taken seriously. Keogh replied that the object

---

1. *Parl. Papers 1851*, xvii (558), p.24, pp.81-2: minutes of evidence J. Timm and T. Keogh, qus.97, 515-6.

2. *Ibid.*, qus.97, 517.

of the Publications Act was to bring within the range of the newspaper laws the publishers of prints in which public transactions were seriously discussed, 'but not in the manner in which "Punch" or any paper of a mere jocular character refers to public events.'[1] Collet's exercise in the art of *reductio ad absurdum* thus provoked, yet again, reactions which ranged from feigned nonchalance to pragmatic expediency, from indifference to concern, over the nature of pictorial humour and its effects. Perhaps, between the *Figaro in London* of 1832 and the *Punch* of twenty years later, that desire only 'to create a laugh' had been strengthened.[2] However, this was by no means true on every level of political caricature. While the authorities floundered in an inconclusive debate as to whether the genre was dangerous or not, the producers of the most radical types of political caricature were free to comment on and to aid their more closely watched colleagues on the unstamped press.

1. *Ibid.*, qu.518.
2. See below, Ch. VI, Section II.

II

The freedom of the press was a source of unremitting anxiety to those in authority throughout the nineteenth century. Hannah More wrote in 1801 how she had observed from the beginning of the French Revolution, 'the arts used by the jacobinical writers to alienate the people from the church, by undermining their respect for its ministers'. She hoped to counteract their 'pestilent pamphlets' with a multitude of little tracts.[1] With a similar aim in view, George Miller, a Dundee publisher, produced in 1814, 'a valuable repository of important information, and moral and religious instruction.'[2] This venture probably inspired Charles Knight to commence his lengthy pilgrimage to save the cause of popular education from undesirable leaders.[3] For not only was there a danger to the established religion, but also the threat 'of lopping and topping the sturdy oak of the constitution till its shelter and its beauty were altogether gone.'[4] After the Napoleonic Wars had ended, the task became more pressing. Cobbett's and Wooler's pamphlets, as well as those of Hone, provoked Southey to write in 1818 of 'the indefatigable zeal with which the most pernicious principles of every kind are openly disseminated, in contempt and defiance of the law and of all things sacred'.[5] In the same year, Knight wrote, 'There is a

---

1. The Letters of Hannah More, selected with an introduction by R. Brimley Johnson (1925), p.180. Letter to the Bishop of Bath and Wells. 1801.

2. A. Somerville, The Autobiography of a Working Man (1848), pp.93-95. Also, R. D. Altick, The English Common Reader (1957), p.320.

3. See Knight, Passages of a Working Life for the most revealing account of the development of middle class attitudes to popular education during the first half of the nineteenth century.

4. Ibid., i. 225.

5. (R. Southey), 'On the Means of Improving the People', Quarterly Review, xix (1818), 93.

new power in society, and they have combined to give that power a direction. The work must be taken out of their hands'. The 'they' referred to were the 'anarchists of that day' who were 'a subtle and acute race':

> They had watched the progress of knowledge amongst the people. Their publications teemed with allusions to the increasing intelligence of the working classes.[1]

The progress of knowledge, the 'March of Mind' throughout society was at the root of this fear. At its most frivolous, this slogan provided the inspiration for a seemingly inexhaustible fund of fun at the expense of the new methods of advertising, new wonders of steam power and the new pretensions of the lower orders.[2] Among these pretensions was their interest in reading matter, which distracted them from their normal course of duty.[3] The most common setting for such malingering was the coffee house or reading room, used by Seymour for three of his Sketches. Two dustmen sit in the Byron Coffee House and Reading Room and engage in conversation (No.26):

> You shall have the paper directly, Sir, but really the debates are so very interesting.
>
> Oh pray don't hurry Sir; it's only the scientific notices I care about.

Again, two dustmen converse in a coffee house in front of a notice which announces M. Fubb's course of fifteen lectures on SCIENCE (No.35). One is reading 'Tales of Love' and the other is deep in a newspaper:-

---

1. Knight, op.cit., i. 235 quoted from a paper he wrote for the Windsor Express, 11 December 1819, entitled 'Cheap Publications'.

2. George, Political and Personal Satires, x. pp.xxxviii-xxxix. See also, B.M. No.15604 &c.

3. See, for example, THE MARCH OF INTELLECT (B.M. No.15604+, 23 January, 1828) by Heath, in which an apple-woman sits against a lamp-post reading Byron, while a boy steals an apple.

> Have you read the Leader in this paper, Mr. Brisket?
>
> No! I never touch a newspaper, they are all so wery wenal and woid of sentiment.

The third print illustrates a scene in an evangelical book and print shop, adorned with busts of clerics and advertisements for the <u>Pulpit</u> and <u>Evangelical Magazine</u> (No.101). A dustman addresses a prim lady at the counter:

> I say Marm, do you happen to have the hair of 'All round my hat, I vears a green villow!'

Thus, Seymour covered the range of reading matter available to the lower classes. Straight political news competed with useful knowledge, with evangelical tracts and with romantic fiction. The most worrying aspect of these trends was not the inconvenience caused by distracted servants, but the pretensions to political knowledge and power they would attain. A letter to Brougham from a 'country gentleman', which appeared in the <u>Edinburgh Review</u> of 1826 summed it up:- 'with the same propriety may the person that <u>claims education</u> from your Lordship on such terms, <u>claim part of your estate!</u>'[1] Owing to the superficiality of their knowledge, he foresaw that the populace would become dissatisfied with their ignorance, before they would be wise enough to profit by their knowledge. In fact, what this amounted to was a condemnation of the preference among the lower classes for Cobbett over Hannah More, cheap politics rather than useful knowledge or evangelical pamphlets.[2]

---

1. 'Diffusion of Knowledge', <u>Edinburgh Review</u>, xlv (1826), 192.
2. Webb, <u>The British Working Class Reader</u> pp.1-102.

Lord Eldon's belief that 'the march of intellect' was 'the rogue's march and think it a tune to which one day or the other a hundred thousand tall fellows with clubs & pikes will march against Whitehall',[1] was echoed in some prints. 'MARCH 1829' (B.M. No.15682) balances on the scales 'Liberality' and the 'March of Intellect' against 'Prudence' and 'Experience', O'Connell against Eldon. The lithograph is the sole work of some private anonymous individual, whose publisher only ever produced two other prints.[2] A less portentous approach was adopted by 'A Sharpshooter' in 'THE SCAVENGER'S LAMENTATION; OR, THE DREADFUL CONSEQUENCES OF SWEEPING STREETS BY MACHINERY' (B.M. No.15757, 16 May 1829), published by Gans, a popular publisher of Southampton Street, Strand.[3] Eldon, dressed as a street scavenger, laments in front of the new machinery:

> Ah! this is what comes of Improvement - this is the happy effects of the March of Intellect - No employment for Scavengers now - when I had the management of the Rubbish concern, I found plenty of employment for all of them.

However, it was not only Eldon and the Tories who had reason to fear the power of the press, but also the Whig government when it attained power. Lord Brougham, indeed, through his association with the Society for the Diffusion of Useful Knowledge, was attacked from all sides.[4] For the

---

1. Brit.Mus., Addit. MSS.35,148 (Place Papers), f.6-6b.J.C. Hobhouse to F. Place.
2. The artist's initials were P.C. (?W.P.), the publisher, J. Chappell, 98 Cornhill, who also put out B.M. Nos.15711 and 15727. George, Political and Personal Satires, xi 100, 806.
3. Ibid., xi.p.liii, 807.
4. For the career of Lord Brougham see A. Aspinall, Lord Brougham and the Whig Party (1939). C. W. New, The Life of Henry Brougham to 1830 (Oxford, 1961).

most conservative element in politics, he was as responsible as Cobbett for fostering political awareness in the lower classes. H.B.'s'"A TALE of a TUB" and the MORAL of the TAIL!'(Political Sketches, No.134, 13 June 1831) predictably takes this line. It illustrates the boat of government being deluged by the 'Popular spray', while Brougham, one of the oarsmen, says, 'It has been discover'd in the March of Intellect that the Tail often outstrips the Head'. The warning also came from the other direction, from the radicals. In 'THE HEAD SCHOOLMASTER THREATENED', a lithograph by C. J. Grant of December 1830, Brougham adopts a Dighton-like pose in profile, wearing his Lord Chancellor's robes, a position he had just attained, with a broom under his arm. He reads a message which says, 'Unless you instantly put aside your Thrashing Machine you may expect a visit from Swing'. Brougham's own thoughts are expressed as:-

> I calculate that this shews the march of Useful Knowledge as much as anything - Verily if this is the case I must begin to Strike for a general Reform amongst my Scholars who seem to have an immoderate attack of a Burning Fever.

The print is shot through with double meaning. First, there is the reference to Brougham's connection with the Society for the Diffusion of Useful Knowledge, his speech of 1828 in which he spoke of the 'schoolmaster' being 'abroad',[1] and his insistence on being in control of the sort of knowledge diffused by 'thrashing' it into the scholars. However, there is a more specific reference to the agricultural disturbances of 1830, and the trial that month which resulted in nine labourers being hanged and 457 transported.[2] This act disenchanted the lower classes with the Whigs, almost as soon as they attained office. Hence, the 'thrashing' also refers to the destruction of the threshing machines and

---

1. Hansard, new series, 1828, xviii. 58. See New, op.cit., pp.328-89 for Brougham's educational activities before 1830.
2. G. Rudé and E. J. Hobsbawm, Captain Swing (1969). Also Webb, op.cit., pp.103-22 on the propaganda which ensued.

the 'burning' of hay ricks by the labourers, and further, to the savage Whig reprisals. In general, the message of the print was, that unless the Whigs did something to reform the lot of the lower classes, they must expect much more trouble at the hands of their newly educated inferiors. Thus in diagnosis, if not in remedy, the print coincides with the conservative view. Lord Wilton was not alone in attributing the riots to:

> the march of education, to the malign nostrums of the schoolmaster, to the spurious morality of the present day, and the dangerous influence of Mr. Henry, now Lord Brougham, and cheap libraries.[1]

The most detailed delineation of the turn this process took in the 1820s and 1830s is presented in a series which begins with 'PREPARING A POTION' 89 in McLean's Monthly Sheet of Caricatures (No.68, 1 August 1835). 'Literary twaddle', 'Agitation' and 'Scotch Feelosophee' are mixed by Brougham, O'Connell and Joseph Hume respectively into a 'Cheap Sedition' brew. 'THE POTION PREVENTED shows John Bull asleep, being protected by Lord Eldon, who is armed with the 'Laws' and 'Stamp Acts'. However, Brougham and his friends manage to administer a dose of 'Cheap Sedition', in 'THE POTION TAKEN'. Finally, in ' EFFECTS OF THE POTION', Brougham and O'Connell run away from a raving John Bull, who is burning the church, trampling over the 'LAW' and the 'GOSPEL', armed with fire and the sword of 'Revolution'. The print is extremely topical, for O'Connell was about to set off on his speech-making tour to rouse the country against the House of Lords. However, the references to well known figures and catch phrases connected with reform since the time of Cobbett suggest an interpretation of greater perspective. The prophecies of the earlier prints were now confirmed in the light of practical experience: the efforts of middle class reformers to control the March of Mind within their own tenets had been futile. The practical experience they had acquired during the first half of the 1830s was the outcome of their own journalistic efforts and the opposition they had encountered in the so-called 'War of the Unstamped'.

---

1. 'The Burnings in Kent and the State of the Labouring Classes', Fraser's Magazine, ii (1830), 572-3.

The middle class reformers in general, and the Society for the Diffusion of Useful Knowledge in particular, based all of their calculations on the simple but unproven assumption that 'good' reading matter would drive out the 'bad'. Furthermore, the problems which prevented the attaining of a mechanical accumulation of knowledge were merely technical.[1] For such people, at their most idealistic when advocating the repeal of the taxes on knowledge in parliament, the 'good' could be spread in newspapers run by them for the benefit of the lower classes.[2] Newspapers furnished:-

> by far the best vehicles for disseminating important truths and useful information ... Every man of good sense must at once perceive what an engine this would be in the hands of the Educator.[3]

At that moment, the opportunity to communicate sound political instruction to the poorer classes was being wasted:-

> But couple useful knowledge with the intelligence which a newspaper deals in, and the doors of those humble dwellings, where so much remains to be done in teaching the inmates, fly open at once to the Schoolmaster.[4]

Unfortunately, Brougham was prevented from playing the star role as Educator or Schoolmaster by the taxes on newspapers. His more ambitious vision declined into the mundane facts of useful knowledge, pure and simple. Nevertheless, even this was not without

---

1. Hollis, op.cit., pp.295-6.

2. See Hansard, 3rd series, 1832, xiii. 619-47; 1834, xxiii. 1193-1223; 1835, xxvii. 85-95; 1835, xxx. 835-62. For a summary of the middle class arguments in favour of the removal of the texts on knowledge, see Hollis, op.cit., pp.12-18. Wiener, The War of the Unstamped, pp.20-51.

3. (Lord Brougham), 'Petition from the Inhabitants of the City of London against the Newspaper Taxes', Edinburgh Review, lxi (1835), 184.

4. 'Lord Brougham's Speech, on presenting the London Petition against the Taxes on Knowledge in the House of Lords', British and Foreign Quarterly Review, i (1835), 171.

its peculiar thrill, it was believed, for those who had previously possessed no cheap reading matter. The principle result of this sort of reasoning was the birth of the Penny Magazine on 31 March 1832:-

> What the stage-coach has become to the middle classes, we hope our Penny Magazine will be to all classes - an universal convenience and enjoyment... we shall endeavour to prepare an useful and entertaining Weekly Magazine, that may be taken up and laid down without requiring any considerable effort; and that may tend to fix the mind upon calmer, and, it may be, purer subjects of thought than the violence of party discussion, or the stimulating details of crime and suffering.

Continuing to make a virtue of its own limitations, it proceeded:-

> Whatever tends to enlarge the range of observation, to add to the store of facts, to awaken the reason, and to lead the imagination into agreeable and innocent trains of thought, may assist in the establishment of a sincere and ardent desire for information.[1]

By the end of its first year, it could rejoice in the fact that it sold over 200,000 copies per issue, enumerated the subjects it had covered 'of the broadest and simplest character', which had 'supplied the materials for exciting the curiosity of a million of readers', while acknowledging that some of its unexampled success was to be ascribed 'to the liberal employment of illustrations, by means of wood-cuts'. The use of artists of eminence, both as draughtsmen and wood engravers, served:-

> to gratify a proper curiosity, and cultivate an increasing taste, by giving representations of the finest works of Art, of Monuments of Antiquity, and of subjects of Natural History, in a style that had been previously considered to belong only to expensive books.[2]

Another useful knowledge publication, the Graphic and Historical Illustrator, expressed even more clearly this belief in illustration as an educational bait, strategically included to draw the reader in to consideration of more serious matters in the same way as the useful knowledge text was intended to:-

1. 'Reading for All', Penny Magazine, i (1832), 1.
2. 'Preface', Penny Magazine, i (1832), iii-iv.

> Graphic Illustration has a charm for almost everyone; and many who have, at first, been attracted by that alone, have insensibly acquired a relish for investigating and inquiring into the subjects thus introduced to them. From careless and casual inspection, they have been led on to make themselves acquainted with the history of the buildings and places they were shown...[1]

It too represented a popular version of a respectable theory, that of the capacity of high art to elevate and refine, now linked to a more utilitarian cause. The Penny Magazine sought to cultivate popular taste because:-

> By diffusing a love of nature and of art amongst the people, the higher faculties of the mind will be awakened, and the impulses under which men seek for excitement in vicious indulgences, will be more easily overcome.[2]

Thus, it is not surprising that Cowper should think of the Penny Magazine as the 'paper currency' of art, which diffused 'science and taste and good feeling, without one sentence of immoral feeling in the whole';[3] or that a writer on the art of wood engraving should find it 'impossible to over-estimate the influence of a well-directed illustrated literature as a lever to educate the masses, and a refining influence on society at large'.[4] Henry Cole believed that men owed no slight obligation to Mr. Charles Knight for the great impulse he had given to wood engraving, the adaptations he had made of it 'and the moral good he has done by it to the poor of the whole civilized world; - thanks and praise be to the man who has multiplied and extended the pleasures of the beautiful where they were scarcely known before!'[5]

1. 'Preface', Graphic and Historical Illustrator, i (1832).
2. 'Cultivation of Popular Taste', Penny Magazine, v (1836), 479-80.
3. See above pp.51-52.
4. Gilks, Sketch of the Origin and Progress of the Art of Wood-Engraving, p.73.
5. Cole, 'Modern Wood Engraving', p.269.

There is some evidence to suggest that the Penny Magazine and other publications of this type could work in this way and stimulate interest in more profound aspects of learning. Francis Place believed:-

> I know that if you teach ignorant men, especially young men, something of geography, and something of natural history, you give them a taste for reading which hardly ever leaves them.[1]

The Penny Magazine itself printed in 1835 a paper entitled 'A Poor Student's Literary Expenditure', in which the writer compared his own 'struggles and difficulties' to obtain cheap reading material in the second decade of the century with the present variety available.[2] Some more specific examples come from the memoirs of articulate working men, who recalled the 1830s. Christopher Thomson went without sugar in his tea to purchase the Penny Magazine, and felt that in common with tens of thousands, he had never bought anything so valuable:-

> The "Penny Magazine" was the first intellectual mile-post put down upon the way-side, wherefrom coming ages may measure their progress towards a commonwealth of books.[3]

When George Jacob Holyoake toured Derbyshire on foot in 1838, he was able to obtain a bed for the night by giving a man, who had never seen a paper with pictures before, some copies of the Penny Magazine, 'They proved as valuable as glass beads in dealing with Indians'.[4] Groves, the wood engraver, recognized the high standards set by John Jackson's neat, skilful engravings of natural history, topography, antiquities and the fine arts.

1. Parl. Papers 1834, viii (559), p.176: Select Committee on Intoxication among the Working Classes, minutes of evidence, qu.2060.
2. 'A Poor Student's Literary Expenditure', Penny Magazine, iv (1835), 227-8.
3. C. Thomson, The Autobiography of an Artisan (1847), p.319.
4. G.J. Holyoake, Sixty Years of an Agitator's Life (1892), i. 70.

He remembered the 'intense enjoyment' he felt as a boy on the rare occasions he was allowed to see a volume at his aunt's house.[1] And on a rather higher level of society, Frederick Harrison in his youth bought the Penny Magazine every Sunday from an itinerant salesman and took half the week to get through it:-

> I doubt if any illustrated serial now has such a high aim and quality. The noble (and lost) art of wood engraving was then in its zenith, and I recall with delight and sorrow Jackson's woodcuts after Raffaelle and the great classical painters ... My early ideas of history, art, geography, and literature were nearly all bound up closely with those simple woodcuts, almost everyone of which I can vividly recall to this day, which I certainly would try to draw or paint on the wet afternoons and dark winter evenings.[2]

Not everyone agreed with them. At the profoundest level, the point was occasionally made that art and taste, learning and moral elevation simply could not be diffused in this manner. In 1836, the Morning Chronicle reviewed the first volume of Knight's 'Library of Entertaining Knowledge' which was devoted to the Townley Gallery of the British Museum. Having castigated the level of accuracy and quality in the illustrations, the article went on to make a larger point:-

> A due regard for the interests of the fine arts, and what is justly due to its industrious professors, compelled us to speak once for all without reserve, in reference to a notion which is beginning to come into vogue of the feasability of 'diffusing a taste for the fine arts' by means of cheap publications like the present. The attempt originates in a creditable intention, but in a mistaken view of the case. As there is no royal road to mathematics, so we say, once for all, there is no Penny Magazine road to the fine arts. Every ingredient in the cultivation of the arts, and in their practice, is expensive in the highest degree ...[3]

More pointedly still, the Quarterly Review of 1844 believed the growth of illustrated useful knowledge was 'a partial return to baby literature',

---

1. Groves, op. cit., p.6.
2. F. Harrison, Autobiographic Memoirs, (1911), p.6.
3. Morning Chronicle, 19 October 1836, pp.2-3.

'a second childhood of learning', in which the eye was appealed to rather than the understanding. It stemmed:-

> not from an acute and accurate perception of beauty and design, as from a low utilitarian wish to give and receive the greatest possible amount of knowledge at the least possible expense of time, trouble, money, and, we may add, of intellect.[1]

Arguing from the highest level of art, seen as the exclusive privilege of the few to achieve, appreciate and profit from, the mechanical lever theory purveyed by Knight, Cowper and Cole to the masses was quite simply inappropriate and futile.[2]

The most frequently voiced antipathy to the Penny Magazine, however, stemmed from more practical down-to-earth objections. Some middle class publications suggested that the Penny Magazine was a private money speculation of Charles Knight. The New Monthly Magazine went on to call it a very feeble periodical of largely stolen material; like the Thief, its motto ought to have been, 'Ex rapto vivens'.[3] Knight himself referred to the emnity of three or four of the large wholesale booksellers, mainly provoked by the 'wonderful success' of the Penny Magazine: 'They complain that this, and similar works, will absorb all the old trade in books. They look forward even with greater dread to the Cyclopaedia'. Apparently, they had gone so far as to hold several meetings on the subject and Longman's even threatened to discourage their

---

1. 'Illustrated Books', Quarterly Review, lxxiv (1844), 171. Wellesley Index to Victorian Periodicals 1824-1900, ed. W.E. Houghton (Toronto, 1972), ii. 1207 suggests, on slender evidence, that this article might have been written by John Holmes.

2. See above p.139.

3. 'The Penny Magazine', Athenaeum, No.235 (28 April 1832), p.274. 'Notes on Periodicals', New Monthly Magazine, xxxix (1833), 427.

correspondents from stocking the penny numbers by charging them retail price.[1] However, they failed to stand united against the relentless technical and commercial momentum of the <u>Penny Magazine</u>. It was appropriate that the first number should adopt the metaphor of the stagecoach to convey its benefits. The preface to the first volume also stressed the high state of civilisation which was necessary to enable the <u>Penny Magazine</u> to be read all over the country. From the artists and writers involved, the compositing and paper purchase, the article went on to consider the more recent boons of machine printing and stereotyping. Communication between the capital and the country was now so perfect, so '<u>cheap</u> and <u>ready</u>' through the use of steam-boat, canal, railway, quick van, and stage coach and mail, that there should be no difficulty in obtaining a copy from a bookseller, even in remote districts:-

> This is a striking illustration of the civilization of our country; and when unthinking people therefore ask, what is the benefit of steam-engines, and canals, and fine roads to the poor man, they may be answered by this example alone. In this, and in all other cases, ready and cheap communication breaks down the obstacles of time and space, - and thus, bringing all ends of a great kingdom as it were together, greatly reduces the inequalities of fortune and situation, by equalizing the price of commodities and to that extent making them accessible to all.

As for the charge that the <u>Penny Magazine</u> was a monopoly, the preface

---

1. University College, London, Brougham Papers, 10,061: Knight to Brougham, 29 August 1832. By the end of its first year, the <u>Penny Magazine</u> was distributed wholesale via twenty nine agents throughout the United Kingdom, and even one in New York, and then through inumerable retail outlets. If it was not available weekly, then it could be obtained in monthly parts for six shillings a year, the difference in cost being made up by the monthly supplements of new books and the wrappers. This method of sale presumably posed less of a threat to the book trade, being more compatible in terms of price to their usual sale.

maintained that it was in fact the opposite: it broke the monopoly of high prices and exclusive readerships by succeeding in circulating as many copies as cheaply as possible. It stood 'upon the commercial principle alone', and derived no subsidy from the Society for the Diffusion of Useful Knowledge, but in fact, subsidized the activities of the latter.[1] As Knight wrote to Brougham, when contemplating the possibility of writing a 'little work' on 'The Economy of the Press' to illustrate these principles more fully and prevent the public being led away by 'stupid denunciations of The Society as Monopolists':-

> it might be easily shewn that no such great experiment could have been tried without the aid of the moral power of an association that saw the extent of the new demand for knowledge; - and that had courage enough to set the example of a bold calculation upon the real desires of the people for sound food for the mind.[2]

Besides these manifestations of commercial jealousy, Knight felt he had to contend with another class of enemies who differed from the Society in principle, and who consisted of 'most open Radicals, including many of the Utilitarians and all of the Cooperatives'. Some (presumably he meant the Utilitarians) believed it was a gross mistake to omit politics:

> and require that we should be always preaching to them the doctrines of political economy, - and what is more they insist we have no right to persuade them that they can find any sources of enjoyment while Tithes and Corn Laws exist.

The Radicals and the Cooperatives, on the contrary, were extremely angry:-

> that the doctrines that the happiness of all is founded upon Security of Property, and that cheap Production, produced by Machinery, is an universal benefit, have been advocated in a popular manner, and have estranged many of their disciples.[3]

1. 'Preface', Penny Magazine, i (1832), iii-iv.
2. Knight to Brougham, 29 August 1832.
3. Ibid.

It is clear from the content of the Penny Magazine, that Knight, while differing from the latter class of enemies in principle, parted from the former only on the question of degree and the style with which the message was conveyed. The whole of the Penny Magazine consists of thinly disguised propaganda for Whig reform and political economy, lightly scattered between snippets of encyclopaedic knowledge. Short homilies were extracted from Adam Smith, Wilderspin's Early Discipline, or Dr. Ure's Philosophy of Manufactures on the advantages of frugality and self-education, the dangers of drunkenness and idleness, the degradation of ignorance, the good effects of industry and the virtuous endurance of poverty. The publication of Hogarth's works, re-engraved by John Jackson, provided the occasion for comment on the history of apprenticeship and the benefits to be accrued by perseverance, the history of gin and the growth of Temperance Societies, dishonest reviewing, corrupt electioneering and, on the subject of 'The Rake's Progress', 'a monument of deep and dire retribution for crimes and follies that even in their completion were but another name for misery'.[1] A review of a poem entitled 'The Village Poor-House', written 'By a Country Curate', in 1832, which only started with an idyllic description, was roundly condemned:-

> But from this description of the village itself the author passes to its inhabitants, and then would prove to us, that this external beauty is but a veil to cover what is in reality a more disgusting place than a charnel-house. For within the village, he says, there is nothing but tyranny and slavery, - pampered luxury on the part of the few, and the most abject poverty on the part of the many... We are fully prepared to admit the existence of evils among the labouring classes of this country, but we are sure that the state of things represented in this poem has no more foundation in truth than those poetical pictures of rural life which our author, justly enough, pronounced to be _only_ poetical.[2]

---

1. 'Hogarth's Works', Penny Magazine iii (1834), 121-8, 209-16, 249-56, 377-84; iv (1835), 81-88, 113-4.

2. Penny Magazine, i (1832), 170. Compare with the favourable review of the poem in the Poor Man's Guardian, 7 July 1832.

Yet, almost ten years later, the Penny Magazine was itself using what can only be termed poetic licence to describe 'Two Hours at a Union Workhouse', under the new poor law. The Windsor Workhouse, illustrated with a sensitive vignette, contrasted strikingly with Grant's savage view half a dozen years previously:

> The Union Workhouse harmonizes with the cheerful peeps over the valley of the Thames, and the massive and venerable trees which form the charm of these woodland solitudes. It is built in the style of two centuries and a half ago, when comfort and elegance, the growth of security, had displaced the rude fortress-mansions of the feudal lords...[1]

Again, the Penny Magazine succeeded in looking on the bright side of the growth of industry and machinery. A correspondent who visited 'A Well-Conducted Factory' in 1833 concluded:-

> The general tenour of the evidence given before the Factory Commissioners goes to show that, although there may be great abuses in many establishments in which children are employed, extensive factories may, and do, exist where the light spirits of youth are still buoyant and unbroken by undue labour and restraint, and where the industry of the young not only contributes to the increase of our national wealth, but also to their own advantage. In many factories they are not only usefully employed, but, at the same time, are trained up in those habits of morality and good feeling which are most likely to ensure their own lasting happiness and make them valuable members of society...[2]

And when, ten years later, the Penny Magazine conducted a series of tours round factories, illustrated with diagrams and old prints, it found in the Potteries, 'very few indications of squalor and wretchedness', excellent conditions in the cotton factories of Hyde, and that those for children in the woollen mills had much improved, since the improvements made by the factory acts and mill owners.[3] Even in the

---

1. Penny Magazine, x (1841), 397.
2. Penny Magazine, ii (1833), 445-6.
3. Penny Magazine, xii (1843), 201-8, 241-8, 457-64.

mining industry, a visit to the northern colliery towns in 1835, for
example, accompanied by topographical and diagrammatic representations,
was more concerned to describe the character of each family as indicated
by the appearance of their dwellings, or the degradation of some of the
pitmen caused by 'the practice of indulging at the public-houses', than
to comment on the statement that boys of seven worked down the pit.
The article noted with satisfaction that women had been relieved from
the unsuitable labour of carrying coal on their backs, and the growth
of prosperity and formation of provident habits as evinced by the
activity of the Savings' Banks of the area.[1] A follow-up article by a
correspondent in 1836 was able to point to the formation of bands and
horticultural societies. It stated that their cottages, particularly
those of the steady and temperate part of them, 'generally exhibit inside an appearance of comparative cleanliness and comfort seldom indeed
to be met with in the abodes of the poorer classes of populous towns'.[2]
Not that the Penny Magazine exactly lingered in these areas of the city.
Its 'Looking Glass for London' series of 1837, took an uncontroversial
stroll round the sights of the metropolis, its public buildings, leading
thoroughfares, clubs and markets, parks and museums being depicted in
topographical views. Once it paused in Bow Street to reflect that public
opinion had undergone a great change since the initial dislike of Peel's
new police.[3] On another occasion, it visited the Rag Fair in Rosemary
Lane, describing it as the 'anti-type' of Hyde Park and explicitly

---

1. Penny Magazine, iv (1835), 121-8, 161-8.
2. Penny Magazine, v (1836), 242-4.
3. Penny Magazine, vi (1837), 38.

contrasting 'ideas of wealth, fashion, grace and beauty' with 'whatever is most sordid, mean, and base'.[1] It peeped into St. Giles and the Seven Dials district and found it 'A filthy, gin-drinking, and obnoxious-looking neighbourhood',[2] while the decay and squalidness it found in Spitalfields it believed did not arise from the poverty of the weavers alone, but from the casual population who moved in to intercept the aid offered:-

> And just as carrion birds scent the carcass, so many of the worthless and idle, on the least whisper of a subscription, flock into Spitalfields, hire some of the miserable and empty apartments, always ready to be let, and endeavour to intercept the bounty from the really destitute weaver.[3]

Thus, it is clear that the Penny Magazine was at best seen as irrelevant to the furthering of man's education; or at worst, as epitomizing everything that stood for political economic doctrine in its various manifestations of large-scale mechanization, the development of industry and social legislation of a peculiarly restricted and unbending nature. A third grievance compounded its sins in the eyes of its most radical opponents. Even Edward Lytton Bulwer was able to isolate this before the House when he gave his interpretation of the Penny Magazine's philosophy:-

> We will give you information; but whoever else gives it to you, him we will punish and destroy; we will tell you about animals and insects, and give you pictures of ruins and churches, with all such infantile trumpery - the hobbyhorse and rattle of education.[4]

The Penny Magazine was seen to be a government supported monopoly which

---

1. Ibid., pp.498-500.
2. Ibid., p.499.
3. Ibid., pp.393-5.
4. Hansard, 3rd series, 1834, xxiii. 1198.

escaped prosecution under the stamp act, while the publishers of the
radical unstamped press suffered. It is Seymour's 'PATENT PENNY
KNOWLEDGE MILL' (McLean's Monthly Sheet of Caricatures, No.34, 1 October
1832. B.M. No.17267) which summed up these views most comprehensively.
The mill is worked by a crank turned by Brougham and Althorp. In Brougham's
pocket there is a 'Ready made Injunction against any new Penny Mag.'.
Into the mill Russell empties a tankard labelled 'Whig Liberalism', while
Bishop Maltby empties a bottle of 'Whig Theology from Chichester', of
which Russell does not want too much. 'Never fear my Piety', the Bishop
replies, 'It will not quarrel with your Philosophy'. Behind Russell is
a large 'MASHING VAT' in which the contents of the Penny Magazine are
being prepared. These include, 'Wonderous condescension & affability',
and several 'Illustrative Wood Blocks', which are stirred by Denman who
says, 'Send out the Police and see that no other unstamp'd things are
selling'. The mixture is being spiced by the Devil with 'A small season-
ing of Infidelity'. Charles Knight, with ass's ears, cuts up newspapers
in the background. On the mill two notices are posted. The first says,
'No one else need attempt to print or publish anything; as we intend to
do all and every thing cheaper and better than it will (by other means)
be done'. The second reads, 'Don't buy any Cyclopaedia but ours'. The
contents of the mill gush forth from two spouts, 'The Proprietor's Pipe'
flowing with 'Pennies', 'The Public's Pipe' with paper labelled 'Twaddle'.
A tube described as 'The Penny Extractor' is connected with John Bull's
pocket, while Knight holds a large funnel to his victim's mouth, into
which he rams paper with a stick saying, 'Never mind your pockets, Mr. Bull
but take this. I am its Publisher, and know it to be good for a
Be-Knight-ed generation'. Behind them is a policeman, acting on instructions
from Denman, who terrifies an emaciated hawker with his baton.

97

Not surprisingly, working class leaders treated the Penny Magazine with contempt. It represented everything they hated: mechanical expansion, moral elevation and monopoly. The Poor Man's Guardian sneered at the 'account of Charing Cross, the Antiquity of Beer, the lost Camel &c.', and woodcuts of 'the bear, the dormouse, the swallow'. It mocked the technical and artistic feats of the Penny Magazine by presenting three of its own cuts, 'executed in a superior style', after the plates in Colonel Macerone's Defensive Instructions for the People, from which it also printed long extracts. In doing so, it posed a choice between this which was 'given in illustration of knowledge that should be deeply studied by every man who desires to be free', and the 'namby-pamby stuff published expressly to stultify the minds of the working people and make them spiritless and unresisting victims of a system of plunder and oppression'.[1] The serial cuts shared this attitude. They consistently championed the victims of the unstamped press and explicitly contrasted them with the protection afforded to the Penny Magazine by Lord Brougham. He ensured he was the principal target by declaring that the Penny Magazine had 'destroyed a great number of those wicked publications, some of the most obnoxious of them, in three or four weeks after it had begun'. Indeed, he considered the attempt to meet 'this great mischief' by providing 'more wholesome food' happily had been attempted, 'and attempted with great success'.[2]

1. Poor Man's Guardian, 14 April 1832. This 'atrocious' number of the paper was sent by Comm. John Debenham to the Home Office in 1833, 'it being nothing other than an incitement of the subject to levy War against the King and also giving instructions as to the means'. P.R.O., Home Office Papers, Series 64, box 16: Police/Secret Service, miscellaneous 1827-33.

2. Taxes on Knowledge. Stamps on Newspapers. Extracts from the evidence of the Right Honourable Baron Brougham and Vaux, Lord Chancellor, before the Select Committee of the House of Commons on libel law, 14 June 1834, p.6.

Throughout the 1820s, Brougham was mocked for his activities in connection with useful knowledge, and his seemingly polymathic talents. In 'The Busy Busy B--'. (The Caricaturist, No.4), he is shown gathering honey from the flowers of the 'PENNY MAGAZINE', 'MECHANICS INSTITUTION', 'REFORM', 'PAMPHLETS', 'THE TIMES', 'LIBRARY OF USEFUL KNOWLEDGE', 'EDINBURGH REVIEW', 'LONDON UNIVERSITY' and 'MISS MARTINEAU'. However, such a list could be expressed with more cynicism, especially with regard to his connection with the Penny Magazine. C.J. Grant revived an old tradition by producing two mock frontispieces for the Penny Magazine, in 1832 and 1833.[1] They include emblematic representations of the range of subjects covered by the paper, but mainly are concerned with attacking Brougham, especially in the second print. Here, the centre-piece is a depiction of him stuffing the Penny Magazine down the throat of a man sitting in the stocks, with a signpost above pointing either to the workhouse or to gaol. His importance is repeatedly stressed through the use of the coat of arms, his 'broom', and the woolsack; he himself is seen variously as a broom-girl, a schoolmaster and a witch scattering pamphlets. Emblems of oppression include a prison inscribed 'County Gaol', and heavy fetters labelled 'Liberty of the Press', 'Passive Obedience' and the 'Poor Man's Guardian'. The Government Stamp - 'The Right Divine of US to Govern Wrong' is illustrated with a foot stamping on 'Cheap Politics' and 'Grant's Caricatures'. The theme was echoed in 'THE PENNY TRUMPETER!' (B.M. No.17258), issued first as a large coloured lithograph by Tregear on 20 September 1832. Brougham, in the character

---

1. See also, his 'FRONTISPIECE TO USEFUL KNOWLEDGE' (?1831). Thomas collection.

of a trumpeter, carries a bundle of Penny Magazines in one hand and a bag on his back containing 'Materials for the Penny Cyclopaedia to commence in 1833 and to end the Devil knows when'. His trumpet proclaims, 'All works not issued by the Society are illegal'. In the background is the office of the Society, composed of various books, all bolstered up by a beam labelled 'Monopoly'. This caricature was singled out for praise by the Poor Man's Guardian, in an article which went on to damn Brougham, the Society and the Whigs.[1] On the same day, 13 October 1832, a new publication commenced, entitled the Fool's Cap, which made a wood engraving of the 'Trumpeter' the subject of its leader. It described how Brougham, 'viewed with dismay the growing intelligence of the age, and the rapid strides with which the intellect of the people was pressing towards that goal, at once so fraught with strength and danger'. Owing to the accumulated weight of the movement, the paper continued, to stem the tide of public opinion was seen to be impossible:-

> but to turn it, to divide it, to 'diffuse' the popular feeling, might yet be effected, with the aid of a little manoeuvring. A 'Society', was, therefore, established for the 'diffusion, alias confusion of Knowledge'; and the worthy individual of whom we write, had the honour of mixing up and administering the first potion to the perplexed and bewildered intellectual-cultivators, who gaped around.

By 1836, Brougham was further damned through his connection with the new poor law and 'THE LITERARY DUSTMAN, or L--d BROOM in Character', (Lloyd's Political Jokes, No.6) places him in front of London University and a 'Poor Law Bastile No.10000'. Thus, the polymathic reputation Brougham had acquired in the caricatures of the 1820s was degraded by his association with the Penny Magazine and with Whig coercion.

101

1. Poor Man's Guardian, 13 October 1832.

The greatest show of hatred for Brougham in the radical and humorous magazine cuts was reserved for his callous disregard of the plight of the vendors so long as his own protegé, the Penny Magazine, did not suffer. Seymour revived the imagery of the 1820s to produce 'THE STAMP ACT' for the Devil in London (No.33, 13 October 1832), which shows Brougham, Althorp and Grey stamping on the body of Britannia, whose mouth is bound with a padlock labelled 'STAMP ACT'. Grant, in the serial cuts, was more specific in his identification. In 'POLITICAL SPORTSMEN; OR, PRACTISING AGAINST THE NEXT SESSION' (Political Drama, No.24), Brougham shoots at The Man, Cosmopolite, Poor Man's Guardian, and the Reformer, in the company of Wellington, Althorp and the bishops. He says:-

102

> Aye, this is my favourite game, I'll have a pop at 'em if I split my broomstick. I'll exterminate the whole fry of 'em. The property of the rich is in jeopardy through them, wherever they fly. I'll clear the board, and stick up the Penny Mag.

A similar point is made in 'FISHING FOR GUDGEONS AND FLATS' (Political Drama, No.54). This shows Brougham fishing from his broomstick with the 'PENNY MAG' and 'CHEAP KNOWLEDGE' as bait. Further along the bank is a Stamp Office Spy, who hooks the unstamped publications' vendor with a penny. The victims named are the Poor Man's Guardian, Political Drama, Pioneer, Twopenny Dispatch and Weekly Police Gazette. In 'THE CHANCELLOR'S DREAM; OR, KING RICHARD III. TRAVESTIE' (Political Drama, No.25), Brougham is asleep on the woolsack, with the 'PENNY MAG' for a pillow. Various ghosts haunt him, including 'the wandering ghosteses of the victims of the UNSTAMP'D murdered in the dungeons of the BASTILES, for the cause of a FREE PRESS'. One of the ghost vendors says, 'A curse, Lord Harry, upon thy march of intellect; my occupation's for ever gone; no old women and children will be affrighted now'.

103

104

The plight of the vendors was treated emblematically by Seymour in 'EFFECTS OF THE STAMP ACTS' (McLean's Monthly Sheet of Caricatures, No.55, 1 July 1834). A medallion in the centre depicting Britannia eating her children is marked, 'WITH ALL DUE CONTEMPT THIS MEDAL IS INSCRIBED TO THE UNBLUSHING ADVOCATES OF THINGS AS THEY ARE'. Behind this, a newspaper vendor in gaol writes, 'I broke no law but am cast into prison because I could not pay the cost of an unjust Trial', while his two children hold up a placard which reads, 'Our father was proved innocent & we are punished with beggary'. The sub-caption to the print adds, 'In these prosecutions should the accused be acquitted, he must pay all costs!!!, the crown pays no costs'. Another case of acquittal was treated in 'FIGARO V. THE BLUE DEVILS'(Figaro in London, No.17, 31 March 1832), which shows the police beating up a crowd and a vendor in gaol awaiting trial, entitled 'HORRORS OF LIMBO'. This vendor, as we have seen, was let off since the Commissioners of Stamps declined to prosecute him.[1] Nevertheless, the paper complained that the vendor had been held in gaol for three days. It repeated that its motive was simply 'to improve many and amuse all by a little harmless satire'. Indeed, in 'REALLY USEFUL KNOWLEDGE' (Figaro in London, No.182, 30 May, 1835), Brougham himself is depicted handing out the magazine with the resolution, 'That every person in England above the age of six years, be furnished with a copy of FIGARO IN LONDON every week, at national expence'.

The serial cuts could ill-afford such waggishness. Significantly, they never included the humorous magazines among the lists of unstamped

---

1. See above p.128.

newspapers victimized by the government: Figaro in London and its genre were acquitted; the true unstamped press were always found guilty according to the law. John Bull's Picture Gallery was prosecuted at least once.[1] In 'MAGISTERIAL JUSTICE - A FACT' (Political Drama, No.14) Grant depicted the prosecution of the vendor of the Political Drama under the Hawkers' Act. The magistrate goes on to say, 'Why can't you sell instead The Penny Magazine, God's Revenge against Murder, The Pulpit or any of the Bible Societies Tracts, which come within the law'. The police superintendent makes the distinction between these, together with Chamber's Journal and Newspaper, The Companion to the Newspaper and The New Metropolitan Police Gazette, which are to be praised not prosecuted, and the Poor Man's Guardian, the Cosmopolite and the Reformer for which the reverse holds true. A better documented outrage is depicted in 'WHIG ROBBERY AND DESTRUCTION OF PROPERTY UNDER THE NAME OF LAW' (Political Drama, No.100), namely the arrest of Cleave and Hetherington and the seizure of their presses. In imagery, it brings up to date the scene represented in A Slap at Slop, in which the Constitutional Association destroyed the radical presses a decade previously.[2] It confirmed in caricature the impression gained by John Cleave that the behaviour of the Stamp Office was worthy of the worst days of the Liverpool administration.[3]

---

1. See above p. 127.

2. See above p. 125. For a remarkably similar depiction of the destruction of presses in France in the same period see J.J. Grandville and A. Desperret, 'DESCENTE DANS LES ATELIERS DE LA LIBERTE DE LA PRESSE', from Philipon's La Lithographie Mensuelle (November 1833).

3. Wiener, The War of the Unstamped, pp.251-3. See also British Museum, Place Newspaper Collection, set 70, which includes this number of the Political Drama.

The Whigs attack the presses on the grounds that the Freedom of the Press is '<u>freedom</u>, with a vengeance to be exposed, calumniated, satirized and caricatured as we have been every week, for the paltry price of Twopence - if the rabble cannot afford Sevenpence for good wholesome and CORRECT intelligence why let 'em go without'. They carry off bundles of Hetherington's <u>Twopenny Dispatch</u>, Cleave's <u>Police Gazette</u>, the <u>Political Drama</u>, <u>Everybody's Album</u>, the <u>Poor Man's Guardian</u> and <u>Roebuck's Pamphlets</u>. However, the representatives of the people who stand by the flag of 'DEFIANCE', which is surmounted by the cap of liberty, on the tower of 'PUBLIC OPINION', have the last laugh. They say:-

> every blow they give, adds to their infamy and ruin and to our fame and advantage ... Why instead of the Stamp'd being against us, they will have good reason to thank us in the end; for without our determined exertions in the cause of Cheap Knowledge, neither the country would have been directed to the subject, nor these villainous Whigs have troubled themselves about it - so three cheers for Cheap Knowledge and defiance to our oppressors.

Thus, the radical wing of political caricature made full use of its freedom from legal restraint to express its antipathy to old and new targets and also self consciously championed its own role and identified itself with the larger good of the freedom of the press generally. It did this in the face of the laws of libel and the taxes on knowledge, as well as the more insidious attacks undertaken by the Society for the Diffusion of Useful Knowledge, the <u>Penny Magazine</u> and Lord Brougham, with their machine to beat the unstamped on its own ground. Their efforts were seen as an affront, not only because of the mealy-mouthed content, but also because their crowing confidence about the technical facilities they had employed, the progress in art, in printing and distribution they had achieved, contrasted so severely with the crude woodcuts, the smashing of the presses and prosecution of the vendors experienced by the unstamped press. It is not therefore surprising that B.F. Duppa, an active member of the Society for the Diffusion of Useful Knowledge, admitted in 1839 that the <u>Penny</u>

Magazine, like other publications put out by the Society, had only to a limited extent reached the humblest classes of the country.[1] W.E. Hickson, looking back from the 1851 Select Committee on Newspaper Stamps, confessed that he had never met a poor man who took in the Penny Magazine,[2] while Collet, before the same Committee, believed that the working classes considered themselves insulted by it:-

> I cannot say exactly where its circulation was, but I can say that there was a very large number of operatives who demanded something else, and who not only wanted something else, but felt themselves oppressed because the "Penny Magazine" was allowed to circulate and the penny papers were not allowed to circulate.[3]

This Whig coercion, both open and covert, provoked the declaration of the serial cuts, and to a lesser extent, the humorous magazines, to identify with the cause of the unstamped and to partake in their fate. A final dimension is added to this analysis by taking into account another type of journal in this which carried illustrated material, the illustrated police gazette.

1. B. F. Duppa, Manual for Mechanics' Institutions (1839), pp.12-13.
2. Parl. Papers 1851, xvii (558), pp.478-80:- minutes of evidence, qus. 3248-59.
3. Ibid., p.151:- minutes of evidence, qus.923-4.

III

The development of the police gazette during the first half of the nineteenth century is central to the understanding of the development of graphic journalism since it involves several of its major themes: first, the old broadside tradition, secondly, useful knowledge and middle class concern, thirdly, working class politics and satire, and finally, the growth of popular literature and illustrated news journalism. The first and last of these will be examined elsewhere.[1] Here, middle and working class use of the genre are studied in relation to the freedom of the press and the constraints of the stamp laws in the first half of the 1830s.

Knowing their own species of useful knowledge was boring, aware of the universal propensity of the lower orders for sensational reading matter, the middle class reformers hankered after the adoption of crime reporting for their own purposes. Brougham, writing in the Edinburgh Review in 1835, introduced the subject in connection with the campaign to repeal the stamp duty on newspapers. If newspapers were cheap, people would be able to acquire a thorough acquaintance with the rules laid down for regulating their conduct, and disposing their rights. There was nothing more useful than to read all that passed at criminal trials, for it afforded one of the best lessons of practical morality the people could learn. It inculcated a reverence for the laws to see them administered with inflexible justice, an affection for them to observe how they were administered in mercy, and a dread of violating them to witness the trial

---

1. See below Ch. VIII.

and punishment of offenders. Finally, he underlined the main advantage of this type of 'useful knowledge': 'Happily there is no kind of reading so great a favourite of all classes, as trials, whether criminal or civil'.[1]

This sensitivity to demand and stress on audience acceptability were themes reinforced by John Stuart Mill in the Monthly Repository, who implicitly compared the police gazette with the Penny Magazine type of publication:-

> What is it likely an unlettered villager will care about the history of a foreign bird, an ancient cathedral, or alluvial deposits, compared with a narrative of proceedings before a justice of the peace in the neighbourhood, or an account of the trials at the County Assizes? Let not the fastidious condemn the taste of the working classes for police intelligence. It has been well observed by Mr. Elliot, that 'police reports are far better digests of the laws which relate to the affairs of the poor, than are the term reports to the lawyers...' Every regulation that affects the poor man, every protection his few affairs require, are there explained, not by mere rules, ill-composed, but by individual and ever recurring facts.[2]

Similarly, W. E. Hickson, in pressing for cheap local newspapers rather than London journals, argued in the London Review:

> As the history of Jack the Giant Killer is a far better book for a child than Newton's Principia, so an account of the trial of a poacher is much better calculated to excite reflection in the mind of a peasant, and create the habit of reading, than a column and a half in the Morning Chronicle upon the politics of Russia and Turkey.

He went on to describe how the leading article in The Times had once been read to a number of agricultural labourers, but they failed to understand what it meant.[3]

---

1. (Lord Brougham), 'Newspaper Tax', Edinburgh Review, lxi (1835), 183.
2. (J.S. Mill), 'The Taxes on Knowledge', Monthly Repository, viii (1834), 108-9:
'The newspaper is the poor man's history of laws, customs, institutions and opinions. By it he learns what is done, and to forbear from what should not be done'.
3. W. E. Hickson, 'Reduction, or Abolition, of the Stamp-Duty on Newspapers', London Review, ii (1836), 350.

This special problem of rural ignorance was first noticed with a vengeance at the time of the agricultural disturbances in 1831-32 when government warnings proved futile. The Westminster Review pointed out that the labouring population was in too high a state of excitement to pay any attention to separate addresses, nor would they have trusted these strange communications if they had read them. Whole parishes of labourers went on committing capital crimes, thinking they were liable to nothing more than fines and imprisonment: 'They were only undeceived when they saw the work of the executioner'.[1] Four years later, Roebuck drew attention to the fact, in relation to the Dorchester labourers, that Francis Place had been forbidden to publish the Combinations Acts even in abridged form.[2] Middle class reformers, therefore, combined the specific claim that knowledge of the legal penalties would have prevented disorder, with a more basic faith in the efficacy of any reading matter to lead men on to higher sorts of learning. The working man would 'thus be raised from that state of semi-barbarism, in which many thousands bearing the name of Englishmen yet remain'.[3] Crime reports and police gazettes were steps in the right direction.

However, a major inhibition prevented middle class reformers from creating their own gazette, namely their unwillingness to break the law by dealing in unstamped news. Only very modest efforts were made to unite theories of utility and political economy with an attractive criminal content. The Bristol Policeman, for example, packaged its

1. 'Taxes on Knowledge', London and Westminster Review, xv (1831), 245.
2. J. A. Roebuck, On the Means of Conveying Information to the People (1835), p.4.
3. Mill, 'The Taxes on Knowledge', 109.

product - a straightforward quarto gazette which commenced publication with the establishment of the city's new police force - in the following up-to-date jargon:-

> Political economists of virtue and eminence, have been of the opinion that the fear of exposure, and the dread of punishment, have a greater influence in deterring persons from the commission of crime than any abstract principles of morality and virtue distilled into the heart, - or, at all events, that if the influence of the former feeling be not more powerful where both exist, by far the greater number of persons are affected by it. May we not, then, boast a higher object than the mere gratification of public curiosity? - May we not hope that the exposure of delinquency in all classes of society, which our pages will contain, will not be without its moral and religious effect?[1]

The Old Bailey Reporter also adopted modern means of expressing its purpose, being more analytical and less emotive than its predecessors. The Compiler's intention, he said, was not to confine himself to 'a mere detail of what passes in Courts of Justic, but to remark sometimes upon the origin, nature, progress and result of Crime'. Backed by learned quotations, he reasoned that it was possible by such means to reform the criminal and to prevent, what had become, the Science of Crime itself.[2] The Lawyer. another quarto penny magazine, believed that whatever faults there might be in the laws were the effect of ignorance of the system and its purpose. It undertook to instruct the people on their legal rights and duties. It started off with the 'Nature and Acquisition of Property' ('the inequality with which property and privileges are distributed in society is no proof of injustice ...') and included articles on Lord Brougham's judgements and legal wit.[3]

1. Bristol Policeman, 6 August 1836.
2. Old Bailey Reporter, ? May 1832.
3. Lawyer, 26 January 1833.

One publication of this type deserves special attention. God's Revenge against Murder ran to at least forty issues between 1833 and 1834. It purported to appeal, not merely to 'the gratification of a vain desire for horrors, and an unnatural longing for excitement', but also to:-

> call the attention of the reader to the particular point at which the guilty person gave himself over to the evil influence of his passions, and at which point, if he had resisted, he would have gained a certain victory, and commenced a life of happiness and prosperity.

A titillating illustration embellished the first number, which was devoted to a story entitled, 'The Factory Boy or the Murdered Overseer', in which the 'extraordinary interference of Divine Providence' brought to light concealed murder. The Editor was indebted to the kindness of a Rev. Mr. Joseph Armstrong for providing the details of the case. This faintly ludicrous echo of a repository tract, no doubt together with its comparative longevity,[1] brought it to the attention of the Political Drama which bracketed it with the Penny Magazine, the Pulpit and Bible Society tracts as publications which escaped prosecution.[2] However, this was a rather minor irritant compared with that provoked by the official Police Gazette and which resulted in the major campaign of the radical journalists.

The official Police Gazette, or the Hue and Cry began in 1828 and was published by authority twice weekly from Bow Street. It was compiled by the Commissioners from the seventeen daily reports which came to them each morning from every division, and published by Mr. John Stafford, chief clerk at Bow Street. It only contained felonies and misdemeanors of an aggravated nature, not trivial cases, nor those which had already been solved, those whose solution might be jeopardized by publication and those

---

1. Only one issue of God's Revenge against Murder seems to be in existence today, that of 27 April 1833, the first number. However, Bell's Weekly Magazine, 8 March 1834, contains an advertisement for a sheet of forty engravings reprinted from this periodical.

2. Political Drama, No.14.

where prosecution was not going to take place. It listed escaped
convicts from New South Wales and deserters from His Majesty's Service,
as well as cases of murder, arson, robbery, house-breaking, felony and
horse and cattle stealing, with descriptions of the animals. Despite
criticism from the magistrates that it was not comprehensive enough,[1]
and the implication from radicals that it was too comprehensive, this
was not the chief means by which information was spread through the
force. The Police Gazette gave information only to the police officers
and commissioners, not to every station, for the mass of the Metropolitan
police constables knew its contents a day beforehand. Whenever a felony
was committed, a report in writing or print was dispatched immediately
from that division to the whole of the Metropolitan police by routes
laid down throughout the police district. Lt.-Colonel Rowan, one of the
commissioners, asserted that by these means, the whole of the division
would know it within two hours, 'They do it in such a way, it is like
the spreading from the centre of a circle when a stone is thrown in the
water.[2]

This description of the Police Gazette, compiled from evidence before
the Select Committee on the Metropolitan Police in August 1833, is necessary
background information for the understanding of the storm which blew up at
the same time in the radical press. In the cut from the Political Drama 85
(No.14), which attacked the non-prosecution of the unstamped Penny Magazine,
Pulpit and God's Revenge against Murder, a paper called the New Metropolitan

---

1. Parl. Papers 1834, xvi (600), pp.96-7, 264: Select Committee on the
   Metropolitan Police, minutes of evidence, qus.1494-5, 1502, 3720.
2. Ibid., pp.299-300: minutes of evidence, qus.4161, 4163, 4165, 4171.

Police Gazette was also mentioned as being 'published under the patronage of the Ministry', and that it was 'the exclusive property of the Police Commissioners, and ... consequently to come into the cognizance of the law'. It is likely that Grant lifted this information from the Poor Man's Guardian, which announced on 31 August 1833 the publication of a new unstamped, 'published from day to day, not only without let or impediment, but the said illegal publication is largely circulated amongst the New Police, under the direction of the highest authorities'. Quoting from the True Sun it added, 'Surely, while this continues, there can be no other prosecution for the sale of an unstamped paper'. The Poor Man's Guardian itself took most of its information from a couple of leaders in the True Sun, but it omitted several interesting details. The True Sun's first leader was much more extreme. On 20 August it announced that it had got hold of a letter from the Commissioners of Police implicating them in the sale of a Police Gazette to individual members of the constabularies. The leader also stated that this 'weekly' paper of large dimensions and varied matter, apologetical of the new police force, was being hawked in almost every street without prosecution. However, on 24 August the paper announced it had received a letter from the Editor of the Police Gazette (presumably Stafford), peremptorily denying this statement and asserting that the True Sun had been imposed upon by some designing person. The True Sun half-heartedly withdrew part of its claim but still maintained that even if it only circulated among the police, the presence of the Police Gazette precluded prosecution of any other unstamped paper.

This incident could be dismissed as a minor example of journalistic exaggeration if it were not for the capital the radical press made out of it. The Poor Man's Guardian of 2 November, quoting The Times, described the case brought against one John Herbert, who had been arrested in the

New Cut for selling unstamped newspapers. When he came up before
Mr. Gregorie, the magistrate at the Queen's Square Court, he defended
himself on the grounds that there was a paper called the Police Gazette,
which he understood was sanctioned by the government. He sold that and
was not molested, and it contained a great deal more news than the
Poor Man's Guardian. He therefore thought that there could be no more
harm in selling one paper than the other, particularly as the Guardian
sold the best of all the penny papers. Such disingenuousness was quickly
slapped down by the magistrate, who said he believed there was a case
pending against the Police Gazette, and it was not sanctioned by the
government. The defendant disputed this, but all the same was sentenced
to a month's imprisonment. Obviously, the magistrate and the vendor
were talking about two different Police Gazettes, or at least appeared
to be. Herbert's record as one of the most outrageously persistent
vendors,[1] is enough to call into question whether he was really selling
an official paper or something else. Sure enough, the following week,
9 November, a meeting was reported in the Poor Man's Guardian of the
National Union of the Working Classes. A man called Wragg stood up and
made a speech which mentioned the official Police Gazette, Herbert's case
and that of another man, Reeve, who had just been sentenced for selling
the People's Police Gazette. The leader in the Poor Man's Guardian of
16 November enlarged on the case and this new gazette, which was a paper
'recently started upon the self-same plan as the Government Police Gazette,
which a short time since circulated among the "Force" with the connivance,
if not the secret support of Government'. Thus the official police gazette

---

1. Hollis, op.cit., pp.173, 181, 182, 188.

occasioned a whole new genre of radical journalism. If the middle class reformers were too scared of the law to use the police gazette formula to put over their ideas, the working class journalists exploited the medium, not only thereby attracting large audiences but also, temporarily at least, confusing the law.

The People's Police Gazette and Tradesman's Advertiser was published by Charles Penny, a stationer and publisher of Chancery Lane. His first venture in this line was a quarto magazine entitled the London Policeman, which started on 6 July 1833 and lasted until the end of the year. What distinguished it from other compilations of police cases was its radical tone. It professed as its object, 'to lay before the reader whatever is most curious, artful, and audacious in London roguery, as well as to keep a look out and watch upon the London Police'.[1] It dedicated itself mockingly to Brougham and placed itself on a par with him in helping to put the law into practice with justice. It condemned all politicians as rogues, all statesmen as thieves and the Metropolitan police as 'a set of idle knaves, dressed up in fine clothes at other men's expence, stealing our sweethearts, and breaking our heads as if they were the only real "Gentlemen of England, who live at home at ease"'. The paper castigated their brutality and their spying, of which Popay had recently furnished a notorious example. In the first number there was a cover illustration of 'The Interior of Bow Street Police Office', not related to any apparent story, but depicting a man looking outraged before a magistrate and a harsh looking gaoler. The following week George Furzey, who had been acquitted on a police murder charge after Cold Bath Fields, was depicted in profile.[2]

1. London Policeman, No.1, 6 July 1833.
2. London Policeman, No.2, 13 July 1833.

Penny's next venture was the People's Police Gazette, and Tradesman's Advertiser, the first folio police gazette, and as such, conspicuously like a newspaper. It began in about August 1833; by November its sale was 12,000 and by January 1834, between 15,000 and 20,000 copies, despite the prosecution of its vendors.[1] In February 1834, Penny was fined £120 and the following May, his goods were confiscated. This proved a bone of contention with Cleave, who had at first worked with Penny to promote the sale of the People's Police Gazette, and then in the spring of 1834, brought out his own paper. On 3 May 1834, Penny wrote:-

> When Mr. Cleave says he took the idea of the Police Gazette from the Penny Magazine, he says what is false. He took from us the notion of this publication and basely used, for his own profit, the means and advantages, which at our peril and our expense he had received. The public may now judge between us.

Penny claimed to have spent upwards of £100 in bringing a case to prove his paper's legality. Cleave, he said, had spent a mere £5 to save himself from prison. If instead, Cleave had joined his 'mite' to Penny's funds, they could together have defended the gazettes. As it was, the Crown had crushed their single-handed efforts by filing numerous and ruinously expensive informations at the same time. Despite this expense, however, the paper defiantly managed to produce a costly wood engraving of Haydon's 'Reform Banquet', which it said was the largest wood engraving ever presented by the proprietor of any newspaper or other publication of any kind whatsoever. It represented a lasting monument to their cause and would be followed by an engraving of a 'Trades' Unionist's Funeral' in the next issue.[2]

1. Hollis, op.cit., pp.122-3.
2. No known copy.

Cleave also made a definite appeal for trade union support, writing to the <u>Pioneer</u> to publicize his donation to the strike fund formed for the Derby lock-out, and offering free space in his paper for resolutions adopted by the Grand National Consolidated Trades' Union. <u>Cleave's Weekly Police Gazette</u> was probably the most successful combination of trial reports and trade union news. Its circulation rose from 20,000 copies in 1834, to around 30,000 the following year and 40,000 at the start of 1836.[1] Other leading politicians of the 'unstamped' followed Cleave's example. The <u>Destructive</u> had decided as early as June 1833, at the request of its readers, to devote more space to police reports. At the beginning of 1834, it announced a change of style, to become 'a comprehensive vehicle of news ... The grand secret of journalism, as in everything else, being to combine the <u>utile dolci</u>'.[2] In June 1834, it became the broadsheet <u>Twopenny Dispatch and People's Police Register</u>, which Hetherington, its owner and publisher, said would be:-

> a repository of all the gems and treasures, and fun and frolic and "news and occurrences" of the week. It shall abound in Police Intelligence, in Murders, Rapes, Suicides, Burnings, Maimings, Theatricals, Races, Pugilism, and all manner of moving "accidents by flood and field". In short, it will be stuffed with every sort of devilment that will make it sell ... Our object is not to make money, but to beat the Government.[3]

It was also a success until 1836, having a circulation of 27,000 copies.[4] Similarly, Richard Lee and George Petrie turned the <u>Man</u> into a broadsheet and produced the <u>People's Hue and Cry</u>.

1. Hollis, <u>op.cit.</u>, pp.122-4.
2. <u>Destructive</u>, 15 June 1833, 25 January 1834.
3. <u>Twopenny Dispatch</u>, 7 June 1834.
4. <u>Memorial of Certain Inhabitants of the City of London</u>, 6 May 1835.

Most of these radical police gazettes continued the tradition of their antecedents by adding a weekly illustration to attract purchasers. The New Legal Observer, a twopenny broadsheet also issued by Penny, included 'Sir Andrew Day versus the Lord's Day' in one number, which depicted in crude fashion a starving family in a bare room, decorated with a copy of the reform bill and a gun.[1] The People's Weekly Police Gazette, owned and published by T. Wilson, one week depicted flogging in the army; while the Political Register; late the London Police Gazette attacked, in primitive cuts, both the corporations and Whig policy towards Ireland.[2] The most consistent, and certainly the most sophisticated use of illustration was Cleave's use of Grant for a front page cut each week on his Weekly Police Gazette. These caricatures, perhaps a quarter of the size of the Political Drama made attacks on the Lords and Commons, the church, the army and the 'stamp office footpads', employing the style and imagery he had evolved on the serial cuts. However, the format of the broadsheet police gazette, as developed by the journalists of the 'unstamped', marked one stage along the road to a popular newspaper, and Grant's 'cartoons' for the genre, strong evidence that by the mid 1830s, political caricature was indeed 'trickling into journalistic channels'.[3]

1. New Legal Observer, No.1, 26 April 1834.
2. People's Weekly Police Gazette, No.9, ii. 2 December 1835.
   Political Register, No.58, 15 August 1835, No.59, 22 August 1835.
3. George, English Political Caricature, 1793-1832, p.259.

In June 1836, the stamp tax on newspapers was reduced to a penny. This proved to be a boon for the stamped newspapers, but drove the unstamped out of business. As the London Review realized:-

> the practical effect of a reduction of the stamp-duty to one penny would be to impose a new tax upon a class of newspapers at present free from duty, and commanding already a circulation equal to half that of the whole daily and weekly London stamped press.[1]

The reaction of Figaro in London was in perfect accord with that of the unstamped press. 'THE NEW STAMP ACT' (No.228, 16 April 1836) depicts Mercury still chained by a weight labelled 'ONE PENNY', at the connivance of the stamped press. The editorial stated, 'The proposal of a penny stamp is not quite so bad as a fourpenny one; but we won't have it'. This cut was singled out for praise by Cleave's Weekly Police Gazette, who reproduced it with the title 'FIGARO AND THE PENNY CHANCELLOR' (23 April 1836). 'OPPRESSION OF THE PRESS' (Figaro in London, No.233, 21 May 1836) again reveals where its sympathies lay. It illustrates the 'abominable principle' of breaking open houses to search for the unstamped, the door of John Bull's house being battered down by the Whigs with a 'PENNY STAMP' mallet.[2]

However, it was the unstamped broadsheets rather than Figaro in London who were driven out of business by the measure. As the cut described above suggests, the act was accompanied by much stricter powers of execution. Cleave wrote a leader on 3 September 1836 in his Weekly Police Gazette which described the 'care and art' taken with the bill. It conferred upon the commissioners for stamps greatly enhanced powers relating to types,

---

1. London Review, ii. (1836), 345.
2. See 6 & 7 Will.IV, c.76, xxiii for the right granted to Constables having been given search warrants, to break open doors on refusal of admittance.

presses and materials, which could be executed in a 'summary and despotic mode'. In the face of this, no unstamped newspaper could be attempted. Furthermore, the cost of the increase would not simply be one penny per paper. As the paper would have to be bought in advance, there would be an inevitable wastage caused by spoilt sheets. Also, the vendor would still demand the same percentage profit on the price. Cleave found it necessary to increase the charge for his Weekly Police Gazette from twopence to threepence halfpenny, although he promised wider circulation, increased size and quantity of matter, and greatly improved appearance. There was one issue of the new series, on 17 September 1836. Then it died. The new stamp act appeared to have succeeded where previous legislation and all of the energies of the Society for the Diffusion of Useful Knowledge had failed, in running to ground the radical unstamped newspaper, and with it, almost inadvertently, the tradition of independence enjoyed by political caricature. By tying itself now almost wholly to the fortunes of the newspaper or magazine, graphic journalism certainly ensured its future prosperity; yet its very dependence on the more complex operations involved in printing and distributing large editions, at the pace demanded by regular weekly issue, suggested that the future lay with operations of the Penny Magazine type. They would have the enormous sale to finance steam presses, competent wood engraving, country wide distribution, not the parochial ad-hoc run of a series dominated by the personality of one artist; they would be bland and universally acceptable, not personal and partisan. Frederick von Raumer was right when he visited England in 1835 and watched the 'unwearied rapidity' of twenty Penny Magazine presses, each turning out a thousand sheets an hour: 'All the censors in the world could not stop the movement of the steam press, but would be hurried along, or torn in pieces by its resistless force'.[1]

1. F. von Raumer, England in 1835 (1836), i. 193.

FROM CHEAP POLITICS TO CHEAP FICTION

1836 - 1846

V

In 1849, at the time of the Manning murder 'mania', Punch printed a large cut by John Leech entitled, 'USEFUL SUNDAY LITERATURE FOR THE MASSES; OR, MURDER MADE FAMILIAR'. It depicts the father of a family, surrounded by seven ragged children, the youngest held by his wife, in a messy garret, reading aloud from an illustrated paper called The Murder Monger the details of the last moments of a 'wretched murderer'. On the wall, above his pipe and beermug, hang pictures of Courvoisier, Greenacre and various gibbets. A bible lies upturned on the floor amidst the children's debris.[1] The moral of the cartoon need hardly be spelt out. Instead of the secular and religious useful knowledge purveyed by Knight and his imitators in the 1830s, by the middle of the century, the masses were reading illustrated murder sheets. Furthermore, the implication was that the working classes had forsaken their politics and now sought chiefly to be amused. This is not to say that the English had ever been exactly free from such a taste. However, several new factors served to strengthen the old chapbook and broadside tradition. This chapter examines what happened to the popular political caricature tradition after the 1836 stamp act, its reactions to Chartism and the Anti-Corn Law League and its connections with sensational journalism and literature. Just as the theme itself is a natural continuation of the development of the popular police gazette, already examined in the last few pages, so too its treatment presents similar problems of approach. It is not possible to isolate the illustrations from the format in which they occur,

1. Punch, xvii (1849), 117.

in other words, the whole of the journalistic framework and sometimes it will seem as if their presence is merely a peripheral factor tagging along beside more important developments. Nevertheless, this changing context is significant since it provides the background necessary for the understanding of developments in graphic journalism during the 1840s and sets the scene for the more spectacular illustrated success stories of both Punch and the Illustrated London News.

I

On Saturday, 14 October 1837, Cleave began his <u>London Satirist and Gazette of Variety</u>. Since, he wrote in the first address, instruction in political things was forbidden, this paper would be a miscellany directed 'at once to the intellect and to the moral feeling'. While it ministered to the amusement of its readers, it would set them a thinking 'by mixing up the graver matters of personal and universal interest with the lighter and more ephemeral gaieties of the passing moment'.[1] Thus, like its later companions in the field, the paper had something of a split personality. It featured scraps of useful knowledge, theatre reviews and poetry, 'Quips and Cranks'. Also, despite Cleave's continuous campaign against the ban on talk of politics and political affairs, which he compared to a 'species of forbidden fruit',[2] each week he printed a leader on both long-standing and topical radical grievances. In addition, C. J. Grant provided the weekly cartoon on the front page, which Thackeray so much reviled in <u>Fraser's Magazine</u> in 1838:-

> Rude woodcuts adorn all these publications, and seem to be almost all from the hand of the same artist - Grant, by name. They are outrageous caricatures; squinting eyes, wooden legs, and pimpled noses, forming the chief points of fun.[3]

The very name of the paper indicates that some evolution took place between 1837 and its death in 1843. <u>Cleave's London Satirist and Gazette of Variety</u> changed at the end of 1837 into <u>Cleave's Penny Gazette of Variety</u>.

1. 'Address', <u>Cleave's London Satirist and Gazette of Variety</u>, 14 October 1837.
2. <u>Ibid</u>., 25 November 1837, 9 December 1837, 15 December 1838.
3. (W.M. Thackeray), 'Half a Crown's Worth of Cheap Knowledge', <u>Fraser's Magazine</u>, xvii (1838), 287.

In October 1839, this became <u>Cleave's Penny Gazette of Variety and Amusement</u>. In 1841, it still classed itself, together with Cleave's other venture, the <u>English Chartist Circular</u>, and Hetherington's <u>Odd Fellow</u>, as a radical publication, not a magazine devoted to useful or entertaining knowledge.[1] However, by the middle of the year it admitted having made permanent provision for 'a succession of Romances of "thrilling interest"'. It had heard whispered 'that however instructive and valuable in itself, yet that much of the "matter" selected by us has been "too heavy"'.[2] It had to keep pace with 'the wonderful march made by the gigantic power of STEAM in periodical Literature', since the days of Spring Rice's prosecution of the <u>Police Gazette</u>. The paper had borne its part in the 'vast revolution of public opinion, of which it has been alternately a cause and a consequence':-

> Now, however when the <u>illustrative art</u> has arrived at such perfection as to enter into every branch of publication; - when even newspapers are carrying its elements into the broadest channels of public life; - when the illustrative and the instructive elements have become synonymous; it has been determined to render this paper a worthy coadjutor in adorning, gilding, reflecting, and interpreting every form of thought; and under the head of '<u>The Comic Journal</u>', in <u>giving pungency to satire</u>, by devoting WEEKLY, the entire front page of the GAZETTE to the development of fun, frolic, and badinage; leaving, as heretofore, the remainder of the paper to the delineation of general literature, theatres, reviews, customs, and well-selected varieties, on every subject that can attract the attention of mankind, whether it be "serious or satirical, trivial or of purpose grave".[3]

Thus, by 1842, Cleave had changed his newspaper from one catering for the political needs of a threatened minority to one which sought a more general readership. It had broadened out to take note and make use of contemporary developments in journalism: to admit the power of steam presses,

---

1. <u>Cleave's Penny Gazette of Variety and Amusement</u>, 27 February 1841.
2. <u>Ibid</u>., 18 September 1841.
3. <u>Ibid</u>., 18 June 1842.

to contemplate the introduction of light literature and to harness itself behind the gaudy pictorial band-waggons of Punch and the Illustrated London News. This is reflected in the illustrations it carried. From 1838 onwards, there appeared a much more varied selection of cuts: humorous puns and jokes, pictures copied from Dickens' illustrations, murder cuts, as well as depictions of fires, new buildings, railways and airships, royalty and personalities. Cleave became an agent for the Novel Newspaper; later, in 1845, he published a large series of his own under the general title of The Penny Novelist and Library of Romance, in addition to individual novels.[1] Hetherington also turned to the sale and publication of non-political literature. We have already seen how his Twopenny Dispatch promised a more varied content than the earlier Destructive.[2] In 1838, he published Actors by Gaslight; or 'Boz' in the Boxes, and the following year, the Odd Fellow, which was edited in turn by the dramatist James Cooke, W.J. Linton and finally, very briefly before it collapsed in 1841, by Ebenezer Jones, an impoverished, radical poet friend of Linton's.[3] During Linton's editorship, which lasted from April 1841 to October 1842, some effort was made to attract new readers with fiction and verse, theatrical and literary reviews and translations. It printed the illustrations to Gil Blas, the life of Napoleon and adventures of Robinson Crusoe.[4] The Odd Fellow's Comic Scrapbook was put out at a penny, with '24 highly amusing Wood Engravings, by first rate Artists'. When the Odd Fellow finally died, Hetherington turned wholly to publishing

---

1. James, Fiction for the Working Man 1830-1850 pp.26-27.
2. See above p.168.
3. Smith, op.cit., p.42.
4. The Odd Fellow, 21 September 1839, 30 November 1839, 11 April 1840.

fiction and moved for a short time into extensive offices in Fleet Street.[1]
In 1840, a survey carried out by C. R. Weld for the Statistical Society
'On the Popular Penny Literature of the day', revealed that out of eighty
publications, nearly half concerned themselves with novels, romances, tales,
lives and memoirs; only nine could be described as political. Fifty-eight
were illustrated with wood engravings.[2] Thus, Cleave and Hetherington were
part of a general trend.

A closer examination of the politics of Cleave's Gazette and
Hetherington's Odd Fellow, as shown in their text and illustrations, confirms the impression of a certain lack of focus compared with their efforts
before 1836. Certainly, Queen Victoria was not quite the stock target of
abuse that William IV had been, at any rate, not when she first came to
the throne. Grant includes the figure of John Bull, being jeered at by
Melbourne, Russell and Spring Rice, in 'THE MORNING AFTER THE CORONATION', 110
who says, 'This is the way I'm used, but it serves me right for being an
ass - my fondness for raree shows, and my easy nature, makes these Scamps
impose upon me, and then they turn round and jeer me; but I deserves to
be laugh'd at'.[3] Significantly, Cleave's leader of 13 June 1838 gave a
detailed account of the order of procession to match the representational
illustrations on the front page. However, in both Cleave's Gazette and
the Odd Fellow, attacks were made in illustration and comment on the

---

1. Todd, op.cit., p.96. Hollis, op.cit., p.135.
2. Quoted in the Athenaeum, No.643 (22 February 1840), p.157. See also, 'Popular Literature of the Day', British and Foreign Review, x (1840) 243.
3. Cleave's Penny Gazette of Variety, 7 July 1838.

expense of the royal wedding, and that incurred by the rapid succession of royal births.[1] Predictably, Prince Albert was the target of xenophobia, being depicted as the leader of a bunch of foreigners out to milk the country.[2]

111

The papers exhibited a strong dislike of the Sabbatarian campaign, but were enthusiastically in favour of the march of temperance, Cleave's other paper during the period, the English Chartist Circular being sub-titled, the Temperance Record for England and Wales.[3] They attacked the new poor law, the new Pentonville 'Bastile',[4] and the metropolitan police. Indeed, when the Metropolitan Police Act came into force in 1839, Cleave

112

113-5

---

1. Grant's cartoons in Cleave's Gazette include 'The Wedding-Dress' (25 January 1840), 'The Royal Honeymoon' (29 February 1840), 'Birth of the Nation's Hope' (5 December 1840), 'A "Crying" Evil for John Bull' (16 January 1841), 'A ROYAL "INVITE"' (23 January 1841), 'Royal Extravagance' (30 January 1841), 'The Cadger's Christening! or, a Loyal Turn-out!' (20 February 1841), 'THE SEVEN AGES OF THE PRINCE OF WALES' (11 December 1841), 'THE ROYAL CHRISTENING' 'THE CHRISTENING CAKE' (29 January 1842).
   The one remaining copy of the new series of the Political Drama, brought out by Benjamin Cousins in the 1840s, and illustrated by Grant also depicts a 'GRAND PROCESSION IN HONOUR OF THE ARRIVAL OF THE PRINCE OF WALES' (No.15).

2. In Cleave's Gazette, 'The Queen's Consort, or the Queen Consort - Which?' (7 December 1839), 'Trying it on' (14 March 1840), 'Prince Albert's Songster' (28 March 1840), 'The Prince Not Suited, or Albert and his Snips' (11 April 1840), 'The Robbery at Windsor Castle' (17 April 1841).
   In the Odd Fellow, 25 January 1840 'COAXING'.

3. In Cleave's Gazette, Grant's 'THE SUNDAY CRUSADE' (16 November 1839), which depicts a police raid on a tobacconist to take away Chartist newspapers. Also, Cleave's leaders on 19 May, 14 July, 28 July, 25 August 1838.
   On the temperance theme see Grant's 'The Drunkard's Coat of Arms' (17 March 1838), 'THE MARCH OF COMMON SENSE' (2 September 1843). Also, Cleave's leaders on 21 October 1837, 21 July 1838, 22 September 1838, 17 August 1839. In the Odd Fellow, 19 October 1839, 4 January, 5 Sept. 1840

4. See the 'POOR LAW SKETCHES' in the Odd Fellow, 8 June, 29 June, 6 July 1839. Also, in Cleave's Gazette, 'THE POOR LAWS IN BRADFORD' by Grant (9 December 1837) and Cleave's leaders on 16 February, 23 November 1839, 24 October 1840.
   On Pentonville prison, Grant's 'THE BASTILLE MONGERS GOING INTO THEIR OWN TRAP' (Cleave's Gazette, 21 January 1843) and 'THE PENTONVILLE BASTILLE' (16 December 1843). Cleave attacked it on 17 October 1840.

brought out a single sheet, in the same format as his collected Cleave's Picture Gallery of Grant's Comicalities, entitled Cleave's Illustrated Metropolitan Police Act. The largest cut by Grant was devoted to displaying the extreme forms of coercion which prevented street life and work from continuing, while both the Gazette and the Odd Fellow published versions of the act.[1] However, Cleave's leaders often went beyond the capabilities of Grant's imagination and the two rarely coincided on a single theme in any one number. Grant found no visual equivalent for Cleave's leaders on the uses or abuses of machinery, the conditions in factories and housing, the theoretical discussions on political science or Owenism.[2] Similarly, the illustrator of the Odd Fellow preferred to

116

1. In Cleave's Gazette, Grant's 'The New Whig Police Act in Full Operation in the City' (23 March 1839), 'The Whigs preparing for the Invasion of the City' (6 July 1839), 'The English Gen'darmerie Act' (7 September 1839), 'Playing Music without a License' (23 November 1839). Cleave believed that the new act was made for the repression of discontent not the increase in crime. 29 June, 6 July 1839. However, he printed the act on 31 August 1839, as did the Odd Fellow, 5 October 1839.

2. See Cleave's Gazette in February and March 1838 for his anti-Malthusian attitude to machinery. On 16 November 1839, he attacked the 'infant slavery' in England, and the following February, apologists for the factory system including Chambers' Journal and the Globe (8 February 22 February, 14 March 1840). Later in 1840 and over the next two years, he commented on the evidence about conditions in the factories and mines, as revealed in the government select committees (7, 14, 21 November 1840, 7 August 1841, 21 May, 28 May, 4 June 1842). On 20 March 1841, he attacked the unhealthy abodes of the labouring classes. He also defended Owen and the New Moral World (25 April 1840).

snipe at the Queen, Cumberland, the Whigs and the Tories, with a few 'Poor Law Sketches' thrown in, rather than get to grips with any of the leaders on temperance, education,[1] or Chartism. Chartism presented both papers and the London based radicalism of the Cleave Hetherington generation with peculiar problems. Although they supported the cause in their leaders, Chartism was not in origin a metropolitan movement, and when London did contribute more towards its momentum in the 1840s, Cleave and Hetherington were not the protagonists.[2] In 1842, at the time of the so-called 'Plug Plot', Linton's account of the events in the Odd Fellow sound, as Dr. Smith has pointed out, as if he were commenting on rebellion in another country: he did not identify with the strikers and even his sympathy appears luke warm.[3] He showed no curiosity

---

1. Both papers displayed a complex attitude towards education. On the one hand, they attacked the sectarianism of the plans for national education, as well as middle class useful knowledge (for example, the Odd Fellow, 15 June 1839, 20 February 1841). On the other, they were open to new proposals. Cleave took note of the article in Tait's Magazine on Brougham's Education Bill (Cleave's Gazette, 6 January 1838) and later praised his S.D.U.K. pamphlets entitled 'Introductory discourse on the objects, pleasures, and advantages of political science', (9 May 1840) though he added, 'It is scarcely to be conceived that we can acquiesce in every principle laid down by a writer who discharges the functions of teacher in such a school as that of Lincoln's-inn-fields'. Cleave also praised Lovett's Chartist education scheme (10 October 1840) and Henry Mayhew's 'What to teach - and how to teach it' (12 March 1842).

2. I. Prothero, 'Chartism in London', Past & Present, No.44 (1969), pp.76-105. For Grant's infrequent references to Chartism in Cleave's Gazette, see 'The Working Men's Association. THE ROMAN BUNDLE OF STICKS CLEARLY ILLUSTRATED' (25 November 1837), 'The National Petition and the Lilliputian Attack' (29 June 1839), 'THE PHOENIX OF CHARTISM' (22 October 1842). For Cleave's attitude see his leaders on 9 June 1838, 29 December 1838, 28 November 1840, 21 August 1841. In the Odd Fellow 26 January 1839, 2 March 1839, 21 March 1840, 28 March 1840, 21 May 1842.

3. F. B. Smith, 'The Plug Plot Prisoners and the Chartists', Australian National University Historical Journal, No.7 (1970), pp.3-15.

about the living conditions of the factory workers and colliers; probably like most Londoners, he was ignorant on the subject. He remained uncertain as to whether to ascribe the turn-outs to Chartist leadership, conspiracy by the Anti-Corn Law League, or the misery of the workers, and put them down to the rather generalized primary cause of 'the monstrous injustice of class legislation.'[1] It was in fact only after he had left that the paper came out with an illustration by William Newman entitled 'LAW MAKING A MEAL IN THE MANUFACTURING DISTRICTS', which depicted workmen being eaten up by the law on the plates of 'CONSPIRACY', 'TREASON', 'SEDITION' and 'MISDEMEANOUR'.[2]

118

Cleave's role during the period is even more ambivalent. On 2 April 1839, at the time of the Chartist Convention, he wrote to Francis Place to ask for advice. He was worried because he had heard the notion that his paper was either 'an obscene work or a rabid "Physical Force" politico Religio melange' was very prevalent. He asked Place, therefore, to circulate some copies to prove that this was not so and to write for the paper himself. Place replied to his 'Fellow Citizen' thus:-

> It is true as you say you have been told that your publication is a disreputable one. I have on more than one occasion lately asserted the contrary to numbers of influential men, and pointed out the utility of the publication in its having inserted the "Scene at Windsor" respecting the Penny Postage and thus causing a very considerable circulation of it among the working people. I will send the copies left with me to members and others as you desire, and I shall have much pleasure in doing so.

However, Place went on to draw attention to two faults:

> The number is a fair specimen and excepting the wood cuts and one fault to be mentioned presently is a good one. The fault alluded to is calculated to make well conditioned people think ill of the intentions of the Editor and Proprietor. I dislike

---

1. 'The Question of Rebellion, 'Odd Fellow, 27 August 1842.

2. Odd Fellow, 10 December 1842.

> it also because it is a substitution of passion for reason, because it is a going out of the way to be abusive, and because it is a Lie. I mean the allusion to Mr. Mott, in p.4, Col.2. I have no doubt at all that among the same number of persons in the Union Workhouses, of the same ages, in Workhouses before there were Union Workhouses, under the new Poor Law Bill, fewer have died than died in the same time in the Workhouses, on the old plan, and I dislike it because it misleads the poorer people and does them injury.[1]

The correspondence is particularly important since it affords a unique insight of the positions adopted by a moderate radical, Place, who was prepared to cooperate with middle class reformers, and by Cleave, his more extreme friend, at the end of the 1830s. Place congratulated the Gazette for inserting the penny postage propaganda which had been written and circulated on a massive scale by Henry Cole.[2] However, Cleave's continual harping on the iniquities of the new poor law was a black mark against him. Furthermore, he implied that the whole look of the publication, with its rough woodcuts by Grant, was inclined to make it seem disreputable to those who did not pause to examine the text; it suggested the lingering on of the old unfocussed anger and abuse into a new political reality and the progress of technology. There is no evidence to suppose that Cleave ever took up Place's recommendations, either to the lengths of praising the new poor law or of sacking Grant. However, it is about this time that Grant referred to himself as 'such an obscure object in the back-ground as myself'.[3]

1. Brit. Mus. Addit. MSS.35,151 (Place Papers), f.154-6: Cleave to Place, 2 April 1839; Place to Cleave, 2 April 1839, referring to the edition of 10 March.

2. See Cole, Fifty Years of Public Work, i.47; ii. 95-101, 105-6. Cole composed an imaginary dialogue between the Queen, Rowland Hill, Melbourne and Lord Lichfield on the subject of the penny postage and distributed 92,000 copies through a variety of means all over the country. 40,000 were stitched in Nicholas Nickleby.

3. Lamb, '"Gallery of Comicalities"', pp.209-10.

And as if to mock such obscurity, to underline Grant's isolation from the technical progress of wood engraving, Benjamin Cousins advertised his newly resurrected Political Drama, which was again illustrated by Grant, with the slogan, 'DESIGNED by STEAM and ENGRAVED by ELECTROMAGNETISM: for which purpose has been engaged, at an Enormous Expense, the unapproachable talent of the Caricaturist General, MASTER OF THE BLACK ART &c'.[1] Perhaps Grant's very obscurity itself is symptomatic of the vague embarrassment working class leaders were beginning to feel about his art. Cleave's side of the correspondence with Place certainly reveals an anxiety to be distinguished from the less respectable elements of working class radicalism in general, and physical force Chartism in particular. His subsequent behaviour confirms this. In 1842, he was one of the people picked out by Sir James Graham, the Home Secretary, for surveillance of his letters.[2] At the conference of the National Charter Association held at Birmingham in December 1842, a National Victim Fund was set up for the workers arrested after the Plug Plot, and Cleave was made treasurer. By July 1843, it had reached over £500, yet none seems to have been distributed. Cleave, who was notoriously tight-fisted,[3] faced repeated attacks, especially from Feargus O'Connor, who wanted the fund to be handled from Manchester. By September, O'Connor had triumphed and Cleave remained only as nominal 'administrator' of it. There must be some connection between these events and the gradual decline of Cleave's Gazette, but the exact circumstances

1. Penny Satirist, 14 August 1841.

2. P.R.O. Home Office Papers, Series 79, box 4: Miscellaneous Private and Secret. For the whole question of government tampering with the mail, an issue in which Linton was deeply involved, see F. B. Smith's 'British Post Office Espionage, 1844, 'Historical Studies, xiv (1970) 189-203.

3. Scott and Howard, op.cit., i.31. Also, Holyoake, Sixty Years of an Agitator's Life, i. 102.

are not clear. Grant continued to churn out his weekly political cuts, but from August 1842, there were no political leaders in the paper, only short sketches on well-known literary figures and justifications for cheap fiction.[1] Whether Cleave was too busy with the National Charter Association or had lost interest in radical journalism is not known. At any rate, by 1844 both the English Chartist Circular and Cleave's Gazette of Variety were dead, and with them, one of the chief vehicles of the illustrated gazette formula.

Grant's other main outlet during this period was on the front page of Benjamin Cousins' Penny Satirist, which lasted from 1837 to 1846. Cousins' first venture after the 1836 stamp act was the Weekly Herald, which lasted for all of two months. It vigorously attacked the stamp laws, the new poor law and campaigned for a more equitable distribution of land. In addition, it contained extensive accounts of parliamentary debates and police cases, as well as a curiously emblematic series of illustrations, each depicting a political target in fable form accompanied by a moral homily.[2] The Penny Satirist lasted long enough to present an up to date image. Thomas Frost thought that it contained more political material than Cleave's paper and reflected the views of the Anti-Corn Law League rather than those of the National Charter Association. He believed

---

1. For example, Cleave's Gazette, 20 August 1842:
   'So long as fiction represents life as it has been and is - vindicates truth and decries injustice, - holding up the mirror to nature, reflecting aright the workings of the vast arcana of society, so long will it be available in improving the heart, and in leading to the greatest of all studies - man himself'.

2. For example, 'THE VENDORS OF CHEAP KNOWLEDGE' (3 July 1836), which depicts a smiling vendor carrying a bundle under his arm, and holding up a broadsheet labelled 'A FREE PRESS', out of the smoke. A bishop with devil's horns attempts to stab him in the back, but is prevented from doing so by an angel with a sword.

that it was probably subsidized by the League, who paid for Grant's woodcuts.[1] Although I can find no documentary evidence in the papers of the League to support this assertion, it is certainly true that from the beginning of 1843, there was a proliferation of cuts relating to the campaign. 'THE MODERN TELL; OR, THE APPLE OF DISCORD' depicts Cobden shooting at the Corn Laws; 'PULL DEVIL; PULL, BAKER!' is a tug-of-war between Cobden and the Devil, representing the landed interest, which he stands firm against also in 'THE ANTI-CORN LAW GIANT, AND THE DWARFS OF MONOPOLY'.[2] On 23 December 1843, the Penny Satirist gave up, rather grudgingly, space to comment on the League in a leader entitled, 'The Truck System; or the Landlord's Mode of Trading':-

119

> It is but seldom that we meddle with the subject of trade; except in our cuts or caricatures, when we give the monopolists the benefit of our artist's ingenuity, and amuse our readers like so many feudal vassals, at the expence of their feudal and Baronial Lords. But we think it right to give the subject one sweeping review in one of our leading ex-Cathedra articles, that our readers may understand in what light we view it...

Needless to say, despite the flippant tone, the paper came down in favour of the repeal of the Corn Laws. In contrast, Cleave and Linton did not share the same view in their respective publications. Although Linton was prepared to write to the League offering to illustrate its

---

1. Frost, op.cit., pp.83-84. According to Hepworth Dixon, the Penny Satirist was a serial which,'for low scurrility and malignity was unequalled. At one time its circulation, amongst the lowest refuse of the populations of London, Manchester, Liverpool, Glasgow, and other large towns, was enormous'. 'The Literature of the Lower Orders', Daily News, 9 November 1847. Unfortunately, however, I can discover nothing about the means or size of its circulation, or whether this was simply another example of Dixon's tendency to exaggerate.

2. Penny Satirist, 28 January, 25 February, 25 March 1843. Also, 'THE BRIDGE OF MONOPOLY' (13 May 1843), 'THE QUACK BETWIXT TWO STOOLS' (3 June 1843), 'ANTI-FREE-TRADE MOVEMENT' (22 July 1843), 'THE MAN OF BRASS; OR, THE COLOSSUS OF MONOPOLY' (19 August 1843), 'CUTTING DOWN THE TREE OF MONOPOLY; OR, TIP-TOP SAWYERS FINISHING THEIR JOB' (14 October 1843), 'A FREE TRADE WIND; OR, MORE GRIST TO THE MILL' (2 December 1843), 'JOHN BULL TO THE BREACH, BACKED BY 100,000 ARTILLERY' (9 December 1843) &c.

Bazaars,[1] nevertheless he refused to back it in the Odd Fellow because he said that if it succeeded as a unilateral pressure group, the middle classes would lose their incentive to back the Chartists' demand for the suffrage.[2] Similarly, Cleave pointed out in response to Ormsby Gore's observation that the operatives refused to join the League, that this was not because they were content with the status quo or preferred starvation to plenty, oppression to freedom, misery to happiness, aristocratic self-pampering to equality of privilege and enjoyment; 'No! it is because the operatives place little faith in the promised relief from the corn law abolition so long as aristocratic oppression is to continue'.[3]

The Anti-Corn Law League made one other, and rather better documented attempt to use graphic journalism for propaganda purposes. On 12 June 1839, Cobden wrote to Henry Cole for advice about a suitable illustrator for the Anti-Corn Law Circular. They had met in Manchester the previous month in connection with the agitation for introducing a uniform penny postage and the following February, Cobden, Place and others tried, unsuccessfully, to persuade Cole to undertake the Secretaryship of the League.[4] For the moment however, Cobden enclosed a rough sketch suggestion of the Poles offering bread on one side of a stream, and the people starving on the other, while a demon in the centre prevented the exchange.[5] Another idea Cobden had

---

1. Feltrinelli, Linton: A. W. Paulton (one of the League's senior agents) to Linton, 22 August 1845:
    'I am instructed to say that as it is not contemplated to make the forthcoming Bazaar in Manchester any thing more than a mart for the relics of the London one, the Council do not intend to make it the subject of pictorial illustrations'.

2. Odd Fellow, 24 April, 8 May 1841, 1 October 1842.

3. Cleave's Gazette, 25 May 1839.

4. Cole, Fifty Years of Public Work, i. 53, 57-58.

5. Ibid., ii. 143.

makes it clear that he was prepared to libel Lord Ashley in the process. A cut to be entitled 'The Landowner and the Factory Child' was envisaged by him of 'Two or three pale & starved children going to work with large bits of bread in their hands':-

> Lord Ashley has taken the bread from the first child & has broken it in two, & whilst putting the larger share in his pocket & returning the smaller to the child, he lifts up his eyes & in a very sanctimonious tone says "I will never rest until the poor factory child is protected by a ten hours bill from the tyranny of the <u>merciless & gripping millowners</u>". This last is a quotation from Lord Ashley. There should be a good likeness...[1]

Ten days later, Cole replied that he had found an illustrator in W.M. Thackeray, 'a genius both with his pencil and his pen. His vocation is literary. He is full of humour and feeling'. Cole tactfully omitted to mention that Thackeray did not think much of the sketch but said he would do anything for <u>money</u>, or that he had worked on the conservative <u>Fraser's Magazine</u>. Instead, he stressed Thackeray's connections with the <u>Westminster Review</u>, his friendship with Charles Buller and played up his general enthusiasm for the scheme:

> Hitherto he has not had occasion to think much on the subject of Corn Laws, and therefore wants the stuff to work upon. He would like to combine both writing and drawing when sufficiently primed, and then he would write and illustrate ballads, or tales, or anything. I think you would find him a most effective auxiliary, and perhaps the best way to fill him with matter for illustrations, would be to invite him to see the weavers, their mills, shuttles, et cetera... We think the idea of an ornamental emblematical reading of the Circular good...[2]

However, there was some delay in producing the first cuts, for Thackeray was tempted to experiment with a new mode of etching by a Mr. Schönberg of Hatton Garden. It was not a success and the drawings he made were eventually entrusted by Cole to his friend John Thompson, for engraving on wood.[3] Only two designs ever appeared, in the latter half of 1839.

1. N. McCord, <u>The Anti-Corn Law League 1838-1846</u> (1958), pp.69-70.

2. <u>The Letters and Private Papers of W.M. Thackeray</u>, ed. G.N. Ray (1945), i. 385. Cole, <u>Fifty Years of Public Work</u>, ii.143-4.

3. Cole Diary. Entries for 22 June - 6 August 1839. For a description of Schönberg's 'acrography' process see E.M. Harris, 'Experimental Graphic Processes in England 1800-1859', <u>Journal of the Printing Historical Society</u> v (1969), 58-63.

Entitled 'ILLUSTRATIONS OF THE RENT LAWS', they take up Cobden's general 120-121 ideas without the pointed quotation from Ashley's speech.[1] Thackeray's own suggestion of 'a howling group with this motto, "GIVE US OUR DAILY BREAD"' was adopted for the masthead. But nothing seems to have come of Thackeray's, or rather Cole's more grandiose schemes. One very feeble illustrated pun entitled 'KEEPING UP THE PRICE OF BREAD', appeared in 1841, together with a large map of the wheat growing areas of North America.[2] The Circular's successor, the League only printed review illustrations, apart from a couple of efforts in 1845, showing decrepit cottages owned by Lady Holland and St. John's College, Oxford, under the heading of 'CONDITIONS OF THE WILTSHIRE PEASANTRY'.[3]

On 25 April 1846, in an address entitled 'Signs of the Times', the Penny Satirist announced its departure from the journalistic scene. It said it had lived long enough to assist in giving a coup de pied to the atrocious Corn Law, which was about to die, and it bequeathed the same struggles to its successor, the unillustrated London Pioneer. It went on to summarize the central dilemma of the radical gazettes during the 1840s:-

> It now remains to be proved whether the people shall have a cheap press - a penny press - that shall advocate their rights, or whether they shall have to depend on a dear, monopolist press, which shifts its opinions according to the weight of the purse presented for the prostitution of its columns. He is aware his task is a difficult one - that if he introduces too much political, philosophical, or educational matter into his paper, his readers will not be sufficiently numerous to enable him to proceed. If, on the other hand, he inserts too much of what is called "light reading", he runs the risk of losing his best and most esteemed supporters. He will do as the "old man

---

1. Anti-Corn Law Circular, 23 July, 10 December 1839.
2. Anti-Bread Tax Circular, 21 April, 4 November 1841.
3. The League, 15 February 1845.

with the ass" did: he will <u>try</u> to please them all - whether with the same, or better, success, remains also to be proved.[1]

---

1. <u>Penny Satirist</u>, 25 April 1846.

II

When the Penny Satirist changed its name in 1846 to the London Pioneer, it did so on the grounds that 'the word "SATIRIST" is associated with untoward events which have happened to the proprietor of a paper bearing that title', and it did not want to be confounded with it.[1] It is evident that Cleave dropped 'Satirist' from the title of his paper in 1837 for the same reason.[2] Furthermore, his letter to Place in 1839 reveals his fear that his paper, if not taken for one which advocated physical force Chartism, was thought to be an 'obscene work'.[3] Similarly, the Odd Fellow came out very strongly against licentious publications, which were allowed to circulate unstamped: 'The government and legislature had much sooner that the public morals were corrupted, than that the political rights of the people were sought after'.[4] It is necessary to take a closer look at such publications for, although scantily illustrated themselves, their presence permeated the whole atmosphere of graphic journalism during the late 1830s and early 1840s. They were a plague spot, against which all manner of illustrated publications hastened to inoculate themselves.

Thackeray isolated the germ in his 1838 collection of 'Half-A-Crown's Worth of Cheap Literature' in Fraser's Magazine. He bought the Star of Venus or Shew Up Chronicle, with its music and brothel guides, and the

---

1. 'Signs of the Times', Penny Satirist, 25 April 1846.
2. Cleave's Gazette of Variety, 16 December 1837.
3. See above p.181.
4. 'The Taste of the Public for Certain Metropolitan Weekly Publications', Odd Fellow, 12 January 1839.

Town, which sold at twopence and contained series devoted to East End gin shops and pawnbrokers. These, together with the Penny Age and the Fly were publications whose 'ribaldry so infamous, obscenity so impudently blackguard and brazen' could hardly be conceived, 'and certainly never was printed until our day'. Their main purpose, he thought, was:

> to familiarise every man in London who can afford a penny with the doings of the gin-shops, the gambling-houses and - houses more infamous still...dismal indications indeed of the social condition of the purchasors, who are to be found among all the lower classes in London.

Thanks to the enlightened spirit of the age, no man scarcely was so ill-educated as not to be able to read them; 'and, blessings on cheap literature! no man is too poor to buy them!' Thackeray's main grievance seems to have been that whereas in olden times, vices were the secret of the aristocracy, now they were common to the serving maid, the poorest artisan, the meanest apprentice and the 'hidden treasure of the charmed schoolboy, who, by this excellent medium, knows as much about town as the oldest rake in it'. He concluded: 'We have our penny libraries for debauchery as for other useful knowledge; and colleges like palaces for study - gin-palaces, where each starving Sardanapalus may revel until he die'.[1]

Other voices swelled the hysteria. Cobden, when serving as a member of the select committee on Newspaper Stamps in 1851, produced a copy of the Town and showed it to Thomas Keogh, Assistant Secretary to the Board of Inland Revenue:

> That is a weekly publication, publishes at a penny, upon very fair paper, and with woodcuts fairly executed, of a very demoralizing

---

[1]. Fraser's Magazine, xvii (1838), 290.

> character. The number that you have in your hand has
> for its frontispiece a large woodcut called "a scene in
> a brothel". You will perceive that the greater portion
> of the contents of that weekly publication, at a penny,
> is news and intelligence relating to the practices and
> scenes in public brothels and similar places.

Cobden went on to suggest that if the stamp tax were abolished and a penny newspaper thus became feasible, then the competition might help to drive out such 'noxious publications'. Keogh, however, was unconvinced, 'That is certainly a benevolent theory, but I am afraid it is not sustained by the facts which are notorious'. Publications which contained 'little else but a collection of all the police reports, murders, and atrocities of every kind' were read by five times as many people as the best Sunday newspaper. Even one, which he omitted to name, selling at sixpence was read by the working classes and, he believed, by scarcely any other class. After some exchange at cross purposes, in which Keogh took Cobden to imply that such publications should be stamped, the former conceded that freer circulation of newspapers would '<u>pro tanto</u>' tend to diminish their influence, but not drive them out.[1]

The facts about this species of journalism are less dramatic. The sixpenny one referred to by Keogh was probably the <u>Satirist</u> (1831-1847), run by Barnard Gregory, which together with Westmacott's the <u>Age</u> (1825-1843), were the longest lived of the genre. Politically, the <u>Age</u> was Tory in its sympathies, the <u>Satirist</u> radical; apart from a few cuts in the first volume of the latter, attacking bishops, both were unillustrated. Barnard Gregory (1796-1852) is one of the characters who crops up most regularly in journalistic memoirs of the period. A bill of reward for his arrest described him as having been 'a schoolmaster, itinerant preacher, druggist, auctioneer, brewer, banker, bankrupt', that he was aged 55, 5 ft.2in. in

---

1. Parl.Papers 1851, xvii (558), pp.75-80: minutes of evidence, qus.471-503.

height, knock-kneed and shabbily dressed. As J.F. Wilson, the printer, said, 'Add to this the occupations of editor, professional blackmailer, and actor, and his career will present a record that "will take a little beating"'.[1] His notoriety derives from two incidents. In 1843, as an amateur actor, he put on a performance of Hamlet at Drury Lane, with himself in the leading role. The Duke of Brunswick, one of his victims packed the theatre with supporters who drove Gregory off the stage. Gregory brought an action against him and lost.[2] The second involves the Satirist's rivalry with the cheaper Town and its owner Renton Nicholson. Their exchanges became so abusive that Gregory brought an action against Nicholson, who was sent for trial. Nicholson proceeded to pose as the champion of morality and got up a subscription to help pay for his defence in the court of Queen's Bench. However, when the case came up, there was no prosecution for Gregory had in the mean time been gaoled for libel and extortion.[3] Such were the types who ran the 'licentious publications'.

Renton Nicholson's Town deserves closer inspection, not only because of its low price of twopence, but also because of the personnel who came to be associated with it and its owner. Renton Nicholson (1809-1861) was born in Islington, was apprenticed to a pawnbroker in Shadwell and in 1830, opened up a jeweller's shop at 99 Quadrant, Regent Street. A year later, he was declared insolvent and paid the first of many visits to the

1. Wilson, op.cit., pp.98-101. Also, Vizetelly, op.cit., i. 174-6.
2. Ibid. Also, Linton, Memories, pp.199-201.
3. Vizetelly, op.cit., i. 168-9. See also, 'Preface', Town, ii (1838). 'Characteristic Sketches No.lxiii' - 'The Extortioner', Town, 11 August 1838. For the irresponsibility, dishonesty, immorality and licentiousness of the press generally during this period, see Aspinall, 'The Social Status of Journalists at the Beginning of the Nineteenth Century', pp.222-7. Balzac considered blackmail to be an invention of the English press, and largely accounted for its secret revenues. Lost Illusions (1837-43), trans. H.J. Hunt (Penguin edn., 1971), pp.421-3.

debtors' prisons of the metropolis.[1] There followed successive forays into the twilight regions of gambling and racing, billiard rooms and wine shops before he was again declared bankrupt in April 1836. Then he composed a series of stories in the Pickwick mould entitled Cockney Adventures and Tales of Town Life but had difficulty in finding a printer for them. Eventually, Joseph Last 'a good man and better printer', agreed to take on the series issued weekly, with illustrations by Grant, who adopted a scribbled Cruikshank style to execute the cuts, 'strikingly emblematic of cockney life'.[2] In addition, an agreement was prepared by Alfred Mayhew whereby Last employed Nicholson to edit and bring out the Town for £3 a week. Nicholson signed and the first number appeared on 3 June 1837.

The prospectus stressed that the new paper was the size of the Satirist, but cost a third of the price, twopence. It would comprise of original sketches of:-

> Metropolitan Gaming Houses - Free and Easies - The Prisons - The Swell Mob - Flats and Sharps - Parish Worthies - Licensed Victuallers - Pawnbrokers and their Assistants - Cigar Shops and Pretty Women - Bow-street Officers - The Doings of Courtesans and Demireps of Quality &c &c; with Criticisms on Actors and the Theatres, and all places of Public Amusement.

Furthermore, it promised not to 'pollute our columns by attacks grounded on malignity or scurrility. We beg it to be understood that we are open to all parties, and influenced by none':-

> We have assumed the title of "THE TOWN", because we treat upon the vices and follies of this great metropolis in the age we live in.[3]

The paper was, by his account, immensely successful from the start and

---

1. The Lord Chief Baron Nicholson, An Autobiography (1860), pp.134-51.
2. Ibid., pp.229-41. R. Nicholson, Cockney Adventures and Tales of London Life (1838), 'Preface'.
3. Nicholson, Autobiography, p.242.

'became a weekly necessity with the fast community of London'. Nicholson not only gave publicity to the business speculations of his friends, but also performed some service by exposing many swindling companies. At first, a Mr. Anderson, once editor of the Marylebone journal, supervised the work, but soon Nicholson took over the entire management, 'Anderson being far too innocent in the ways of the world to conduct such a periodical'. Other contributors included John Dalrymple, a writer of burlesques who died in Newgate in 1839 on a forgery charge, Henry Pellatt, afterwards known as the double of Lord Brougham, John George Canning, who wrote under the pseudonym of Theophilus Pole, Dr. Maginn and Edward Leman Blanchard.[1]

Each week on the front page, the paper ran a column entitled 'Characteristic Sketches,' rather like the Odd Fellow's 'The World We Live In', which was illustrated by 'Gilray the Younger', in other words, Archibald Henning, and engraved by Landells. The series, which featured metropolitan 'types' was well within the tradition which had commenced in the eighteenth century with prints of street criers and itinerant tradesmen. Of these, Francis Wheatley's The Itinerant Traders of London, issued between 1793 and 1797, was probably the most popular, but Thomas Rowlandson's Characteristic Sketches of the Lower Orders (1820) certainly gave a less idealized impression.[2] In 1829, the sporting paper run by William Clement, Bell's Life

---

1. Ibid., pp.243-79. Also, 'Preface', Town, i (1837): 'Our induction to the public was admitted upon all hands to have been one of the most racy, spicy, and figging specimens of literature ever produced'.

2. See C. Hindley, A History of the Cries of London, Ancient and Modern (1884). A. W. Tuer, Old London Street Cries and the Cries of Today (1885). F. Bridge, The Old Cryes of London (1921). W. Roberts, The Cries of London (1942). S. Rayner, Cries of London (1929). M. Webster, 'Francis Wheatley's Cries of London', Auction, iii (1970), 44-49.

in London began a series of wood engraved sketches from the designs of George Cruikshank (who never gave his permission),[1] Robert Seymour, Kenny Meadows and from May 1837, John Leech. These were republished at irregular intervals between 1834 and 1840 in a four-page broadsheet entitled the Gallery of Comicalities, costing threepence and covered with a mass of cuts accompanied by short verses. It claimed to have sold over two million copies.[2] Its contents included 'PHISOGS OF THE TRADERS OF LONDON', 'LEGAL PHISOGS', 'MEDICAL PHISOGS', and 'THEATRICAL PHISOGS'; 'PARISH WORTHIES', 'POLITICAL WORTHIES' and 'CORPORATION WORTHIES'; 'PARIS ORIGINALS' and 'AMATEUR ORIGINALS'; 'FEATURES OF INSOLVENT LIFE' and 'UPS AND DOWNS OF LIFE; or the vicissitudes of a swell'.[3] The tone of the periodical was 'a compound of slang, backslang, and the wise crack';[4] the style of the cuts that of hastily drawn sketches. They operated in the same way as political caricature, nudging their way round the metropolis,[5] yet they were too general and too poor a likeness to be able to aspire to its strength of motivation and direction. They offered a knowing wink at the routine, the pastimes and the pleasures of the city rather than confronting their audience with political controversy.

---

1. Jerrold, op.cit., p.93-94. See also 'Comicalities', Notes and Queries, 4th Ser., iv. (1869), 478. W. Bates, 'Gallery of Comicalities', Ibid., v (1870) 43-44.

2. Gallery of Comicalities, No.7 (1 May 1840).

3. Gallery of Comicalities, No.1 (1 October 1834), No.4 (1 January 1836), No.6 (1 May 1838), No.7 (1 May 1840).

4 S. Morison, The English Newspaper 1622-1832 (Cambridge, 1932), p.247.

5. See above p.95.

Nicholson, with his slang filled writings and libellous innuendo and Henning, with his suggestive sketches of 'The Saloon Lady' or 'The Amorous Old Gentleman' were part of the same mode, but relishing a greater degree of freedom from standards of decency.[1]

The Town managed to survive until 1843, whether under Nicholson or not is uncertain; he once managed to contribute to it from the Queen's Bench prison.[2] By 1841, however, he had established the 'Judge and Jury Society', which first met in the Garrick's Head and later moved between this locale and two other well-known haunts of the fast life, the Coal Hole in Fountain Court, Strand and the Cyder Cellars in Maiden Lane, until 1858. Here, he presided over mock trials acted from sham law reports and 'poses plastiques' - live representations of classical sculpture groups - all of a more or less indecent nature, patronized by the 'swells of the town'.[3] He was aided by Pellatt and Canning, while an immense painting at the corner of Wellington Street and the Strand, by Henning, containing portraits of many of the celebrities of the day, advertised the proceedings for many years.[4]

---

1. Town, 29 December 1838, 20 October 1838.

2. Nicholson, Autobiography, pp.168-72.

3. Ibid., pp.308-23. Vizetelly, op.cit., i. 169-70. C. Scott, 'The Old Coal Hole', Daily Telegraph, 20 November 1896. Plate III of George Cruikshank's The Drunkard's Children (1848), 'FROM THE GIN-SHOP TO THE DANCING-ROOMS, FROM THE DANCING-ROOMS TO THE GIN-SHOP, THE POOR GIRL IS DRIVEN ON IN THAT COURSE WHICH ENDS IN MISERY', depicts the dancing-rooms adorned with posters for 'JUDGE and JURY', and 'LES POSES PLASTIQUES'. See below p.300. For descriptions of these night spots, see Guildhall Library, Norman Collection: 'Inns and Taverns', ii. 63-67.

4. 'The Lord Chief Baron Nicholson', Notes and Queries, (8th series), iii. 7 January 1893, pp.3-5. Vizetelly, op.cit., i. 169.

It is not the purpose of this study to give a full account of the London demi-monde during the first half of the nineteenth century, nor to assert that it was any more permissive than at any other time. However, for those who watched over the public's progress, its political and moral welfare were often inextricably connected, and they were alive to anything that threatened this in the form of cheap, suggestive works. Furthermore, it is important to understand the background it provided to the development of graphic journalism during the late 1830s and 1840s. The lengths to which Gregory, Nicholson and their ilk went in producing 'obscene', 'licentious' and 'scurrilous' material with which to fill their pages made a deep impact on the men who shared their profession, journalism, and their neighbourhood and places of entertainment, the area of the Strand. As we have seen, the radical journalists also sought to disassociate themselves from the tone of these periodicals. Nothing, after all, could be more different from Cleave's English Chartist Circular or Temperance Record for England and Wales (1841-44), than the paper Last and Nicholson ran for a few months in 1838-9, the Crown, a weekly publication supporting beer sellers.[1] In addition, as I hope to show in the next chapter, the mainstream of humorous journalism during the 1840s was strenuous in its efforts to rise above such a level of gutter humour. At the time when Nicholson's notoriety was packing the drinking dens of Covent Garden, Last, Landells and Henning found themselves isolated from their fellows in graphic journalism, kept in quarantine lest the marks of their disease should contaminate the purer images of others.

---

1. Nicholson, Autobiography, p.280. 'The Lord Chief Baron Nicholson', p.4.

III

In 1846, Charles Knight attributed the winding up of the Penny Magazine at least in part to the successful circulation of Newgate romances 'all of the same exciting character' amongst the least informed class of the population: 'All the garbage that belongs to the history of crime and misery is raked together, to diffuse a moral miasma through the land, in the shape of the most vulgar and brutal fiction'.[1] Writing to Brougham a dozen years later on the state of popular literature at this time, he confessed, 'I was almost out of heart about its tendencies; for some of the worst of the Weekly Penny Sheets, such as Reynolds' Mysteries of London (a most infamous book) and Lloyd's Newgate Novels had a very large circulation'.[2] M. J. Whitty, the editor, proprietor and conductor of the Liverpool Journal, was more optimistic, taking a longer term view. In 1851 he stated before the select committee on Newspaper Stamps that he thought the unstamped newspapers of Hetherington and his fellows had killed off immoral publications in dozens, and that they 'did a great deal of good, because though bad in themselves, they displaced what was a great deal worse'. He believed that the present reading matter of the working and poorer classes, namely Lloyd's publications and the News of the World, must have an immense circulation in order to make a profit, as they contained no advertisements and thus were entirely dependent on sales. Though infinitely better than

---

1. 'Address', Penny Magazine, ii. new series (1846), 231-4.
2. U.C.L., Brougham Papers, 10,622: Knight to Brougham, 2 November 1858.

the old unstamped, their character, however, was not wholly good, 'and they are not conducted with any kind of literary ability, not much at all events, nor with very proper feeling'. Cheap newspapers, he thought, would help to drive them out of business.[1] S. G. Bucknall, the printer and publisher of the penny Stroud Observer (which had been stopped by the Stamp Office) and the Stroud Free Press, expressed similar sentiments:-

> I think that the good will always drive out the bad, and that if you referred back 10 or 12 years you would find that the penny scurrilous publications, for instance, the "Penny Satirist" and "Cleave's London Gazette", circulated to a large number; and that inasmuch as they have been driven out of circulation, it has been by a better class... I contend that the most effectual way of doing it is by supplying them with news. News is what we all care about, almost beyond anything else.

He described the type of periodicals which needed to be replaced:-

> what unstamped publications they have are, generally speaking, rather of a demoralizing class than otherwise; large numbers of them are novels, such as "Dick Turpin", "Jack Sheppard", the "Highwayman", and the "Black Pirate", all those, the foulest filth of the printing press, are read by those persons eagerly, and they encourage a love of adventure which may be natural but which certainly, I think, ought not to be encouraged beyond very restricted limits; and it presents to them cuts of daring and heroism which, however morally wrong, they cannot but view in their uneducated state with admiration; and consequently to their education, such reading as they get is bad instead of good.[2]

Thus, the familiar theme of the inevitability of good reading matter replacing bad,[3] churned on into the middle decades of the century. Again, the source of the disorder was the penny press; again the panacea espoused was the cheap newspaper. However, by the 1840s it was not so much cheap

---

1. Parl. Papers 1851, xvii (558), pp.92-94: minutes of evidence, qus. 588-604.
2. Ibid., pp.196-8: minutes of evidence, qus. 1214-7.
3. See above p.137.

politics which provoked these displays of moral outrage, as cheap fiction. As the 1836 stamp act had put an end to the unstamped press[1] and as men like Cleave and Hetherington revolted against using titillating obscenities to attract a large readership, the only alternative lay, as we have seen, in incorporating some measure of fiction into their periodicals. They were joined, during the 1840s, by printers and publishers ready to exploit to the full the lower class predilection for romance and adventure, for variety.

It is not my purpose to examine the development of cheap fiction for the masses, nor the relationship between nineteenth century novelists and their illustrators; both areas have been studied before.[2] However, it is important to place the decline of the tradition of radical caricature in the 1840s in this context. It is important to see where the artists who had produced such cuts went when the radical journals with whom they were involved had largely turned to producing fiction; if they joined them, what level of fiction they illustrated. Only in this way can other, topical currents in graphic journalism - the development of humorous and news magazines - be properly appreciated.

Grant's collaboration with Edward Lloyd had commenced in 1836 with the short running serial cuts entitled Lloyd's Political Jokes.[3] At the same time, Lloyd collaborated with George Purkess and William Strage to publish such penny fiction as the History of the Pirates of All Nations and Lives of the Most Notorious Highwaymen Footpads and Murderers.[4] The

1. See above pp.170-1.

2. See, for example, M. Dalziel, Popular Fiction a Hundred Years Ago (1957). James, Fiction for the Working Man. J.R. Harvey, Victorian Novelists and their Illustrators (1970). F.R. and Q.D. Leavis, Dickens the Novelist (1970), pp.332-71.

3. See above p.80.

4. Wiener, Descriptive Finding List, Nos.182, 241. See also, J. Medcraft, Bibliography of the Penny Bloods of Edward Lloyd (Dundee, 1945).

latter combined excursions into the not too well authenticated past with more topical accounts. In April 1837, for example, Lloyd printed an account of the Edgware murder and the subsequent trial of James Greenacre and his mistress, Sarah Gale. This was illustrated with a particularly gruesome depiction of the murder and portraits of the prisoners in the dock.[1] More usually, however, both periodicals were enlivened by superior versions of Catnach type illustrations, better cut and printed on better paper,[2] although still retaining the theatrical postures, stiff hatching and strong contrasts of the old tradition. This style was retained for the large broadsheet newspapers Lloyd began to put out from 1840 onwards. The Penny Sunday Times and People's Police Gazette, the Companion to Lloyd's Penny Sunday Times and Lloyd's Illustrated London News all combined illustrated fiction with various topical conflagrations cut in the manner of a Catnach broadside; they will be examined more fully in connection with the development of illustrated news.[3] However, in addition to the large front page cut, the Penny Sunday Times carried each week two small illustrated jokes or puns executed with a little more finesse by Grant. And Lloyd employed Grant to illustrate what was perhaps the most important breakthrough in the field of popular fiction during the 1830s and 1840s: the imitations and plagiarisms which followed in the wake of the success of Charles Dickens.

---

1. Lives of the Most Notorious Highwaymen, No.50 (supplementary number, 1 April 1837), No.51 (8 April 1837), No.52 (15 April 1837). For an account of the murder see R.D. Altick, Victorian Studies in Scarlet (1972), pp.37-40.

2. See James, op.cit., pp.29-33 for an account of Lloyd's publishing methods.

3. See below p.276.

Dickens' first attempts at literature took a conventional form: they were short tales and 'sketches' for the Monthly Magazine, Evening Chronicle and Bell's Life in London from 1833 onwards, in addition to the parliamentary reports he wrote for the Morning Chronicle. The genre was one which had been exploited by Pierce Egan in his Life in London, but Dickens' tone lacked the slangy affectations of the earlier work, although they shared the same illustrator, George Cruikshank. In 1835, Dickens was introduced to John Macrone, the publisher, who commissioned him to write a collection of tales. These Sketches by Boz, accompanied by Cruikshank's etchings, were first published on 8 February 1836 and made Dickens' reputation. On the basis of this success, Chapman and Hall asked Dickens to supply the text for a series of Cockney sporting plates created by Robert Seymour. Seymour had in fact already illustrated an anonymous story by Dickens which appeared in the Monthly Magazine in 1834, and later in the Library of Fiction, another monthly periodical published by Chapman and Hall. It was not uncommon for illustrated works to be published in monthly parts if the plates were considered more important than the words, as opposed to the usual three volume edition of the novel. This mode was adopted by the publishers but in fact proved to be the inauguration of a new method of issuing fiction. Dickens made himself the dominant member of the partnership; Seymour died, and his eventual replacement, Hablôt K. Browne was young and compliant. The Pickwick Papers, as they were issued month by month from 31 March 1836 to 20 November 1837, with two illustrations by 'Phiz' rather than the four Seymour had produced, took the shape of a novel. Furthermore, this form enabled Dickens to gauge the popularity of his plot and characters with a much wider audience than ever before, owing to the cheaper and larger sale of the parts.[1]

For some, however, it was not cheap enough. Immediately the success of Dickens' work became apparent, Edward Lloyd, never one to shrink from exploiting a new taste, put out a series of cheap plagiarisms, and other purveyors of popular fiction jumped on the band-waggon.[2] Besides the long extracts which were printed in the Odd Fellow and Cleave's Gazette, many 'new' titles appeared: The Penny Pickwick, The Sketch Book by 'Bos', Oliver Twiss, Nickelas Nicklebery, as well as scrapsheets, song books and stage plays based on Dickens' characters. Lloyd was fortunate in being able to enliven these early plagiarisms adapted for a lower class audience with illustrations by Grant which were equally suitable. Instead of the etched plates of the originals, each eight-page number of the penny Dickens contained two approximately half-page woodcuts executed in a coarse, vulgar yet lively style. A brief perusal of those in Mister Humfries' Clock, which Lloyd published in 1840, with illustrations by some anonymous hack, highlights the virtues of Grant's work. As in those he did for Nicholson's Cockney Adventures,[3] the lines are finer than in his serial cuts or political cartoons for the radical newspapers, the design reduced to a more organized whole; yet, they retain the boldness of characterization, the obviousness of facial expression and confidence of handling in the bodily proportions which is far more sophisticated

---

1. J. Forster, Life of Charles Dickens (1872), i. 86-119. F.G. Kitton, Dickens and his Illustrators (1889), pp.29-46. Harvey, op.cit., pp.6-18. M. Steig, 'Dickens, Hablôt Brown, and the Tradition of English Caricature', Criticism, xi (1969), 219-33.

2. James, op.cit., pp.45-71.

3. See above p.194.

than the primitive cuts in Lloyd's later publication. The Pickwick Papers had sold 40,000 copies per issue by its fifteenth instalment; the Penny Pickwick claimed a sale of 50,000 copies a week. For both audiences, the style of production and publication was appropriate as was the content of the novels and their illustrations. The etched plates by Seymour and Cruikshank were works of imagination by artists in their own right and for both, claims were made that they had been the real initiators of Dickens' success.[1] Grant's status is, inevitably, of a more elusive kind, yet the reprint of many of his 'Dickens' cuts in Cleave's Gazette late in 1838 suggests a certain rapport with an audience hitherto accustomed to his large scale work. Similarly, on its higher level, Cruikshank's illustrations were introduced to magazines when Oliver Twist was first published in the periodical Dickens had been engaged to edit, Bentley's Miscellany. Thus, by 1840 there was a range of illustrated fiction in magazine form which to a large extent was reinforcing the divisions in style, personnel and audience which had been experienced in the field of political caricature. They were strengthened further with the commencement of the humorous and news magazines.

During the 1840s, currents in the publication of cheap fiction did not remain stationary. George William MacArthur Reynolds (1815-1879) was the son of an admiral, was educated at Sandhurst, inherited a fortune and lost it in Paris through dabbling in periodicals.[2] When he returned to England, he made use of his experience by writing for Bentley's

---

1. For Seymour, by his wife in An Account of the Origin of 'Pickwick Papers', (1849). This is refuted by Roe in 'Seymour, the "Inventor" of "Pickwick"', 67-71. For Cruikshank's claim to have suggested Oliver Twist, see Harvey, op.cit., pp.199-210.

2. For the career of G.W.M. Reynolds, see Reynold's Miscellany ii (1845), 191. J.V.B.S. Hunter, 'George Reynolds', Book Handbook, i (1947), 225-36. For the most recent bibliography of his writings see M. Summers, 'G.W.M. Reynolds', Times Literary Supplement, 4 July 1942, p.336.

Miscellany and editing the Monthly Magazine, in which there first appeared his serial, Pickwick Abroad; or, the Tour in France late in 1837. Then it was issued in twenty parts with illustrations by A.H. Forrester ('Alfred Crowquill'), John Phillips and George Bonner. The preface to the bound volume proudly acknowledged its success and added:

> The spirited proprietor of the copyright also incurred, at the outset, additional expenses beyond those sustained by any other publisher of a work issued in livraisons of a similar kind. Besides the two steel engravings by an eminent artist, every Number contained two exquisite wood-cuts representing some of the public buildings or scenes of interest in Paris and its environs. These wood-cuts, which are executed in the first style of the art, alone demanded a very considerable sale of the work to defray their cost. It is however, hoped that they form no inconsiderable feature in a book, which, by their aid, and on account of the information it contains, may almost be termed a manual for English travellers in France.[1]

Each of Bonner's small, neat vignettes of Parisian topography referred to the text on the same page. However, since Bonner had died the previous year and as the cuts did not accompany Crowquill's and Phillips' etchings until the second number, it is probable that Reynolds followed on their subject matter rather than the reverse. However, the high standard of illustration through specially commissioned etchings was maintained in Reynolds' other Dickens' plagiarism, Master Timothy's Book-Case, which came out in 1842.

The sophistication of Reynolds' work, compared with Lloyd's publications, becomes evident, as Margaret Dalziel has pointed out,[2] when he began to write for a truly popular market in the penny numbers of the London Journal, which began in 1846. He was asked to edit it by its proprietor, George Stiff, an engraver who had been sacked from the Illustrated London News. It is probable that Reynolds' connections gained for the paper its French translations

---

1. G.W.M. Reynolds, 'To the Reader', Pickwick Abroad (1837). p.6.
2. M. Dalziel, op.cit., pp.35-45.

and Parisian publisher, Galignani, as well as George Vickers in London; thus, the blocks were probably stereotyped. Certainly, they were of a high standard. Besides the engravings by Stiff himself, the paper contained Reynolds' serial entitled 'Faust', which was illustrated by Henry Anelay and John Gilbert, both of whom worked on the Illustrated London News.[1] Furthermore, when Reynolds quarrelled with Stiff and started his own Reynolds's Magazine of Romance, General Literature, Science and Art (Reynolds's Miscellany from the fifth number, 5 December 1846), Anelay portrayed him as the editor and proprietor on the first page (7 November 1846), as well as designing the engravings for his serial, 'Wagner: the Wehr-Wolf'. If any publication epitomizes these changes, it is Reynolds' Mysteries of London, a rather daringly sensuous and bloodthirsty serial copied from Eugene Sue's feuilletons, published by Vickers, which sold nearly 40,000 copies a week. At first, George Stiff designed and executed the sometimes titillating illustrations. They still retained the theatricality of pose and stiffness of line of a Lloyd penny dreadful, but occasionally, drapery and foliage were treated with a looser hatching technique. When Anelay began to make some of the designs, he introduced an altogether livelier style, more certain proportions and a handling of texture which echoed that of his more talented fellow illustrator, John Gilbert. Throughout 1847 and 1848, this metamorphosis from the 'cut' to the 'sketch' continued, and when Thomas Miller took over the serial in 1849, William Gorway's designs, engraved by Henry White, had the appearance of a pen and ink line and wash, and could be favourably compared with the best work on the Illustrated London News and Punch.

1. See below pp.306-7.

In contrast, the efforts Lloyd made in this direction were backward-looking. Unlike Reynolds, who was willing to use his portrait to publicize his products, Lloyd later tried to suppress his early efforts.[1] In 1846, after issuing several unillustrated penny miscellanies of fiction and general interest,[2] the fourth number of the People's Periodical and Family Library (21 October 1846) appeared illustrated. The first serial to be so treated, called 'Ross Sommerville', is probably the first of Lloyd's publications to make use of the progressive, looser and finer style of wood engraving. Though far from skilful, the characters and poses thus executed were far more convincing than the stiff cuts he had used previously, and there was some attempt to suggest texture in the line and shading. However, this did not last. The second serial, entitled, 'The Dream of Life. A Romance', which began on 13 February 1837., reverted to a rougher drawing technique and a far coarser style of hatching. Probably, Lloyd's attempts to cut corners in the cost of printing extended to the treatment of his contributors, both in writing and illustration. But they also stigmatized his publications as being out of date. By 1850, the Catnach broadsides, the cuts of Grant and the

1. Medcraft, op.cit.

2. For example, Lloyd's Penny Weekly Miscellany (1843-46), Lloyd's Penny Atlas and Weekly Register of Novel Entertainment (1843-5), Lloyd's Entertaining Journal (1844-7), Lloyd's Weekly Volume of Amusing and Instructive Literature (1845-7).
All were produced after Lloyd had moved to new premises in Salisbury Square, Fleet Street from Shoreditch, and had two new presses. See Todd, op.cit., p.120.

Lloyd penny dreadfuls, as Mayhew found when he talked to the costermongers,[1] had had their day.

The title of Lloyd's last-named publication is symptomatic of a strain which had begun to make itself felt in the field of cheap publishing since George Biggs had introduced his Family Herald in 1842.[2] This was aimed to provide reading matter for the whole family; its keynote was domesticity. It provoked many imitations, some of which were illustrated with crochet and knitting patterns, as well as chess problems.[3] In 1845 Linton commenced the Illustrated Family Journal, price twopence which promised 'historical romances, legendary tales, poetry, essays, anecdotes', as well as original designs by himself, Kenny Meadows and others. The masthead incorporated the design of paterfamilias reading aloud to his wife, busy sewing, surrounded by children. Indeed this motif can be said to be the emblem of the family periodical of the 1840s and 1850s, as much as the printing press was for the radical publications

1. Mayhew, op.cit., i. 25-26: '"They've got tired of Lloyd's bloodstained stories", said one man, who was in the habit of reading to them, "and I'm satisfied that, of all London, Reynolds is the most popular man among them".' Also, 'The First Style of Art', Puppet Show, i (1848), 14:
   Our attention has been called to the fact that whenever one of Lloyd's novels for the billion is advertised it is sure to be "embellished in the first style of art". At first thought one would imagine that to the advertisers truth was "strange- far stranger than fiction"; but the statement is, nevertheless, perfectly correct, for the first, or primitive, style of art was such, that it was necessary to write "this is a cow", "this is a horse", underneath the representations of those animals.

2. James, op.cit., pp.39-40.

3. For women's periodicals of this decade see C. L. White, Women's Magazines 1693-1968 (1970), pp.41-46.

of the 1820s and 1830s.[1] The magazine included some small vignettes of country churches, studies of birds and plants and illustrated poetry by Longfellow, Ebenezer Elliott and others. Some of these have a definite German flavour, such as the design by William Bell Scott which illuminated Longfellow's poem, 'Excelsior'.[2] Furthermore, Linton adopted a Nazarene, linear style to illustrate such medieval romances as 'Claudius and Gertrude' and 'Philippo and Bruno.'[3] However, such subtleties appear to have been lost on the audience; the magazine failed after four months leaving behind a trail of debts.[4] This did not seem to deter Linton from getting involved in the production of the People's Journal, a magazine edited by John Saunders. The aim of the publication was to combine amusement, general literature and instruction with 'an earnest and business-like inquiry into the best means of satisfying the claims of industry', in order to be 'an efficient helpmate to the Working Man.'

1. See also, for example, the frontispiece to the Family Circle (1849), designed by William Harvey and engraved by C. Branston, and that by John Gilbert to Leisure Hour (1852), engraved by C.P. Nicholls, on the same theme. Compare with those to the Ragged School Union Magazine, from 1850 to 1853, in which the role of protector of children is taken by the teacher, or Christ Himself.
For an account of the allowance made by the most important 'select' circulating library of the period in order to cater for a family audience see G.L. Griest, Mudie's Circulating Library and the Victorian Novel (Newton Abbot, 1970), pp.32-33, 137-40.

2. Illustrated Family Journal, No.2, 15 March 1845, p.24. Although he did not visit Munich until 1854, Scott was familiar with German art through engravings, and the work of his brother, David and friend Thomas Sibson, both of whom had been with the Nazarenes in Rome. Autobiographical Notes of the Life of William Bell Scott, ed. W. Minto (1892), i. 153-6, 214-7, 317-20.
Other possible sources of the increasing German influence in English illustration are James Burns's 'Fireside Library', a series of cheap illustrated works published in the early 1840s as vehicles for his Germanic taste. S.C. Hall's The Book of British Ballads (1842) was dedicated to the King of Bavaria and many of the illustrations are suggested by the works of German artists.

3. Ibid., No.16, 21 June 1845, p.241; No.19, 12 July 1845, p.289. See also, the illustrations to 'The Nun of Leicester', No.7, 19 April 1845, 102-3.

4. See above p.36. When Palmer wrote to Linton in 1848, the latter still appeared to owe him nearly £150 in connection with the periodical.

It intended to do this by reporting on the state of philanthropic societies of every type, inquiring into domestic management, providing an almanac and a calendar, reviewing new books, plays and exhibitions; in sum, providing matter to 'vivify, elevate, and spiritualize' life.[1] Linton also hoped to make it the organ of European and American liberal movements through a network of foreign correspondents. However, except for an important article entitled, 'Thoughts upon Democracy in Europe', contributed by Mazzini, Linton's hopes proved over-sanguine. One of the proprietors, William Howitt, withdrew at the end of 1846 and although Linton persisted for over a year after this, the magazine was a failure.[2] Nevertheless, it did fulfil its promise to offer illustrations of quality, rather than quantity. Linton interpreted paintings for the series 'People's Picture Gallery', while 'The People's Portrait Gallery' included Dickens, Wordsworth, Southwood Smith, Harriet Martineau and Leigh Hunt. 'Scenes from Society' were drawn by Kenny Meadows to a commentary by Angus Reach. Thus Reynolds' and Linton's cheap publications, employing as they did the staff of both Punch and the Illustrated London News, effectively swamped the old styles and accustomed the lower classes to expect from their reading matter far more sophisticated illustrations than Catnach or Lloyd were prepared to offer. In the mid 1840 s, the Penny Magazine died and the illustrations to the Art-Union were only just getting under way, yet the pace and the standards they set pervaded the whole atmosphere of graphic journalism. The age of the sectionally motivated amateur was dead.

---

1. People's Journal, No. 1, 3 January 1846, pp. 1-2.
2. Smith, op.cit., Feltrinelli, Linton. Scott wrote to Linton on 14 December 1847 asking how he was getting on with the People's Journal, 'I am told there has been a meeting of creditors and that Howitt has been made liable for a swinging sum ...'

Leech's depiction of the working class family sitting down to its police gazette was by 1850 little more than a caricature. It contained a kernel of truth, but by the middle of the century, the diet of popular reading matter was much more varied than Leech's cartoon would suggest. In addition, the lower classes enjoyed access to much more sophisticated forms of illustration than had previously been the case, and furthermore, it was applied to material they enjoyed, namely fiction. Dickens' success in the mid 1830 s came at exactly the right time so far as the publishers of cheap fiction were concerned. Plagiarisms of his work provided the shot in the arm of penny fiction which hitherto had repeated itself ad nauseam in the face of the enforced absence of penny politics and ever-changing, topical news items. However, they provoked new fears on the part of the middle classes. Perhaps the most hysterical attack was launched by Hepworth Dixon in the Daily News of 1847, on the 'viciousness' of Lloyd's and Reynolds' publications.[1] Yet even he granted the possibility of a glimmer of hope:

> Even the poor and ignorant would not prefer the literature of Salisbury-square and Holywell-street to that of Paternoster-row and Fleet-street, if they could procure the latter, and had the elementary education necessary to enable them to understand and enjoy it.

Furthermore, he did allow there to be a 'perceptible improvement' and some 'contact with moralities' in the London Pioneer, the London Journal and Family Herald.[2] To some extent, the image of the respectable paterfamilias reading aloud to his adoring family was replacing Leech's more cynical view. If in some ways this chapter appears to be more concerned with the background development of journalistic trends, rather than the foreground spotlight on graphic journalism, this is because the multiplying options both set

---

1. (H. Dixon), 'The Literature of the Lower Orders', Daily News, 26 October, 2 November 1847.

2. Ibid., 9 November 1847.

constraints and provided scope for new types of illustrated journalism. Against a backcloth of reaction against any suspicion of immorality, there developed journals of a more generalized family appeal, with fun rather than wit, travels abroad rather than troubles at home. The following chapters are concerned with exploring these areas more fully: the role filled by the humorous magazine and that of the news journal, both of which transported illustration into new fields of progress.

PUNCH AND ITS RIVALS

1841 - 1850

VI

It is the destiny of the artist, as well as the author, who labours principally for the Art, or Literature, of the existing moment, to labour - chiefly - in vain. The interest of to-day will be pushed aside by the interest of the morrow; a new topic is continually taking the place of an old one - one whose age is four-and-twenty hours, or, at greatest, a week; and the eloquence of pen or pencil will be considered to have served its purpose if it has been a theme of talk and admiration from sunrise to sunset of a whole day. It is notorious that some of the grandest and most beneficial productions of mind have been born to die in the columns of a daily newspaper; and it is not too much to say that, of late years, some of the finest efforts of genius have made their entrances and exits with the ephemera they were created to illustrate.[1]

The Art-Union thus recognized with regret the ambivalent status of the graphic artist, as well as the journalist, in the mid 1840's. On the one hand, it was clear that such an artist was no longer producing libellous caricatures, nor needed to be bribed into silence. On the other, he was not exactly representing the permanent and lasting qualities to be found in high art and great literature. It is the contention of this chapter that Punch gradually consolidated a middle path for humorous illustrated journalism throughout the decade. First, it examines how Punch obtained a stability of organization altogether lacking in its rivals. Secondly, its staff and policy ensured that its content lay somewhere between elevated moral lessons and scurrilous squibs. Finally, this role is emphasized by a comparison with other humorous magazines of the decade which never obtained this stability of organization and tone.

---

1. 'Shakespeare. The Illustrations by Kenny Meadows. Introductory Remarks', Art-Union, vii (1845), 165.

I

> With the publication of 'Punch', commenced a new era for caricature. Novelties came so rapidly and in such profusion that it left the old school of satirical artists nothing to do. Society found itself illustrated to the fullest possible extent. It cared not for entertainment on a larger scale, and the caricature-shops died a natural death.[1]

The relentless regularity of Punch's weekly issue, compared with its predecessors, was much remarked upon towards the end of the first decade of its existence. The London Journal in 1847 believed that John Doyle's day had passed. The rapidity of production which was associated with such a publication as Punch and its many imitators had literally 'cut out' the H.B. Sketches.[2] Instead of a batch of drawings published at irregular intervals during the parliamentary session, each week Punch's 'big cut' commented on the political scene of the moment. As one writer at the turn of the century perceived, this task was comparatively easy when there were no penny papers and the electric telegraph was in its infancy. News travelled slowly 'and the interval of a week was, in respect of news, equivalent to the space of time between night and morning as it is counted now'.[3] Nevertheless, within this week Punch had to rely on an infallible organization which would not, and did not break down.

It is clear that Punch would have gone the way of all of its predecessors and most of its rivals were it not for the support of Bradbury and Evans, first its printers and then its proprietors. They, more than anyone, virtually fulfilled Vizetelly's dream of 'the philanthropic capitalist with funds for all manner of journalistic enterprises, and a

---

1. Berkeley, op.cit., iv. 141.
2. 'George Cruikshank', London Journal, vi (1847), 178.
3. H. W. Lucy, Sixty Years in the Wilderness (1909), p.373.

sneaking desire to acquire social standing through a connection with the press.'[1] However, Punch's beginnings did not seem any more auspicious or less seedy than the circumstances surrounding the false starts and vague suggestions made by individual members of the original personnel during the latter part of the 1830s.[2] Many had worked together on George Cruikshank's Comic Almanac (1835-53): Thackeray, à Beckett, the Mayhew brothers Henry and Horace, Robert Brough and Albert Smith. Most had frequented the Mulberries Club, held in the Wrekin tavern, Broad Court, Drury Lane.[3] Later, they patronized the Shakespeare's Head in Wych Street, where Mark Lemon was manager briefly,[4] and during the time of the preliminary proposals, the Edinburgh Castle gin palace in the Strand and an upper room in the Crown, Vinegar Yard. So although the contracts were drawn up in a solicitor's office, as Mayhew's son puts it, without such habitats 'there would have been no Punch, for it was from these three hostelries the first literary staff... was recruited'.[5]

The original idea would seem to have come collectively from Henry Mayhew, Joseph William Last, the printer, and Ebenezer Landells, the engraver, who had been working together on the Cosmorana, and also on Nicholson's Town. Last, in Crane Court, though apparently an excellent printer and an unflagging worker, possessed a 'mercurial' temperament and was already fairly notorious for starting up periodicals which folded

---

1. Vizetelly, op.cit., i. 166.
2. Ibid. Also, W. Jerrold, Douglas Jerrold and 'Punch' (1910), p.10. A. A. Adrian, Mark Lemon First Editor of Punch (1966), p.29.
3. Scott and Howard, op.cit., i. 60-64. A. Mayhew, op.cit., pp.27-36.
4. Ibid., pp.58-60, 94-96.
5. Ibid., p.93. R.G.G. Price, A History of Punch (1967), pp.44-45.

a few weeks later.[1] Landells, perhaps with greater claim to be its originator, contributed £25 capital and spent £111 12s on advertising. In his house at 22 Bidborough Street, St. Pancras, he already had a staff of engravers - Birket Foster, Edmund Evans, J. Greenaway and William Galter - and could call upon the Dalziels, Armstrong and Charles Gorway to act as outworkers.[2] Mayhew, not on good terms with his family, was at this point living with a fellow journalist, R. B. Postans, above a haberdasher's shop in Hemming's Row, a dingy little thoroughfare adjacent to Leicester Square at the back of St. Martin's workhouse. He got together most of the staff, writing to Jerrold in Boulogne, and to Lemon, who was also at the seaside, with the dubiously accurate line of 'come to town - here's a man with a notion for a comic paper and he has £2000 to lose'.[3]

The initial agreement settled that the proprietors were to be Last, Landells and the third share to be divided equally among the three editors, Mayhew, Lemon and Stirling Coyne. The prospectus announced that the new work would cost threepence and the first number appeared on 17 July 1841. Byrant, the publisher at 13 Wellington Street, Strand ordered a reprint making the first sale 10,000 copies, but after this initial success, the circulation did not rise above 5-6,000 copies, which resulted in a loss.

---

1. A. Mayhew, op.cit, pp.89-91. The Real Life in London and Comic Times indicted Last for using the name of a famous prize-fighter, Tom Spring, in the title of a 'Life in London' periodical, without obtaining the fighter's permission. On 23 August 1840, it dubbed Last 'Printer, Puffer and Publisher of rubbish in general, and vendor of offal in particular', and listed nearly a dozen of his publications which had failed.

2. Spielmann, op.cit., pp.15-16.

3. A. Mayhew, op.cit., pp.49-55. R. B. Postans, 'The Origin of "Punch"', Notes and Queries, 7th series, vii (1889), 401-2. Silver diary, 7 March 1866.

Lemon sold a two-act drama 'The Silver Thimble', to the Strand Theatre for £30 to enable the third number to go to press, and repeated the gesture with his farce 'Punch' a few months later. Leech's first large drawing, 'FOREIGN AFFAIRS', arrived late for the fourth number; publication had to be deferred for a day while it was engraved by the Dalziels, and circulation dropped drastically.[1] In the second half of 1842, there were virtually no large cuts, a sure sign that costs were outweighing profits. Finally, after the printer had lost £600, the only hope seemed to lie in finding a financial backer. Bradbury and Evans eventually took over the printing after Last had sold his share in the proprietorship to Landells. At the end of 1842, following protracted negotiations between Bradbury and Evans and the remaining owners, they bought out Landells for £350 and become sole proprietors.[2]

The expansion of the firm of Bradbury and Evans would seem to follow the typical pattern of a Victorian business success story. William Bradbury came from Bakewell, Derbyshire, and after living in Lincoln, came to London in 1824 and set himself up as a printer in partnership with William Dent, his brother-in-law, at 76 Fleet Street.[3] During the remainder

---

1. See Harvey, op.cit., pp.189-90 for Leech's delay over the illustrations for Surtees' novels at the end of his career.

2. The clearest analysis of the conflicting accounts of Punch's early history is given in Appendix 3 to Price, op.cit., pp.353-5. Also, J. Hatton, 'The True Story of Punch', London Society, xxviii (1875), 49-56, 152-61, 237-46. Spielmann, op.cit., pp.10-35. Silver diary, 15 February, 1860, 30 July 1862, 7 March 1866. Punch offices: Schedule of deeds and documents contained in the deed box, Bundle No.7.

3. 'Some London Printing Offices, No.5 - Bradbury, Agnew & Co.', London, Provincial & Colonial Press News, xix (1884), 27-29. 'Mr. Punch at Dinner. Centenary of a Famous Printery', 'British & Colonial Printer and Stationer, lxcviii (1926), 63.

of the decade, the firm acquired another partner, Manning, and made a series of moves in Fleet Street, Warwick Lane and Bouverie Street. This partnership was dissolved and in 1830, Frederick Mullet Evans, who had been a printer in Southampton, joined the firm, replacing Bradbury's previous partners. This partnership of William Bradbury, described in Spielmann's History of Punch as 'the keenest man of business that ever trod the flags of Fleet Street',[1] with 'Pater' Evans lasted over forty years. In July 1833, they gave notice of their removal from Bouverie Street to the premises formerly occupied by the late Thomas Davison in Lombard Street, Whitefriars. Davison's business had been renowned for the high standard of its work, printing the poems of Byron and Samuel Rogers. However, Davison had stuck to hand machines. The Bradbury and Evans business, at first still largely of a 'jobbing' character, announced the erection of a 'Printing Machine, of the largest size, best construction, and with all the most recent improvements' and that they would be glad to undertake the management of a newspaper, or periodical, requiring 'regularity and dispatch'. Their first volume was a law book, undertaken for an old friend of Bradbury's, Alexander Maxwell, the law booksellers of Bell Yard, who continued during the 1830s to be one of their regular customers. By 1835, their annual wage bill was well over £6,000. They were undertaking work for other printers, from Cleave to Chapman and Hall and William Clowes. However, undoubtedly their largest source of income came from W.S. Orr, the London agent for Chambers' publications. Bills for

1. Spielmann, op.cit., p.36.

reprinting the Journal and Cyclopaedia rose from around £1,400 in 1833 to over £6,000 in 1835.[1] It is probably this debt which enabled Bradbury and Evans to arrange for Punch's national circulation to be on a sale or return basis through Orr's organisation. Vizetelly believed that for a time Punch's survival owed more to his efforts than to Jerrold's pen or to Leech's pencil.[2] Unfortunately, owing to the disappearance of the ledgers relating to Punch, it is not possible to assess the exact financial state of the periodical, nor the growth of its circulation during the 1840s. In 1845, the London Journal reported that it had reached 40,000 copies.[3] Furthermore, despite some financial set-back with the ill-fated Daily News in 1846,[4] Bradbury and Evans were printing the whole of the literary output of Dickens, Thackeray, Jerrold and other Punch contributors,[5] as well as works on the fine arts and law reports. They expanded steadily down Bouverie Street and Lombard Street, as well as acquiring a Punch office in Fleet Street.[6] It became necessary to fit up a special room for the printing of Punch as it grew.[7] Thus, as

1. Punch offices: General Ledger, 1830-35.

2. Punch offices: Vizetelly to Spielmann, 26 July 1892.

3. 'The Newspaper and Periodical Press of London', London Journal, i (1845), 407. Hansard, 3rd series, 1855, cxxxvii. 781 quotes the same figure.

4. Vizetelly, op.cit., p.248.

5. The records relating to Dickens' publications are in the Victoria and Albert Museum, Forster collection; those for Jerrold's and Thackeray's in Punch offices.

6. Todd, op.cit., p.23. Punch offices: Schedule, Bundle Nos.2 and 3.

7. 'Incidents of My Life!, London, Provincial & Colonial Press News, xxi (1886), 18.

in Swain's wood engraving establishment, the growing organisation and division of labour eventually distanced the editorial staff somewhat from the production of the periodical.[1]

However, accounts of the internal organization of Punch during the 1840s reveal that there was still a good deal of common ground. Mark Lemon, the first editor after the Bradbury and Evans take-over, received a salary of thirty shillings a week. He was responsible for organizing and administering the practical make-up of the paper. He managed the copy, arranged the series, dealt with outside applications and visited the artists who produced the illustrations, helped at first by Horace Mayhew as sub-editor. He believed in letting each man write what he chose, so long as he wrote economically and got his contributions in early.[2] On Friday evening, he corrected what was necessary and passed it on to the printers. Meanwhile, the big cut, the subject of which had been decided upon at the weekly dinner, was drawn on one block of wood to be engraved by Swain and his workers in time for the print-off on Monday morning. Saturday was the busiest day in Whitefriars for the proofs were finally checked by two in the afternoon and the publication made up for the press; the printing at machine commenced very early on Monday morning. A few of the staff always came up to the printing office, Lemon being greeted 'with a cheer and a most cordial reception'. Mayhew fiddled clumsily with the compositors' boxes and Jerrold, somewhat more expertly, corrected his own proofs. The copy, the head printer recalled, varied from Lemon's fair readable hand to Jerrold's microscopic script and à Beckett's oblique scrawl.[3]

---

1. See above p.70.

2. Spielmann, op.cit., pp.254-7. Adrian, op.cit., pp.48-49.

3. 'Incidents of My Life', pp.17-19. Spielmann, op.cit., pp.249-53. W. P. Frith, John Leech: his Life and Work (1891), ii. 33-34.

In the evening there was a dinner in one of the Covent Garden or Bouverie Street hotels, or by the river in summer.

The closeness of the editorial staff to the proprietors is underlined by the many letters, still in the Punch offices, begging Bradbury, or more usually 'Pater' Evans, to lend them money on account. Once his father had stopped managing his affairs, Richard Doyle was particularly bothersome, asking frequently for loans even when he knew his work was late.[1] Leech too seems to have been hard pressed: 'Will it be possible without "breaking the Bank" for you to let me have twenty pounds on account of the Pocket Book ... p.s. I have just brought more drawings!!' Again: 'My dear B & E - a trifling monetary obligation - in fact (as Mr. Micawber would say) an acceptance, of mine has to be arranged tomorrow - Can you let me have £40 without inconvenience, or interfering with my salary'.[2] A Beckett adopted a more responsible tone, at one time mentioning the heavy demands being made upon him on account of his brother's business in the North being wound up, and on another, because he wanted to take out some life insurance before the premium went up on his birthday: 'As I know you have an objection to make advances on work not actually done I would suggest that unless I place in your hands before a certain day ... the prize comedies complete the whole of my Punch money should be stopped

---

1. One undated, but obviously early letter from Doyle to his employers reads:-
   My object in calling yesterday was ... partly to hand you the enclosed account which I have made up by my Father's directions, as nearly as I was able at the same scale of prices as in the former settlement. My Father observed upon looking over it, that he would not say that I had made the most accurate estimate in detail, but that he thought the total was not too much.
   H.B. was none too keen on his son's attendance at the Punch dinner table. Spielmann, op.cit., p.455. This does not seem too surprising in view of what appears to be the financial chaos exposed in his letters to Evans. A typical specimen starts, 'I am sorry to make a financial request so soon again, but I must ask you to allow me to draw upon my new work for 50 pounds more ...'

2. Leech was apparently not only a very generous man but had a difficult father to support. Frith, op.cit., i. 92-93. Hodder, op.cit., pp.81-88.

to repay you the advance I am now asking for'.[1] Lemon asked for money, and Vizetelly rather maliciously told Spielmann that Jerrold only recommended to Vizetelly that Lemon should be drama critic of the new *Pictorial Times*, 'not because he thought him a competent critic but the rather to put two or three guineas a week into Lemon's pocket and secure his good offices when he (Jerrold) made one of his constant applications for an increase in salary to the proprietors of "Punch"'.[2]

Thus it seems the case that all of the *Punch* staff relied on Bradbury and Evans as a never-failing kitty whenever their own financial affairs became too precarious. Bradbury and Evans not only saw the paper through to a stability of issue, but also to a stability of content by ensuring that the major contributors did not spend their time in and out of bankruptcy courts and debtors' prisons as they had done in the previous decade. The staff, for their part, were now all in their thirties and had their own families to support; they could not afford to run the hand-to-mouth existence of their youth. It is significant that the only member of the *Punch* crowd to be declared bankrupt in the decade of the 1840s was Henry Mayhew, who had left the paper before 1845. Vizetelly, wrote that he was careless in money matters, 'was a persistent borrower but made it a point of honour never to repay a loan'.[3] Although he made a considerable

---

1. *Punch* offices.

2. *Punch* offices: Vizetelly to Spielmann, 26 July 1892.

3. *Ibid*. Mayhew's bankruptcy case, reported in *The Times*, 12 February 1847, reveals that he was over £2,000 in debt. He had earned £300 in 1844 and again in 1845. In 1846, he had received from Bradbury and Evans for his work on *Punch* £200, with an extra £50 for the Almanack and Pocket Book. He had left them, however, in May 1846 and now claimed a further £200 was owing from them, as he believed it was the custom to give a year's notice of severing the connection. He also claimed £200 from Mark Lemon, 'in consequence of an agreement entered into ten years ago, which was now disputed. He had not pressed the claim before, being in the habit of meeting Mr. Mark Lemon daily and not liking to raise a question of money, which might cause a rupture'. The money claimed was for joint dramatic productions.

sum from his writings, he never seemed to have a shilling. Most of his letters were from creditors, but he handed them all over to his wife to deal with, which she did, presumably rather inefficiently.

II

Charles Knight believed, with others, that if it had not been for the weekly Punch dinner, which preserved the magazine's vitality and unity of tone by the interchange of thought between writers and artists, it might have degenerated into a vehicle for random caricatures and miscellaneous jokes.[1] Henry Silver, however, heard over twenty years later, that at the early dinners, 'rows were generally the order of the night... The new number used at one time to be handed round at the meeting and endless squabbles arose therefrom - every writer finding fault with every article inserted in preference to his own'.[2] In its early issues, Punch may have successfully obtained regularity of issue, but owing to the variety of its contributors, it took longer to establish a unity of tone.

First and foremost, there were political differences; to complicate matters, there were personal and social rifts. The greatest political breach existed between Jerrold and Thackeray, and until quite late in the 1840s, Jerrold was the more prominent contributor. Silver noted that his 'Q Papers' had a marked success and influence, and that the Caudle Lectures (1845) decidedly raised the circulation.[3] Thackeray, by comparison was only half-hearted in his participation at first. He began to write in June 1842, against the advice of Edward Fitzgerald who urged a common friend, 'Tell Thackeray not to go to Punch yet'.[4] He expressed his own ambivalence

---

1. Knight, Passages of a Working Life, iii. 269. Also, Spielmann, op.cit., pp. 53-58. The practice of having a regular staff dinner was not confined to Punch. See J. Gross, The Rise and Fall of the Man of Letters (1969), pp.10-11, 16.

2. Silver diary, 23 July 1862.

3. Ibid.

4. Spielmann, op.cit., p.308.

in a letter to his mother on 11 June; Punch, he thought, was 'a very low paper... only its very good pay, and a great opportunity for unrestrained laughing sneering kicking and gambadoing'.[1] He felt rather diffident about his early efforts,[2] and it was not until 1844 when Albert Smith left, that Thackeray established a firm connection through his articles signed 'Our Fat Contributor', and the series entitled 'Jeames's Diary' and 'The Snobs of England'. They reveal his willingness to attack snobbery and privilege at the same time as his essential indifference to social reform, his dislike of personal attacks and the radical view of politics. This set him at odds with Jerrold, who, fulfilling his early promise, as diagnosed by the Poor Man's Guardian when it examined his Punch in London,[3] still wrote on the side of progress and reform. He took the side of the poor and the weak, writing as a moralist and a censor, rather than as a political journalist taking a broader view.[4] According to Thackeray's biographer, it was precisely this lack of balance which Thackeray disliked and mocked. In one of his papers 'On Clerical Snobs', he hinted that among 'those eminent philosophers who cry out against parsons the loudest, there are not many who have got their knowledge of the church by going thither often'.[5] This uneasy relationship continued, the tension no doubt heightened by personal remarks of the nature of Thackeray's jibe that Jerrold was not

1. Ray, op.cit., ii. 54.
2. Spielmann, op.cit., p.310.
3. See above p.85.
4. W. B. Jerrold, The Life and Remains of Douglas Jerrold (1859), pp.191-224.
   W. Jerrold, op.cit., pp.43-68.
5. G. N. Ray, Thackeray The Uses of Adversity (1955), pp.370-3.

fit company as he ate his peas with a knife.[1] Jerrold, for his part, found Thackeray, 'uncertain. Today he is all sunshine, tomorrow he is all frost and snow', and when he was advised to get Thackeray's help in the 1850s to be elected to the Garrick Club, retorted that though they were very good friends, 'our friend T. is a man so full of crotchets, that, as favour, I would hardly ask him to pass me the salt'.[2]

If Jerrold and Thackeray represented the two opposite extremes of the Punch political viewpoint, the other contributors grouped round them. Lemon was neutral with a tendency towards radicalism. It was he who stood up for Hood's 'Song of the Shirt' when the rest of the staff objected to its publication. He wrote the leaders on 'The Pauper's Christmas Carol', (23 December 1843), 'Substance and Shadow' (13 July 1843) and 'Famine and Fashion' (4 November 1843). Like Jerrold, he was somewhat wary of Thackeray, never feeling quite at home with him. He said, 'he was always so infernally wise. He was genial; but whatever you talked about, you felt he would have the wisest views upon the subject. He seemed too great for ordinary conversation.'[3] Some of the more prejudiced spectators of the Punch team give an unfavourable impression of Lemon. Sala found him unctuous.[4] Vizetelly said that he owed everything to his position on Punch, and that most of his confrères openly expressed a very poor opinion of his abilities. Jerrold, Thackeray and Tom Taylor occasionally spoke most contemptuously of him, while Mayhew felt

1. Adrian, op.cit., p.37.
2. C. Mackay, Forty Years Recollections (1877), ii.284-8.
3. Adrian, op.cit., p.38
4. Sala, Things I have Seen, i. 62-63.

he had been unfairly ousted from the editorship by him.[1] Vizetelly, never one to mince his words, added that he never heard Lemon say a smart thing and his jokes did not extend beyond a feeble pun. His manners too were vulgar:

> partaking of the Wych Street Shakespeare's Head, until his constant consorting with men of a superior social stamp improved them somewhat. He was a great swiller of strong liquor, was brusque and obsequious by turns according to the social status of the individual he had to do with.[2]

A change in the manner of Gilbert à Beckett was also noted since the days when he wrote the copy for Figaro in London locked up with a gin bottle.[3] His son describes him as neutral politically, especially after he had been appointed a Metropolitan Police Magistrate at the age of thirty-eight, with a tendency to follow the politics of The Times, for which he wrote leaders. He sobered down, having outgrown his 'journalistic wild oats', and like Thackeray believed that Punch could be comic without descending to the level of the pawn-shop and public house.[4] Other staff changes bear witness to the continuous sifting process which took place to obtain some unanimity of social standpoint. Albert Smith was a part time dental surgeon who lived in Percival Street, Tottenham Court Road, and had spent his youth carousing with Percival Leigh and John Leech, both fellow students. Smith, however, seems to have lacked something of Leech's breeding and Leigh's scholarship although he was a

---

1. Punch offices: Vizetelly to Spielmann, 26 July 1892. Also, A. Mayhew, op.cit., pp.124-5.

2. Punch offices: Vizetelly to Spielmann, 26 July 1892. A more flattering picture of Lemon is given in J. Hatton, With a Show in the North (1871), although Vizetelly remarked spitefully that Hatton 'as a young man no doubt toaded Lemon'.

3. See above p.83.

4. A Beckett, op.cit., p.88. Also, Punch offices: A. W. à Beckett to Spielmann 3 June 1895.

reliable enough contributor to Punch. He liked to talk about fast life in London, the charms of ballet girls and the humours of medical students. Vizetelly again seems to have taken a dislike to him for he describes him as 'vulgar and bumptious in manner' until he became polished by consorting with swells after the success of his entertainments in the 1850's. He always had a keen eye for the main chance and never neglected any opportunity for self-advertisement. Thackeray and Jerrold detested him, the latter openly showing it by making him the butt of many of his rather cruel jokes.[1] He eventually got the sack, perhaps because of his meanness or other undesirable qualities, perhaps for plagiarism, perhaps because of his habit of showing his copy round the Cheshire Cheese before it went to press.[2]

The make-up of the artistic staff reveals a similar consolidation in the direction of respectability. The artists whom Landells had recruited, and who had worked on such publications as the Town or the Odd Fellow, were swiftly dispatched. William Newman, probably the most important until eclipsed by Leech, had drawn for Figaro in London after Seymour's death and had contributed to the Odd Fellow, but, according to Spielmann, owing to his lack of breeding and common manners, he was never invited to the weekly dinner, nor did his colleagues care to associate with him. He was a prolific worker and was responsible for most of the punning 'blackies' in the first numbers, for which he was paid eighteen shillings a dozen.[3] Brine and John

---

1. Punch offices: Vizetelly to Spielmann, 26 July 1892. Again to be tempered with the more favourable description of Smith in E. Yates, Recollections and Experiences (1884), i. 224-44.

2. Spielmann, op.cit., pp.303-6. Silver diary, 28 June 1860. A Beckett, op.cit., pp.256-61, who found these reasons a little absurd. Plagiarism was not thought to be a particularly grave crime and Smith was on the best of terms with the Punch crowd in the 1850's, apart from Jerrold whose politics he disliked. See also, Punch offices: Silver to Spielmann, 11 November 1895, 'I wonder if Smith was knowingly a plagiarist'.

3. Spielmann, op.cit., pp.413-4.

Phillips, the latter a scene-painter, were poorly paid at three shillings and sixpence for a small cut; they were sacked by Bradbury and Evans. H.G. Hine, who specialized in grotesques, had little knowledge of drawing on wood and was principally a water colour artist. Archibald Henning, Kenny Meadows' brother-in-law, had been the illustrator of Nicholson's Town, on which Landells and Last had also worked. Again, according to Vizetelly, Henning was

> of somewhat dissipated habits and vulgar manners and kept low company and was looked down upon by the men with whom he was brought into accidental contact. He had not even a spark of ability to recommend him and was never admitted to the social gatherings at which his brother-in-law Meadows was received with open arms.[1]

Of their principal replacements, William Harvey had no sense of humour; Birket Foster, although taught by Landells to be a wood-engraver and helped by Brine and Crowquill, was not felt to be really suitable; nor was John Gilbert, of whom Jerrold said, 'We don't want a Rubens on Punch!'[2] Richard Doyle was only fifteen when he illustrated the 'Comic Histories' and required the chaperonage of his father to protect him from the trials of bills and the Punch dinner table. Once launched into his own sphere, the 'Manners and Customs of Ye Englishe' in 1849-50, he could not always be relied upon as a letter dated 9 March ?1851 to Bradbury and Evans reveals:

> He (Doyle) has signed a paper owning that he has been constantly late, that he has had many warnings from you, and 3 distinct ones from me, and acknowledging that at his first delay hereafter he puts himself out of our undertaking.[3]

Perhaps it was his failure to meet this promise rather than his dislike of the anti-Catholic attitude Punch adopted which was responsible for his departure from the paper.[4]

1. Punch offices: Vizetelly to Spielmann, 26 July 1892.
2. Spielmann, op.cit., pp.444-6, 450.
3. Punch offices.
4. Punch offices: W. Holman Hunt to Spielmann, 28 December 1891 put Doyle's departure down to religious differences.

John Leech's first large cut 'FOREIGN AFFAIRS' was also late for the fourth number, which appeared on 7 August 1841. Although he had a slight mechanical knowledge of drawing on wood from Orrin Smith and had received a few lessons in etching from George Cruikshank, Leech lacked an all-round artistic education. Nevertheless, after a sojourn in France, he did not owe much to his most famous predecessor, Robert Seymour, and professed to find him unfunny. There was little sympathy and less intimacy between him and Cruikshank; according to Frith, the extravagant caricature of the latter blinded Leech to his serious work. Cruikshank admitted that his work was clever, and of the new school, and the public always took to novelty.[1]

Leech's novelty lay in a combination of style and tone. Mayhew is said to have been responsible for insisting on one large cut per issue in Punch, as in the copies of the Parisian Charivari which he had seen. Landells, on the contrary, preferred lots of little cuts. However, it was only with Leech that these 'PUNCH'S PENCILLINGS' developed their full potential. The early numbers tended to be small drawings put together to fill the page, or one drawing blown up, with no sense of overall design. Leech, more than anyone, successfully introduced what amounted to a vignette approach, a large oval which focussed attention on the subject matter. Furthermore, it was he who popularized the half or quarter-page two-line caption joke which is now taken to represent archetypal Victorian humour, in his series 'THE RISING GENERATION' (1847), 'DOMESTIC BLISS' (1847) and 'FLUNKEIANA' (1848).[2] Although obviously derived from theatrical dialogue, the model was not present from the commencement of Punch. Its early volumes relied much more on the simple illustration or a word pun translated into visual terms.

1. Frith, op.cit., i. 76-77, 101-2; ii. 20, 224-6.
2. There were, however, odd examples of dialogue captions before this time, the first in Punch being a 'big cut' by Newman entitled 'JINKS TRYING HIS OWN COALS', Punch, ii (1842), 37.

Alfred Bunn was the first to direct what was to become a fairly frequent jibe at the paper, 'so thoroughly worn out is what little humour they once possessed, that your pages, PUNCH, are now sought after solely for their wood-cuts.'[1] The Man in the Moon published a cut entitled 'PUNCH'S LIFE BUOY', (DEDICATED WITHOUT PERMISSION TO MR.JOHN LEECH), which depicted Mr. Punch clinging to Leech's emblem, a leech in a bottle, on a stormy sea.[2] In 1854, Thackeray wrote:

> in Mr. Punch's cabinet John Leech is the right-hand man. Fancy a number of Punch without Leech's pictures! What would you give for it? The learned gentlemen who write the work must feel that, without him, it were as well left alone.[3]

The article, which appeared in the Quarterly Review, aroused some protest from Thackeray's former colleagues on Punch; yet in all of his lengthy apologies, Thackeray never once expressed doubt as to the justice of the statement, only regret as to his lack of tact for actually saying so in public.[4] Leech was perhaps Thackeray's closest friend on Punch; they both had experienced an early drop in social position and they both took care to recover it. He had developed his art under pressure of trying to maintain his former style of life and he too was conservative compared with Jerrold, 'and he had .... the greatest contempt for and detestation of the

---

1. A Word with Punch, 11 November 1847.

2. Man in the Moon, iii (1848), 256.

3. (W.M. Thackeray), 'Pictures of Life and Character', Quarterly Review, lxcvi (1854), 82.

4. To Percival Leigh he wrote:
    Of all the slips of my fatal pen, there's none I regret more than the unlucky ½ line wh has given pain to such a kind and valued old friend as you have been, and I trust will still be to me. I ought never to have said that 'Punch' might as well be left unwritten but for Leech - it was more than my meaning, wh is certainly that the drawing is 100 times more popular than the writing - but I had no business to write any such thing ....

    See also the letters he wrote to the Rev. Whitwell Elwin, Mrs.Carmichael-Smyth and G. Smith. Ray, Letters, iii. 413-8.

Chartists'.[1] He expressed a certain disdain for his art and once remarked to his hunting friend, Dean Hole, 'There is always a boy from the Punch office, diffusing an odour of damp corduroy through the house, and waiting for fresh supplies'.[2]

Leech was praised for the gentlemanlike point of view of his drawings and for their beauty. Dean Hole admired the 'exquisite delicacy of touch' in his drawings, their lack of exaggeration and caricature, 'How superior in the good taste which designed, as well as in their form of execution, to the coarse, personal, malignant caricatures of Gillray and Rowlandson, who put sharp stones in their snowballs, and shot with poisonous darts!'[3] For Dickens, Leech was the first to make beauty a part of his art.[4] Leech had done more than any man to refine a branch of art to which the facilities of steam printing and wood engraving were giving an almost unrivalled diffusion and popularity, one of his biographers wrote. Newspaper art was an utter novelty, 'and he gave to that novelty, the dignity, the grace, and the nameless attraction of genius'.[5] Millais stated before a Royal Commission that he thought Leech one of the greatest artists of the day.[6] Leech's career lasted from the days when he produced caricature lithographs in

---

1. Punch offices: Vizetelly to Spielmann, 26 July 1892.

2. Hole, op.cit., p.27.

3. Ibid., pp.28,56. Also, Mackay, Forty Years Recollections, ii. 302-4. Berkeley, op.cit., pp.141-3, who remembered those times in the stately homes of England when the weather was bad and the party bored:
   then the works of my departed friend (Leech) circulate from hand to hand, attracting round them groups of animated commentators, whose mirth makes the capacious chamber ring with the heartiness of their enjoyment.

4. C. Dickens, 'The Rising Generation', Examiner, 30 December 1848, p.838.

5. F.G. Kitton, John Leech. Artist and Humourist (1884), pp.32-33.

6. Parl. Papers 1863, xxvii (3205), p.186: Royal Academy Commission, minutes of evidence, qu.1676.

quod to those in the 1860s when all the first painters were taking to drawing on wood.[1] He, as much as anyone, contributed to its change in status.

Leech was not the only graphic artist to receive this sort of acclaim even in the 1840s. In 1845, the Art-Union commented upon the illustrations made by Kenny Meadows to Shakespeare. Meadows had first met Jerrold through his friend Laman Blanchard in 1828, and had produced the Heads of the People with him in 1840. He was a member of the Shakespeare and Mulberries clubs, enjoyed drinking and was always hard up.[2] He was fifty-one when he first worked for Punch, for which he produced good ideas, often of a phantasmagorical nature, not always particularly well drawn.[3] The Art-Union, which previously had praised his work on several occasions,[4] now sought to put his art in perspective, believing that men who adopted the humorous as a sort of 'profession' seldom obtained credit for thoughts loftier than those which humour suggested. Meadows' work was singled out from the ephemeral material in the rest of Punch, from the badinage of all sorts, which was beginning to dwindle into sarcasm and threatened to degenerate into slander:-

> Nearly every week (surrounded, it is true, by infinitely too much that degrades Art to the purpose of caricature, and renders personal the satire that should be only universal) we meet, in that widely popular publication, some "little bit" that merits

---

1. Silver diary, 1 February 1860. Frith, op.cit., pp.92-93. See above p.65.
2. Spielmann, op.cit., pp.446-9. Scott, op.cit., i. 113-5.
3. For example, 'THE WATER DROP' and 'THE GIN DROP' Punch, v (1843), 220-1. 'THE WATER THAT JOHN DRINKS', Punch, xvii (1849), 144-5. 'THE WONDERS OF A LONDON WATER DROP', Punch, xviii (1850), 188.
4. See, for example, Art-Union, i (1839), 32; iv (1842), 54; v (1843), 250.

immortality for the lesson it inculcates - of integrity, or sympathy, or duties even higher.[1]

Such a complex and pompous article can be unravelled to reveal what seems like a theory as to what humour should provide: first, like high art, it should have a moral lesson, and secondly, that it should never degenerate into the personal, the excessive, the slanderous attack. Exactly how this could be achieved was not stated, but Punch vigorously counter-attacked with a piece which sounds as if it comes straight from the pen of Jerrold:-

> It is true, Punch is sometimes personal. His dealings are, at times, with the knaves and simpletons of the world - the knaves and simpletons in chairs of authority - and, whenever truth calls for the right word, why, be it ever so hard a one, that word is administered. But the Art-Union has no such serious mission. The Art-Union is established as a twelvepenny temple, whereto men are invited that they may therein ponder on the beautiful; where there are no politics, no social iniquity, no want, no human suffering to ruffle and distress the prejudices and sympathies of the reader. In the Art-Union personality would, indeed, be a foul thing - a very toad in a porphyry temple. And therefore, even as the most delicate lady would avoid the aforesaid reptile, therefore is personality avoided by the Art-Union...[2]

In fact, the core of the argument was the problematic nature of humour in this period, what sort of content people wanted to find in a light illustrated periodical. Below the level of Punch lay the pits of libel and obscenity in caricature and satire. Above lay the elevating clouds of high art. Punch, in its radical attitudes and personal attacks from the Jerrold camp occasionally seemed rather closer to the former than the latter position. When Jerrold hit out against the Art-Union for its bland disregard of 'personality' and the feelings and sufferings of the people, he echoed what we have seen was the Art-Union's policy

1. Art-Union, vii (1845), 165-7.
2. Punch, viii (1845), 256.

on wood engraving: much talk of the improvement of mankind generally, but no sympathy whatsoever for the lot of a single wood engraver whose livelihood might be threatened by a glut of competitors.[1] However, in the main, in seeking to avoid the excesses of both, Lemon, aided by Leech and Thackeray steered an uneasy middle course during the first ten years of its existence, hoping to hit the taste of an audience sufficiently large to sustain its life. It succeeded.

The Westminster Review in 1842 was one of the first to discern its 'moral superiority' to the publications with a similar aim by which it was preceded. The Satirist, Age and John Bull had endeavoured to avail themselves of the weapons of wit and humour, but their best puns rarely rose above the level of obscene jests, and none such disgraced the columns of Punch. This, the periodical believed, was a favourable sign of the progress of opinion, on a par with the decaying taste for blood and horror and the desire for somewhat more healthful and intellectual means of pleasurable excitements than police reports.[2] The newspapers agreed. The Sunday Times found it 'mirthful without malice, witty without grossness, and pointed without partisanship', while provincial gazettes expressed their surprise at anything so healthy:-

> There is nothing low or vulgar; it may be safely introduced into the family circle, where it will provoke many a hearty laugh, but can never call a blush to the most delicate cheek.

---

1. See above p.67.

2. 'The Philosophy of Punch', Westminster Review, xxxviii (1842), 316-7.

It is almost the first comic periodical we ever saw which was not vulgar.[1]

The point of the famous cartoon which appeared in 1848, entitled 'AUTHORS' MISERIES', by Thackeray, which shows him and Jerrold listening in on a railway conversation between an old gentleman and a young lady, was not that Punch was thought to be politically dangerous and socially disreputable, but that it was not.[2] Thackeray embroidered the image during the 1850s in his notorious article on Leech. He compared Punch with the material to be found in 'two or three mottled portfolios' in an old gentleman's library in the country, full of Gillray, Bunbury, Woodward and Cruikshank prints:-

> We swiftly turn over those prohibited pages. How many of them there were in the wild, coarse, reckless, ribald, generous book of old English humour! How savage the satire was - how fierce the assault - what garbage hurled at opponents - what foul blows were hit - what language of Billingsgate flung! Fancy a party in a country house now looking over Woodward's facetiae or some of the Gillray comicalities, or the slatternly Saturnalia of Rowandson...

In contrast, Punch was respectable and well-mannered, having put aside his mad pranks and tipsy habits; 'and frolicsome always, has become gentle and harmless, smitten into shame by the pure presence of our women and the sweet confiding smiles of our children'.[3] Similarly, Charles Knight

---

1. Somerset's County Gazette. The Derbyshire Courier found it 'untainted by either profanity or indelicacy'; the Manchester Advertiser saw within it follies exposed 'without one atom of malice; nor is there an expression that could raise a blush, or excite any other feeling than hilarity and joyousness'; the Salopian Journal found it 'Witty without coarseness'; the Sunderland Herald 'free from satiric spleen and coarse ribaldry'; the Post Magazine 'no lurking innuendo to shock female delicacy'; the New Monthly Belle Assemblée that its
   > humour is that of the harmless kind which admits of his presence on the breakfast-table, in the drawing room, and even in the boudoir. The success of this work proves that grossness need never be associated with the broadest humour, and that delicacy and wit may be cleverly associated.

   All quoted from an advertisement for Punch which appeared in Bentley's Miscellany, xi (May, 1842).

2. Punch, xv (1848), 198.

3. Thackeray, 'Pictures of Life and Character', pp.78-80.

believed Punch to be:-

> the shrewdest observer, the most good-humoured satirist, the most inoffensive promoter of merriment, and one of the most trustworthy of portrait-painters, that ever brought the pencil to the aid of the pen, for harmless entertainment and real moral instruction.

It had gathered together the materials for a political and social history of its times, 'as viewed in broad day-light of a laughing philosophy'.[1] Both Thackeray and Knight believed that Lemon was partly responsible for this high tone. Thackeray thought that through Lemon, 'there is decorous wit, and fun without its general attendant, coarseness'.[2] For Knight, even the unifying effect of the weekly dinner would not have prevented the writers from degenerating into malice and the grossness of satirists, had it not been for the 'presiding mind' which directed their career, 'It is the rare merit of Mark Lemon that no impurity ever sullied the work of which he is the Editor, - that under his guidance Wit has thought it no restraint "to dwell in decencies for ever"'.[3] Silver reports that Lemon said Punch had blotted out the Age and Satirist, 'and other vile publications', which before Punch existed, were the only amusing journals of the day.[4] He took care not to include jokes of a violent or sexual nature as well as to preserve the paper's integrity. He refused insertion to an article puffing some railway Bradbury was interested in, and an article of Fonblanque's which he thought libellous.[5] On his death in 1870,

1. Knight, Passages of a Working Life, iii. 247-8.
2. Hatton, 'The True Story of Punch', pp.345-6, quoting Thackeray's lecture on 'Men of Humour' given in 1855 at Birmingham.
3. Knight, Passages of a Working Life, iii. 269.
4. Silver diary, 27 June 1866.
5. Ibid., 30 July 1862.

Mrs. Lemon was awarded a pension from the Civil List of £100 by Gladstone, who said Lemon had 'raised the level of comic journalism to its present standard'.[1]

It is further clear that Punch was taken in good part by the most eminent people who read it from quite early in its career. Lord Beauvale wrote to Lady Palmerston on 9 January 1846:-

> I forgot to mention that I told the Queen to read that paper in the Examiner, and as some of the things I told her out of it about Ld Grey amused her highly, I have no doubt She will. She did not seem to know much about the Examiner and rather thought it a paper in the style of Punch... She still sees Punch inspite of his misdeeds, for I found She had seen that caricature of "You're not strong enough for the place, John", and She split her sides with laughing at it, so I hope she will have been equally amused with "The Artful Dodger", which is charming.[2]

The Prince Consort, although attacked continually for his foreignness, his over-swift army promotion and designs for uniforms, his hunting, his dabbling in the arts and interference in politics, nevertheless appears to have appreciated Punch and made a large collection of the caricatures of the day, in the belief that in them alone could the true position of the public man be felt.[3] Disraeli bought a dozen copies of Punch whenever he was depicted in it.[4] In 1845, he tried to ingratiate himself with Punch in a speech at the Printers' Pension Society dinner, making witty and flattering references to Leech; this did nothing to stop the paper's hostility to him, as was noted with some smugness.[5]

---

1. Spielmann, op.cit., p.267.
2. M. Ogilvy, Countess of Airlie, Lady Palmerston and Her Times (1922) ii. 106, referring to Punch, x (1846), 6, 27.
3. Sir T. Martin, Life of the Prince Consort (1875-80), ii. 299.
4. Groves, op.cit., p.12.
5. Vizetelly, op.cit., i. 302-4.

Lord John Russell's biographer believed that Leech's cartoons of the politician, usually being depicted as a naughty child, fixed his public image to his detriment.[1] However, Leech's wife did obtain Russell's sponsorship for her son to a place at Westminster school, after her husband's death.[2] Brougham was still a leading victim. According to Lord Carlisle, Brougham believed 'those Punch people... never get my face, and are obliged to put up with my plaid trousers'. Another writer contradicted him, saying Brougham 'himself admits that the Punch likenesses are the best'.[3] A Beckett certainly corresponded with him on legal matters in the mid 1850s, and after his death, Brougham was especially kind to his widow, using his influence to obtain a £100 per annum pension for her, and an appointment in the Audit Office for her second son, Albert.[4] Gladstone himself praised the paper at its anniversary dinner:-

> in his early days, when an artist was engaged to produce political satires, he nearly always descended to gross personal caricature, and sometimes to indecency. Today he noted in the humorous press a total absence of vulgarity and a fairer treatment, which has made this department of warfare always pleasing.[5]

Not everyone received as fair a treatment as Gladstone did at the hands of Punch. The Westminster Review article which had praised the paper's general decency, went on to criticize the lack of taste exhibited in a

1. Sir S. Walpole, Life of Lord John Russell (1889), ii. 462-3.
2. Punch offices: Silver to Spielmann, 11 November 1895.
3. Spielmann, op.cit., pp.200-2.
4. U.C.L., Brougham Papers, 2,364, 30,712: G. A. à Beckett to Brougham, 7 April 1855, M. A. à Beckett to Brougham, 28 April 1858.
5. Spielmann, op.cit., p.172.

couple of puns and the capriciousness in the choice of some of _Punch_'s favourite targets - the 'Quixotic tilting at upper-class windmills' to which Spielmann referred:-[1]

> We regret the scurrilous paragraphs to which we allude, because the spirit of detraction which assails all public men, and chiefly those who have been the most indefatigable in favour of popular objects, is one great reason the public are not better served.

These remarks, it said, were offered in a friendly spirit 'because we hold it by no means unimportant that a right direction should be given to the light artillery of the press'. Wit, or that which was received as such, had an influence not to be despised. The fear of ridicule was a power greater than the force of reasoning, 'Certain it is that man, by the constitution of his nature, is a laughter-loving animal, and society would be nearer perfection than it is if he only knew well what to laugh at'.[2] Such blemishes marred what was envisaged as a far higher role for humour. Implicitly and sometimes explicitly woven into the theme of the cleanliness of _Punch_'s humour, as in the _Art-Union_ article on Meadows, or Charles Knight's comments, was the promise of higher things: universal truths, moral instruction. Yet how far could _Punch_ ascend on this scale without becoming a rather insipid, certainly humourless, fine art magazine? Throughout the 1840s it definitely rejected this role in a campaign waged against Samuel Carter Hall in particular and high art in general. _Punch_ failed to be moved by Hall's complaints to Bradbury and Evans about the gross personal attacks made on him[3] and went on to let off a continuous philistine chortle at anything which smacked of his Pecksniffian pretensions.

1. _Ibid._, p.101.
2. 'The Philosophy of Punch', pp.317-8.
3. _Punch_ offices: Hall to Bradbury and Evans, 11 December 1847.

Punch continued the long-standing joke over useful education[1] and applied it specifically to the improvements which could be brought about, supposedly, through art. It ran a campaign against the Art Unions, first with a leader attacking their lottery nature and the manner in which the pictures were chosen. Later, it depicted the Royal Academicians breathing down the necks of the prize-winners at the Annual Exhibition and it ridiculed the tardiness with which the free engraving was produced. Its most elaborate joke, in 1851, took the form of a wafer, designed by Horace Mayhew, sending up the annual free engraving. A lithograph of a cracked willow-pattern plate was dedicated: 'To the Subscribers to the Art Union this beautiful plate (from the original in the possession of the Artist) is presented as the finest specimen of British Art, by Punch'. And the whole philosophy of the Unions was reduced to a mockery in the 'Umbrella Art Union', the engravings and works of art for distribution being made up of the cheap wares sold in the street by hawkers.[2] It attacked the 'School of Bad Designs' under Wilson and 'Drawing for the Million' with a letter purporting to come from one of the pupils, illustrated with his own childish efforts.[3] As for the extension of art to manufactured goods, the Man in the Moon jibbed at the prices of Felix Summerly's 'Art Manufactures', and Punch

---

1. See for example, 'Punch's Information for the People', i (1841), 41,58,82,119,179,261; 'Grand National Project for Moral and Intellectual Advancement', - a University for Ladies in Pimlico, iii (1842), 105-6, 'Useful Knowledge; Read! Mark! Learn! 262. Under 'New Curiosities of Literature' it listed:
    A volume of Chambers's Journal without the description of a tea-party given by the proprietors to their poor workmen, made lively with a tremendous blowing of their own trumpets ...
    A work of Mr. Charles Knight, in which you had not some recollection of having seen the woodcuts five or six times before.
   Punch, xiii (1847), 132.

2. Punch, i (1841), 108, 112; iv (1843), 110-1; xi (1846), 87. There is a wafer in Punch offices. It was rather a costly jape, the 250 copies being printed for £52. 7s. 6d. For the sale of prints in umbrellas, see H. Mayhew, op.cit., i. 302-4.

3. Punch, iii (1842), 89; iv (1843), 104; ix (1845), 21, 117.

following on the example of the Art-Union itself announced a 'Tour in the Manufacturing Districts:-'

> Punch is suddenly smitten with the spirit of utility; he therefore purposes to throw open his pages - wide as his heart - to fac-simile engravings of all that is new and beautiful in household decoration.[1]

Motivated by the same spirit, it suggested that the hat pegs, key holes, door knockers and bells of the new Palace of Westminster be open to a design competition.[2] This was part of a much larger attack upon the whole decorative scheme of the parliamentary buildings. Punch ridiculed the subjects of the frescoes, applied pseudo-historical themes to the decoration of railway stations and extended their style and critical language to cope with nursery rhymes.[3] It attacked the 'German school' of art, while the Royal Academy was said to be divided between the Mediaeval-Angelico-Pugin-Gothic, or flat style, and the Fuseli-Michael-Angelesque school:-

> The alarming spread of the German School in Art has created considerable astonishment; but the phenomenon has at length been accounted for, by it having been discovered that the Committee of the Art Union cannot understand, and will not patronize any other class of drawing. Every competitor for the Art Union Prizes is driven, in self-defence, to adopt the serpent-like hair for the countenance, inflamed gooseberries for the eyes, and tufts of tow for the mustaches, which are the principal features of the German School of drawing.[4]

It made inumerable jokes at the expense of the National Gallery's

---

1. Punch, x (1846), 123. Man in the Moon, ii (1847), 253, 317.
2. Punch, v (1843), 102, vi (1844), 205.
3. Punch, v (1843), 38, 68; vii (1844), 192, viii (1845), 247; ix (1845) 88, 150; x (1846), 9; xii (1847), 25, 55, 87, 180, 267; xiii (1847), 8-9, 19.
4. Punch, ix (1845), 103, 186; x (1846), 145; xiv (1848), 197.

cleaning and purchasing policy.[1] It even concocted letters from a Mr. Cimabue Potts in defence of High art, a practice echoed in the Man in the Moon's Mr. Raphael Van Eyck Glazings, the forger from Camden Town, who was quite prepared to dole out advice to pupils who wanted to make good sales and to run up some ancient art to fill up the recesses in the House of Lords.[2] Indeed, Punch was only one of the many outlets the humourists of this period used to give vent to their feelings about high art; others ranged from Cruikshank's Comic Almanack to Thackeray's The Newcomes, with Mr. Gandish's Academy.[3]

Such a catalogue of charges against high art helps to explain why some of the most striking of the 'big cuts' of the first decade of Punch's existence took their framework from the art and design movement. In each individual cut with its topical reference, it was as if Punch said these are the real priorities, not the beauty and elevated moral ideals of the original. From July to December 1843, for example, Punch

---

1. Punch, ix (1846, 42; Almanack, 1847. Both Punch and the Man in the Moon also mocked the hanging arrangements in the new Vernon Gallery, which was so dark it was called the Vernon Pit. Punch, xiii (1847), 108; xv (1848) 138, 170, 208, 221; xvi (1849), 166. The Man in the Moon, iv (1848), 252, 282-83, 320, 351. However, Punch was in favour of the liberalization of opening hours, especially on Sundays, as in France. Punch, viii (1845), 224; xviii (1849), 10.

2. Punch, xii (1847), 218-9. Man in the Moon, iii (1848), 21-22, 224-5; v (1849), 159-61.

3. In Cruikshank's Comic Almanack, for example, 'Guy Fawkes treated Classically- An Unexhibited Cartoon', 'Humbugs of the Day', which included fresco painting, 'The Legal Art Union', 'Critical Essay on the Prize Cartoons', (1844), pp.31, 39, 50, 55-56. 'Movement of the Fine Arts', (1848), pp.103-5. 'Valuable advice to Persons about to Marry - Don't buy your furniture at Felix Summerly's Cheap Art-Manufacture Mart', 53-58. Also, an article for Our Own Times, illustrated by Cruikshank with the text by à Beckett and Reach, entitled 'High Art in 1846', which attacked German art, fresco painting and the Westminster decorations:
    Never before did a nation rear such a temple to the genius of quackery, and never before did the spirit take such entire and stifling possession of a sanctuary. There will be enough of the concentrated essence of humbug bottled up in that building to infect a world.
pp.89-93. For Thackeray's attitude see The Newcomes (1853-5), ch.xvii.

ran its own series of 'Cartoons' based on the exhibition of fresco cartoons which had taken place in Westminster Hall.[1] The most famous was Leech's 'SUBSTANCE AND SHADOW', a vignette showing a group of beggars and cripples looking at pictures of the bourgeoisie and their style of life, in the Royal Academy. Meadows introduced a mock high art theme in the 'BATTLE OF THE ALPHABET', in which four clergymen, in the shadow of the devil, attempted to dismember a child.[2] 'CAPITAL AND LABOUR' surrounded the cross-section of a pit in which the poor grovelled and laboured, with pictures of luxury, ease and good fortune. The accompanying leader referred to the recently published, illustrated report and evidence of the royal commission which investigated conditions of employment for children in mines and manufactures:-

> The public mind has been a good deal shocked by very offensive representations of certain underground operations, carried on by an inferior race of human beings, employed in working the mines, but Punch's artist has endeavoured to do away with the disagreeable impression by showing the very refined and elegant result that happily arises from the labours of these inferior creatures.[3]

At the end of the decade it proposed 'SPECIMENS FROM MR. PUNCH's INDUSTRIAL EXHIBITION OF 1850. (TO BE IMPROVED IN 1851),' in which Mr. Punch shows to Albert 'AN INDUSTRIOUS NEEDLE-WOMAN', 'A LABOURER AGED 75', 'A DISTRESSED SHOEMAKER' and 'A SWEATER' all in glass display

---

1. In fact, even in its first volume, Punch exhibited a 'CARTOON OF MR. DANIELL O'CONNELL, TAKEN FROM RAPHAEL', i (1841), 259. See also, 'Prince Albert's Stock', ii (1842), 49 described as an 'inimitably comic cartoon'.

2. Punch, v (1843), 23, 27.

3. Punch, v (1843), 49. See below p.282 . The series ran to six in all: Punch, v (1843), 23, 27, 35, 39, 49, 59. See also xv (1848), 121. 'Father Thames Introducing his Offspring to the Fair City of London', (a design for a Fresco in the new Houses of Parliament), xxxv (1858), 5.

cases.[1]

However, apart from the 'big cut' and Jerrold's 'Q Papers', the great bulk of material in Punch was non-political. No doubt, this was in part a continuation of the type of humour the staff had indulged in while working for George Cruikshank's Comic Almanack, which preceded and ran alongside Punch. Naturally, it was chiefly a show-case for Cruikshank's etchings, one for each month, and based on themes concerning the climate, the seasons or traditional festivals.[2] Many made use of verbal puns, in a manner Punch was to exploit, for example in 1839, 'JANUARY - The birth of the Year', which depicted a husband nursing a squawling baby, or 'SEPTEMBER - Plucking a Goose', in which a Jewish money-lender called on a shocked paterfamilias while his wife fainted in the background. In addition, there were the small punning woodcuts and 'blackies' favoured in the early numbers of Punch, essays attached to sketches and general almanac information. Cruikshank's humour dealt with man in the most generalized sense, in types, in human folly, occasionally in grotesqueness. The humour was very rarely political, more often it was vaguely topical: a comparison of Cruikshank's 'COMMENTARY upon the "New Police Act"' in his Omnibus (1841-42) with Cleave's depiction of the same theme clarifies the point.[3] It was the increase in this type of humour that Jerrold noted and frowned upon;

---

1. Punch, xviii (1850), 145. The paper conducted a virulent campaign against the Exhibition and its protagonist, Prince Albert, many of its cuts concentrating on the destruction of the trees and open space for the people in Hyde Park. Punch, xix (1850), 2, 10, 22, 28, 32, 142, 167.

2. See below p. 277.

3. George Cruikshank's Omnibus (1841-42), pp.33-34. 'The New Whig Police Act in Full Operation in the City', Cleave's Gazette, 23 March 1839.

in a letter to Dickens of 1846 he wrote:-

> Punch, I believe, holds its course... Nevertheless, I do not very cordially agree with its new spirit. I am convinced that the world will get tired (at least I hope so) of this eternal guffaw at all things. After all, life has something serious in it. It cannot be all a comic history of humanity... unless Punch gets a little back to his occasional gravities, he'll be sure to suffer.[1]

Thackeray felt that, on the contrary, too much had been said on the Jerrold side, and his view prevailed. The extremes were, as we have seen, a paper composed of scurrilous personal attacks on politicians, or the art of moral elevation. Punch turned down both in favour of 'healthy genuine fun'.[2] This prevalence of 'fun' was noted by the Literary Gazette when it reviewed the early numbers of the Man in the Moon; it 'displays a fair share of that sort of fun and drollery of which the professional humorists of the day are now so lavish in almost every form of publicity'.[3] Or, as the Art-Union, equally drily, said:

> The pen and the pencil are alike labouring after 'fun', and it seems to be considered something like 'an achievement' to discover a new mode by which a double meaning may be conveyed by a single word.[4]

It added that 'Genius should look upon such themes rather as play things of idle moments, than as leading duties to occupy thought'. James Hannay was to isolate one of the causes of this situation. By the middle of the century, the humorous magazine was not catering for men with political purpose, and certainly not for the isolated genius; it was dealing with

---

1. W. Jerrold, op.cit., p.67.
2. A. Beckett, op.cit., p.45.
3. Quoted in the Man in the Moon, i (1847), 123.
4. Art-Union, vii (1845), 167.

the Great British Public and the wholesome British family. From <u>Cleave's Gazette</u> to <u>Punch</u> what was produced to appeal to the largest common denominator was 'fun, frolic and badinage':-[1]

> The public now is the baron, and has his jester, who comes tumbling up to the side of its good-natured ears with his jibe. He makes merry with it over the day's events, and the changes of governments and fashions, and awakens laughter in its lazy eyes. But this outward sheen of pleasantry, which has nothing to say to the heart, and very little to the intellect, introduces a giggling murmur into the day's conversations and peoples our streets and our thoroughfares with a legion of buffoons. All this may be fun (though this is doubtful); but it is not literature![2]

---

1. See above p.175.

2. J. Hannay, <u>Satire and Satirists</u> (1854), pp.275-6. Also, Hannay's unfinished autobiographical novel, 'Bagot's Youth', <u>Idler</u>, i (1856), 169:
    > At this period the British public was rapid for comic literature. To do the B.P. justice, it is always willing to be amused, and liberal to its buffoons. But in those days it bought funny journals and little books with voracity; and funny journals and little books were showered upon it accordingly...

III

In order to understand more fully the reasons for Punch's success, it is necessary to compare it with the other humorous periodicals which were started up - and closed down - during the 1840's. What was it that Punch had which they did not? Of course, Punch had the capital of Bradbury and Evans behind it; it had regularity of issue. They did not. Puck attempted, unsuccessfully to come out daily, the Man in the Moon monthly.[1] But Punch had been there the longest and by the end of the decade was surrounded by all the trappings of Victorian journalistic publicity: a Christmas almanack, a yearly pocket book, occasional special numbers and even decorated pocket handkerchieves.[2] The majority of its rivals treated it as a touchstone for their style, a yardstick for their own measurements: it was the father, they were the dashing young men or the naughty children. In fact, one of them billed itself as 'a chip off the old block' and had a cover depicting Punch's abdication in favour of his son.[3] For the writers of the Puppet Show the Punch team were 'Eminent Men'.[4] The aim was to try and make Punch somehow seem stodgy, boring, and old-fashioned. They each took one of its elements and extended it beyond the norm of the safe respectable audience's taste, and failed. Some were too

---

1. After two months Puck announced its change to a twice weekly issue, but merged with the Great Gun instead. The thirtieth number of the Man in the Moon announced that it would be coming out weekly from 9 June 1849. Instead, however, it disappeared altogether.

2. Punch's pocket book had an average sale of around 11,000 copies between 1843 and 1850, the peak year being 1845, with around 18,000. In 1844, 20,000 Anti-Graham Wafers were sold and 12,000 Anti-Graham Envelopes. A silk handkerchief, with a design of Mr. Punch and attendant figures in blue, was produced towards the end of the decade.
Punch offices: Paper and Print Ledger 1839-1853.

3. Penny Punch, No. 1, 23 June 1849.

4. Puppet-Show, i (1848), 16.

sweet and elevated; some were too raffish and fast; others were too radical and working class in appeal. Punch had found an audience who did not want art with a purpose, were bored with useful knowledge and high art, and yet did not want to descend to the pub' joke and gutter journalism. Its public wanted, and got, good clean fun.

The first of these rivals was probably the Squib, which appeared on 28 May 1842. Like many of its successors, its staff was largely made up of dissenters from the Punch fold, and its printer was Joseph Last. It was a close imitator of Punch although it only cost a penny (1½d from No. 16, 10 September 1842) and much larger in page size, but it was only four pages long. A Beckett is reputed to have started it,[1] and it contained cuts by Henning, Newman and Henry Alken. It included small 'blackies' and like Punch, a large political cut each week, usually on the subject of Peel or the Queen. It pronounced itself anti-Charter, calling it 'the People's ruin'; but steadily, like most humorous publications uncertain of their audience, it increased its light social content with 'physiologies' and comments on society occasions. It died on 17 December.

The Squib was followed by Judy, started by Leman Rede in 1843, which did not get beyond a few parts, and Puck in 1844. This was the first effort by Albert Smith, with Tom Taylor and E.L. Blanchard, to establish a rival to his former employers. The printers were Palmer and Clayton of Crane Court, the engraver Landells, and Hine produced most of the rather feeble caricatures directed against O'Connell, Wellington, Brougham and the polka. The Great Gun, its successor, began on 16 November 1844, and survived rather longer. The

---

1. Punch offices: A.W. à Beckett to Spielmann, 3 June 1895:
    I do not know what connection my father had with 'the Squib' but I do know that he was proud to feel that all through his life (from 1841) he had been perfectly faithful to Punch and Bradbury and Evans. He said over and over again in my presence that there had never been a number of Punch to which he had not contributed. He used to paste weekly his contributions to Punch in a book which I have seen. Consequently your reference to the Squib and my father's reputed connection with it does not altogether coincide with my impressions on the subject.

cast expanded to include F.W.N. Bayley as editor for the first three numbers, and now promoted the work of a number of bohemian artists who supported Smith: Henry Doyle, Meadows, Crowquill, Sargant, Henning and Hine. Palmer and Clayton were again the printers, Edward Evans the engraver. The paper sold for threepence and stated its intention to be '"A PAPER FOR EVERY HOME", binding classes together, and blending features which, although fairly mixable, have never met before'. By this it meant a combination of the comic and the serious, family features, criticism and fiction, in other words, a light-hearted version of the family papers which were becoming popular about this time.[1] Edward Leman Blanchard recorded in his diary for November, '16th. Great Gun came out this day, first number ... 22nd. - Second number of Great Gun published. As far as it has yet gone, a decided failure.'[2] Nevertheless, the paper staggered into a second volume and died late the following year. In the mean time, it made a special point of attacking O'Connell and Prince Albert, and displayed violent anti-semitism and anti-catholicism.[3] In addition, it succeeded in illustrating its series entitled 'Our French Express' with the work of Gavarni, Daumier and Cham.[4] It delighted in depicting its take-over of the old Punch office at 194 Strand, after a long siege.[5] On 3 May 1845, the first number of another periodical, Joe Miller the Younger, came out. It followed the Punch formula quite closely, being of quarto size, sixteen pages long yet only costing 1½d. It

1. See above p. 209.
2. Scott and Howard, op.cit., i. 35-39.
3. For example, 'LOOK UPON THIS PICTURE. AND ON THIS', (No. 7, 28 December 1844) which compares the luxurious conditions in the Prince's pig-sty with the conditions in which the poor lived. Also, 'THE JEW'S PROGRESS', (No. 17, 8 March 1845), 'THE REMOVAL OF JEWISH DISABILITIES, OR THE VISION OF LITTLE BENJAMIN', (No. 20, 29 March 1845), 'THE MAYNOOTH ROOKERY', (No. 25, 3 May 1845), 'THE MAN OF MANY CREEDS', (No. 27, 17 May 1845).
4. Great Gun, No. 20, 29 March 1845, No. 25, 3 May 1845, No. 26, 10 May 1845.
5. 'THE SIEGE OF THE OLD PUNCH-OFFICE BY THE GREAT GUN', (No.20, 29 March 1845), 'SURRENDER OF THE OLD PUNCH-OFFICE TO THE GREAT GUN', (No.25, 3 May 1845).

was printed by Ingram and Cooke of Crane Court, and presumably the success of the Illustrated London News which they owned, permitted the production of a couple of large cuts each week, one political and the other social. This latter series was printed by a process which resembled aquatint, but which was, according to the advertisement, 'The New Galvanic Engraving - an extraordinary novelty in typographical illustration'.[1] Most of these engravings seem to be taken from Gavarni's 'Les Debardeurs' or 'Le Carnival à Paris', except one entitled 'A MOMENTOUS QUESTION FOR THE PREMIER', in which Victoria asks Peel to give up the Corn Laws.[2] On 5 July 1845, a new series was started, each number being twelve pages long and printed by William Clark of Warwick Lane. The cuts by Hine and Henning, engraved by P. Starling, concentrated on attacking Punch for stealing its cuts and condemning railway speculation. In the twenty third number, on 6 December 1843, it announced that from the following week it would change its name to Mephystopheles and sell at threepence. One number came out on 13 December, with a large cut of Russell by Hine, printed and published by Michael Cooke back in the Palmer and Clayton office in Crane Court. Then it disappeared.

All of these periodicals betray serious faults compared with Punch. Their frequent changes of printer suggest that few had the capital to survive long enough to make a permanent impact on the market. Secondly, all followed much too closely on the Punch formula of one large cut, many

---

1. For a description of the 'galvanoglyphy' process, or glyphography as it was more commonly known, see Harris, 'Experimental Graphic Process in England 1800-1859', 63-80. Henry Cole and the Linnells were not particularly impressed with the method. See Cole, Fifty Years of Public Work, ii. 162-5.

2. Joe Miller the Younger, i (1845), 113.

smaller ones and lots of fun. Their light-weight writing was feeble and bore no trace of individuality, even if it was occasionally relieved by something more than crude art-work. However, on 2 October 1847, Punch went too far with one of its many attacks on Alfred Bunn, the theatre manager and playwright. Bunn, aided and abetted by George Augustus Sala and possibly Shirley Brooks, retaliated in A Word with Punch, issued on 11 November. Aping the Punch format, adorned with cuts by an equally vengeful Landells, Bunn produced a sustained attack on the Punch trio of 'Wronghead, Sleekhead and Thickhead' (Jerrold, à Beckett and Lemon). He charged them with their own failed plays, poems and newspapers; he dug up à Beckett's record from the books of the Insolvent's Court; he created a series of mock theatricals and advertisements which insinuated that Punch was about to be wound up through its plagiarism and lack of material. Bunn received many letters of congratulation and the printer, W.S. Johnson, had to bring out a second edition.[1] The Punch staff never replied, nor did they attack Bunn again.

On 1 January 1847, Albert Smith and Angus B. Reach launched a periodical that bore no similarity in style to Punch: the Man in the Moon. Like the early number of Joe Miller the Younger, it was printed by Clark of Warwick Lane. However, unlike that failure, it was a monthly and the size of the Comic Almanack or Bradshaw's railway guide - its announcements said it was sold at every railway station, pierhead and bookseller in the country. The literary portion was conducted by Smith, Reach, Shirley Brooks and Charles Kenny. The illustrations were by 'Phiz', Meadows, Hine, Nicholson,

---

1. Punch offices: appended to a book compiled by Bunn on the subject of A Word with Punch.

Thomas A. Mayhew, Smythe, 'Cham' and others. Reach was an author and journalist from Inverness, then aged twenty-six, and a stand-by shorthand writer in the House of Commons for the Morning Chronicle.[1] Brooks was in his early thirties, the son of an architect and had trained as a solicitor. He worked on the Argus, Ainsworth's Magazine and the Illustrated London News. He had a capacity for providing witty and satirical verses at a moment's notice, and probably provided the political content of the magazine, for which, according to Burnand, 'neither Angus Reach nor Albert Smith cared a dump'.[2]

Of course the Man in the Moon believed it made better jokes than Punch and jeered at its predictability: jokes in Punch when it first came out, it said, 'ran principally on Lord Brougham, the Duke of Wellington, the Public Monuments, George Jones and the Poet Bunn'. Years rolled along. Time however, 'attacked Punch in vain; the subjects of jokes, and the faces of the caricatures, rival the Pyramids in immutability.'[3] One of Punch's most frequent victims was singled out by the Man in the Moon as 'PUNCH'S BOY OF ALL WORK'. It captioned 'Johnny Russell' (the ill-used boy) saying, 'If you please, sir, will you be so kind as to give me a holiday. Everyone says it's time I had one. I've been put to a deal of very heavy work lately'.[4] Its 'Rewards Offered' section included one for

---

1. Sala, Life and Adventures, i. 199.
2. Sir F. C. Burnand, 'Mr. Punch, Some Precursors and Competitors', Pall Mall Magazine, xxix (1903), 260-2. G. S. Layard, A Great Punch Editor. Life Letters and Diaries of Shirley Brooks of 'Punch' (1907), pp.1-55.
3. Man in the Moon, iii (1849), 29.
4. Ibid., iv (1848), 14.

'A laugh produced by one of <u>Punch</u>'s late jokes'; and an illustration entitled 'A REAL CASE OF DISTRESS' depicted a bedraggled Mr. Punch saying, 'I HAVE NOT MADE A JOKE FOR MANY WEEKS'.[1]

Francis Burnand said that the <u>Man in the Moon</u> appealed rather to 'fast men about town, to the rapid Stock Exchange man, the youthful Guardsman and those interested in theatrical and light literary matters'.[2] Indeed, the social life of its contributors revolved round the Museum Club where, in one of Brooks' parodies, he, Smith and Reach sat around discussing their own plays, and the Café de L'Europe in the Haymarket, kept by the actor Henning, which also attracted the more raffish element from <u>Punch</u>.[3] However, by 1850 the majority of the <u>Punch</u> staff did not care to be too much associated socially with Smith, his friends and their loud attitudes. Although it is difficult to detect the nuances of such a cliquish world, odd hints illuminate felt differences in status and position. Silver reported, for instance, that the <u>Punch</u> table believed it could 'get on very well without Sala & Co., and shouldn't like to dine with them once a week. <u>Punch</u> keeps up by its keeping to the gentlemanly view of things and its being known that Bohemians don't write for it'.[4] 'Bohemia',

---

1. <u>Ibid</u>., ii (1847), 42, 195.

2. Burnand, 'Mr Punch', pp.261-2.

3. <u>Man in the Moon</u>, i (1847), 302-6. Horace Mayhew was the most insatiable sampler of this level of city society. Silver said he was 'only known in the back slums of the Haymarket'. When he married, Lemon joked about 'the Haymarket night houses being closed in consequence'. Silver diary, 27 June 1866, 28 October 1868. When Mayhew took over the editorship of Cruikshank's <u>Comic Almanack</u> in 1847, there was a dramatic increase in the number of articles dealing with such pleasures. For example, 'The Universal Smasher', 'Every Day-Recipes. By a Very Fast Man', and 'The City "Fast Man",' in the <u>Comic Almanack</u> for 1848, pp.40-45, 45-46, 110-1.

4. Silver diary, 28 June 1860. Lemon called Sala a 'graceless young whelp', although later they grew to be friends. Sala, <u>Things I have Seen</u>, i. 86-90.

'the fast life', 'vulgarity' smacked too much of what many of its staff had encountered in their youth during the 1830s. Now, for the most part, respectably middle aged, they did not want to be reminded of their past, nor of a world at its most base, contaminated by Gregory and Nicholson, of the twilight society of the clubs and drinking cellars.

The differences between the two periodicals is further underlined in a mock general election dreamed up by the Man in the Moon, and supposedly held at the Café de L'Europe. The Man in the Moon attacked Punch for chastising the Queen because she did not go to see long winded five act plays, nor ask literary men to the Palace. He criticized Punch's sanctimonious political attitudes and himself adopted the tone of the plain-speaking, plain-thinking man about town: He:-

> didn't believe in The People. (Tremendous Cheering). He did not mean to say that he despised his fellow-creatures who were not so well off as himself - God forbid: but he hated the humbug of the wrongs of the poor man class of writing, when any sneaking, idle, rascal in the country was found poaching, and punished for it.

This last jibe was clearly directed against Jerrold's anti-game law campaign. The Man in the Moon went on to condemn all 'the trash urged about "mutual improvement" and "mutual culture"',to approve of hanging and to insist on seeing the proper barriers preserved between the various degrees of society, assured that it was happier for all. He saw no use in constantly abusing the army, and all those military institutions which had assisted England in making it the powerful nation it was. Loud cheering followed the speech; Mr. Punch spoke in confusion and was heavily defeated.[1]

---

1. Man in the Moon, ii (1847), 69-70.

Such a manifesto seems to confirm all we have observed about the determination of a large section of humourists by the late 1840s to maintain a truce over all serious matters of political, intellectual and moral purpose. They condemned the Jerrold camp who sought to keep some radical attack within the humourist's repertoire as determinedly as they mocked high art. These attitudes were displayed in the reaction to Chartism in 1848. Punch's attitude was ambivalent. Ideally, it wished for the situation illustrated in 'THE RECONCILIATION; OR, AS IT OUGHT TO BE' could take place, whereby the rich conceded the 'POOR LAWS' and 'GAME LAWS' which Punch had always opposed, and the poor the force of their cudgels.[1] In 1848, Leech's cuts mocked equally the bravado of the special constables (who included among their number both himself and Lemon), and the number of false signatures to be found on the Chartist petition.[2] One big cut warned Russell to 'keep moving': to reduce expenditure, extend the suffrage and redress grievances.[3] However, the underlying message of both Punch and the Man in the Moon was that revolution, no matter how much it could be condoned in countries with despotic monarchies like France, would not be tolerated in England. Punch's 'A PHYSICAL FORCE CHARTIST ARMING FOR THE FIGHT' resembles a rather glum, simianized Tweedledum preparing for the fray; two big boots are all that can be seen of his inevitable downfall.[4] The Man in the Moon contributed 'Dips into the Diary of Barrabas Bolt Esq., Late delegate for Smokeley-on-Sewer', who turns out to be a

---

1. Punch, viii (1845), 123-4.
2. Punch, xiv (1848), 166, 170-2, 175.
3. Punch, xiv (1848), 167.
4. Punch, xv (1848), 101, 163.

charlatan, ending up in Middlesex House of Correction. It produced 'The Chartists', a historical tragedy in five acts, and reported a 'Chartist Conspiracy', supposedly discovered by its own detective.[1] It reserved a special antipathy for the Irish leaders, O'Brien, Meagher and Mitchell, once depicting their heads on pikes,[2] while it envisaged a Carlylean vision of 'The Millenium of Manufactures', featuring Cobden and Bright. An imaginary dialogue on the blessings of equality included:-

> No patriotism then; no pluck - no spirit - no fun - no leisure - no sunshine - no generosity - no chivalry - no gaiety - no landscapes - but the vistas of grimy mills - no architecture but tall chimneys - no art but the drawing of patterns - and no books but ledgers.

Such a place would be their 'Model Republic'.[3]

The most vitriolic attack on the fruits of liberalism and radicalism was launched in the Puppet Show, a paper started by the brothers Vizetelly. It commenced on 18 March 1848 and, according to its owner, 'leapt at once into temporary success'.[4] It was eight pages long and cost a penny, and Vizetelly was fortunate in procuring the services of James Hannay and H. Sutherland Edwards, both aged twenty, to write for it. The previous year they had combined to produce eight or ten numbers of the Pasquin:-

> a clever and exceedingly pungent satirical journal, which after a transitory existence, had either frightened by its brutal boldness, or tired out with its weekly losses, the timid capitalist who financed the speculation.[5]

1. Man in the Moon, iii (1848), 235-44; iv (1848), 16-24, 141-4.
2. Ibid., iii (1848), 261.
3. Ibid., iii (1848), 269-71; iv (1848), 52-53.
4. Vizetelly, op.cit., i. 323.
5. Ibid.

In fact, Hannay and Edwards were at exactly the same stage of life as à Beckett, Jerrold and Mayhew had been almost twenty years previously. The difference between them was that whereas the Punch men started on the left side of politics, in an atmosphere of government press repression, Hannay and his followers were emphatically right wing, at least in posture.[1] Hannay, a Scotsman, had entered the navy at the age of fourteen, came out and married a lady in Islington, wrote for the Morning Chronicle, left and attacked it in the Pasquin. He earned his nick-name of 'blood and culture' through his fondness for spouting and railing against the lower orders. A man who first met him in the 1850s thus described him:-

> In politics, Hannay was at heart a sincere and thorough conservative, unwavering in his devotion to his principles and party; but his conservatism was so tricked and bedecked with the conceits of Young England romanticism, that some people were more inclined to ridicule it than believe in it.[2]

John Bridgeman was the editor of the Puppet-Show and he was assisted by William North, a clever but unappreciated poet and mystic, Reach and Brooks, Dr. Mackay, Edward Leman Blanchard and Sala. The frontispiece was designed by Gavarni, who also contributed a series of 'Social Sketches'. He had arrived in England to escape creditors and to make some money in the November of the previous year.[3]

---

1. In Hannay's 'Bagot's Youth', however, he wrote:
   > His set tilted at all comers. They had no particular politics, or, rather, what they called their politics were determined by accident... This is an age of hybrids; and if you weigh strictly what any man says or writes before five-and-twenty, you will find that in trying to prove other people scoundrels you have proved yourself an ass.

   pp.256-7.

2. J. C. Jeaffreson, A Book of Recollections (1894), i. 143-6. Also, G. J. Worth, James Hannay His Life and Works (Lawrence, Kansas 1964), pp.1-64.

3. P.-A. Lemoisne, Gavarni Peintre et Lithographe (Paris, 1924), i. 195-6, ii. 1-82.

The <u>Puppet-Show</u> predictably mocked <u>Punch</u>'s price of threepence, saying that the articles were so heavy they could not sell it for less, and it accused <u>Punch</u> of stealing its own worst jokes. It vehemently attacked the Chartists in its leaders:-

> '<u>You</u> talk of obtaining universal suffrage! first fit yourselves for it by learning to behave after the manner of your betters: when you have succeeded in that, it will be time enough to think about letting you share in their rights.'[1]

It depicted the 'Chartist Bombastes', included a poem denouncing the Red Republicans, produced a model Chartist uniform and warned that the penalty of Chartism was transportation.[2] Its cut entitled 'THE CHARTIST "ORANGE TREE"', also struck out against G.W.M. Reynolds, who had exploited the taste of the working classes by producing his <u>Political Instructor</u> and <u>Weekly Newspaper</u>, promoting radical ideology and news, illustrated with portraits of leading radicals at home and abroad.[3]

The <u>Puppet-Show</u> died before the end of 1848, the <u>Man in the Moon</u> after successive changes in editorship and ownership by 1849. Again, one of the main reasons for their failure seems to have been lack of continuity in personnel. The <u>Man in the Moon</u> announced in January 1848 that Smith had ceased to be editor and Reach went after the twenty-ninth number, the following year. Similarly, on the <u>Puppet-Show</u>, Edwards went

---

1. <u>Puppet-Show</u>, i (1848), 16, 32, 43.
2. <u>Puppet-Show</u>, i (1848), 44, 129, 202.
3. <u>Reynold's Political Instructor</u> ran from 10 November 1849 to 11 May 1850, being somewhat smaller than quarto size and costing a penny. On 11 May 1850, in its twenty seventh issue it addressed its readers on the dropping of this 'pilot balloon' in favour of a 'grander enterprise', <u>Reynold's Weekly Newspaper</u>. This paper, which commenced on 5 May 1850, was broadsheet size, unillustrated and cost fourpence. Later in the same year, however, it was reduced in size and price to 2½d and continued until 1924.

over to Punch in 1848 and Hannay followed him there two years later, the same year as the most talented of the younger generation of humourists, Shirley Brooks. In addition, Burnand says that the French artists proved unsatisfactory. The Man in the Moon mocked the Puppet-Show's use of Gavarni in an illustration of 'HOW GAVARNI IDEALIZES', showing a London cabman as he really was, and how Gavarni had made him.[1] Gavarni in fact also produced a series of 'Heroes of the Revolution' for the Man in the Moon, as well as illustrating 'Gavarni in London', which was edited by Smith. However, it was obvious that both periodicals were in serious difficulties when the Puppet-Show announced a price increase to 1½d, and the Man in the Moon decided to come out weekly. With their novelty and their best contributors gone, there was very little left to interest the public.

If the Puppet-Show and the Man in the Moon were to the right of Punch politically, the Penny Punch, which began on 23 June 1849, was to the left. The address of the publisher, Winn in Holywell Street, already gives a clue to the low social origins of its contributors and market. It made jokes largely at the expense of the Jews, the Irish, the Pope and London aldermen who prevented the city from receiving a decent water supply. Some of the cuts were in dubious taste, one of which depicted the Queen running after Landseer; it even accused Punch of stealing material from the Satirist.[2] After twenty-six numbers, it produced a new series which had a more prominent strain of social criticism than had previously been exhibited. It ran two

---

1. Man in the Moon, iv (1848), 226-7. Burnand, 'Mr Punch', p.262. Vizetelly, op.cit., i. 338-9, who said Gavarni behaved morosely and failed to respond to the advances made by Thackeray and the Punch set; besides, 'Gavarni's drawings had too much of a French character about them'. For Gavarni's early impressions of the English, see J. and E. de Goncourt, Gavarni L'homme et L'oeuvre (Paris, 1873), pp.285-92.

2. Penny Punch, i (1849), 60, 145.

series, one entitled 'Labour and the Poor' and the other, 'Social Troubles'. The first in the 'Labour and the Poor' series depicted a scene in the minories in which a Jewish manufacturer threatened a girl worker; the second, the means of hiring labour in the docks; the third, the plight of needlewomen; the fourth, the truck system with a shopkeeper giving a worker short weight. The paper found it necessary to add, for the benefit of its metropolitan readership:-

> The above system, which is chiefly practised in our manufacturing districts, is that of paying wages partly in cash, and partly in tickets on tradespeople. It is a curse to the poor man, and cannot be too severely reprehended.[1]

The burden of maintaining this and attracting enough readers, however, seems to have proved too much, for the paper disappeared after the sixth issue of the new series.

At the opposite extreme, Life, the Mirror of the Million arrived on the scene in February 1850, priced twopence. Spielmann rightly describes it as 'a sort of sanctimonious joker, with the sententious motto of "Love the Motive, Truth the Power"', and proclaiming the message that life ought to be fed with love.[2] The sugary sweetness of the journal, reminiscent of the annuals which were now going out of fashion,[3] is revealed in its illustrations of such subjects as 'THE GOVERNESS', 'THE FIRST VALENTINE', and 'A SUMMER SHOWER', which were interdispersed

---

1. Ibid., i. new series (1849), 41.
2. M.H. Spielmann, 'The Rivals of Punch', National Review, xxv (1895), 659.
3. Vizetelly, op.cit., i. 143-4.

with jokes.[1] The paper died after its fourth number. Pasquin was reborn at the same time, this time making use of a frontispiece by Gavarni and Meadows' illustrations. Later on in the year, a newspaper size Journal for Laughter was created, price threepence, with a large front cut and several inside dealing with the theatre, but this also swiftly died. Thus, by 1850, Punch's monopoly was proven.

---

1. Life, i (1850), 5, 25, 35. On the 'Fine Arts' it wrote:
    Prints - as known to the public by means of a general accessibility are really beginning to have an educational influence over public taste. There is no doubt that associations of poetry and the calling in of domestic subjects have tended to this important result. With a view to prepare a feature of family interest in "LIFE", we begin, then, to avail ourselves of such associations and subjects in pointing from time to time at the popular engravings of the day, whenever they teach any of the experiences of destiny, and truthfully point a moral or adorn a table.
    i (1850), 27. For Punch's send-up of this type of illustration see 'The Charity-School of Art', xviii (1850), 229-30.

In 1851, a new publication came out, edited by Albert Smith and with illustrations by John Leech, published by Bradbury and Evans. The Month, as it was called, announced that it would be a view of passing subjects and manners, home and foreign, social and general. It would be a light periodical which might beguile a railway or steamboat journey and it would not interfere with any other. Its subject would be chiefly social:-

> We shall avoid all politics and personalities, believing that such matters furnish small amusement to general readers; but, should some one prominently before the public tempt us to indulge in a little fun at his expense, we hope this shall be so ordered that the object may be the first to laugh at it.[1]

Such an introduction epitomized all the characteristics of a humorous magazine which Punch had created. By 1850, they were accepted as the sine qua non of success. What had seemed to be the very essence of amusement in journalism until the 1830s, namely politics and people, was entirely abandoned. The malice, the barb of wit which could be recognized by political supporters or metropolitan cognoscenti was taken out to please the generality. By assiduously avoiding the dirt and immorality of the Town, or the Satirist, by courting the tastes of the family audience, Punch paralleled the progress of other developments in journalism - in the spheres of literature, as we have seen, and news, as will become apparent in the next chapter - and itself paved a safe middle path to light amusement. Furthermore, it was extending itself, via the railways and its own machine presses, into parts of the country never before visited with such speed from the metropolis. Like the illustrated newspapers, Punch fixed the image of its interests onto a grateful,

---

1. Month, i (1851), 1.

uncomplaining, country-wide audience.[1]

It was a vain hope uttered by Charles Knight when he wrote:-

We have got beyond the scurrilous stage - the indecent stage - the profane stage - the seditious stage. Let us hope that the frivolous stage, in which we are now to some extent abiding, will in time pass on to a higher taste, and a sounder mental discipline.[2]

---

1. Disraeli and Palmerston were both recognized in the country on the basis of their caricatures in <u>Punch</u>. Spielmann, <u>op.cit</u>., pp.198, 203.
J. Hannay, 'English Political Satires', <u>Quarterly Review</u>, ci (1857), 394:
He whose business or inclination takes him to the lobby of the House of Commons during the sitting of Parliament will often be amused at the peculiar mixture of awe and comedy with which a stranger from the country may be seen contemplating some famous statesman as he passes in. How does he recognize him? for he evidently knows who he is without having consulted a policeman. The answer is simple. He knows his face from the caricatures of him in "Punch".

2. Knight, <u>The Old Printer and the Modern Press</u>, p.300.

THE ILLUSTRATION OF NEWS

1840 - 1850

VII

First, says the "Age", came the "Observer", with its picture of Thurtell's cottage,[1] then the "Hive", then the "Mirror", then this and that, then the "Illustrated London News", then the "Pictorial Times". Well _après_? as the French say. The "Hive" was better than Thurtell's cottage, the "Mirror" was better than the "Hive", the "News" better than the "Mirror", and the "Times" better than the "News", and (though the "Times" readers may fancy the thing impossible) the day will come when something shall surpass even the "Times", and so on to the infinity of optimism.[2]

We have already seen how the illustrated newspaper was, to some extent, the outcome of illustrated crime reporting. In this chapter first, the antecedents of news illustration will be examined in greater depth. Secondly, the content of the range of illustrated newspapers published during the 1840 s will be studied with especial reference to their art and their relation to society. Finally, the chapter will show how the pace of news events went hand in hand with the development of techniques to cope with them at speed. The increasing sophistication of the concept and techniques of illustrated news are exemplified in two moments of great potential: first the revolutions in Europe during 1848 and finally, the Great Exhibition of 1851.

---

1. For details of the notorious murder of William Weare by John Thurtell in 1823, see R.D. Altick, _Victorian Studies in Scarlet_ (1973), pp.19-28. In fact, the cottage in the case belonged to William Probert, one of Thurtell's associates.

2. (W.M. Thackeray), 'Letters on the Fine Arts No.2. The Objections against Art Unions. M.A. Titmarsh, Esq. to Sanders McGilp, Esq.' _Pictorial Times_, 1 April 1843.

I

Herbert Ingram was born in 1811 at Boston, Lincolnshire. He left school at the age of fourteen and became apprenticed to the printer Joseph Clarke in the same town. At the age of twenty he went to London as a journeyman printer for a couple of years and in 1834, set up in partnership with his brother-in-law, Nathaniel Cooke, as printer, bookseller and news-agent in Nottingham. There, he was the agent for Morrison's Life Pills as well as for the London papers, among them the Weekly Chronicle. On the basis of this experience, he set up on his own account in both fields: he revived the 'Old Parr' legend and began to sell Parr's Life Pills and he put out an illustrated crime broadsheet about the Greenacre murder in 1837. From these profits he moved to Crane Court, Fleet Street, apparently stuffing the entrance with boxes of pills and meeting the journalistic fraternity which inhabited the neighbourhood. His first encounter with Henry Vizetelly came about because Ingram wanted a woodcut for Old Parr's Life Pills, a commission which Vizetelly sent on to John Gilbert. However, it was soon clear that Ingram's ideas were on a somewhat larger scale. According to Joseph Hatton, Ingram said, 'What first led me to start the "News", was this: living in the country, I noticed that when a newspaper published a picture the sale was wonderfully increased; so I thought to myself what a success a paper would be all pictures; and the idea never left me till I did it'.[1]

Ingram met Vizetelly and Frederick Marriott, the editor of the Weekly Chronicle, in the Cock Tavern, Temple Bar. If Vizetelly's account is to

---

1. Hatton, 'The True Story of "Punch"', pp.51-52. For accounts of Ingram's career see Mackay, Forty Years Recollections, ii. 64-75. Jackson, The Pictorial Press, pp.306-11. Illustrated London News, 29 September, 6 October 1860.

be believed, Ingram wanted an illustrated criminal record along the lines of the Greenacre number of the Weekly Chronicle, padded out with police cases, Old Bailey and assize trials, as well as factory riots, rick burnings, coining, sacrilege, horse stealing and the like, some of which he believed could be prepared in advance. Vizetelly says he strongly combatted the notion. Together with F.W.N. Bayley, the impecunious friend of Vizetelly's who was appointed editor, and who had strong conservative instincts believing in the advantages of clerical and family support, he 'weaned' Ingram away from his original notion to a much broader ideal.[1] Although the opening address did promise to bring before its public all the 'pith and marrow' of justice and crime, the following week it added to its principles:

> Whenever society is shocked and degraded by crimes so vast in magnitude and so deep in dye as those we have recently seen committed and condemned, we will seek to infuse a healthier tone of morality into the popular mind upon the subject of such dismal atrocities - to diminish the wild and dreadful excitement which at such moments agitate the public frame, and to cleanse that bad and brutal spirit which is fond of revelling in execration, and makes a holiday spectacle of the crisis which sends the murderer before his God.[2]

Nevertheless, at the end of the same number there appeared the portrait of Daniel Good, witnessed as to its accuracy by his attorney, which was explained rather apologetically on the grounds that this crime and its

---

1. Vizetelly, op.cit., i. 221-31. This account was disputed by Ingram's widow, Lady Watkin and a friend, Jabez Hogg. Lady Watkin insisted that her husband's original scheme included 'a very large measure of social and moral aspiration', mingled with hope of worldly success. Ibid., i. 234-7. Vizetelly's version is supported by Jackson, op.cit., pp.284-6 and by the Dictionary of National Biography, xxix (1892) 13 as well as an account written in the anniversary number of the Illustrated London News, 14 May 1892, by Clement Shorter. However, later Shorter contradicted himself, no longer believing that Ingram published a Greenacre murder sheet. Shorter, 'Illustrated Journalism', p.486. As Ingram's papers have probably been destroyed, there is no final version, but the centenary number of the Illustrated London News, 16 May 1942, more or less accepts Vizetelly's version.

2. 'Our Principles', Illustrated London News, 21 May 1842.

general circumstances were of a more general interest than ordinary offences of that nature possessed.[1]

Vizetelly, who drew up the original prospectus, mocked the pretentious language used by Bayley in his opening address, the high-flown rhetoric which hood-winked the public. He refuted Bayley's contention that the paper would be 'oracular with the spirit of truth' by pointing out that in the first number no single engraving came from an authentic source. The drawing of the fire in Hamburg on the front page was adapted from a print in the British Museum; the portraits were wretched; Gilbert had got together the fancy-dress ball at Buckingham Palace from the description in the Morning Chronicle; the representations of the assassination attempt on the Queen verged on the ludicrous.[2] Nevertheless, it is useful to examine the opening address and the principles of the paper, the prefaces of succeeding volumes and the opinions of the rest of the press on the new journal, in order to get some idea, even in exaggerated form, of the sort of audience the paper was aiming at and the sort of content it believed it was producing.

The opening address placed the Illustrated London News firmly within the developing tradition of periodical literature at whose side illustrative art had marched. First there had been illustrated natural history, then literature and poetry, then cheap publications like the Penny Cyclopaedia and Saturday Magazine, then 'the merry aspect of fun, frolic, satire and badinage'. Finally, it progressed into the very heart and focus of public life, the world of newspapers:

> The public will have henceforth under their glance, and within their grasp, the very form and presence of events as they transpire, in all their substantial reality, and with evidence visible as well as circumstantial.

1. Ibid., p.30.
2. Vizetelly, op.cit., i. 231-8.

Bayley went on to list the subjects he intended to cover. In political matters, he made the same point which had been made in connection with Punch, namely the advantages that regularity of issue would bring:

> we lend muscle, bone and sinew to the tone taken and the cause espoused, by bringing to bear upon our opinions, a whole battery of vigorous illustration. What "H.B." does amid the vacillations of parties, without any prominent opinions of his own, we can do with the double regularity and consistency, and therefore with more valuable effect.

He stated the 'homely illustration' which nearly every public measure would afford - Poor-laws, Corn-laws, Factory bills, Income taxes, as well as the field for portraiture in both Houses of Parliament.[1] The following week in expressing the paper's principles, Bayley enlarged on the politics of the paper. It would avoid party politics and instead, concentrate on matters domestic, in particular, the Poor Laws, the Factory Laws and the working of the Mining system. However, although promising to support the work of Lord Ashley, he admitted, 'We are no friends to innovation - we rush at no wholesale changes and reforms'. Furthermore:

> The Poor Laws will be attacked by us only in their clauses of cruelty and of wrong - only when they starve rather than relieve - only when they intrench upon the domestic affections, make poverty a crime, and pour their bitter punishments upon suffering rather than upon sin.[2]

The paper promised the illustration of diplomacy and foreign policy, reportage both in peace and war, giving the literature, customs, dress, institutions and localities of other lands. Another fruitful branch of illustration would be 'the pleasures of the people! - their theatres, their concerts, their galas, their races and their fairs!', as well as those of the aristocracy, 'their court festivals, their bals masqués, their levees, their drawing rooms - the complexion of their grandeur, and the circumstance

---

1. 'Our Address', Illustrated London News, 14 May 1842.
2. 'Our Principles'.

of all their pomp!' It would review illustrated literature and explore the fine arts.[1]

The opinions of the press were full of praise for the venture: the beauty and number of its pictorial embellishments, the high standard of its typography and above all, echoing again what had been written about Punch, the tone of the whole publication. The Morning Post believed:

> It is, without exception, the newspaper which is more calculated for a family, where the younger branches are more numerous, than any other of the periodical journals, from the utter absence of all matter which can offend the most delicate, and the varied nature of its contents.

The Morning Advertiser found 'a further recommendation from the good taste with which it is conducted, and its studied avoidance of whatever should create a blush, or induce an impure sentiment. It is precisely the weekly periodical for the drawing-room table and "evenings at home".'[2] At the end of its first volume the Post congratulated the paper on the unprecedented success with which its endeavours to improve public taste and morals had been attended and hoped that its healthful influence would counteract that of the infamous trashy prints which had long disgraced the weekly press of the country. The Morning Herald continued on the same theme:

> The weekly prints to which we allude have long enjoyed a factitious reputation, founded ostensibly upon their assuming to address themselves more particularly to the wants and wishes of the people at large, but, in reality, working for the abasement of all moral feeling, subverting all religious principle, and widely extending opinions of the most disloyal and pernicious character. These publications had unhappily absorbed a large number of that class of readers who have only the opportunity of seeing a newspaper once a week, and to their evil influence may be attributed much of the discontent which has from time to time manifested itself among the working people.[3]

1. 'Our Address'.

2. 'Opinions of the Press', ibid., 18 June 1842.

3. 'Opinions of the Press', ibid., 28 May 1842. Also, London Journal, i (1845), 328 which described it as a political organ with little influence; 'nor do we believe that it aspires to the exercise of any. It is chiefly got up with a view "to please"; and its circulation is mostly amongst families where there are young persons'. Walter Crane remembers as a child colouring in the ceremonies. Op.cit., pp.9-10.

The paper went on to state that the scope and tendency of the Illustrated London News was the reverse of that which it had condemned; its purpose was to improve at the same time both the mind and the taste of the people: to elevate the moral tone of the weekly newspaper readers, and combine amusement with instruction, and it had drawn within its vortex not only the readers of papers which gave knowledge of 'vice and infidelity', but also the well-informed and highly-educated.

That the Illustrated London News itself was peculiarly aware of its appeal is revealed in subsequent prefaces to the volumes. In July 1843, it declared its superiority to its rivals, as proven by the increase in circulation. It believed its 'real faithful and influential patrons' to be the 'respectable families of England' for whom 'we have kept the printing of our columns inviolate and supreme'.[1] The clergy too had given their approval, boosted no doubt by the distribution of 11,000 free copies to the clergy on the consecration of five new colonial bishops, which was illustrated.[2] As for its tone, like its orthodox colleagues on the daily press, it too grew hysterical in a leader against blasphemous and obscene publications, 'of the vilest order - the most horrible and loathsome impiety - the most cantankerous and leprous in their defiling and brutalizing spirit - and calculated to work upon the minds of the lower classes with the most disgusting and vitiating effect'.[3] Besides disassociating itself from

---

1. 'Prospectus', Illustrated London News, ii. 8 July 1843.

2. 'A Few Select Words to the Clergy', ibid., 27 August 1842. The paper said that its circulation of 24,000 had been increased to 35,000 that week, to celebrate and record the consecration in that issue:
    and which, by its general contents, might not unaptly indicate something like a sympathy of ordinary but interesting intelligence with that tone of purity in the conveyance of the pabulum of news to society which neither religion nor morality would forbid.
   It hoped it would thereby be recommended to new friends.

3. Ibid., 17 December 1842.

the radical or low grade Sunday press, the other theme reiterated in the prefaces was the service to history the paper was performing. Sometimes its aspirations to immortality reached a grandiloquent crescendo worthy of the Art-Union:

> We know that the advent of an Illustrated Newspaper in this country must mark an epoch - give wealth to Literature and stores to History, and put, as it were mile-stones upon the travelled road of time. Here is alone one fine subject of contemplation in such a work - What will it do for the future? Judge by comparison with the past. What would Sir Walter Scott or any of the great writers of modern time have given - whether for the purposes of fiction or history, or political example and disquisition - for any museum-preserved volume such as we have here enshrined. The life of the times - the signs of its taste and intelligence - its public monuments and public men - its festivals - institutions - amusements - discoveries - and the very reflection of its living manners and costumes - the variegated dresses of its mind and body - what are - what must be all these but treasures of truth that would have lain hid in Time's tomb, or perished amid the sand of his hour-glass but for the enduring and resuscitating powers of art - the eternal register of the pencil giving life and vigour and palpability to the confirming details of the pen.[1]

However, despite such rhetorical flights on the theme of its own uniqueness, the Illustrated London News had borrowed much from the journalistic traditions of the past. The Weekly Chronicle itself and those papers owned by William Clement - the Observer and Bell's Life - did not exclusively rely on murders to provide them with illustrated subject matter. They had depicted events surrounding the Cato Street Conspiracy, the Queen Caroline trial, George IV's coronation and his visit to Ireland. In the 1830s, like many broadsheets, they depicted the destruction of the Houses of Parliament by fire, the funeral of William IV, the coronation of Queen Victoria and

---

1. Ibid., i. 6 January 1843. See also that to vol. iii:
    If you have grandchildren open it for them - it will show faithfully what these times were, and it will reflect their living action with pictured fidelity, so that the historian may reap his harvest in that field, and the novelist feed his fiction out of that granary, and the dramatist gather his incidents from that store!
Vol. iv. spoke of the 'pictured register of the world's history;' vol.vi. felt that it aided 'Art and Literature, as well as the Christian Policy, and Concentrated General Intelligence, and Universal History'.

the building of the London to Birmingham railway.[1] Nor was this practice confined to the full-price Sunday newspapers. As we have seen, the radical gazettes, <u>Cleave's Gazette of Variety</u>, the <u>Penny Satirist</u> and the <u>Odd Fellow</u> towards the end of the decade were featuring news events besides their caricatures. <u>Cleave's Gazette</u>, for example, featured well before the <u>Illustrated London News</u> came into existence a bird's-eye view of London from the Duke of York's column, new railways, spectacular fires in the city, straightforward depictions of royal pageantry and celebrated stage actors.[2] Even the provinces were not entirely bereft of illustrated news reportage, although as in the field of political caricature this was sporadic and occurred only at times of political upheaval. In Bristol, the riots which broke out in 1831, were depicted by the Bristol 'school' of artists, who were on the spot to sketch the burning of municipal buildings and the rioting in the streets. These were converted into lithographs for a wider sale, and later, into dramatic, fiery oil painting of the sublime.[3] However, the lithographs were drawn on the stone by Louis Haghe, of the firm of Day and Haghe, Lithographers to the King, of Gate Street, London.[4] Catnach also produced at least two broadsides of the riots and the subsequent trials and executions of the rioters.[5] Similarly, over a decade

1. See Jackson, <u>op.cit</u>., pp.219-75. Also, Morison, <u>op.cit</u>., pp.247-50.

2. <u>Cleave's Gazette of Variety</u>, 24 March, 14 April, 28 April, 2 June, 30 June, 21 July, 28 July, 8 September 1838 &c.

3. The Bristol artists who covered the riots included Samuel Jackson (1794-1869), William James Muller (1812-1845) and Thomas Leeson Rowbotham Senior (1783-1853). A watercolour and bodycolour by Muller and Rowbotham, signed and dated 1833, of 'The Charge of the Dragoons in Queen Square during the Riots of 1831', was commissioned by Thomas Garrard, possibly as one of a set of the riots. It was lithographed by Haghe and published by George Davey. City Art Gallery, Bristol.

4. For the firm of Day and Haghe see Twyman, <u>Lithography</u>, pp.208-9, 219-20, 225.

5. From a scrapbook entitled <u>Troubles in Bristol by Politics, Fire and Pestilence</u>. Bristol City Library, Reference department.

previously, the Peterloo Massacre had been the subject of a drawing by George Cruikshank, and was depicted in a large woodcut published by the firm of J. Evans & Sons, whose neighbour, G. Thompson, in Long Lane, West Smithfield, was putting out similar works on incidents in London.[1] Such contacts with the metropolis suggest the inadequacy of provincial production and marketing techniques compared with the capital. Nevertheless, throughout the 1830's and 1840's, a few successful print-sellers in the larger cities did manage to feed the country-wide market for commemorative prints after paintings of large meetings or the leading personalities connected with reform agitation, Chartism and the Anti-Corn Law League.[2]

Other newspapers existing contemporaneously with the Illustrated London News blur the frontiers of its originality. The Portfolio and London Free Press specialized in fashion plates of leading society ladies as well as odd political cartoons. Similarly, the Penny Weekly Dispatch combined cartoons with melodramatic illustrations of the Chinese war. The Real Life in London and Comic Times copied Bell's Life in London for its sporting illustrations and the Town for its libidinous tone, scraps on

---

1. Cruikshank's original drawing and the engraving taken from it are in the City Art Gallery, Manchester. There are at least two copies of the large sheet, 'DREADFUL SCENE AT MANCHESTER MEETING OF REFORMERS Augt. 16. 1819', one in Manchester, the other in the London Records Office, County Hall, Prints department, together with 'SMITHFIELD MEETING LONDON' and similar cuts.

2. See, for example, 'THE GATHERING OF THE UNIONS ON NEW HALL HILL BIRMINGHAM, May 7th 1832', a lithograph after an original drawing, published in 1832. Birmingham Political Scrapbook iii. 'REFORM MASS MEETING BIRMINGHAM. Drawn on Stone from Sketches taken during Three Successive Meetings in May 1832 by HENRY HARRIS Birmingham'. 'THE ATTACK OF THE CHARTISTS ON THE WESTGATE INN NEWPORT, November 4th 1839', drawn by W. Howel, lithographed by W. Clerk, 202 High Holborn and published by R. Taylor, St. Mary's St. Chepstow. Klugman collection. 'THE NATIONAL CONVENTION as it met on Monday 4th February 1839 at the British Coffee House'. Bishopsgate Institute, Howell collection. 'The Meeting of the Council of the Anti-Corn Law League', engraved by S. Bellin after the painting by J.R. Herbert, R.A. 1847. Published by Thomas Agnew, Manchester. 25 March 1850. Manchester central library, local history department, J.B. Smith's Corn Law and Election Papers.

secret agents and courtesans of fashion.[1] Bell's Penny Dispatch, Sporting and Police Gazette, and Newspaper of Romance and Penny Sunday Chronicle, as the name implies, combined as many of these strands as possible, from the death of Corsican brigands and the explosion of a firework factory to sketches of popular stage performers and executions in Afghanistan.[2] And as usual, the line between fact and fiction was drawn very fine. Edward Lloyd, whose Penny Sunday Times and Companion to the Penny Sunday Times and People's Police Gazette specialized mainly in murder cuts, whether fictitious or actual, went on to issue Lloyd's Illustrated London Newspaper in November 1842, priced at twopence and unstamped. The first number contained odd topographical sketches, one of a wreck and another of the Queen. The second illustrated the life of the Emperor of China; by the third, murder cuts had been resorted to. By the eighth, there were no illustrations and the paper had changed its name to Lloyd's Weekly London Newspaper, perhaps fearing an injunction from the Illustrated London News, more likely through a combination of lack of finance and a warning from the Stamp Office.[3]

152-154

1. Penny Weekly Dispatch ran from March to June 1840, printed and published by J. S. Frampton. Real Life in London and Comic Times, published by William Strange, ran from about May to August in the same year. To trace all of these short-lived attempts to combine illustration with newspapers would be an impossible task. Others include:
Penny Newspaper and Universal Post Bag, Last and Strange, No.1, 9 May 1840.
Penny Times, Davidson and Berger, No.1, 23 January 1841.
Clark's Weekly Dispatch, W. M. Clark, 23 May - August 1841.
Weekly Express, Jonathan Seaver, October - December 1841.
Weekly Dispatch and Modern Astrologer, Last and Clark, No.1. new series, 22 May 1842.

2. Bell's Penny Dispatch, printed by W. Dugdale, Holywell Street. See editions for 6 March, 27 March, 25 September 1842 &c. For the explosion at D'Ernest's Fire Work Factory, in which four people were killed, compare Bell's Penny Dispatch, 13 March 1842 with Cleave's Gazette of Variety, 12 March 1842 and Lloyd's Companion, 13 March 1842.

3. Vizetelly, op.cit., i. 277 suggested the injunction reason. C. N. Williamson 'The Development of Illustrated Journalism in England', Magazine of Art, xiii (1890), 336 gives the more probable grounds of a threat from the Stamp Office.

So in fact the Illustrated London News was part of a fairly common process of adaptation from the old broadside tradition, and on a higher level, that of commemorative prints, to the new broadsheet newspapers. What lifted the Illustrated London News out of the commonplace was the number and regularity of its illustrations. It was not simply a case of being lavishly illustrated, but that it remained lavishly illustrated, indeed improved as the months passed by. The idea of an all-the-year-round illustrated cycle of the social scene was present in William Hone's Every-day Book.[1] Hone's illustrations included saints' feast days, festivals and customs and it is possible that they, together with the monthly engravings in Cruikshank's Comic Almanack, formed the basis for Ingram's idea of stock-fillers, which could be prepared in advance and so confound those critics who said an illustrated newspaper could not hope to be topical and succeed. The Illustrated London News took up the tradition and revelled in it, from harvest homes to valentines, May Day and Guy Fawkes, seasons of the year and days of the month. The climax was reached in the Christmas supplement, first directed by Mark Lemon, in which William Harvey and Kenny Meadows specialized in putting over the holiday bathed in a peculiarly rosy glow of nostalgic content, aided by Alfred Crowquill at the Pantomimes.[2]

As for the 'pleasures of the aristocracy', it has been suggested that

1. The full title of the Every-day Book, or, the Guide to the Year related to: Popular Amusements, Sports, Ceremonies, Manners, Customs and Events, incident to the 365 Days in Past and Present times, being a Series of 5000 Anecdotes and Facts; forming a History of the Year, a Calendar of the Seasons and a Chronological Dictionary of the Almanac; With a Variety of Important and Diverting Information for Daily Use and Entertainment, compiled from Authentic Sources.
The Book came out in monthly parts from 1825 to 1827, and was subsequently much reissued.

2. For example, 'GUY FAWKES DAY', 5 November 1842; 'THE CHRISTMAS PANTOMIMES', 31 December 1842; 'TWELFTH NIGHT CHARACTERS', 31 December 1842; 'FRENCH VINTAGE. ENGLISH HARVEST HOME', 7 October 1843 &c.

the concentration on upper-class social events in the illustrated newspapers in part recall the eighteenth century portrayal of manners in an aristocratic milieu.[1] There were, however, also practical reasons for the emphasis. A royal occasion was described in minute detail in the court circulars of the press - the order of procession, dress and so forth - and thus could be illustrated without any artist necessarily being on the spot.[2] A royal tour was always announced in advance and therefore some sort of topographical illustration could always be found.[3] The Dalziels believed that it was Ebenezer Landells who suggested to Ingram that an artist should be sent to follow the progress of the Queen on her first journey to Scotland, Landells himself undertaking the commission. The paper proudly drew attention to the accuracy of its sketches, and pointed out the stimulus such journeys afforded to trade and employment.[4] The Queen, apparently, was so much pleased that she bought all Landells' original drawings;[5] indeed, she appears to have been exceptional in her support of graphic artists. As Vizetelly pointed out, the graphic artist

1. N. G. Sandblad, Manet, Studies in Artistic Conception (Lund, Sweden 1954), pp.48-50. Sandblad makes this observation in relation to the precursors of Manet's realism in 1862. He traces the tradition back to the engravings of Callot and Bosse in the seventeenth century, which reached its full flowering in the black and white work of the eighteenth century. In nineteenth century France, he sees this continuing not so much in the work of Daumier and Gavarni as that of Constantin Guys and the other newspaper artists who worked for L'Illustration, founded in 1843.

2. As for example was the case with Gilbert's illustrations of the Queen's Costume Ball in the first number of the Illustrated London News, 14 May 1842.

3. For example the 'Pictorial Histories' of Manchester and Newcastle in the Pictorial Times, August - November 1843, July 1846. When the Queen visited Scotland, however, in 1844, the paper perpetrated a howler by depicting a reported reference to 'sheering' as a sheep shearing, not the Scottish sense of cutting the corn. Pictorial Times, 21 September 1844.

4. Illustrated London News, 3 September 1842.

5. The Brothers Dalziel, op.cit., p.6.

met with scant favour in official quarters and facilities were afforded only very occasionally, the illustrated newspaper not being 'then the social power it has since become'. He was allowed to sketch inside Westminster Abbey and at the western entrance on the occasion of the Queen's coronation for Bell's Life in London and the Observer, but the editor, Vincent Dowling, was refused permission for Vizetelly to sketch from the roof of Apsley House.[1] Andrew Spottiswoode, the Queen's printer and owner of the Pictorial Times, succeeded in obtaining a place for John Gilbert in St. James' Palace,[2] and in 1845, when the Queen visited Germany, the Illustrated London News was graced with drawings of the scenery loaned by her husband:-

> A peculiar interest is associated with the authenticity of these Illustrations of the Royal Visit; his Royal Highness Prince Albert having, with his characteristic kindness and condescension, granted our artists access to the originals in his Royal Highness' collection of beautiful Drawings, for the Special Illustration of this Journal.[3]

That relations with the Pictorial Times did not continue quite so cordially is revealed by Vizetelly, who says the Queen was not amused by the caricatures made by 'Cham' on his visit to England in 1843 and printed in the paper, commemorating the Queen's visit to the king of France.[4] However, on the whole, Victoria was well served by the early numbers of the illustrated newspapers and that this was the case is in no small part due to John Gilbert's predilection for flattering portrayals of grand occasions. From the time when he worked in an estate agent's near the Mansion House,

---

1. Vizetelly, op.cit., i. 155-7, 232-3.
2. Ibid., i. 253.
3. Illustrated London News, 16 August 1845.
4. Vizetelly, op.cit., i. 260. Compare Cham's sketches in Pictorial Times 6 January 1844 with the dignified depiction of the same scene, 9 September 1843.

he was always most confident when depicting pomp and ceremony.[1] His 158 work for the Illustrated London News and the Pictorial Times advanced a view of royalty that was at once splendid and elevating. And he was backed up with leaders and articles which not only praised the extension of peace at home and abroad through such progresses, but also the prosperity and encouragement to industry an event like a state costume ball would bring.[2] Yet also the developing scope of such depictions has a wider significance. In its search for novel appeal, the illustrated newspaper was confronted with entirely new problems. On the one hand, it stressed the accuracy, the documentary reality of such a parade. On the other, it is clear from the Queen's reaction to Cham's illustrations that any slight shift in viewpoint could throw the whole scene into the obvious partiality of a caricature. Even the ostensibly straightforward depiction of such events was circumscribed by the choice of subject matter, the predilections and resources of the artist and the requirements of the audience. That the world as revealed through the pages of the Illustrated London News was only a partial vision and fell far short of its claims to universal fidelity is further highlighted when its treatment of the rest of society is examined in detail.

1. For John Gilbert's career see the M. H. Spielmann, 'A Memorial Sketch', Magazine of Art, xxii (1898), 53-64. His drawings as an amateur came into the hands of John Sheepshanks. He showed them to Mulready who advised Gilbert to become a draughtsman on wood. Gilbert began in 1838 with nursery rhymes, was soon known to the booksellers of Paternoster Row and worked on Punch when it first began.
See above p.230.

2. 'Preface', Illustrated London News, vi (1845).

II

> The staple materials for the steady-going illustrator to work most attractively upon are, Court and Fashion; Civic Processions and Banquets; Political and Religious Demonstrations in crowded halls; Theatrical Novelties; Musical Meetings; Races; Reviews; Ship Launches - every scene, in short, where a crowd of great people and respectable people can be got together, but never, if possible, any exhibition of vulgar poverty.

This was the opinion of Charles Knight on the Illustrated London News and its 'endless repetitions', in which the 'scenery is varied; the actors are the same'.[1] The problem is to decide whether this was an isolated view. Why should the Illustrated London News conform to what we take too much for granted, in these photo-documentary days, to be one of the principal functions of illustrated reportage, namely the revelation of unacceptable social conditions? Yet the whole fabric of assumptions out of which the philosophy of the Illustrated London News was constructed argued against the adoption of such a role. First, as we have seen, it purported to be a family magazine and therefore had to observe a certain decorum in what it depicted. Secondly, it had pretensions to impartiality and thus could not take up any partisan cause too obviously. It endeavoured to divert the mind of England, 'too exclusively devoted to politics and the incessant calls of faction, from the threadbare ground of party to the only practically-explored high places of religion, morality and literature'.[2] Thirdly, it had aspirations to elevate and educate through art; and nobody, except possibly Hogarth, could do this through illustrations of the squalid, the vulgar and profane:

> We perceived that a love of art, not merely for its own sake, but from a deep and dearly-cherished consciousness of those high aims which its cultivation will promote and perpetuate, was growing up in the national soul of our beloved country; we determined, at all hazards, to lend our aid towards the work of directing this love of art to those high and noble purposes which we believed it best

1. Knight, Passages of a Working Life, iii. 246-7.

2. Illustrated London News, 27 May 1843.

282

> qualified to subserve – to plunge into the great ocean of human affairs, and to employ the pencil and burin in the work of illustrating not only the occurrences of the day, but the affections, the passions, the desires of men, and the faculties of the immortal soul ... Conscious of our power for good or evil, we shall pursue the course of which we have hitherto given our earnest, unbiassed by temporary considerations, unawed by the frowns of power, from whatever quarter directed, and hoping one day to see realized that ever-glorious prophecy of "Peace on earth, good will to men".[1]

Such sentiments were not quite high-falutin' rubbish: they echoed those voiced by the Penny Magazine, and later, the Art-Union.[2] Furthermore, the paper, as we have seen, had one eye cocked on immortality and the legacy it hoped to bequeath to future historians was very similar to Knight's own summary of its contents.[3]

Given such a philosophy, it is not surprising that the Illustrated London News should concentrate on the glorious side of life rather than the seamy. A few examples help to show this. In discussing its principles in 1842, the paper singled out the working of the mining system for its attention:

> The recent horrible disclosures that have been made upon the last subject will be dragged by us into a broader and a brighter daylight – and the mark, the impress of their atrocity rendered more hideous and inhuman under the burning gaze of national indignation and the loathing of the public disgust.[4]

In the same month of May, the Report of the Inquiry into the Employment and Conditions of Children in the Mines and Manufactures had been published.[5] This proved to be a sensation through its exposure of the degradation and hardship undergone by children at work. What was more, the reports and evidence were illustrated with sketches made by the Sub-Commissioners

1. Ibid.
2. See above pp. 64, 138-9.
3. Compare p.273 with p.281.
4. 'Our Principles'.
5. Parl. Papers 1842, xv, xvi, xvii (380, 381, 382): Children's Employment (mines). Royal Commission, Report and Appendices.

themselves. The Times commented on the variety of woodcuts, 'illustrative of the horrible and degrading labours to which too many of the unfortunate children employed in the coal-mines, &c. appear to be subjected'. It continued:

> One of these woodcuts represents a child dragging a small waggon full of coal on all-fours, just like a beast of burden, and in a state of nudity! To the naked persons of these children is buckled a broad leathern strap, to which is attached in front a ring and about 4 feet of chain, terminating in a hook! Other woodcuts represent children pushing the waggons forward, and apparently using the severest exertions to accomplish their task. Almost all are more than half-naked; and it appears, that in the district of Halifax these wretched beings work perfectly naked, in low, dark, heated, and dismal chambers.[1].

159-161

When the Bishop of Norwich presented petitions in the House of Lords calling for reform in the conditions of employment for women and children in the mines, two leading colliery-owners, the Marquess of Londonderry and Earl Fitzwilliam, protested that the reports were exaggerated, the children were as healthy as those in agriculture and any restrictions of their work should not be lightly imposed.[2] The Times and the Morning Chronicle attacked them, spoke out against the cruelties of the apprenticeship system in the mines and commented favourably on Lord Ashley's introduction of a bill in the House of Commons, limiting such employment.[3] Ashley believed that never:

> since the first disclosure of the horrors of the African slave-trade, has there existed so universal a feeling on any subject in this country, as that which now pervades the length and breadth of the land in abhorrence and disgust of this monstrous oppression.[4]

His abhorrence was shared by Bell's Penny Dispatch, which on 15 May, under the headline of 'Wholesale Murder of the Working Classes', published several pages of illustrations from the reports, showing girls crawling in the mines, girls and boys ascending the shaft together and in general stressing the

---

1. The Times, 29 April 1842.

2. Hansard, 3rd series, 1842, lxiii. 196-9.

3. The Times, 7 May, 8 June 1842.
   Morning Chronicle, 7 May, 12 May, 13 May, 17 May, 24 May 1842.

4. Hansard, 3rd series, 1842, lxiii. 1336.

'revolting indecency' of such conditions.[1] A year later, in May 1843, when petitions were filed by the large mine owners to change the law back: Douglas Jerrold's Illuminated Magazine stated:-

> The degraded condition of the children and young persons in mines was rendered the more apparent to comprehension by the introduction of certain diagrams and sketches, made on the spot by the Assistant-Commissioners. The sight of them caused great commiseration among all those who could feel for the poor people; and great annoyance and disgust to the fine senses of all those who could not, or would not. Lord Londonderry declared that the sketches were offensive - made him quite sick - and were "calculated to inflame the passions". The passions - what passions? The passions of pity and indignation. True, the sketches were often "disgusting", but for that very reason the cause, not the explanatory sketches, should be removed.[2]

It too published some of the sketches, a few of which were published for the first time 'with a view more fully to show the recent condition of these women and infant labourers who have only been just emancipated'.[3] Jerrold's indignation echoes that with which he was to defend Punch against the attack made on its attitudes by the Art-Union; indeed, his view was backed up in the Punch by Leech entitled 'CAPITAL AND LABOUR'.[4] The Illustrated London News, by contrast, failed to publish any of the engravings, lost its nerve at the prospect of printing anything which did not conform to the highest standards of decency and impartiality. Like the Penny Magazine,[5] it preferred to retain a safe academic distance rather than to explore fully subjects which could arouse the partisan passions of pity and indignation, disturb the comfort of the family circle, or pass on such images of the age to posterity.

1. Bell's Penny Dispatch, 15 May 1842.
2. Illuminated Magazine, i (1843), 46.
3. Ibid.
4. See above p. 245.
5. See above p. 147.

Again, the marked lack of documentary depiction of social conditions in the Illustrated London News is emphasized when the paper is compared to its nearest rival in the 1840s, the Pictorial Times. The Pictorial Times was founded in March 1843 by Henry Vizetelly with Andrew Spottiswoode. Vizetelly said he was sick of dancing attendance on Ingram and he managed to get a strong team to support him. Jerrold wrote on social topics, Thackeray was art critic and literary reviewer, Lemon became theatre critic and à Beckett wrote a humorous column. Peter Cunningham was made anecdotal commentator on living literary celebrities, who were drawn by Charles Martin. Frederick Knight Hunt was sub-editor and John Gilbert became principal artist.[1] The paper started in much the same way as the Illustrated London News. It expressly disassociated itself from the illustrated crime sheet, from 'all participation in the acts of those who cloud and desecrate the brightness and natural beauty of the highest moral organ by making it the communicant of the foulest abominations, by fantastically smearing it with blood'.[2] On its first anniversary, similarly, it stressed its value 'preparing a record of news for the moment, and history for the future',[3] while the preface to the second volume compared the effect of an ugly brutalising print which could cause moral injury, with a beautiful print which would give grace, health and sweetness to the soul. Illustrated newspapers were:-

> children of the fancy as well as of the actual world; they are not only papers of news, but pictures of nature and art; they are intended to instruct and refine the feelings and the taste, as well as to convey information... and we venture to think that the amount of intelligence and good feeling which may be acquired through

---

1. Vizetelly, op.cit., i. 242-59.

2. 'To Our Readers', Pictorial Times, 18 March 1843.

3. Pictorial Times, 16 March 1844.

the medium of the eye alone, from works of art, in truthfulness, entireness, and in its immediate effect upon the sensibilities and the mind, has never yet been sufficiently estimated.[1]

Again, in 1845, when discussing the 'embellished' almanacs for the following year, the paper dwelt on the importance of illustrations which 'contribute at the present day to communicate either knowledge of error'.[2] However, two years later the Pictorial Times had come round to the view that to depict the ugly side of life need not necessarily be bereft of value or be positively harmful. Indeed, depending on circumstances, as the Illuminated Magazine believed, such illustrations could have a positively salutary effect. In connection with the 1847 monetary crisis, depicted in a sketch of a bankrupt dealer being refused entrance to the work-house, the Pictorial Times commented:-

> In periods of national prosperity, it is usual to gratify the aggregate vision with pictures of palaces, and amuse the general ear with tales of happiness. At this moment, when by the operation of a wretched financial legislation, our merchant princes are sinking into parish paupers, representation of the workhouse is a subject of national interest - happily for many of the men who were but a few weeks since eminent "on 'Change'".[3]

The reasons for such a change of heart are difficult to discover. It is clear, however, that the actual mechanism of documentary investigative illustration was rarely initiated by the illustrated newspapers themselves. Furthermore, the principal catalyst to action seems to have been the publication of The Times reports from its special correspondents. For example, in 1846, O'Connell was revealed to have property in Ireland which was in a deplorable state of upkeep.[4] On 10 January, the Illustrated London News

---

1. 'Preface', Pictorial Times, ii (1844).
2. Pictorial Times, 29 November 1845.
3. Pictorial Times, 23 October 1847.
4. The Times, 25 December 1845, pp.5-6.

announced:-

> The great interest excited by the "proven" account of the condition of the tenantry of the O'Connell Estate, by "the <u>Times</u> Commissioner", has induced us to dispatch an Artist to the spot, to sketch the principal localities so vividly described in the above communications. Our Artist's report is almost exclusively <u>graphic</u>; but, he had appended to his sketches a few pencil notes, of which we avail ourselves.[1]

Whether the artist was peculiarly inept, or whether he never got beyond Liverpool is hard to decide. The result, at any rate, was two pages of small views, which, but for one interior 'of Chevane's hut', could easily be taken for topographical vignettes of the scenery. The <u>Pictorial Times</u> was rather more thorough in its approach. Two weeks after the efforts of the <u>Illustrated London News</u>, it announced:-

> The prominent career of Mr. O'Connell; the graphic reports of "The Times Commissioner"; the descriptions of Mr. Howitt; and the very general discussion which the two latter have given rise to - these circumstances strengthened and determined an intention we had long entertained to send a PICTORIAL COMMISSIONER to IRELAND, and to direct his first efforts towards Derrynane. On the 26th day of December, an artist (Mr. Frederick N. Sheppard) left our office for Cahirciveen, <u>via</u> Liverpool, and the first fruits of his pencil (with many valuable facts) are now placed before our readers. <u>That justice may be done to Ireland - Ireland must be known as she really is</u> in 1846. Let us make an offering in her behalf of PICTORIAL FACTS.[2]

There followed no less than a dozen pages devoted to his findings, not mere perspectives of distant mountains, but close-up details of villages, housing and families, often explicitly named and constantly reinforced with accounts stressing their authenticity:-

> It should be kept in mind that the sketches from which our engravings are executed, have just been transmitted by our artist, who made them on the spot, and they may therefore be received as faithful transcripts of the objects he beheld. Our aim from the first has been truth, nor shall anything induce us to swerve from it: truth alone can prove satisfactory;

---

1. <u>Illustrated London News</u>, 10 January 1846.

2. <u>Pictorial Times</u>, 24 January 1846.

truth alone can do good; and its motto is, and ever must be, "A clear stage, and no favour".[1]

Again it urged, 'We wish, so far as possible, to annihilate distance, to bring our leaders into contact with the peasantry of the sister isle, and to contribute our part to the urging of appropriate means for the amelioration of their wretched condition'.[2]

The Pictorial Times also displayed a more daring approach in its treatments of conditions at home. On several occasions, it adopted the formula of a double-page spread, consisting of four large drawings facing each other symmetrically and covering different aspects of the subject in question.[3] The most striking use of this technique was reserved for the poor law. When in 1846 the conditions of the Andover workhouse were exposed, the Illustrated London News responded with two isometric drawings of workhouses, the one representing the rather spartan collection of buildings at Andover, the second, the lavish plan for a model workhouse to be built at Canterbury. The latter, with its gothic detailing, closely resembled the idyllic view of the 'Antient Poor Hoyse' of Pugin's Contrasts.[4] No clearer picture of the inhabitants was given than the tiny token figure of a woman and child creeping to the front door in both sketches. By comparison, the Pictorial Times was lavish.

164

1. Pictorial Times, 31 January 1846.

2. Pictorial Times, 7 February 1846.

3. For example, that for the Corn Law agitation, 21 February 1846 which juxtaposed the free traders of the Westminster election and the hustings outside St. Paul's, Covent Garden beside a sketch of the ministerial benches of the House of Commons during the 'Great Debate' on repeal, and beneath it, the Protectionists in the House. Also, 'THE GREAT QUESTION OF NATIONAL EDUCATION', 24 April 1847, which contrasted the friends of the proposed Education Grant, Ashley and the Bishop of Westminster, and beneath them, 'THE EVIL TO BE REMEDIED', against the opponents of the proposed grant, Baines and Bright, who were coupled with an illustration of 'THE GOOD TO BE SECURED'.

4. Illustrated London News, 7 November 1846. A.W.N. Pugin, Contrasts 1841.

A leader condemning the poor law was appended to a portrait of Chadwick, leaning on a book covered table beneath notices announcing, 'RETURNS DEAD' and 'DIETARY SUNDAY GRUEL 1 PINT'. The ironic caption said, 'Rich in good works, ready to distribute, willing to communicate'.[1] The same week there was a double-page spread on 'The Crime of Poverty and its Punishment'.[2] It argued that since the poor law had come into existence twelve years before, nothing but evil had come of it: 'Time has been given for the experiment. What are the results?... behold its character as displayed in the report of the Andover Union Inquiry Committee - peculation and fraud, selfishness and inhumanity'. There had been no compensating side to the act, no reduction in the poor rates, no diminution in crime, no obliteration of pauperism. The four illustrations enhanced their impact by being placed together and by the use of a dead-pan caption to point the moral of each. 'POOR LAW DIVORCE' depicted the punishment of the aged pauper through his separation from his wife in the male and female wards. 'TRANSPORTATION OF THE CASUAL POOR' showed 'THE HALT, THE LAME, THE BLIND; IN SEARCH OF A SUBURBAN FAMINE HOUSE'. 'POOR LAW IMPRISONMENT' showed 'THE UNION WINDOWS ALWAYS LOOKING INWARDS, COUNTRY PROSPECTS ARE EXCHANGED FOR EXPANSIVE VIEWS OF THE WALLS', which was the 'Punishment of the Intelligent Pauper'. 'POOR LAW EXERCISE' depicted hemp and oakum picking, the 'Punishment of the Able-bodied Pauper'.

Such a view had more in common with the scorching caricatures of Grant, more than a decade previously, than the isometric tricks of the Illustrated London News, or the lyrical vignettes employed by the Penny Magazine.[3] In its documentary approach, it provided a visual parallel

1. Pictorial Times, 29 August 1846.
2. Ibid.
3. See above pp. 108, 146.

to the paths of social reportage which were gradually being developed in the government Blue Books, and their coverage in the newspapers. It also resembled the illustrated propaganda put out by societies seeking to draw attention to the causes they upheld. They made the greatest progress in widening the scope of illustrated journalism during the 1840's because they did not have to worry about the needs of a family audience, cater to an illusion of impartiality or glorify the dignity of city life for art and posterity. Such publications could use the darker side for their own purposes. One of the first of these investigative journals was an eight page octavo number, the Poor Man's Guardian, started on 6 November 1847, and published as the organ of the Poor Man's Guardian Society.[1] To accompany articles written by the Chairman of the Society, Charles Cochrane, to the Editor, W.G. Mason went along as pictorial reporter. Together they visited and recorded the huddles of people outside the main London workhouses and the squalor within. Sometimes Mason stressed Cochrane's points by employing visual devices such as cutting sections of the lodging houses to reveal conditions on every level. In 'ENON CHAPEL CEMETERY AND DANCING SALOON' the unhealthy proximity of the dead and the living was graphically depicted, and contrast again was used to compare city balls for the Poles with city beds for the poor, and English pigs with the English poor.[2] Fortunately, the paper was able to illustrate in neat order the

---

1. The Poor Man's Guardian Society apparently worked closely with the National Philanthropic Association and professed its aims in the introductory address to the paper. Having realized the severe trials, the labour and misery of the poor and their helplessness in the face of severe Poor Laws and a harsh administration, it hoped to influence the legislature towards providing a remedy and to encourage sympathy for the poor. It abstained from party or political allusions, 'and from anything which is not strictly in accordance with the one great object to the accomplishment of which we address ourselves, namely, the vindication of the rights and the redress of the great and manifold wrongs of the poor'. 'Our introductory address', Poor Man's Guardian, 6 November 1847.

2. Poor Man's Guardian, No.5, 4 December, No.7, 18 December, No.8, 25 December 1847.

improvements made by the Society: able-bodied paupers employed as street orderlies, a model lodging house in St. Giles and a soup kitchen in Leicester Square.¹ These were the only illustrations in the Illustrated London News which it permitted itself to run, especially when the soup kitchen was visited by Prince Albert.² The Pictorial Times, however, did not flinch from depicting the other side of the story. In a front page article on the conditions of the poor in London, it wrote:-

> London is the city of contrast... not merely poverty, ... not merely filth,... but it is a combination of squalid want, of utter filth and abject misery, such as makes the flesh creep again with disgust and horror.³

The article was attached to one of its most striking images, a picture of a mudlark, 'Sketched on the banks of the Thames, between Lambeth Palace and Vauxhall Gardens'. This was the 'vulgar poverty' which the Illustrated London News refused to face.

In contrast to this developing documentary style, the Illustrated London News tended to stick to conventional types of illustration when it so much as approached subjects of social importance. Take, for example, its view of the metropolis. When it published a panorama of the city, taken from the top of the Duke of York's column, The Times commented:-

> There could not be a more appropriate and acceptable present (in so portable a form) for country friends: and we can imagine the interest with which the "young ones", to whom London is "but a dream", would gaze upon this fine picture of its glories.⁴

1. Poor Man's Guardian, No.4, 27 November, No.6, 11 December 1847. 'RELIEF OF METROPOLITAN DESTITUTION. Able Bodied Paupers Employed as Street Orderlies' appeared as the frontispiece to Sanatory Progress: - being the 5th Report of the National Philanthropic Association (1849), which reprinted many of the cuts from the Poor Man's Guardian. The Report of Progress in the Employment of the Poor; and in the Promotion of Health and Cleanliness (1853) also reprinted the 'street orderly' cut.

2. Illustrated London News, 19 February 1848.

3. Pictorial Times, 10 October 1846.

4. The Times, 10 January 1843.

Yet during the first ten years of its existence, the paper rarely seemed to break through the dream, to depict anything but distant glories. It diligently recorded the improvements to the city, the new prisons and parks, the new streets, drainage and paving schemes, the new government, civic and commercial buildings, the statues and exhibition halls.[1] Always there was progress, always improvement. On the building of New Oxford Street through the middle of the worst west end slum in London the paper commented:-

> Had it merely swept away the squalor and filth of St. Giles's, it would have been a great public benefit; but, if to this we add that upon the site of wretched tenements are fast rising lines of stately houses - mansions, indeed, they would be styled, were they not to be appropriated to trade - our readers at a distance, aided by the annexed Illustration, may form some idea of the splendid appearance which this new thoroughfare will ultimately present.[2]

Similarly, on the building of the elegant New Coventry Street and Cranbourne Street, the paper drew attention to the scheme of the Improvement Commissioners to redesign the area of the Inns of Court with new streets and new Law Courts, which 'will indeed be a boon to the public, as well as a vast advantage to the metropolis in a healthful as well as a moral point of view'.[3] Again on the site chosen for the Public Records Office:-

> By this means, knots of courts and passages, unhealthy almost to pestilence, would be swept away, a narrow and tortuous street (Fetter Lane) got rid of, and an immense amount of benefit insured to this overpeopled metropolitan locality.[4]

---

1. See, for example, the special numbers devoted to the opening of the Royal Exchange, 2 November 1844; Wyatt's statue of Wellington, 30 October 1845; the new Coal Exchange, 3 November 1849 &c.

2. Illustrated London News, 2 January 1847.

3. Illustrated London News, 18 October 1845.

4. Illustrated London News, 20 November 1847.

The same theme of physical airation and health going hand in hand with moral purity, the clearing away of what was foul, both physically and spiritually, cropped up when the colonnade of the Regent's Quadrant was removed in 1848. The upper promenade had not been used and made the mezzanine floor dark and gloomy, obstructing the ventilation necessary for comfort and health:-

> in addition to which, the value of the house property was considerably lessened by the great number of doubtful characters to whom the sheltered portions of the street presented an attraction to the great discomfort and prejudice of the shopkeepers.[1]

Rarely did the Illustrated London News stop to think what the cost was in social terms to the inhabitants of the dwellings swept away. On only one occasion did it go beyond the most noticeable improvements - the widening of streets, 'the sweeping away of so many vile courts and alleys... to make room for architectural displays of sumptuous character', the investment potential - to inquire what had become of the poor persons who had become unhoused by these great changes.[2] Fortunately, the remedy was at hand. The Society for Improving the Condition of the Labouring Classes was busy putting up 'model housing' in Pentonville, while the Metropolitan Society for Improving the Dwellings of the Industrious Classes had constructed baths and washhouses in St. Pancras and artisans' homes. The Ragged School Union had schools in Lambeth and Clerkenwell, the Philanthropic Society, a farm at Red Hill.[3] All were conscientiously

---

1. Illustrated London News, 4 November 1848.
2. Illustrated London News, 11 April 1846.
3. See for example, 'ST. PANCRAS' BATHS AND WASHHOUSES', 3 January 1846; 'MODEL LODGING-HOUSES, PENTONVILLE', 'THE LAMBETH "RAGGED SCHOOL"', 11 April 1846; 'LAMB AND FLAG RAGGED SCHOOLS, CLERKENWELL', 12 January 1849; 'THE PHILANTHROPIC SOCIETY'S FARM, AT RED HILL', 14 June 1851.

depicted with clarity and neatness, or occasionally, in a more lyrical topographical mood.

The only thorough investigation into the less laudable aspects of metropolitan improvement schemes during this period was launched by George Godwin in the Builder during the course of 1853. Godwin had founded this weekly periodical on 31 December 1842 to provide, by means of plans, diagrams, elevations and topographical sketches, a guide to developments in building and architecture, both contemporary and in history. Up to 1853, the only attention paid to lower class housing was in sketches and descriptions of model dwellings planned for the poor by various philanthropic societies, similar to those depicted in the Illustrated London News.[1] However, a leader for 26 February 1853 announced:-

> Deep are the "Mysteries of London", and so environed by dangers that few can penetrate them. The condition of large sections of its inhabitants is wholly unknown to the majority of those above them in the social pyramid, the wide base of which is made up of poverty, ignorance, degradation, crime and misery. Much has been written on the subject within the last few years, and a large amount of good has been done. Still the great bulk of the people are ignorant and apathetic on the subject. Viewing the evil as a mighty one, and strongly impressed by the helpless - almost hopeless - condition of many thousands of fellow creatures, who cannot make themselves heard unless the press speak for them, we propose entering into some particulars respecting the lodging-houses and other dwellings in London inhabited by the poorer classes.

Although it realized the difficulties, even danger, of intruding into these districts, it nevertheless aimed to be comprehensive, asserting that many districts of London were as bad, if not worse, than the once fashionably notorious, but now improved, 'Rookeries' of St. Giles.[2]

1. For example, 'LUMSDEN'S MODEL DWELLINGS FOR WORKING CLASSES', 'DESIGN FOR LABOURERS' COTTAGES, vi (1848), 523-4, 606-7; 'MODEL LODGING-HOUSE, HATTON-GARDEN', 'MODEL HOUSES FOR FAMILIES, STREATHAM-STREET, BLOOMSBURY', vii (1849), 325-7; 'THE ARTIZANS' HOME, SPICER-STREET, WHITECHAPEL', viii (1850), 31; 'PRINCE ALBERT'S MODEL HOUSES', ix (1851), 343; 'COTTAGES FOR THE WORKING CLASSES', x (1852), 468-9.

2. Builder, xi (1853), 129.

The survey continued at fortnightly intervals, with illustrations by John Brown, until the end of the year, receiving fresh impetus from correspondents, action in parliament and the cholera epidemic in the autumn. In 1854, it came out as a book entitled <u>London Shadows; A glance at the "Homes" of the Thousands</u>. Two specific themes were continually reiterated, giving the series its underlying motive. First, it stressed, in contrast to the <u>Penny Magazine</u>,[1] the environmental influence on the character of the inhabitants: 'homes are the manufactories of men, – <u>as</u> the home, <u>so</u> what it sends forth'. It was certain that one important and leading cause of the degradation of many of the poorer classes was the nature of the dwellings in which they were born, lived and died. Again, 'It cannot be too often repeated that the health and morals of the people are regulated by their dwellings'.[2] Secondly, and closely connected, 'What we maintain is this, that it is possible to house the poorer classes comfortably and healthfully at as little cost to the community as they now pay, and at infinitely less cost to the community at large; and what we desire is to aid in bringing this about'. As a result, the paper believed that the dwellings of the London poor should not be demolished without providing places which, under good regulations, they could occupy at a moderate, yet fair cost: the alternative was overcrowding or the workhouse.[3] The <u>Builder</u> maintained a dialogue both through its correspondence columns and more generally in the country as to the actual effect of its campaign. After two weeks of graphic depictions of conditions in Berwick Street, Agar Town and the 'valley of the Fleet', it was flooded with

1. See above p.148.
2. <u>Builder</u>, xi (1853), 129-30, 258.
3. <u>Builder</u>, xi (1853), 129-30, 202, 465-6.

offers of pecuniary assistance for the individual households depicted. It declined to take any part in this: its object was 'permanent improvement and general amelioration... The attention which these papers have already excited, encourages us to proceed, and makes us hopeful as to their effect'.[1] It continued to move through Whitechapel and Spitalfields, feeling generally satisfied with the impression it was making in London and the country, 'and we may fairly anticipate improvements as a consequence'. Some readers had said, '"Your statements are too truthful, too minute, and they give us pain"'. The Builder, echoing Jerrold's responses to such sentiments, regretted that this should be so, but felt it its duty to tell the whole truth. It admitted that the examination of conditions disheartened and distressed, but 'Nothing short of personal experience would have led us to believe in the frightful amount of ignorance, misery, and degradation which exists in this wealthy and luxurious city',[2] and it continued with its account of conditions in Spitalfields. This drew the 'sincere and heartfelt thanks' from a Spitalfields labourer, for exposing the misery. He had lent his copy to several of his fellows and all agreed that the conditions were accurately described.[3] Similarly, an article condemning the Spitalfields model building erected by the Metropolitan Association for Improving the Dwellings of the Industrial Classes as being only for single men, was reinforced by a correspondent who said that it was badly placed for work and too expensive.[4] The depiction of drainage arrangements and the cess-pools in the neighbourhood of Drury Lane, in the

1. Builder, xi (1853), 200.
2. Builder, xi (1853), 257, 337.
3. Builder, xi (1853), 257-8, 337-8, 360.
4. Builder, xi (1853), 337, 360, 465.

wake of the September cholera outbreak, was used by the medical officers of health as evidence, but the church wardens of St. Giles protested at their account for its inaccuracy. The Builder reaffirmed its views and gently reminded its readers that the church wardens were not exactly unprejudiced, since the St. Pancras grave-yard scandal had also been exposed by the paper.[1] Another correspondent, grateful for the account of sanitary conditions hitherto conveyed to the public, drew the paper's attention to those south of the river, which were equally bad. The Builder followed up the suggestion with a page full of illustrations attached to descriptions of the squalor.[2] A final letter suggested the extension of suburban railways to rehouse the poor.[3]

Neither the Penny Magazine nor the Illustrated London News had any equivalent for Godwin's role as what might be termed, an architectural Mayhew. In the Penny Magazine, the nearest approach had been its 'Looking Glass for London'; in the Illustrated London News, it was Thomas Miller's long running series, 'Picturesque Sketches of London', which included both a rookery in St. Giles and the dry arches of the Adelphi in its literary runaround.[4] This attitude was part of a much larger tendency to convert the grim realities of the city into the dramatic or the picturesque. Kenny Meadows depicted the crossing sweeper as a sentimentalized urchin. The pauper child begging on the pavement was treated in a similar fashion in one Christmas supplement of the Illustrated London News.[5] Despite the mockery of Punch,[6] the

---

1. Builder, xi (1853), 465-6, 601-2, 625-7.
2. Builder, xi (1853), 646, 673-5.
3. Builder, xi (1853), 687.
4. Illustrated London News, 22 September 1849, 20 April 1850.
5. Illustrated London News, 17 June 1848, 27 January 1849.
6. See above p.263.

temptation was particularly strong for papers like the Illuminated Magazine and Douglas Jerrold's Shilling Magazine, which crossed the divide between fiction and social comment. An uneasy balance had to be struck between downright social comment and elevating cultural qualities, as Jerrold's prospectus to the first volume of the Illuminated Magazine suggests:-

> It has been the wish of the Proprietors of this work, to speak to the MASSES of the people; and whilst sympathizing with their deeper and sterner wants, to offer them those graces of art and literature which have been too long held the exclusive right of those of happier fortunes.[1]

And of his novel, St. Giles and St. James, first serialized in the Shilling Magazine, Jerrold wrote of his endeavour to show 'the picture of the infant pauper reared in brutish ignorance, a human waif of dirt and darkness', who was the victim of an ignorant disregard of the social claims of the poor upon the rich.[2] The use of romantic contrast between rich and poor was also the theme of 'Death and the Drawing Room or the Young Dress Makers of England', written by 'A Lady' for the Illuminated Magazine. She concluded her article with pious gratitude to the Association for the Relief and Protection of Young Persons Employed in the Dress-Making and Millinery Departments in London, which had been founded by aristocratic ladies.[3] The Pictorial Times commented sourly on this help offered to

---

1. Illuminated Magazine, i (1843). Similarly, that of Douglas Jerrold's Shilling Magazine (1845), i. pp.iii-iv, began:- 'It is intended that this work shall be mainly devoted to a consideration of the social wants and rightful claims of the PEOPLE; that it shall appeal to the hearts of the Masses of England'. It continued that its chief object was:
    'to make every essay - however brief, and however light and familiar its treatment - breath WITH A PURPOSE. Experience assures us that, especially in the present day, it is by a defined purpose alone, whether significant in twenty pages or in twenty lines, that the sympathies of the world are to be engaged, and its support ensured... It will be our earnest desire to avail ourselves of all and every variety of literature, if illustrating and working out some wholesome principle...

2. B. Jerrold, op.cit., pp.228-9.

3. Illuminated Magazine, i (1843), 97-100. See also, 'The Song of the Pauper', i (1843), 139; 'The Orphan Milliners. A Story of the West End', by Miss Camilla Toulmin, ii (1844), 279-85.

the 'slaves of the needle', in a leader entitled 'Fashionable Philanthropy', which revealed that the annual subscription levied by the duchesses was only one pound per annum.[1]

Again, the problem with such subject matter, as the humorous magazines had discovered, was how to reconcile the requirements of both art and life, elevation and information, and again, there were plenty of commentators to draw attention to cases in which the prevailing standards had been breached. The British and Foreign Review, in covering Harrison Ainsworth's Jack Sheppard and Mrs. Trollope's Michael Armstrong the Factory Boy in 1840 struck the nub of the question. Although it was glad 'that the press should raise its voice, and declare that this attempt to reproduce in the novel the jail-bird and the house-breaker, is vicious and offensive', it did not protest merely from 'astonished Innocence suddenly awakened in the midst of a dream of human perfectability', nor from 'compulsory advertence to decorum'. The problem was more basic, even for such a writer as Dickens whose object was to win sympathy for the oppressed:-

> it is questionable whether the amount of justice for the wronged thus obtained is not more than counterbalanced by the amount of morbid irritation excited by details of crime and cruelty.[2]

The Review protested against what could be described as the moral open-endedness of such works, which at best represented 'slices of life', and at worst, were dangerously close to the attractions of the Newgate Calendar.

As for their illustrations, they too were objectionable. On Cruikshank's 'vivid tableaux' for Jack Sheppard it commented, 'alas! how sadly sunk from the high moral position he might have occupied as Hogarth's far-off successor!'[3]

---

1. Pictorial Times, 20 May 1843, 3 June 1843.
2. 'Popular Literature of the Day', pp.223-32.
3. Ibid., p.224. For the connections between Hogarth, Cruikshank and Ainsworth see Harvey, op.cit., pp.44-49.

Hogarth was the great exception to the unspoken laws relating to the depiction of vice. Even the Penny Magazine had depicted a series of his works, anticipating any moral outcry with quotations from Charles Lamb and its own point of view:-

> Those who are acquainted with the works of Hogarth will be aware that in this selection we have not introduced a single print that can offend the most fastidious taste. In many of them there will be found representations of human nature in its degradations of vice and imprudence; but such representations are redeemed from the possibility of exciting disgust by the exquisite skill of the artist.[1]

What made Hogarth acceptable was his genius for relating a moral fable through a series of prints and sealing up the fate of the transgressors by the end. There was no ambiguity of moral standpoint, no relish in the sordid details for their own sake but only as means to the greater end. This then was the device which Cruikshank exploited when he wanted to put over his own moral message of temperance and escape the charges of sensationalism. His two series of plates, issued in 1847-48, entitled The Bottle and The Drunkard's Children slowly expose the plot set in the sordid surroundings of cheap lodgings, gin palaces and dance halls and move in carefully worked-out stages towards their inexorable conclusion of death, transportation and suicide.[2] In publishing two of the plates the Pictorial Times congratulated the artist:-

180-184

> He has been content to help out an author's feebleness or make clear his obscurity, without asserting the true dignity and usefulness of his own profession. The brush is as great a moral teacher as the pen, and capable of exercising its influence independently of the sister instructress. Of this truth George is now aware.[3]

Thus, the Pictorial Times happily slotted in the series to its own philosophy of depicting social conditions that they might prove an example

---

1. Penny Magazine, iii (1834), 121-8.

2. The Bottle is said to have sold 100,000 copies at a shilling a print. The process used was the tinted glyphograph. See above p 252.

3. Pictorial Times, 4 September 1847.

to its audience. Other periodicals were not slow to follow. The
Ragged School Union Magazine for example, produced a series in 1850
entitled 'Scenes in the History of a Ragged Boy', which took him from
a background of poverty and idleness leading to crime, through his   185-187
schooling and emigration, aided by the Union, to an idyllic life in
the bush and eventually, a happy family of his own.[1] Similarly, the
True Briton, which went out of its way to condemn most of the recent
cheap publications as 'earthly sensual devilish', was quite happy to
depict graphically the 'Life of a Reformed Drunkard', whose path,
illustrated by George Measom, contrary to Cruikshank's victim, took   188-190
him from the gin palace to 'THE DEATH-BED OF THE HOLY'.[2]

These evangelical tracts extended the range of illustrated social
reportage, through their reliance on the Hogarthian convention, as much
as The Times commissioner extended it in the illustrated newspapers proper.
However, the pronounced lack of viewpoint which the pretensions to impartiality, the aspirations to moral elevation and the concern for the
decorum of the family could impart was precisely the quality which prevented the Illustrated London News from being more adventurous. Rather
than risk condemnation for pandering to sensationalism or concentrating
on the worst elements in society, it glided through the higher ranks
cushioned by the patronage of royalty and 'pictures of palaces'. The
large scale panorama and literary vignette were employed to insulate its
view of the city, which carefully avoided both the illustrated reportage
of more committed journals and the 'literature of debasement'. It serenely
covered one of the most important political manifestations of the decade

1. Ragged School Union Magazine, ii (1850), 89, 185, 205, 257, 282, 300.
2. True Briton, i. new series (1853) 548, 581, 613, 645, 677, 708.

at home, Chartism, with a few stock sketches in 1842, and a picture
of the police force lolling in Bonner's Fields in 1848, together with
some rather distant views of the crowds.[1] By this time, the whole
of its energies were concentrated on the excitement of events abroad
and it had no competition at home. The <u>Illuminated Magazine</u> had died,
perhaps because of its unwieldy size, more probably because of a mistaken
sense of its own readership.[2] The <u>Pictorial Times</u> had also sunk with a
debt of £20,000.[3] Despite its 'endless repetitions' at home, the
<u>Illustrated London News</u> enjoyed the changes and pace of events abroad,
and what is more, had the capital and organization to cope with them.

1. <u>Illustrated London News</u>, 20 August, 27 August 1842; 15 April, 17 June 1848.
2. Hodder, <u>Memories of my Time</u>, pp.29-38.
3. <u>Dictionary of National Biography</u>, xxix (1892), 14.

III

The 1840s was a decade of increasing technical momentum. The railways and the telegraph together facilitated the speedy transmission of news throughout the country. The telegraph, which was first adopted by the railways to improve their resources for traffic control, began to acquire an increasing source of revenue from contracts with the press and thus enabled the provincial newspapers to print lengthy extracts from the parliamentary and general news.[1] Furthermore, by 1848, government offices made use of its services, the government Board of Health to instruct its medical inspectors during the cholera epidemic, the Home Office to obstruct the Chartist lines of communication and strengthen its own during the disturbances in April of that year.[2] In addition, the multiplication of foreign expresses, correspondents and intelligence improved the quality of reporting from abroad. Such news was mocked by both Punch and the Man in the Moon, with skits on correspondents and expresses contradicting each other, music and chit chat by electric telegraph and even illustrated parliamentary reports.[3] Occasionally, however, such facetiousness had a deeper purpose as when Thackeray devoted two of his 'Jeames' papers to a journey which drew attention to the misery and inconvenience caused by the lack of a uniform rail gauge in England. Thackeray's actual journey had been undertaken in the company of the ubiquitous Henry Cole, who headed the campaign and it is therefore not surprising to learn that the two illustrations by

---

1. J. Kieve, The Electric Telegraph (Newton Abbot, 1973), pp. 49-50.

2. Ibid. Also, F. C. Mather, 'The Railways, the Electric Telegraph and Public Order during the Chartist Period 1837-48', History, new series xxxviii (1953), 40-53.

3. Punch, xvii (1849), 11, 40-41, 235; xviii (1850), 13. Man in the Moon iv (1848), 62.

J. H. Townsend in the <u>Illustrated London News</u> on the same subject, were inserted at Cole's instigation.[1]

Besides publicizing the cause of technological progress in general, the illustrated newspapers were not averse to blowing their own trumpets at each succeeding mechanical feat which facilitated the speed of their publication. When the <u>Illustrated London News</u> had completed a survey of the history of wood engraving, it complimented itself on the boldness of its undertaking and the confidence it felt in its ability to gain the active cooperation of artists and engravers, an inexhaustible supply of interesting subjects and the support of a large audience. In the face of some criticism of the result, the paper asked its readers to consider the difficulties under which it was produced:-

> that the drawing, which might have been made at the distance of two or three hundred miles, may have been sent to London, drawn on the block, engraved, and printed in scarcely more time than was required to travel the same distance about a hundred years ago. A consideration of the various contrivances of human ingenuity which must have been available in order to produce such a cut, and to print it off tens of thousands, in so short a time, would perhaps induce a person of charitable feelings and reflecting mind to excuse rather than to exaggerate any of its presumed defects.

Even with the best minds, the paper continued, and much time and labour, excellence was not always attained:

> surely designers and engravers on wood may be excused becoming occasionally drowsy, after having sat up for the greater part of two or three preceding nights, anxiously labouring to produce cuts <u>just in time</u> to most seasonably gratify public curiosity. Those cuts, however, displaying passing scenes and events, though necessarily drawn and engraved in haste, possess more than a merely ephemeral interest; they not only aid the mind at the present hour in realizing the written description of places and persons, but also form an interesting pictorial record for future times.[2]

---

1. Cole, <u>Fifty Years of Public Work</u>, i. 82-83; ii. 149-57. For the use of graphic propaganda to promote technical innovation, first in relation to gas, and later for railways, see F.D. Klingender, <u>Art and the Industrial Revolution</u> (1947. Ed. and rev. Sir A. Elton 1968), pp.141-63. I am indebted to the late Sir Arthur Elton for showing me his collection of drawings, aquatints and lithographs related to these subjects. For the practical results of such propaganda see Charles Dickens, <u>American Notes</u> (1842), ch.i.

2. <u>Illustrated London News</u>, 22 June 1844.

Similarly, the Pictorial Times wondered at its own efficiency in illustrating the explosion of the steamboat 'Cricket' in 1847:

> By extraordinary exertion, backed by liberal expenditure, we were able to present our subscribers and the public with illustrations in the short space of twelve hours after the accident had occurred, and which appeared contemporaneously with the accounts contained in the journals - a feat in illustrated journalism never before equalled.[1]

Besides stressing the topicality of its visual reportage, the Illustrated London News constantly drew attention, as the Penny Magazine had done,[2] to the technical means it was employing. Ingram's intuitive faculty for judging what would please the public never seemed to fail and was reflected in a circulation rise from 26,000 for the first number to 66,000 by the end of the first year.[3] The demand was always ahead of supply and during the first six months it had to be announced that two editions would be printed: one for the country which would be printed all day Friday, containing news up to the morning of that day, and successive editions which would be printed at intervals of twelve hours up to Sunday morning. The paper would then be reset if there was still not enough. It urged people to order in time through their booksellers.[4] In 1848, however, at the height of revolutionary fever in Europe, the demand was so great that the publisher was pelted with flour for not being able to supply the demand.[5] In order to accommodate this sale, successively improved printing machines were installed. By the end of 1843, the paper had two new steam presses,

---

1. Pictorial Times, 4 September 1847.
2. See above p.143.
3. Jackson, op.cit., p.300. According to Lemon, the paper did make a loss at the start and Ingram and his family sat around in the evening to weep over the week's takings. Hatton, 'The True Story of "Punch"', p.52. The story is contradicted by Vizetelly, op.cit., i.239. According to the London Journal, i (1845), 328 its circulation then was 45,000 and it made a net profit of £16,000 per annum, mainly from advertising.
4. Illustrated London News, 25 June 1842.
5. Jackson, op.cit., p.302.

one for printing each side, with an output of 2,000 perfect sheets an hour.[1] By 1846, the paper illustrated a Double Action machine, with four cylinders, which could turn out 8,000 sheets an hour.[2] By 1851, an edition was printed inside the Crystal Palace on one of Applegarth's vertical printing machines. The accompanying article stated that it would 'enable the proprietors to facilitate the Saturday morning early delivery', and 'gratify the millions of enquiring visitors to the Great Exhibition'.[3]

An article on the printing of the large panorama of the city of London reveals the stages taken in the engraving process. The daguerrotypes, a number of small silver plates, taken by Claudet, were first of all touched up and copied by Henry Anelay, one of the Illustrated London News' draughtsmen. It was then drawn on wood by Sargeant, sixty blocks for the purpose being supplied by Mr. Wells of Lambeth. Landells then supervised the engraving of eighteen other engravers, 'all eminent in their particular departments', one for buildings, another for foliage, a third tints and so on. This took two months. Then it was stereotyped by the firm of Knight and Hawks. Finally, it was mounted on blocks, retouched and inspected, and printed by steam press.[4] Besides Landells, Ingram seems to have relied on a number of engraving firms for work, including Vizetelly, Sly and Linton for the 'fine art' work, until the paper set up its own

---

1. Illustrated London News, 2 December 1843.

2. Illustrated London News, 21 November 1846.

3. Illustrated London News, 31 May 1851.
   This was not the first time the Ingrams had publicized their technical prowess within an exhibition building. In June 1840, they printed off specimens of typography from the Exchange Rooms, Nottingham, during the Nottingham Mechanics' Exhibition. I am indebted for this information to Mrs. H.H.C. Ingram.

4. Illustrated London News, 31 December 1842.

engraving department at the end of the decade.[1] He also relied on John Gilbert. Reported to have executed 30,000 drawings for the paper, he was renowned for the speed of his draughtsmanship and his promptitude in business dealings. It is said that a messenger sent from the paper to his home in Blackheath with the subject and the block, was told to take a turn on the heath while he completed the drawing. If it was a large jointed block, Gilbert was known to complete the drawing section by section in order for the engravers to start on it the sooner.[2] As a result, he developed the sketchy open style which loosened up the whole manner of wood engraving to something which more approximated to a pen sketch. As Mason Jackson wrote, he stands out as the first great popular illustrator of the Victorian era:

> He it was who first gave a distinctive character to the illustration of news. He seems to possess an inborn knowledge of the essentials of newspaper art, and could express by a few freely drawn lines and touches the hurried movement of street crowds or the state and dignity of Court ceremonies. Whether he had to draw a knight in armour or a gentleman in a paletôt he did it in a way exactly suited to rapid engraving and printing. The feeling which, in his pictures, made him delight in battle-fields, blazoned banners, velvet and gold, made his drawings on wood brilliant in handling and always picturesque. It was most fortunate that the commencement of his career was coincident with the foundation of the pictorial press.[3]

The greatest test of the illustrated news process came when events abroad required depiction. It was common practice in the eighteenth century, following on the new interest in the picturesque, and in geographic and scientific exploration, to take draughtsmen on archaeological, antiquarian, architectural and topographical tours to furnish views of distant corners

---

1. Vizetelly. op.cit., i. 232. According to a rather complicated reckoning made out by Linton for his partners, from January to October 1846, his firm received £1,764.15.6 worth of business from Ingram and Cooke, by far his largest account. Feltrinelli, Linton collection.

2. The Brothers Dalziel, op.cit., pp.66-80. Vizetelly, op.cit., i. 231-3.

3. Jackson, op.cit., pp.355-6.

of the world, on voyages of discovery and the foreign missions of statesmen and soldiers.[1] Furthermore, the Seven Years War and the Napoleonic Wars had created a market for the lives and deaths of popular heroes, conforming to the traditions of history painting, as well as for battle scenes on land and sea, and views of the costume and scenery in lands where the British armies had fought.[2] The market had readily been exploited by print dealers like the Boydells, so such a range of engraved depictions as the Illustrated London News presented was scarcely a novelty, except in so far as wood engraving enabled it to be produced in larger numbers and for less cost. In its first address, the paper promised pictures of the wars in China and Afghanistan, and after a month included a map and an extremely stylized battle scene from the latter country, as well as a few topographical illustrations.[3] Rather closer to home, the paper was caught unprepared by an insurrection in Poland in 1846. It dreamed up some 'POLISH INSURGENTS', engraved by a 'Polish Volunteer', from a painting owned by the Literary Association of the Friends of Poland, found a portrait of Adam Czartoryski, one of the leaders, and filled in with sketches of Polish folk costumes and topographical drawings of Cracow and Posen.[4] The same year, when trouble broke out in India, the paper relied on the traditional source of amateur sketches: by G.T. Vigne Esq., in the Punjab, an officer in the Bengal Engineers and Captain G.P. Thomas.[5] In January

1. See S.T. Prideaux, Aquatint Engraving, (1909), pp.84-86, 215-57.

2. Ibid., pp.215-28. Also, E. Wind, 'The Revolution of History Painting', Journal of the Warburg Institute, ii (1938), 116-27. C. Mitchell, 'Zoffany's "Death of Captain Cook"', Burlington Magazine, lxxxiv (1944), 56-62; 'Benjamin West's "Death of General Wolfe" and the Popular History Piece', Journal of the Warburg and Courtauld Institutes, vii (1944), 20-33; 'Benjamin West's "Death of Nelson"', Essays in the History of Art presented to Rudolf Wittkower, ed. D. Fraser, H. Hibbard, M.J. Lewine (1967), pp.265-73.

3. Illustrated London News, 11 June 1842.

4. Illustrated London News, 14 March, 28 March, 11 April 1846.

5. Illustrated London News, 28 March, 11 April, 25 April 1846.

1848, when there was a massacre of British officers in the Kaffirland War, a full-page sketch of the terrain encircled the page, taken from a sketch lately received from a Cape Town artist:

> It shows the general character of the vegetation of the country, especially the <u>bush</u>, behind which the Kaffirs lie in wait for trains of waggons, which they attack and plunder with frequent success. The waggon drawn by yoked oxen is the usual goods and produce conveyance of the Colony.[1]

However it was the 'year of revolutions' in Europe which brought out the best in the paper and gave the greatest boost to the role of the 'special artist'.[2] When revolution broke out in Paris in February, pictures of Guizot and Barrot were hastily reprinted, but in addition there were a few drawings illustrating the reception of the news and proclamations in the city:

> We are enabled by the activity of our Artists in Paris (from whom we have received the Sketches) to present the reader with the accompanying illustrations of some of the scenes detailed in the adjoining columns.[3]

The 'team of artists' included Valentin, Forest and Guys. How they all became involved specifically with the <u>Illustrated London News</u> is unfortunately not known, but Guys had worked for the paper before.[4] In London, Gavarni who had fled from Paris the previous November to escape arrest for debt, was employed to transfer Guys' drawings onto the block and also to draw his own gallery of types and scenes. Of two of his pictures, 'DEFENDERS OF THE BARRICADE' and 'BEHIND THE BARRICADE' the paper commented flatteringly:

---

1. <u>Illustrated London News</u>, 29 January 1848.
2. For the role of the special artist see W. Simpson, <u>Autobiography</u> (1903). Also, the fictional account in R. Kipling, <u>The Light that Failed</u> (1897).
3. <u>Illustrated London News</u>, 26 February 1848.
4. Mackay, <u>Through the Long Day</u>, i. 124-5.

Both Pictures are rife with the vigour of Gavarni's characteristic pencil; and they present vivid portraits of the classes by whom "the Great Revolution" has been achieved.[1]

The paper appeared to be ubiquitous. Besides depicting in ever enlarging double numbers events in France, it dispatched Duncan to Newhaven to catch the landing of Louis Philippe in England, and even showed the rush to buy outside its own offices.[2] Never behindhand when there was a possibility of self-congratulation, it printed a letter from one of its Paris correspondents:

> It may not appear very good taste to begin my letter with what is a compliment to the ILLUSTRATED NEWS; but as a matter of fact I feel bound to state that the excellent Illustrations which appeared in the last number of your journal have created quite a sensation here, and have called forth universal expressions of astonishment and delight. These good Parisians know not what to admire most, the number, the extraordinary correctness, or the admirable execution of your designs, or the almost incredible rapidity with which they have been brought forth. Like their Revolution, the double number of the ILLUSTRATED LONDON NEWS seems something not very far removed from the miraculous, and they hold that like it, it is entitled to the designation "glorious".[3]

Punch, always ready to parody what was fast becoming a visual cliché presented its own 'CUT FOR AN ILLUSTRATED PAPER. A BARRICADE TAKEN ON THE SPOT BY OUR ARTIST'.[4] By the middle of the year, as the revolutionary spirit spread to Italy and Germany, the Illustrated London News was able to produce an illustrated guide to the 'History of the Revolutions in Europe 1848'.[5] Each country, undoubtedly, had its own artists, its own caricatures, to cover the same events in their own terms, ranging from

1. Illustrated London News, 18 March 1848.
2. Ibid.
3. Illustrated London News, 11 March 1848.
4. Punch, xv (1848), 39.
5. Illustrated London News, 1 July 1848.

high art to scurrilous squibs.[1] But no other country besides England possessed to quite such a developed degree that combination of capital, organization and technology which could diffuse its art on such a massive scale and at so low a cost throughout Europe. In less than quarter of a century since the death of Bewick, the trade of wood engraving had advanced from a provincial to an international market.

1. For the relationship between the political events and leading artists in France in 1848 see T.J. Clark, The Absolute Bourgeoisie, The Image of the People (1973). For Germany, see Kunst der Bürgerlichen Revolution 1848/49 (Berlin, 1973). Also, W.A. Coupe, 'The German Cartoon and the Revolution of 1848', Comparative Studies in Society and History, ix (1966-67) 137-67.

In 1847, an advertisement for the Illustrated London News appeared in the Man in the Moon. It believed that the increasing prosperity of the journal and the development of this system of news illustration would enable its picturesque attractions to be appreciated more widely, 'by all classes of the intelligent public'. The advertisement went on to summarize the position of the Illustrated London News in the journalistic spectrum and to pick out those characteristics which I have suggested in this chapter mark its significance. Firstly, it continued to win '"golden opinions"' for the 'rapidity and precision with which its artists illustrate the stirring events, scenes, and incidents of the great world before us'. But it also stressed the 'taste and judgement which have uniformly characterised the choice of these subjects for the pencil; in each instance, investing the realities of life with a superior interest, by the aid of the exhaustless and ennobling graces of art'. It went on to suggest what these subjects were: the pageant splendour of royalty, the homelier festivals of the people, the spirit of public improvement and scientific advancement, the 'false' glories of war, the great creations of genius in architecture, painting and sculpture, steam transit by land and sea, the growth of our colonies, the 'master minds' of the age. In its literary conduct, party opinions had been studiously avoided, and social improvement only sought — never demanded — 'if it have any politics, they are those of the hearth and the home'. This was the cosy comfort of its outlook:

> Its tone is that which is best suited to good and general society; and, while it presents all the utilities of a newspaper, especial care is taken that not a line shall appear in its pages which shall offend decorum, or offer violence to the courtesies of life. Hence the "Illustrated London News" may be placed, with equal advantage and safety, upon the tables of the library, the drawing-room, and the public institution.

It assured its readers that all of this world, this level of perception would be mirrored in the journal, 'be chronicled with photographic fidelity', to ensure 'the life-like reality' of the illustrations. That this is only a partial vision is clear to us today. However, in the middle of the nineteenth century, its status was different. The precise point to which pictorial journalism had reached at this time will be examined in a concluding chapter.

CONCLUSION

VIII

On 11 February 1851, Lord Granville agreed to admit the artist of the <u>Illustrated London News</u> to draw the building of the Great Exhibition. It had not been a foregone conclusion. It was seriously proposed to exclude the press. Henry Cole, ever attuned to the requirements of good public relations, protested that this would be an unprecendented step, that the interest of the Exhibition was to attract the Press as much as possible, to facilitate their freedom of access rather than the reverse. In his own words:-

> I entreated the Commissioners not to make so fatal and suicidal a rule. A member of the Commission exclaimed, "Alas! we are a press-ridden people!" and then the Commissioners present gave up the proposal, and Dilke said to me "You get your way when you are in a minority of one".[1]

The <u>Illustrated London News</u>, therefore, through Cole's good offices was allowed to cover the Exhibition, even, as we have seen, to the extent of printing off an edition inside the Crystal Palace, on one of Applegarth's vertical printing machines.[2] The propriety of the gesture did not go unnoticed. The <u>Economist</u>, in an article entitled 'Speaking to the Eye' compared the function of the Great Exhibition to that of a large illustrated newspaper:-

> It is the history of modern art and invention taught by their actual products. Like sun painting, it speaks all tongues. It wants the facility of spreading that history over the world, and the illustrated paper, without which it is doubtful if it could itself have ever existed, comes to its aid, dispenses the knowledge so scientifically gathered and arranged, and so graphically displayed in Hyde Park, over all the nations of the earth. The Exhibition can only diffuse knowledge by inviting persons from all quarters to come and see it at a great charge and great inconvenience; but its own classified and illustrated catalogues, and the illustrated newspaper, spread the gathered knowledge, for the charge of a few

---

1. Cole, <u>Fifty Years of Public Work</u>, i. 194-5.
   From Cole's diary, 25 January 1851, we learn that the protesting Commissioner was Lord Overstone. See also, entries for 5, 9 and 11 February 1851.

2. <u>Illustrated London News</u>, 31 May 1851.

shillings, over distant lands and diversified nations. The Exhibition would be a comparatively feeble instrument for helping forward improvement, without the assistance of illustration and letter-press to convey a knowledge of its wonderful palace and its contents to the many millions who cannot possibly visit it.[1]

Thus, the Economist proved itself true heir to the doctrines of the Anti-Corn Law League, and the utilitarian function of art as manifest in its trade bazaars, its emphasis on progress and diffusion by mechanical means.[2] The Great Exhibition and the illustrated newspaper worked together to produce a cheap universal shorthand for the masses, to echo the Quarterly Review, 'at the least possible expense of time, trouble, money, and, we may add, of intellect'.[3] The Economist fully accepted the necessary characteristics of such an art without any academic scruples:-

> Representations of the material world and of common life do not constitute what is called high art; and it cannot escape observation, that the Exhibition, though it contains a few statues, is much more a collection of products of the arts that minister to the comforts and enjoyment of the millions, than of the products of high art. Instruments from a steam engine to a bodkin, house furniture of all descriptions, and materials for clothing, from the most comfortable woollen to a gossamer web of lace, make up a large part of its contents. The common and the useful predominate far above fine and high art. In like manner, it is with common events, with subjects that interest the multitude, that illustrated newspapers fill their columns. To give illustrations they must have many customers, and the arts they cultivate must attract the multitude. Historical paintings, grand compositions, even fine groups, and, above all, allegorical groups of sculpture, constituting high and fine art, have no charms for the people, and will not be encouraged.

In other words, the artists had to become the equivalent of the 'constitutional statesman', going out to catch 'the floating sentiment of society', and administering it, embodying it, in his work; he could no longer afford to be like the politician aloof within the fading frescoes of 'the palace of the

---

1. Economist, ix (1851), 533.

2. For an account of the free-trade bazaar to display British manufactures, held by the Anti-Corn Law League in March 1845, which anticipates the Great Exhibition, see A. Prentice, History of the Anti-Corn-Law League (1853), ii. 315-41.

3. See above p.142.

senatorial body'.[1] And, as if to add insult to the injury suffered by the academic artist, the Economist went so far as to impugn his motives by concluding on a suitably cynical, materialist note, and then blandly twisting it into a backhanded compliment to the remnants of high art ideals:

> When those make large fortunes who carefully minister to the common wants, men of genius and talents will not long pursue any species of art which is less handsomely rewarded. Hitherto, though much talent has been engaged in illustrating passing events, the art has not done for it all of which it is susceptible. Now that it is becoming so extensively popular, it must attract to it the highest talents, and effect a revolution in art itself, making it more than ever subservient to the uses of the multitude, and in improving them by all the talents and genius that are now wasted on many profitless and unimproving pursuits.

However, neither the Great Exhibition nor the illustrated newspaper presented such a comfortably lined progress for the genius or the masses as the Economist would have wished. Even in 1850, the masses could not be relied upon to lead the way entirely without assistance. Just as the government had interfered with the freedom of the press in the 1830's, with the post office and telegraph in the 1840's, so too the Great Exhibition, as yet another channel of communication, had to be controlled. As Cole himself admitted, 'fear of the working classes caused most anxiety'. In 1850, plans were made to form a Central Working Classes Committee to collect money, diffuse information and promote visits among the working classes. It was composed of what amounted to a stage army in the battle for popular education. It included Lord Ashley and Monckton Milnes, Robert Chambers,

---

1. See above p. 20 . For an unfavourable view of the decoration of the Houses of Parliament see (J.W. Croker), 'Life of Haydon', Quarterly Review, xciii (1853), 582-3, who wondered whether, 'when the first novelty is over, these works will appear deserving of the - we may call it - eternity for which they are destined':

    > We do not think that the climate of our country, the capacity of our public edifices, or the genius of our people, is favourable to this style of decoration, and we fear that the greatest advantage to be hoped from it - the employment of a dozen artists practising a style incompatible with domestic decoration, and therefore incapable of supplying an adequate personal livelihood to its professors - will not at all fulfil the expectations that are formed from it.

    Also, T. Carlyle, 'Jesuitism', Latter Day Pamphlets (1850).

Charles Knight and William Tait, Dickens and Thackeray, J. S. Mill, Southwood Smith and Jeremy Bentham, Francis Place, William Lovett and Henry Vincent. The latter predictably reported that the working classes regarded the Exhibition as a movement to wean them from politics, though he confessed that he himself was quite friendly to it. There was trouble over the site of the building in a public park, as well as opposition to the overall priorities of the Exhibition, as Punch revealed.[1] Eventually, after disputes about the exact status of the Committee and its disturbingly variegated personnel, it dissolved itself on the grounds that without the official recognition of the Royal Commission, it could neither efficiently render the services it sought to perform, nor command the confidence of the working classes.[2] Instead, all questions about the visits of the working classes were referred to Mr. Alexander Redgrave, who was appointed by the Home Office to look into questions of transport and accommodation, as well as the precautions taken for the maintenance of order, health, employment and welfare generally in the metropolis. His report, although it highly commended the conduct of the visitors, the 'most remarkable quietude and good order' which prevailed, and the lack of any significant alteration in the social condition of the city, nevertheless, did underline the very real apprehension which was felt before the Exhibition took place, albeit in somewhat apologetic tones:-

> An uninterrupted succession of arrivals of large numbers of all classes, both from the provinces and from abroad, the absence of experience as regarded their conduct under circumstances so new and unprecedented as those of the present year, and the impossibility of conjecturing the course which might be taken by unscrupulous agitators, led many most intelligent persons to

---

1. See above p. 246.

2. Cole, Fifty Years of Public Work, i. 188-93.

anticipate these arrivals with anxiety and even with alarm, and although their fears have not been realized, yet there were many considerations pregnant with doubt, if not apprehension; the recent revolutionary movements on the Continent, the freedom of access to this country to men proscribed in their own, and the temptations to the increased activity of our own disorderly population, were matters which, at the time, required serious attention as affecting the public tranquility.[1]

International exchange, universal peace and harmony was one thing, universal revolution another. The identification of art with mass audiences by the writer in the Economist and the Parisian readers of the Illustrated London News raised dangerous possibilities.

This whole incident is characteristic of many of the themes which have been explored in the preceding chapters. In the first place, it illustrates yet again the close connection that was seen to exist between graphic journalism during this period and the larger function of art to elevate and educate, to help to increase the well-being and the wealth of the country. Again, the same people were involved: popular educators like Sir Henry Cole with a flare for publicity, who did not blench at utilizing the fruits of industrial growth to foster the diffusion of art, taste and middle class mores to the masses. Furthermore, they had the decisive backing of technological expansion to support them. The overall commercialization of wood engraving, as well as the specific financial arrangements made by successful illustrated periodicals like Punch and the Illustrated London News, were crucial in determining the expansion and continuing importance of this section of communications. However, a constant theme which counterpoints this march during the 1830s and 1840s was, as I have shown, the opposition

---

1. Parl. Papers 1852, xxvi (1485), pp.111-26: Report of Mr. Alexander Redgrave on the Visits of the Working Classes. Appendix XXIV to the First Report of the Commissioners for the Exhibition of 1851.

voiced to the relentless force of the process. These growing pains ranged from the engraver's own fears about his loss of identity and the anger expressed as the pressure of the Penny Magazine, which was itself part of a larger reaction against the results of Whig government, to the stand taken by Douglas Jerrold on Punch in the 1840s for social and political justice, as well as the illustrated campaigns launched by small pressure groups in the field of documentary depiction. By 1850, however, the reputation of graphic journalism was regarded in the main as synonymous with bland respectability and universal comprehensibility. The Economist reiterated the belief that the artist spoke a universal language, extending the theory of high art advanced by Burke and other eighteenth century theorists to cover the value-free qualities of illustrated reportage:[1]

> A Turk or a Chinese understands him at once, though to make either of them understand a written or spoken description would require a long time and much instruction. Hence it has become practicable to establish in London French and German journals, which, by means of illustrations, speak at once to the natives of France and Germany. Pictures, then, have the great advantage over words, that they convey immediately much new knowledge to the mind; they are equivalent, in proportion as they approach perfection, to seeing the objects themselves; and they are universally comprehended. They may make every one participate in the gathered knowledge of all. Artists cannot yet catch and pourtray spiritual abstractions; many of the thoughts of the great historian, of the philosopher, and the poet can only have symbolical and suggestive signs; but all that can be seen - all the material world - may be represented by the artist; and now that his skill can, by the improvements in art, be made cheaply available, it will in future be more and more employed to spread knowledge through every society.[2]

However, in retrospect we can see that just as the idealized vision of universal comprehensibility down through society proved abortive, so too an even profounder hope in the perfectibility of graphic representation

---

1. See above pp.2-3.

2. 'Speaking to the Eye', p.533. Also, Jackson, op.cit., p.1.

in the world at large was over-optimistic. When the Illustrated London News billed itself as doing its utmost to ensure the 'life-like reality', the 'photographic fidelity' of its illustrations,[1] it was deluding itself. 1850 marked the zenith of optimism on behalf of the illustrated press, but the clouds of doubt were never far away. Ironically, only five years later James Fenton, the photographer of the Crimea, had punctured its pretension in a letter he wrote home to William Agnew:-

> Have you seen that picture in the 'Illustrated London News' of Sebastopol from the sea? It has caused a good deal of astonishment and amusement here, as it is a regular 'Punch' sketch. Goodall's sketches seem to astonish everyone from their total want of likeness to the reality, and it is not surprising that it should be so, since you will see from the (photographic) prints sent herewith, that the scenes we have here are not bits of artistic effect which can be effectually rendered by a rough sketch, but wide stretches of open country covered with an infinity of detail.[2]

William Goodall's 'bits of artistic effect' were not isolated examples; the glorification of war and its backcloth in the illustrated newspapers continued into the twentieth century.[3] However, in contrast to the decades of the 1830s and 1840s which had witnessed the building up of momentum and confidence behind the far reaching claims made by the illustrated newspaper, the latter part of the century saw the steady decline of its powers to convince. Dickens' tongue-in-cheek description in Bleak House (1853) symbolizes the trend:-

> Then, there comes the artist of a picture newspaper, with a foreground and figures ready drawn for anything, from a wreck on the Cornish Coast to a review in Hyde Park, or a meeting in Manchester, - and in Mrs. Perkins's own room, memorable evermore, he then and there throws in upon the block, Mr. Krook's house, as large as life;

1. See above p.313.

2. H. and A. Gernsheim, Roger Fenton. Photographer of the Crimean War (1954), pp.21, 62.

3. See, for example, the illustration of the surrender of Sedan at the close of the Franco-Prussion War, which appeared in the Illustrated London News, 17 September 1879, compared with the original sketch, which had been made by Moulin while 'under fire' on the vellum of a discarded drum head and reproduced in Jackson, op.cit., pp.318-9.

in fact considerably larger, making a very Temple of it. Similarly, being permitted to look in at the door of the fatal chamber, he depicts the apartment as three-quarters of a mile long, by fifty yards high.[1]

Fenton too was of course circumscribed by his technical equipment, and the whole context which helped to determine his choice of subject matter and the requirements of his audience.[2] Increasingly, however, the camera seemed to offer more freedom and greater speed for competing with the 'word-picture', which could be 'flashed over the telegraph wires, written out, set up in type, and printed off long before an artist had made the sketch to illustrate the same fact.'[3] Through the invention of the stereoscopic camera in 1853, and a number of other small hand-held cameras soon afterwards, it became possible to take instantaneous views of street life, domestic views and action photographs.[4] Over the next thirty years, successive innovations were made by which photography gradually took over many of the reproduction processes involved in graphic journalism,[5] leaving wood engraving by the turn of the century in a demoralized condition.[6] Despite all the faith exhibited on his behalf by politicians and manufacturers, educators and philanthropists, proprietors, editors and journalists, the wood engraver was not elevated towards perfection. He and his work were products of his age, circumscribed by society, its perceptions and resources, and eventually, all but eliminated by its requirements. The relentless drive to cut costs, to save time, trouble, and perhaps also, intellect, proved too strong.

1. C. Dickens, Bleak House (1853), ch.xxxiii.

2. Gernsheim, op.cit., p.13.

3. W. Gamble, 'Pictorial Telegraphy', Penrose's Pictorial Annual, iv (1898), 2.

4. H. Gernsheim, 'Aesthetic Trends in Photography Past and Present. Documentation and Reportage', Motif, No.3 (1959), 71-85.

5. See Jackson and Chatto, Treatise (1861 ed.), pp.576-7. Also, Shorter, 'Illustrated Journalism', 490.

6. Booth, op.cit., iv. 109-18.

BIBLIOGRAPHY

BIBLIOGRAPHY

1. UNPUBLISHED SOURCES

I   Print Collections

When the final volume of Dr. M.D. George's Catalogue of Political and Personal Satires in the British Museum ends in 1832, there is no continuation of such an authoritative guide to this material for the rest of the nineteenth century in England. However, the British Museum still provides an essential starting point for any work in this field, not only through its volume of Penny Political Caricatures, collections of H.B. prints and drawings and McLean's Monthly Sheet of Caricatures, but also in its separate folders of prints for the reigns of William IV and Queen Victoria. Other useful public collections of prints and caricatures in London are those of the Victoria and Albert Museum and the Guildhall Library, while that of the London Records Office at County Hall provides an especially valuable topographical survey. There is no guide which describes collections in the rest of the country, whether they be housed in a local library, art gallery, museum or private collection. I have found that some central libraries, notably those of Birmingham and Bristol, have valuable scrapbooks of material compiled on the history of these cities. Others, such as the Picton Library, Liverpool and the Guildhall Library, London have been bequeathed personal collections of prints and satires. The most interesting collections of political material made in the nineteenth century, including newspapers and some prints, are the invaluable Place collection in the British Museum, the Howell collection at the Bishopsgate Institute and J.B. Smith's Corn Law and Election Papers in Manchester Central Library. The John Johnson collection in the Bodleian Library provides a unique repository for ephemeral material in this country, including prints, broadsides and first numbers of periodicals. The Society of Antiquaries and the St. Bride Printing Library both have collections of broadsides, the latter - like the Victoria and Albert Museum - also housing rare examples of wood blocks, and printing and engraving materials. Finally, I am deeply indebted to the late Sir Arthur Elton, James Klugman and E.P. Thompson for allowing me to see their private collections, founded on their interest in the technology and politics of the period.

Birmingham Public Library: Birmingham Scrap Book.

Bishopsgate Institute, London: Howell Collection.

Bodleian Library, Oxford: John Johnson Collection.

Bristol City Art Gallery.

Bristol City Library: Reference Department. Troubles in Bristol by Politics, Fire and Pestilence.

British Museum, London: Prints and Drawings Department.

Sir Arthur Elton Bart. (deceased): Private Collection.

Guildhall Library, London: Prints and Drawings Department. Sir John Key Collection.

James Klugman: Private Collection.

Laing Art Gallery and Museum, Newcastle upon Tyne: Prints Department.

London Records Office, County Hall, London: Prints Department.

Manchester Central Library: Local History Department. J.B. Smith's Corn Law and Election Papers.

Manchester City Art Gallery: Prints and Drawings Department.

Picton Library, Liverpool: William Thelwall Thomas Collection.

Saint Bride Printing Library, London: Wilson Collection of Street Literature.

Society of Antiquaries, London: Broadsides Collection.

E.P. Thompson: Private Collection.

Victoria and Albert Museum, London: Prints and Drawings Department.

II Manuscript Collections

Artists' Annuity Fund and Artists' Benevolent Fund Minutes 1825-1847:
  in Private Hands.
British Museum: Place Papers. Additional MSS 27,789; 27,790; 27,791;
  27,797; 27,834; 35,148; 35,150; 35,151.
British Museum: Place Newspaper Collection. Sets 17 (General Election 1831-1833
  21 (Distress, Riots, Luddites, Incendiaries), 32 (Law, Church, Distress,
  Improvement), 41 (Morals, Manners), 65 (Specimens of Unstamped Illegal
  Newspapers), 66 (Chartists), 70 (Newspaper Specimens 1770-1837).
Feltrinelli Institute, Milan: W.J. Linton Papers.
Guildhall Library, London: Norman Collection.
Punch Library, London: Ledgers, Letters, Schedule of Deeds and Documents.
Henry Silver Diary (typescript prepared by J.L. Bradley). J.B. Groves,
  Rambling Recollections and Modern Thoughts by an Old Engraver (MS).
Post Office Records Office, London: Post 23/7 (Postal Packets opened under
  Secretary of State's Warrant. Press Comments).
Public Records Office, London: Home Office Papers. Series 40/28, 40/29, 40/33
  (Disturbances 1831, 1835), 64/12, 64/13, 64/14, 64/15, 64/16, 64/17, 64/18,
  64/19 (Police Secret Service. Seditious and Libellous Publications),
  75/1-10 (Police Gazette), 79/4 (Miscellaneous. Private and Secret).
Stationers' Hall, London: Copyright Registers.
University College, London: Brougham Collection. Society for the Diffusion
  of Useful Knowledge Papers.
Victoria and Albert Museum, London: Cole Papers.

2. PARLIAMENTARY PAPERS

Hansard

Accounts and Papers 1828 xviii (Address on the King's Speech).

1832 xiii (Taxes on Knowledge).

1834 xxiii (Stamps on Newspapers).

1835 xxvii (Newspaper Stamp - Cheap Literature).

1835 xxx (Newspaper Stamp Duties).

1842 lxiii (Employment of Children in Collieries. Employment of Women and Children in Mines and Collieries).

Reports

Select Committee on Intoxication 1834, viii (559).

Select Committee on the Police of the Metropolis 1834, xvi (600).

Select Committee on Art and the Principles of Design 1835, v (598); 1836, ix (568).

Select Committee on National Monuments and Works of Art 1841, vi (416).

Royal Commission on Children's Employment (mines) 1842, xv, xvi, xvii (380, 381, 382).

Census of Great Britain. Occupation Abstract 1844, xxvii (587).

Select Committee on Art Unions 1845, vii (612).

Select Committee on the Schools of Design 1849, xviii (576).

Select Committee on Newspaper Stamps 1851, xvii (558).

First Report of the Commissioners for the Great Exhibition 1852, xxvi (1485).

First Report of the Department of Practical Art 1852-3, liv (1615).

Census of Great Britain. Tables on Ages, Civil Condition, etc. 1852-3, lxxxviii part 1 (1691-i).

Royal Commission on the Royal Academy 1863, xxvii (3205).

3. PRINTED SOURCES

I Illustrated Periodicals and Serial Prints

These are located in the British Union Catalogue of Periodicals, unless otherwise stated. The most useful finding list for the period 1830-1836 is J.H. Wiener's Descriptive Finding List of Unstamped British Periodicals 1830-1836. In the few cases where the following periodicals do not appear in either bibliography, I have given further details.

Anti-Corn Law Circular (1839-41) - Anti-Bread Tax Circular (1841-43) - League (1843-46).

Asmodeus, or the Devil in London (1832).

Bell's Life in London and Sporting Chronicle (1822-86).

Builder (1842-   ).

Cleave's London Satirist and Gazette of Variety (1837) - Cleave's Penny Gazette of Variety (1837-44) - Cleave's Gazette of Variety (1844).

Cleave's Weekly Police Gazette (1834-36).

Comic Almanack (1835-53).

Douglas Jerrold's Shilling Magazine (1845-48).

Everybody's Album and Caricature Magazine. Johnson collection. Nos. 4, 6, 29, 32 (14 February 1834 - 15 April 1835). 6d plain, 1s coloured. Pub. J. Kendrick.

Figaro (1836). Wiener.

Figaro in London (1831-39).

Figaro's Life in London and Literary Times (1836). Wiener.

Fool's-Cap. Wiener.

George Cruikshank's Omnibus (1841-42).

George Cruikshank's Table-Book (1845).

Giovanni in London (1832). Wiener.

God's Revenge against Murder (1833-34).

Graphic and Historical Illustrator (1832-34).

Great Gun (1844-45).

H.B.'s Political Sketches (1829-51). British Museum and many public and private print collections throughout the country.

History of the Pirates of All Nations (1836-37). Wiener.

Illustrated Family Journal (1845).

Illustrated London News (1842-   ).

Joe Miller the Younger (1845).

John Bull's Picture Gallery (1832). Wiener.

Journal for Laughter. Johnson collection. Nos. 1, 2 (16 May - 23 May 1850). Price 3d.

Judy (1843).

Leisure-Hour (1852-1905).

Life. The Mirror of the Million (1850).

Lives of the Most Notorious Highwaymen, Footpads and Murderers (1836-37). Wiener.

Lloyd's Illustrated London Newspaper (1842-43).

Lloyd's Political Jokes (1836). Wiener.

London Journal and Pioneer Newspaper (1845-46).

London Policeman (1833).

Looking Glass, or McLean's Monthly Sheet of Caricatures (1830-36).

Man in the Moon (1847-49).

Mephystopheles (1845-46).

Month (1851).

Odd Fellow (1839-42).

Pasquin (1847).

Pasquin (1850).

Penny Magazine (1832-45).

Penny Punch (1849).

Penny Satirist (1837-46).

Penny Sunday Times and People's Police Gazette (1841-47).

People's Journal (1846-49).

People's Periodical and Family Library (1846-47).

People's Police Gazette and Tradesman's Advertiser (1833-34). Wiener.

People's Weekly Police Gazette (1834-36).

Pictorial Times (1843-48).

Political Drama (1833-36). Wiener.

Political Drama (1841-42). Johnson collection. No.15. Price 1d plain. Pr. and pub. B.D. Cousins.

Political Play Bill (1835). Wiener.

Political Stage (1835). Wiener.

Poor Man's Guardian (1847).

Punch (1841-   ).

Punch in London (1832).

Punchinello (1832).

Puppet-Show (1848-49).

Quizzical Gazette and Merry Companion (1831-32).

Ragged School Union Magazine (1849-75).

Real Life in London (1840).

Reynold's Miscellany (1847-69)

Satirical Puppet Show (1833). Wiener.

Slap at the Church (1832).

Slap at the Times (1832).

Squib (1842).

Town (1837-42).

True Briton (1851-54).

Weekly Herald (1836).

Weekly Show-up (1832). Wiener.

II Primary Sources

The Journal of Mrs. Arbuthnot, 1820-1832, ed. F. Bamford and the Duke of Wellington (1950).

'Art Union of London', Art-Union, ix (1847), 74, 109.

H. de Balzac, Old Goriot (1834), trans. M. A. Crawford (1951).

H. de Balzac, Lost Illusions, (1837-43), trans. H. J. Hunt (1971).

C. Baudelaire, The Painter of Modern Life and other Essays, ed. and trans. J. Mayne (1964).

The Hon. G.C.G.F. Berkeley, My Life and Recollections (1865-6).

Edward Laman Blanchard, ed. C. Scott and C. Howard (1891).

C. Booth, Life and Labour of the People of London, second series (1903).

J. Britton, Autobiography (1849-50).

The Rev. R. A. Bromley, A Philosophical and Critical History of the Fine Arts (1793-95).

Lord Brougham, Taxes on knowledge. Stamps on newspapers. Extracts from the evidence of the Right Honourable Baron Brougham and Vaux, Lord Chancellor, before the Select Committee of the House of Commons on libel law, 14 June, 1834.

Lord Brougham, 'Newspaper Tax', Edinburgh Review, lxi (1835), 181-5.

Lord Brougham, 'Lord Brougham's Speech, on presenting the London Petition against the Taxes on Knowledge, in the House of Lords', British and Foreign Quarterly Review, i (1835), 157-72.

Lord Brougham, 'George the Fourth and Queen Caroline - Abuses of the Press', Edinburgh Review, lxvii (1838), 1-80.

A. Bunn, A Word with Punch (1847).

E. Burke, A Philosophical Enquiry into the Origin of our Ideas of the Sublime and the Beautiful (1757), ed. J. T. Boulton (1958).

'The Burnings in Kent, and the State of the Labouring Classes', Fraser's Magazine, ii (1830), 572-81.

Life of John, Lord Campbell, ed. the Hon. Mrs Hardcastle (1881).

'The Caricatures of H.B. in 8 volumes. From 1828 to 1837', London and Westminster Review, xxviii (1838), 261-93.

T. Carlyle, Latter-Day Pamphlets (1850).

H. Cole, 'Modern Wood Engraving', London and Westminster Review, xxix (1838) 265-78.

H. Cole, 'Wood Engraving among Female Artists', London and Westminster Review, xxxviii (1838), 215-8.

H. Cole, Fifty Years of Public Work (1884).

W. Collins, The Woman in White (1860).

W. Crane, An Artist's Reminiscences (1907).

J. W. Croker, 'Life of Haydon', Quarterly Review, lxciii (1853), 558-600.

G. Cruikshank, Our Own Times (1846).

G. Cruikshank, The Drunkard (1847).

G. Cruikshank, The Drunkard's Children (1848).

P. Cunningham, A Handbook for London, Past and Present (1849).

The Brothers Dalziel, A Record of Work 1840-1890 (1901).

Destructive (1833).

C. Dickens, American Notes (1842).

C. Dickens, 'The Rising Generation', Examiner, 30 December 1848.

C. Dickens, Bleak House (1853).

'Diffusion of Knowledge', Edinburgh Review, xlv (1826), 189-99.

J. Diprose, Some Account of the Parish of Saint Clement Danes (Westminster) Past and Present (1868-76).

B. Disraeli, Coningsby (1844).

H. Dixon, 'The Literature of the Lower Orders', Daily News, 26 October, 2 November, 9 November 1847.

A Journal kept by Richard Doyle in the year 1840, introd. J. Hungerford Pollen (1885).

B. F. Duppa, A Manual for Mechanics' Institutions (1839).

H. Sutherland Edwards, Personal Recollections (1900).

'English Artists on Wood', Art-Union, viii (1846), 11.

The Reminiscences of Edward Evans, ed. and introd. R. McLean (Oxford, 1967).

T. H. Fielding, The Art of Engraving (1841).

T. Frost, Forty Years' Recollections: Literary and Political (1880).

W. Gamble, 'Pictorial Telegraphy', Penrose's Pictorial Annual, iv (1898), 1-9.

'George Cruikshank', London Journal, vi (1847), 177-82.

T. Gilks, The Art of Wood Engraving (1866).

T. Gilks, A Sketch of the Origin and Progress of the Art of Wood Engraving (1868)

G. Godwin, London Shadows; a Glance at the "Homes" of the Thousands (1854).

J. Grant, Sketches in London (1838).

The Greville Memoirs, ed. L. Strachey and R. Fulford (1938).

S. C. Hall, Retrospect of a Long Life: from 1815 to 1883 (1883).

Mrs. S. C. Hall, 'A Visit to the Female School of Design', Art-Union, vii (1845) 231.

P. G. Hamerton, Thoughts about Art (1873 ed.).

P. G. Hamerton, 'Wood Engraving', Encyclopaedia Britannica, viii (Edinburgh, 9th ed., 1878), 436-9.

J. Hannay, Satire and Satirists (1854).

J. Hannay, 'Bagot's Youth', Idler, i (1856).

J. Hannay, 'English Political Satires', Quarterly Review, ci (1857), 394-441.

T. C. Hansard, Typographica (1825).

F. Harrison, Autobiographical Memoirs (1911).

H. T. Hartley, Eighty-Eight Not Out (1939).

A. S. Hartrick, A Painter's Pilgrimage through Fifty Years (Cambridge, 1939).

J. Hatton, With a Show in the North (1871).

J. Hatton, 'The True Story of Punch', London Society, xxviii (1875).

J. Hatton, Journalistic London (1882).

The Life of Benjamin Robert Haydon, ed. T. Taylor (1853).

H. von Herkomer, The Herkomers (1910).

W. E. Hickson, 'Reduction, or Abolition, of the Stamp-Duty on Newspapers', London Review, ii (1836), 336-55.

G. Hodder, Memories of my Times (1870).

F. Reynolds Hole, Memories (1892).

G. J. Holyoake, Sixty Years of an Agitator's Life (1892).

G. J. Holyoake, Bygones Worth Remembering (1905).

W. Hone, The Three Trials of William Hone (1817-8).

W. Hone, Aspersions Answered (1824).

W. Hone, The Every-Day Book (1825-6).

'Illustrated Books', Quarterly Review, lxxiv (1844), 167-99.

'Incidents of my Life', London, Provincial and Colonial Press News, xxi (1886).

J. Jackson and W. A. Chatto, Treatise on Wood Engraving (1839. 2nd ed. 1861).

J. C. Jeaffreson, A Book of Recollections, (1894).

J. Johnson, Typographica or the Printer's Instructor (1824).

C. Knight, Cyclopaedia of London (1851).

C. Knight, The Old Printer and the Modern Press (1854).

C. Knight, Passages of a Working Life during Half a Century (1864-5).

J. Landseer, Lectures on the Art of Engraving (1807).

Lawyer (1833).

J. B. Leno, The Aftermath (1892).

W. J. Linton, The Masters of Wood-Engraving (1889).

W. J. Linton, Memories (1895).

H. W. Lucy, Sixty Years in the Wilderness (1909).

C. Mackay, Forty Years Recollections (1877).

C. Mackay, Through the Long Day (1887).

D. Masson, Memories of London in the 'Forties (1908).

The Young George du Maurier, ed. D. du Maurier (1951).

H. Mayhew, London Labour and the London Poor (1861-2. Dover ed. 1968).

Selections from London Labour and the London Poor, ed. and introd. J. L. Bradley (1965)

A Memorial of Certain Inhabitants of the City of London to the Chancellor of the Exchequer, 6 May 1835.

J. S. Mill, 'The Taxes on Knowledge', Monthly Repository, viii (1834), 103-9.

'Misapplication of Wood Engraving', Art-Union, ii (1840), 23-24.

Memoirs, Journal and Correspondence of Thomas Moore, ed. Lord J. Russell (1853-6).

The Letters of Hannah More, ed. R. Brimley Johnson (1925).

R. Nicholson, Cockney Adventure and Tales of Town Life (1838).

R. Nicholson, An Autobiography (1860).

Sir Robert Peel from his Private Papers, ed. C. S. Parker (1899).

'Notes on Periodicals', New Monthly Magazine, xxxix (1833), 424-31.

'Our Weekly Gossip', Athenaeum, No.839, 25 November 1843, pp.1048-9.

'The Penny Magazine', Athenaeum, No.235, 28 April 1832, p.274.

Pigot and Co.'s London and Provincial New Commercial Directory (1822-48).

'The Philosophy of Punch', Westminster Review, xxxviii (1842), 265-318.

Political Register (1834-5).

Poor Man's Guardian (1831-5).

'Popular Literature of the Day', British and Foreign Review, x (1840), 223-46.

Post Office London Directory (1840-50).

J. Pye, Patronage of British Art (1845).

F. von Raumer, England in 1835 (1836).

G.W.M. Reynolds, Pickwick Abroad (1839).

G.W.M. Reynolds, Master Timothy's Bookcase (1842).

G.W.M. Reynolds, The Mysteries of London (1846-50).

Sir J. Reynolds, Discourses on Art (1769-90).

The Correspondence of Henry Crabb Robinson with the Wordsworth Circle (Oxford, 1927), ed. E. J. Morley.

Robson's London Directory and Classification of Trades (1821-42).

J. A. Roebuck, On the Means of Conveying Information to the People (1835).

G. A. Sala, Life and Adventures (1894).

G. A. Sala, Things I have Seen and People I have Known (1894).

W. Savage, A Dictionary of the Art of Printing (1841).

Autobiographical Notes of the Life of William Bell Scott, ed. W. Minto (1892).

A. Senefelder, A Complete Course of Lithography (1819).

Mrs. R. Seymour, An Account of the Origin of the Pickwick Papers (1854).

Sketches by Seymour, ed. J. C. Hotten (1867).

'Shakespeare. The Illustrations by Kenny Meadows. Introductory Remarks', Art-Union, vii (1845), 165-8.

M. A. Shee, Rhymes on Art (1805).

C. K. Shorter, 'Illustrated Journalism: its Past and its Future', Contemporary Review, lxxv (1899), 481-94.

The Autobiography of William Simpson (1903).

C. Manby Smith, The Working Man's Way in the World (1853).

C. Manby Smith The Little World of London (1857).

A. Somerville, The Autobiography of a Working Man (1848).

R. Southey, 'On the Means of Improving the People', Quarterly Review, xix (1818), 79-118.

'Speaking to the Eye', Economist, ix (1851), 533.

'Taxes on Knowledge', Westminster Review, xv (1831), 238-67.

W. M. Thackeray, 'Half a Crown's Worth of Cheap Knowledge', Fraser's Magazine, xvii (1838), 279-90.

W. M. Thackeray, 'Parisian Caricatures', London and Westminster Review, xxxii (1839), 282-305.

W. M. Thackeray, 'George Cruikshank', London and Westminster Review, xxxiv (1840), 1-60.

W. M. Thackeray, Pendennis (1848-50).

W. M. Thackeray, The Newcomes (1853-55).

W. M. Thackeray, 'Pictures of Life and Character', Quarterly Review, lxcvi (1854) 75-86.

The Letters and Private Papers of William Makepiece Thackeray, ed. G. N. Ray (1945-6).

C. Thomson, The Autobiography of an Artisan (1847).

J. Timbs, Club Life of London (1866).

'View of the Present State of Lithography in England', Library of the Fine Arts, i (1831), 201-16.

H. Vizetelly, Glances back through Seventy Years (1893).

C. R. Weld, 'On the Popular Penny Literature of the Day', Athenaeum, No.643, 22 February 1840, p.157.

J. F. Wilson, A Few Personal Recollections by an Old Printer (1896).

'The Wood Engravers', Art-Union, v (1843), 271; vi (1844), 123.

'Wood Engraving', Art-Union, i (1839), 25-32; vi (1844), 45-46.

'Wood Engraving', Chambers' Miscellany, ix. No.85 (1846), 1-16.

E. H. Yates, Recollections and Experiences (1884).

III Secondary Sources

A. A. Adrian, Mark Lemon First Editor of Punch (1966).

B.W.E. Alford, 'Government Expenditure and the Growth of the Printing Industry in the Nineteenth Century', Economic History Review, 2nd series xvii (1964-5), 96-112.

R. D. Altick, The English Common Reader (1957).

R. D. Altick, Victorian Studies in Scarlet (1972).

A. Aspinall, Lord Brougham and the Whig Party (Manchester, 1927).

A. Aspinall, 'The Social Status of Journalists at the Beginning of the Nineteenth Century', Review of English Studies, xxi (1945), 216-32.

A. Aspinall, Politics and the Press, 1780-1850 (1949).

W. Bagehot, 'The Character of Sir Robert Peel', National Review, iii (1846), 146-74.

I. Bain, 'Thomas Ross and Son. Copper- and Steel-plate Printers since 1833', Journal of the Printing Historical Society, ii (1966), 3-22.

I. Bain, 'James Moyes and his Temple Printing Office of 1825', Journal of the Printing Historical Society, iv (1968), 1-10.

W. Bates, '"Gallery of Comicalities"', Notes and Queries, 4th series v (1870), 43-44.

W. Bates, George Cruikshank: the artist, the humourist, and the man (Birmingham, 1878).

A. W. à Beckett, The A Becketts of 'Punch' (1903).

D. P. Bliss, A History of Wood-Engraving (1928).

F. Bridge, The Old Cryes of London (1921).

A. Briggs, 'Middle-Class Consciousness in English Politics 1780-1846', Past & Present, No.9 (1956), pp.65-74.

Sir F. C. Burnand, 'Mr Punch, Some Precursors and Competitors', Pall Mall Magazine, xxix (1903).

J. W. Burrow, Evolution and Society (1966).

Caricature and its Role in Graphic Satire (Providence, Rhode Island 1971).

H. Carter, Orlando Jewitt (1962).

T. J. Clark, The Absolute Bourgeois (1973).

T. J. Clark, The Image of the People (1973).

A. M. Cohn, George Cruikshank. A catalogue raisonné (1924).

'Comicalities', Notes and Queries, 4th series iv (1869), 478.

F. R. Cooper, Nothing Extenuate. The Life of Frederick Fox Cooper (1964).

W. A. Coupe, 'The German Cartoon and the Revolution of 1848', Comparative Studies in Society and History, ix (1966-7), 137-67.

W. A. Coupe, 'Observations on a Theory of Political Caricature', Comparative Studies in Society and History, xi (1969), 79-95.

M. Dalziel, Popular Fiction a Hundred Years Ago (1957).

A. Dobson, Thomas Bewick and his Pupils (1884).

C. Driver, Tory Radical. The Life of Richard Oastler (1946).

The Victorian City, ed. H. J. Dyos and M. Wolff (1973).

C. S. Felver, Joseph Crawhall (Newcastle, 1973).

K. J. Fielding, 'Charles Dickens and the Department of Practical Art', Modern Language Review, xlviii (1953), 270-7.

A. Fletcher, Allegory, the Theory of a Symbolic Mode (Ithaca, 1964).

J. Forster, Life of Charles Dickens (1872-4).

P. Fraser, 'The British Government's Use of Parliamentary Publicity in the Past', Gazette, xi (1965), 192-202.

R. Freeman, English Emblem Books (1948).

W. P. Frith, John Leech, his Life and Work (1891).

M. D. George, Catalogue of Political and Personal Satires, ix, x, xi (1949-54).

M. D. George, English Political Caricature to 1792, 1792-1832 (1959).

H. and A. Gernsheim, Roger Fenton. Photographer of the Crimean War (1954).

H. Gernsheim, 'Aesthetic Trends in Photography Past and Present. 3. Documentation and Reportage', Motif, iii (1959), 71-85.

E. H. Gombrich and E. Kris, 'The Principles of Caricature', British Journal of Medical Psychology, xvii (1938), 319-42.

E. H. Gombrich and E. Kris, Caricature (1940).

E. H. Gombrich, Art and Illusion (1960).

E. H. Gombrich, Meditations on a Hobby Horse (1963).

D. J. Gray, 'A List of Comic Periodicals published in Great Britain, 1800-1900,' 'Victorian Periodicals Newsletter, No.15 (1972), pp.2-39.

F. Greenwood, 'The Newspaper Press. Half a Century's Survey', Blackwood's Edinburgh Magazine, clxi (1897), 704-20.

G. L. Griest, Mudie's Circulating Library and the Victorian Novel (Newton Abbot, 1970).

J. Gross, The Rise and Fall of the Man of Letters (1969).

F. W. Hackwood, The Life and Times of William Hone (1912).

C. G. Harper, English Pen Artists of To-day (1892).

E. M. Harris, 'Experimental Graphic Processes in England, 1800-1859', Journal of the Printing Historical Society, iv (1968), 33-86, v (1969), 41-80, vi (1970), 53-89.

J. R. Harvey, Victorian Novelists and their Illustrators (1970).

C. Hindley, The Life and Times of James Catnach (late of Seven Dials) Ballad Monger (1878).

C. Hindley, A History of the Cries of London, Ancient and Modern (1884 ed.).

C. Hindley, The History of the Catnach Press (1886).

P. Hollis, The Pauper Press (1970).

G. J. Holyoake, The History of Cooperation in England (1875-7).

E. Howe, The London Compositor 1785-1900 (1947).

G.V.B.S. Hunter, 'George Reynolds, Sensational Novelist and Agitator', Book Handbook, i (1947), 225-36.

W. M. Ivins, Prints and Visual Communication (1953).

M. Jackson, The Pictorial Press. Its Origins and Progress (1885).

L. James, Fiction for the Working Man 1830-1850 (1963).

W. B. Jerrold, The Life and Remains of Douglas Jerrold (1859).

W. B. Jerrold, The Life of George Cruikshank (1882).

W. C. Jerrold, Douglas Jerrold and 'Punch' (1910).

J. Kieve, The Electric Telegraph (Newton Abbot, 1973).

F. G. Kitton, John Leech, Artist and Humourist (1884 ed.).

F. G. Kitton, Dickens and his Illustrators (1899).

F. D. Klingender, Art and the Industrial Revolution, ed. and rev. A. Elton (1968)

Kunst der Bürgerlichen Revolution 1848/49 (Berlin, 1972).

J. J. Lamb, '"Gallery of Comicalities"', Notes and Queries, 4th series v (1870), 209-10.

G.S. Layard, A Great "Punch" Editor. Life, Letters and Diaries of Shirley Brooks (1907).

F.R. and Q.D. Leavis, Dickens the Novelist (1970).

P.-A. Lemoisne, Gavarni (1924).

K. Lindley, The Woodblock Engravers (Newton Abbot, 1970).

N. McCord, The Anti-Corn Law League 1838-46 (1958).

S. MacDonald, The History and Philosophy of Art Education (1970).

J. Macdonnell, State Trials, new series ii. 1823-31 (1889).

T. McLean, An Illustrative Key to the Political Sketches of H.B. (1844).

Sir T. Martin, The Life of His Royal Highness the Prince Consort (1875-80).

F.C. Mather, 'The Railways, the Electric Telegraph and Public Order during the Chartist Period 1837-48', History, new series xxxviii (1953), 40-53.

A. Mayhew, A Jorum of "Punch" (1895).

J. Medcraft, Bibliography of the Penny Bloods of Edward Lloyd (Dundee, 1945).

'Mister Punch at Dinner', British and Colonial Printer and Stationer, lxcviii (1926), 63.

C. Mitchell, 'Zoffany's "Death of Captain Cook"', Burlington Magazine, lxxxiv (1843), 56-62.

C. Mitchell, 'Benjamin West's "Death of General Wolfe" and the Popular History Piece', Journal of the Warburg and Courtauld Institutes, vii (1944), 20-33.

C. Mitchell, 'Benjamin West's "Death of Nelson"', Essays in the History of Art presented to Rudolf Wittkower, ed. D. Fraser, H. Hibbard, M.J. Lewine (1967), pp.265-73.

S. Morrison, The English Newspaper 1622-1932 (Cambridge, 1932).

C.W. New, The Life of Henry Brougham to 1830 (Oxford 1961).

G.D. Nokes, A History of the Crime of Blasphemy (1928).

M. Ogilvy, Countess of Airlie, Lady Palmerston and her Times (1922).

J. Physick, The Duke of Wellington in Caricature (1965).

R.B. Postans, 'The Origin of "Punch"', Notes and Queries, 7th series vii (1889), pp.401-2.

R.G.G. Price, A History of Punch (1957).

S.T. Prideaux, Aquatint Engraving (1909).

I. Prothero, 'Chartism in London', Past & Present, No.44 (1969), pp.76-105.

G.N. Ray, Thackeray. The Uses of Adversity 1811-46 (1955).

S. Rayner, Cries of London (1929).

F. Reid, Illustrators of the Sixties (1928).

J.C. Reid, Bucks and Bruisers (1971).

Radical Squibs and Loyal Ripostes, ed. E. Rickword (Bath, 1971).

F.D. Roberts, 'More Early Victorian Newspaper Editors', Victorian Periodicals Newsletter, No.16 (1972), pp.15-28.

W. Roberts, The Cries of London (1924).

F. Gordon Roe, 'Seymour, the "Inventor" of "Pickwick"', 'Portrait Painter to "Pickwick", or, Robert Seymour's Career', Connoisseur, lxxvii (1927), 67-71, 152-7.

G. Rude and E.J. Hobsbawm, Captain Swing (1969).

N.G. Sandblad, Manet, Three Studies in Artistic Conception (Lundl, 1954).

L. Shepard, John Pitts, Ballad Printer of Seven Dials (1969).

L. Shepard, The History of Street Literature (Newton Abbot, 1973).

F.B. Smith, 'British Post Office Espionage, 1844', Historical Studies, xiv (1970), 189-203.

F.B. Smith, 'The Plug Plot Prisoners and the Chartists', Australian National University Historical Journal, No. 7 (1970), pp.3-15.

F.B. Smith, Radical Artisan. William James Linton 1812-97 (Manchester, 1973).

'Some London Printing Offices. No.5. - Bradbury, Agnew, and Co.,' London Provincial and Colonial Press News, xix (1884), 27-29.

M.H. Spielmann, The History of "Punch" (1895).

M.H. Spielmann, 'The Rivals of "Punch"', National Review, xxv (1895), 654-66.

M.H. Spielmann, 'Sir John Gilbert. A Memorial Sketch', Magazine of Art, xxii (1898), 53-64.

G.H. Spinney, 'Cheap Repository Tracts: Hazard and Marshall Edition', Library, 4th series xx (1939), 295-340.

M. Steig, 'Dickens, Hablôt Brown, and the Tradition of English Caricature', Criticism, xi (1969), 219-33.

N. St. John Stevas, Obscenity and the Law (1956).

L. H. Streicher, 'On a Theory of Political Caricature', Comparative Studies in Society and History, ix (1966-7), 427-45.

M. Summers, 'G.W.M. Reynolds', Times Literary Supplement, 4 July 1942, p.336.

W. L. Thomas, 'The Making of the Graphic', Universal Review, ii (1888), 80-93.

E. P. Thompson, The Making of the English Working Class (1963).

E. P. Thompson, 'Time, Work-Discipline and Industrial Capitalism', Past & Present, No.38 (1967), pp.56-97.

The Unknown Mayhew, ed. and introd. E. P. Thompson and E. Yeo (1971).

W. B. Todd, A Directory of London Printers and Others in Allied Trades 1800-1840 (1972).

G. M. Trevelyan, The Seven Years of William IV (1952).

A. W. Tuer, Old London Street Cries and the Cries of To-day (1885).

H. Twiss, The Public and Private Life of Lord Chancellor Eldon (1844).

M. Twyman, 'The Lithographic Hand Press 1796-1850', Journal of the Printing Historical Society, iii (1967), 3-50.

M. Twyman, Lithography 1800-1850 (1970).

J. Vincent, The Formation of the British Liberal Party 1857-68 (1966).

Sir S. Walpole, The Life of Lord John Russell (1889).

R. K. Webb, The British Working Class Reader, 1790-1848 (1955).

M. Webster, 'Francis Wheatley's Cries of London', Auction, iii (1970), 44-49.

Lord G. Wellesley and J. Steegman, The Iconography of the first Duke of Wellington (1935).

H. R. Westwood, Modern Caricaturists (1932).

C. L. White, Women's Magazines. 1693-1968 (1970).

G. White, English Illustration: 'The Sixties': 1855-70 (1897).

W. H. Wickwar, The Struggle for the Freedom of the Press 1819-1832 (1928).

J. H. Wiener, A Descriptive Finding List of Unstamped British Periodicals 1830-1836 (1970).

J. H. Wiener, The War of the Unstamped (1969).

C. N. Williamson, 'The Development of Illustrated Journalism in England', Magazine of Art, xiii (1890).

E. Wind, 'The Revolution of History Painting', Journal of the Warburg Institute ii (1938), 116-27.

S. F. Woolley, 'The Personnel of the Parliament of 1833', English Historical Review, liii (1938), 240-62.

G. J. Worth, James Hannay: his Life and Works (Lawrence, Kansas, 1964).

GRAPHIC JOURNALISM IN ENGLAND DURING THE 1830s AND 1840s

II

ILLUSTRATIONS

1. R.W. Russ (1804-75), A Studio or Workroom showing a Wood Engraver (? John Jackson) at work on a Block. Oil on panel. Victoria and Albert Museum.

2. J. Crawhall (1793-1853), 'NORTHUMBRIA weighing the Claims of her CANDIDATES 1826.' Etching. Laing Art Gallery and Museum, Newcastle upon Tyne.

3. R. Seymour (1798-1836), 'ARMS OF THE BOROUGHMONGERS,' Figaro in London, No. 15, 17 March 1832. Wood engraving.

4. Seymour, 'ARMS OF THE CHURCH,' Figaro in London, No. 32, 14 July 1832. Wood engraving.

5. Seymour, 'FIGARO'S PROPHETIC ALMANACK,' Figaro in London, No. 30, 30 June 1832. Wood engraving.

6. Seymour, 'A BIT OF PROPHECY,' Figaro in London, No. 156, 29 November 1834. Wood engraving.

7. Seymour, 'MAY DAY,' Figaro in London, No. 22, 5 May 1832. Wood engraving.

8. C.J. Grant, 'TWELFTH NIGHT CHARACTERS,' Political Drama, No. 31. Woodcut. British Museum, Prints and Drawings Department.

9. Seymour, 'GUY FAUX,' Figaro in London, No. 153, 8 November 1834. Wood engraving.

10. Grant, 'The Devil's Menagerie of State Paupers,' John Bull's Picture Gallery, No. 15 (B.M. No. 17276). Woodcut.

11. Seymour, 'THE REFORM MILL FOR GRINDING THE OLD CONSTITUTION YOUNG,' Figaro in London, No. 28, 16 June 1832. Wood engraving.

12. Grant, 'GRINDING THE OLD CORPORATORS YOUNG,' Political Drama, No. 123. Woodcut.

13. ? 'The Reform Boat, in Full Sail,' Political Play Bill, No. 3. Woodcut. British Museum, Prints and Drawings Department.

14. Grant, 'THE ROYAL GERMAN SAUSAGE; OR, THE ADELAIDE AERIAL SHIP,' Political Drama, No. 97. Woodcut.

15. Grant, 'THE GREAT BALLOON,' Lloyd's Political Jokes, No. 9. Woodcut. British Museum, Prints and Drawings Department.

16. Seymour, 'THE BALANCE OF JUSTICE,' Figaro in London, No. 48, 3 November 1832. Wood engraving.

17. Seymour, 'TIMES REVOLUTIONS,' Figaro in London, No. 56. 29 December 1832. Wood engraving.

18. Grant, 'THE OLD TORY HACK COME TO A STAND,' Political Drama, No. 73. Woodcut.

19. J. Doyle (1797-1868), 'DAME PARTINGTON and the OCEAN (OF REFORM),' H.B. Political Sketches, No. 163, 24 October 1831 (B.M. No. 16801). Lithograph.

20. Doyle, 'FANCY BALL-JIM CROW DANCE & CHORUS,' H.B. Political Sketches, No. 478, 17 April 1837. Lithograph.

21. Grant, 'THE INFERNAL MACHING; OR, BLOWING ALL THE RUBBISH TO HELL AT AN ANGLE OF FORTY-FIVE,' Political Drama, No. 102. Woodcut.

22. Grant, 'OLD NICK'S GATHERINGS,' John Bull's Picture Gallery, No. 6. (B.M. No. 17152). Woodcut.

23. Grant, 'THE FIVE PLAGUES OF THE COUNTRY,' Political Drama, No. 19. Woodcut.

24. Grant, 'THE RAT HUNT,' John Bull's Picture Gallery, No. 7. (B.M. No. 17156). Woodcut.

25. Grant, 'Present State of John Bull,' John Bull's Picture Gallery, No. 12 (B.M. No. 17202). Woodcut.

26. ? 'THE STEPPING STONE; OR, JOHN BULL PEEPING INTO FUTURITY,' Weekly Show-Up, 30 June 1832. Woodcut.

27. Grant, 'THE POLITICAL CHEAT. John Bull in the Character of Diogenes on the look out,' John Bull's Picture Gallery, No. 17. Woodcut.

28. Grant, 'That old Irish Bunter, Mother Church, undergoing the operation of Purgation and Phlebotomy,' Political Drama, No. 81. Woodcut.

29. G. Dorrington? 'THE PROMOTION OF PRIESTIANITY,' A Slap at the Church, No. 8, 10 March 1832. Wood engraving.

30. Grant, 'THE BENCH OF BISHOPS IN THE HOUSE OF LORDS DURING A DEBATE CONCERNING THE CHURCH,' Political Drama, No. 26. Woodcut.

31. Seymour, 'CASE OF SURFEIT IN A BISHOP,' Figaro in London, No. 6, 14 January 1832. Wood engraving.

32. Seymour, 'APPLYING THE STOMACH PUMP TO THREE GREAT CORPORATE BODIES,' McLean's Monthly Sheet of Caricatures, No. 46, 1 October 1833. Lithograph.

33. ? 'Corporation Reform, or Lord John Russell's Specific for a System of corruption,' Political Play Bill, No. 11. Woodcut.

34. ? 'Corporation Fed Witnesses being Examined by the Comic Sir Charles Wither-H-ell, before the Seraglio of Torys',' Political Play Bill, No. 18. Woodcut.

35. Grant, 'REVIEWING THE BLUE DEVILS, ALIAS THE RAW LOBSTERS, ALIAS THE BLUDGEON MEN,' Political Drama, No. 11. Woodcut.

36. Seymour, 'THE KING'S SPEECH,' Figaro in London, No. 114. 8 February 1834. Wood engraving.

37. Grant, 'THE ROYAL MOPSTICK PRO-ROGUE-ING THE HUMBUG PARLIAMENT; OR, CROSS READING THE SPEECH,' Political Drama, No. 22. Woodcut.

38. Grant, 'DOES ADELAIDE KNOW HE'S OUT?,' Lloyd's Political Jokes, No. 11. Woodcut.

39. Grant, 'GETTING READY FOR OPENING PARLIAMENT,' Lloyd's Political Jokes, No. 15. Woodcut.

40. Grant, 'BILLY'S BIRTH DAY!,' Political Drama, No. 36. Woodcut.

41. ? 'SILLY BILLY'S BIRTH-DAY,' Political Play Bill, No. 8. Woodcut.

42. Grant, 'MEN AND MEASURES,' Political Drama, No. 65. Woodcut.

43. ? 'The Royal Review at Woolwich, or Addle-head as General a-la-German, Political Play Bill, No. 16. Woodcut.

44. Grant, 'Patience on a Monument Smiling at Grief,' 1831. Coloured etching. Guildhall Library, Prints and Drawings Department.

45. Grant, 'THE OXFORD INSTALLATION! OLD SLAUGHTER ALIAS PADDY O'KILLUS, ALIAS NOSEY, ALIAS THE DUKE OF BUTCHERLOO AS CHANCELLOR!! READING HIS LATIN! SPEECH,' Political Drama, No. 40. Woodcut.

46. Grant, 'THE MODERN SAINT PATRICK; OR, THE IRISH TUTELAR SAINT DRIVING THE VERMIN OUT OF IRELAND,' Political Drama, No. 117. Woodcut.

47. Grant, 'DANIEL IN THE LION'S DEN,' Political Drama, No. 108. Woodcut.

48. Doyle, 'THE CHANCELLOR OF THE UNIVERSITY OF OXFORD ATTENDED BY DOCTORS OF CIVIL LAW,' H.B. Political Sketches, No. 350-1, 1 December 1834. Lithograph.

49. Doyle, 'A CHRISTMAS FIRE-SIDE,' H.B. Political Sketches, No. 236, 8 January 1833. Lithograph.

50. Grant, 'POOR LAWS IN ENGLAND,' Lloyd's Political Jokes, No. 13. Woodcut.

51. Doyle, 'SLEEPING PARTNERS IN A DOUBTFUL CONCERN,' H.B. Political Sketches, No. 268, 13 June 1833. Lithograph.

52. Seymour, 'THE FACTORY FEROCITIES,' Figaro in London, No. 71, 13 April 1833. Wood engraving.

53. Seymour, 'A FEMALE PHILOSOPHER,' Figaro in London, No. 121, 29 March 1834. Wood engraving.

54. Grant, 'INTERIOR OF AN ENGLISH WORKHOUSE UNDER THE NEW POOR LAW ACT,' Political Drama, No. 57. Woodcut.

55. Grant, 'A TETE A TETE. A COUPLE OF GOOD JUDGES AT ALL EVENTS.' JOHN BULL TRYING ON HIS WORKHOUSE SUIT PROVIDED FOR HIM BY THE WHIG POOR LAWS AMENDMENT BILL,' Political Drama, No. 41. Woodcut.

56. ? 'THE FRUITS OF THE NEW POOR LAW BILL,' Figaro in London, No. 249, 10 September 1836. Wood engraving.

57. Grant, 'EFFECTS OF THE NEW BASTARDY LAW,' Political Drama, No. 60. Woodcut.

58. ? 'Innocent Pastime; or, the Blue Devils in their Glory,' Satirical Puppet Show, No. 2, 23 May 1833. Woodcut. Johnson Collection, Bodleian Library.

59. Grant, 'THE GLORIOUS VERDICT OF COLD BATH FIELDS; OR, A HARD PULL FOR JUSTICE,' Political Drama, No. 7. Woodcut.

60. Seymour, 'THE WOLVES LET LOOSE AT WOLVERHAMPTON,' Figaro in London, No. 183, 6 June 1835. Wood engraving.

61. Grant, 'THE FREEDOM OF AN ENGLISH ELECTION; OR, THE DRUNKEN DRAGOONS SHOOTING OLD WOMEN AND CHILDREN AT WOLVERHAMPTON BY WAY OF KEEPING THEIR HAND IN,' Political Drama, No. 91. Woodcut.

62. ? 'MILITARY PASTIME; OR, THE BASTARDS IN THEIR GLORY,' Weekly Show-Up, No. 6, 4 August 1832. Woodcut.

63. Grant, 'THE LATE BLOODY AND BRUTAL EXHIBITION OF HORRID MILITARY TORTURE; OR, ARISTOCRATIC BASTARDS IN THEIR GLORY!!!,' Political Drama, No. 46. Woodcut.

64. Grant, 'POPAY THE SPY, addressing a Political Meeting in the garb of a brother Mechanic. POPAY GIVING IN HIS REPORTS TO HIS EMPLOYERS,' Political Drama, No. 20. Woodcut.

65. Grant, 'THE DORCHESTER UNIONISTS IMPLORING MERCY!!! OF THEIR KING,' Political Drama, No. 32. Woodcut.

66. Seymour, 'THE DAEMON OF MONOPOLY,' Figaro in London, No. 146, 20 September 1834. Wood engraving.

67. Seymour, 'COMBINATIONS,' McLean's Monthly Sheet of Caricatures, No. 52, 1 April 1834. Lithograph.

68. Seymour, 'A MEETING OF THE TRADES' UNIONS. A SUNDAY "TURN OUT" OF THE TRADES' UNIONS,' McLean's Monthly Sheet of Caricatures, No. 53, 1 May 1834. Lithograph.

69. Seymour, 'A TRADES' UNION COMMITTEE. PUTTING DOWN THE TRADES' UNIONS,' McLean's Monthly Sheet of Caricatures, No. 53, 1 May 1834. Lithograph.

70. Seymour, 'A DEDICATION TO THE TEMPERANCE SOCIETY-O'ER ALL THE ILLS OF LIFE VICTORIOUS,' McLean's Monthly Sheet of Caricatures, No. 49, 1 January 1834. Lithograph.

71. Seymour, 'THE TWO FISHERMEN. A DEDICATION TO THE TEMPERANCE SOCIETY,' McLean's Monthly Sheet of Caricatures, No. 53, 1 May 1834. Lithograph.

72. Grant, 'THE DRUNKEN PARLIAMENT DISCUSSING THE PREVENTION OF DRUNKENNESS BILL,' Political Drama, No. 49. Woodcut.

73. Grant, 'JOHN BULL; or, an Englishman's Fireside!,' Political Drama, No. 4. Woodcut.

74. Grant, 'THE SINNERS BEFORE SAINT ANDREW,' Political Drama, No. 6. Woodcut.

75. ? 'Church Fanaticism and the Gentlemen in Black,' Satirical Puppet Show, No. 1, 16 May 1832. Woodcut.

76. Grant, 'THE FOUR FACTIONS, WHICH DISTRACT THE COUNTRY,' Political Drama, No. 12. Woodcut.

77. George Cruikshank (1792-1878), 'LIBERTY SUSPENDED! with the Bulwark of the Constitution!,' March 1817. (B.M. No. 12871). Etching.

78. Cruikshank, 'A FREE BORN ENGLISHMAN!,' 15 December 1819. (B.M. No. 13287). Etching.

79. Cruikshank, 'Poor BULL & his Burden--or the Political MURRAION!!!,' 15 December 1819 (B.M. No. 13288). Etching.

80. Cruikshank, 'THE THING,' Political House that Jack Built, (1819). (B.M. No. 13296). Wood engraving.

81. Cruikshank, 'THE SHOWMAN,' Political Showman - At Home! (1821). (B.M. No. 14149). Wood engraving.

82. Cruikshank, 'THE TRANSPARENCY,' Political Showman - At Home! (1821). (B.M. No. 14150). Wood engraving.

83. Cruikshank, 'THE "DAMNABLE ASSOCIATION;" OR THE INFERNAL INQUISITION OF BLACK FRIARS,' A Slap at Slop and the Bridge Street Gang (1821). (B.M. No. 14221). Wood engraving.

84. William Heath (1795?-1840), 'THE MAN WOTS GOT THE WHIP HAND OF 'EM ALL,' 30 May 1829. (B.M. No. 15776). Etching.

85. Grant, 'MAGISTERIAL JUSTICE - A FACT,' Political Drama, No. 14. Woodcut.

86. Sketches by Seymour, No. 35. Etching.

87. Doyle, '"A TALE of a TUB" and the MORAL of the TAIL!,' H.B. Political Sketches, No. 134, 13 June 1831. (B.M. No. 16711). Lithograph.

88. Grant, 'THE HEAD SCHOOLMASTER THREATENED,' December 1830. Lithograph. Private collection.

89. Seymour, 'THE POTION,' McLean's Monthly Sheet of Caricatures, No. 68, 1 August 1835. Lithograph.

90. 'The arts offering their Tributes to Education. From a Design by Moreau in the Musee Francais,' Penny Magazine, v (1836), 513. Wood engraving.

91. ? 'Workhouse of the Windsor Union,' Penny Magazine, x (1841), 397. Wood engraving.

92. ? 'Power-looms. - Cotton Manufacture,' Penny Magazine, xii (1843), 241. Wood engraving.

93. ? 'South Hetton Colliery,' Penny Magazine, iv (1835), 121. Wood engraving.

94. ? 'Mining,' Penny Magazine, iv (1835), 127. Wood engraving.

95. ? 'Rag Fair,' Penny Magazine, vi (1837), 500. Wood engraving.

96. ? 'Hyde Park - Entrance from Piccadilly,' Penny Magazine, vi (1837), 497. Wood engraving.

97. Seymour, 'PATENT PENNY KNOWLEDGE MILL,' McLean's Monthly Sheet of Caricatures, No. 34, 1 October 1832 (B.M. No. 17267). Lithograph.

98. W.C. Walker, wood engraving after a plate in Colonel Macerone's Defensive Instructions to the People. Poor Man's Guardian, 14 April 1832.

99. ? 'The Busy Busy B--,' The Caricaturist, No. 4. Lithograph.

100. Grant, 'FRONTISPIECE FOR THE PENNY MAGAZINE,' Vol. 2, 1833. Lithograph. British Museum, Prints and Drawings Department.

101. Grant, 'THE LITERARY DUSTMAN, or L--d BROOM in Character,' Lloyd's Political Jokes, No. 6. Woodcut.

102. Grant, 'POLITICAL SPORTSMEN; OR, PRACTISING AGAINST THE NEXT SESSION,' Political Drama, No. 24. Woodcut.

103. Grant, 'FISHING FOR GUDGEONS AND FLATS,' Political Drama, No. 54. Woodcut.

104. Grant, 'THE CHANCELLOR'S DREAM; OR, KING RICHARD III. TRAVESTIE,' Political Drama, No. 25. Woodcut.

105. Seymour, 'EFFECTS OF THE STAMP ACTS,' McLean's Monthly Sheet of Caricatures, No. 55, 1 July 1834. Lithograph.

106. Seymour, 'FIGARO V. THE BLUE DEVILS. THE POLICE FORCE ON DUTY,' Figaro in London, No. 17, 31 March 1832. Wood engraving.

107. Grant, 'WHIG ROBBERY AND DESTRUCTION OF PROPERTY UNDER THE NAME OF LAW,' Political Drama, No. 100. Woodcut.

108. Seymour, 'THE NEW STAMP ACT,' Figaro in London, No. 228, 16 April 1836. Wood engraving.

109. J. Leech (1817-64), 'USEFUL SUNDAY LITERATURE FOR THE MASSES; OR, MURDER MADE FAMILIAR,' Punch, xvii (1849), 117. Wood engraving.

110. Grant, 'THE MORNING AFTER THE CORONATION. THE NIGHT OF THE CORONATION,' Gleave's Penny Gazette of Variety, 7 July 1838. Woodcut.

111. ? 'COAXING,' Odd Fellow, 25 January 1840. Wood engraving.

112. Grant, 'THE MARCH OF COMMON SENSE,' Cleave's Gazette, 2 September 1843. Woodcut.

113. ? 'POOR LAW SKETCHES. - "A DOG IN OFFICE.",' Odd Fellow, 8 June 1839. Wood engraving.

114. Grant, 'THE POOR LAWS IN BRADFORD,' Cleave's Gazette, 9 September 1837. Woodcut.

115. Grant, 'THE PENTONVILLE BASTILLE,' Cleave's Gazette, 16 December 1843. Woodcut.

116. Grant, 'THE WHIG NEW POLICE ACT IN FULL OPERATION,' Cleave's Illustrated Metropolitan Police Act (1839). Woodcut. British Museum, Prints and Drawings Department.

117. Grant, 'THE PHOENIX OF CHARTISM,' Cleave's Gazette, 22 October 1842. Woodcut.

118. W. Newman, 'LAW MAKING A MEAL IN THE MANUFACTURING DISTRICTS,' Odd Fellow, 10 December 1842. Wood engraving.

119. Grant, 'THE ANTI-CORN LAW GIANT, AND THE DWARFS OF MONOPOLY,' Penny Satirist, 25 March 1843. Woodcut.

120-1. W.M. Thackeray (1811-63), 'ILLUSTRATIONS OF THE RENT LAWS,' Anti-Corn Law Circular, 23 July, 10 December 1839. Wood engravings.

122. A. Henning, 'The Saloon Lady,' Town, 20 October 1838. Wood engraving.

123. Grant, wood engraving for the Penny Pickwick (1837), p. 133.

124. ? woodcut for Mister Humphries' Clock (1840, p. 1.

125. G. Stiff, illustration for G.W.M. Reynolds, The Mysteries of London (1846-50, p. 1. Wood engraving.

126. H. Anelay, illustration for The Mysteries of London, ii. 281. Wood engraving.

127. W. Gorway, wood engraving for The Mysteries of London, vi (1850), 265.

128. Leech, 'FOREIGN AFFAIRS,' Punch, i (1841), 43. Wood engraving.

129. Leech, 'THE CHARITY BALL,' Punch, iv (1843), 87. Wood engraving.

130. ? 'PUNCH'S LIFE BUOY,' Man in the Moon, iii (1848), 256. Wood engraving.

131. Kenny Meadows (1790-1874), 'A DROP OF LONDON WATER,' Punch, xviii (1850), 188. Wood engraving.

132. Thackeray, 'AUTHOR'S MISERIES, No. VI,' Punch, xv (1848), 198. Wood engraving.

133. Leech, 'THE ARTFUL DODGER,' Punch, x (1846), 27. Wood engraving.

134. R. Doyle (1824-83), 'HIGH ART AND THE ROYAL ACADEMY,' Punch, xiv (1848), 197. Wood engraving.

135. Leech, 'SUBSTANCE AND SHADOW,' Punch, v (1843), 23. Wood engraving.

136. ? 'CAPITAL AND LABOUR,' Punch, v (1843), 49. Wood engraving.

137. Leech, 'SPECIMENS FROM MR. PUNCH'S INDUSTRIAL EXHIBITION OF 1850,' Punch, xviii (1850), 145. Wood engraving.

138. ? 'A TRIO OF PUNCHITES,' Puppet Show, i (1848), 16. Wood engraving.

139. ? 'A REAL CASE OF DISTRESS,' Man in the Moon, ii (1847), 314. Wood engraving.

140. Leech, 'THE RECONCILIATION; OR, AS IT OUGHT TO BE,' Punch, viii (1845), 124. Wood engraving.

141. Leech, 'A PHYSICAL FORCE CHARTIST ARMING FOR THE FIGHT,' Punch, xv (1848), 101. Wood engraving.

142. ? 'THE CHARTIST "ORANGE TREE",' Puppet Show, i (1848), 97. Wood engraving.

143. P. Gavarni (1804-66), 'LONDON POLITENESS,' Puppet Show, i (1848), 126. Wood engraving.

144. ? 'HOW GAVARNI IDEALISES,' Man in the Moon, iv (1848), 226. Wood engraving.

145. ? 'HOW GAVARNI IDEALISES,' Man in the Moon, iv (1848), 227. Wood engraving.

146. ? 'A SCENE IN THE MINORIES,' Penny Punch, i. new series (1849), 1. Wood engraving.

147. ? 'THE TRUCK SYSTEM,' Penny Punch, i. new series (1849), 41. Wood engraving.

148. ? 'THE GOVERNESS,' Life, i (1850), 5. Wood engraving.

149. ? 'View of the Conflagration of the City of Hamburgh,' Illustrated London News, 14 May 1842. Wood engraving.

150. W.J. Muller (1812-45) and T.L. Rowbotham (1783-1853), 'THE CHARGE OF THE DRAGOONS IN QUEEN SQUARE DURING THE RIOTS OF 1831,' Watercolour and bodycolour. City Art Gallery, Bristol.

151. ? Full Particulars of the Dreadful and Tremendous Riots at Bristol. Catnach broadside woodcut. Bristol City Library, Reference Department.

152. ? 'EXPLOSION OF A FIREWORK MANUFACTORY, IN PRINCES ST. LAMBETH,' Cleave's Gazette, 12 March 1842. Woodcut.

153. ? 'TERRIBLE EXPLOSION OF D'ERNEST'S FIRE-WORK MANUFACTORY,' Bell's Penny Dispatch, 13 March 1842. Woodcut.

154. ? 'DREADFUL EXPLOSION OF THE FIRE-WORK MANUFACTORY OF MONS. D'ERNST, IN DOUGHTY STREET, LAMBETH WALK, AND LOSS OF FOUR LIVES!,' Lloyd's Companion to a Newspaper, 13 March 1842. Woodcut.

155. ? 'COBURG. SCHLOSS KALENBERG,' Illustrated London News, 16 August 1845. Wood engraving.

156. ? 'LOUIS PHILIPPE INTRODUCING QUEEN VICTORIA TO THE QUEEN OF THE FRENCH,' Pictorial Times, 9 September 1843. Wood engraving.

157. A.C.H. de Noe (1819-79), 'ARRIVAL AT TRERORT - THE ROYAL GREETING,' Pictorial Times, 6 January 1844. Wood engraving.

158. J. Gilbert (1817-97), 'Costume Ball,' Illustrated London News, 14 May 1842. Wood engraving.

159. Parl. Papers 1842, xvii (382): Reports to the Commissioners on the Employment of Children, p. 65. Wood engraving.

160. Parl. Papers 1842, xvii (382): Reports to the Commissioners on the Employment of Children, p. 158. Wood engraving.

161. Parl. Papers 1842, xvii (382): Reports to the Commissioners on the Employment of Children, p. 61. Wood engraving.

162. ? 'THE REAL SUFFERERS BY THE MONEY PRESSURE. - A SKETCH FROM LIFE IN THE FACTORY DISTRICTS,' Pictorial Times, 23 October 1847. Wood engraving.

163. ? 'VIEWS OF THE O'CONNELL PROPERTY IN IRELAND,' Illustrated London News, 10 January 1846. Wood engraving.

164. ? 'THE UNION WORKHOUSE TO BE ERECTED AT CANTERBURY. THE ANDOVER UNION WORKHOUSE,' Illustrated London News, 7 November 1846. Wood engraving.

165. ? 'POOR LAW DIVORCE,' Pictorial Times, 29 August 1846. Wood engraving.

166. ? 'TRANSPORTATION OF THE CASUAL POOR,' Pictorial Times, 29 August 1846. Wood engraving.

167. ? 'POOR LAW IMPRISONMENT,' Pictorial Times, 29 August 1846. Wood engraving.

168. ? 'POOR LAW EXERCISE,' Pictorial Times, 29 August 1846. Wood engraving.

169. W.G. Mason, 'FIELD-LANE LODGING-HOUSE,' Poor Man's Guardian, No. 3, 20 November 1847. Wood engraving.

170. Mason, 'ENON CHAPEL CEMETERY AND DANCING SALOON,' Poor Man's Guardian, No. 5, 4 December 1847. Wood engraving.

171. ? 'MODEL LODGING-HOUSE, GEORGE STREET, ST. GILES'S,' Poor Man's Guardian, No. 4, 27 November 1847. Wood engraving.

172. Mason, 'SOUP KITCHEN IN LEICESTER SQUARE,' Poor Man's Guardian, No. 6, 11 December 1847. Wood engraving.

173. ? 'VISIT OF HIS ROYAL HIGHNESS PRINCE ALBERT TO THE SOUP KITCHEN, LEICESTER SQUARE,' Illustrated London News, 19 February 1848. Wood engraving.

174. ? 'CONDITION OF THE POOR,' Pictorial Times, 10 October 1846. Wood engraving.

175. 'LONDON IN 1842,' (Northern prospect), Illustrated London News, ii (1843), wood engraving from a daguerrotype by Claudet.

176. ? 'ST. PANCRAS' BATHS AND WASHHOUSES,' Illustrated London News, 3 January 1846. Wood engraving.

177. ? 'THE PHILANTHROPIC SOCIETY'S FARM, AT RED HILL,' Illustrated London News, 15 June 1851. Wood engraving.

178. ? 'THE HOUSES OF THE LONDON POOR,' Builder, xi (1853), 137. Wood engraving.

179. ? 'SOUTHWARK,' Builder, xi (1853), 674. Wood engraving.

180. Cruikshank, 'COLD, MISERY AND WANT DESTROY THEIR YOUNGEST CHILD,' The Bottle, V (1847). Glyphograph.

181. Cruikshank, 'FEARFUL QUARRELS AND BRUTAL VIOLENCE ARE THE NATURAL CONSEQUENCES OF THE FREQUENT USE OF THE BOTTLE,' The Bottle, VI (1847). Glyphograph.

182. Cruikshank, 'NEGLECTED BY THEIR PARENTS, EDUCATED ONLY IN THE STREETS AND FALLING INTO THE HANDS OF WRETCHES WHO LIVE UPON THE VICES OF OTHERS THEY ARE LEAD TO THE GIN-SHOP TO DRINK AT THAT FOUNTAIN WHICH NOURISHES EVERY SPECIMEN OF CRIME,' The Drunkard's Children, I (1848). Glyphograph.

183. Cruikshank, 'BETWEEN THE FINE FLARING GIN PALACE AND THE LOW DIRTY BEER SHOP, THE BOY THIEF SQUANDERS AND GAMBLES AWAY HIS ILL-GOTTEN GAINS,' The Drunkard's Children, II (1848). Glyphograph.

184. Cruikshank, 'THE MANIAC FATHER AND CONVICT BROTHER ARE GONE. - THE POOR GIRL, HOMELESS, FRIENDLESS, DESERTED AND GIN-MAD, COMMITS SELF-MURDER,' The Drunkard's Children, VIII (1848). Glyphograph.

185. ? 'THE FIRST THEFT,' Ragged School Union Magazine, ii (1850), 185. Wood engraving.

186. ? 'LIFE IN THE BUSH,' Ragged School Union Magazine, ii (1850), 282. Wood engraving.

187. ? 'THE HOME IN AUSTRALIA,' Ragged School Union Magazine, ii (1850), 300. Wood engraving.

188. G. Measom, 'INTERIOR OF A GIN PALACE,' True Briton, i. new series (1853), 548. Wood engraving.

189. Measom, 'THE HOME OF THE DRUNKARD,' True Briton, i. new series (1853), 581. Wood engraving.

190. Measom, 'THE DEATH-BED OF THE HOLY,' True Briton, i. new series (1853), 708. Wood engraving.

191. ? 'THE RIOTS IN THE COUNTRY,' Illustrated London News, 20 August 1842. Wood engraving.

192. ? 'CHARTIST EXCITEMENT. - THE POLICE FORCE IN BONNER'S FIELDS, ON MONDAY LAST,' Illustrated London News, 17 June 1848. Wood engraving.

193. ? 'OUR TROOPS RECOVERING THEIR CANNON,' Illustrated London News, 11 June 1842. Wood engraving.

194. ? 'THE POLISH INSURRECTION,' Illustrated London News, 14 March 1846. Wood engraving.

195. H. Valentin, 'SKETCHES FROM THE BARRICADES. BARRICADE ON THE BOULEVARD MONTMARTE,' Illustrated London News, 11 March 1848. Wood engraving.

196. Gavarni, 'BEHIND THE BARRICADE,' Illustrated London News, 18 March 1848. Wood engraving.

197. Gavarni, 'SKETCHES FROM THE FRENCH REVOLUTION,' Illustrated London News, 25 March 1848. Wood engraving.

198. ? 'A CUT FOR AN ILLUSTRATED PAPER,' Punch, xv (1848), 39. Wood engraving.

199. ? 'PATENT VERTICAL PRINTING MACHINE, IN THE GREAT EXHIBITION,' Illustrated London News, 31 May 1851. Wood engraving.

1. R.W. Russ   A Studio or Workroom showing a Wood Engraver (? John Jackson) at work on a Block

2. J. Crawhall 'NORTHUMBRIA weighing the Claims of her CANDIDATES 1826

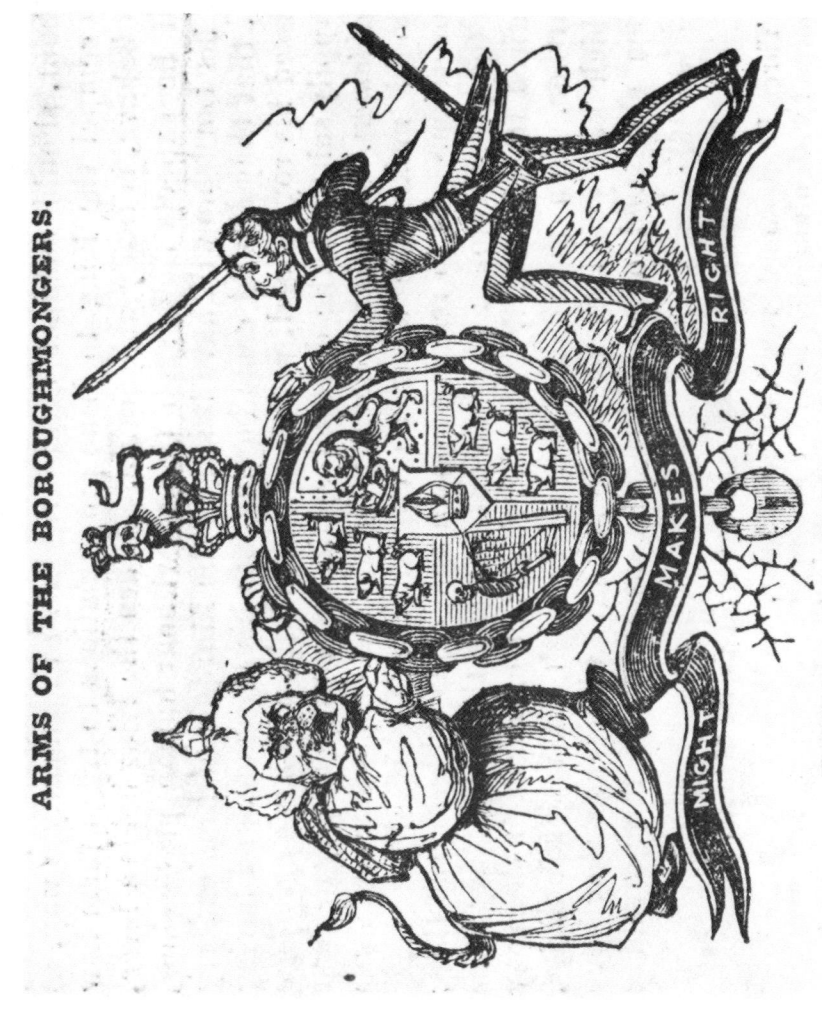

3. R. Seymour 'ARMS OF THE BOROUGHMONGERS,' Figaro in London

4. Seymour 'ARMS OF THE CHURCH,' Figaro in London

The sun of England is represented to be setting in great glory, while the moon whose face will be recognized on the other side, having performed a number of the most eccentric orbits,

5. Seymour 'FIGARO'S PROPHETIC ALMANACK,' Figaro in London

6. Seymour   'A BIT OF PROPHECY,' <u>Figaro in London</u>

7. Seymour   'MAY DAY,' Figaro in London

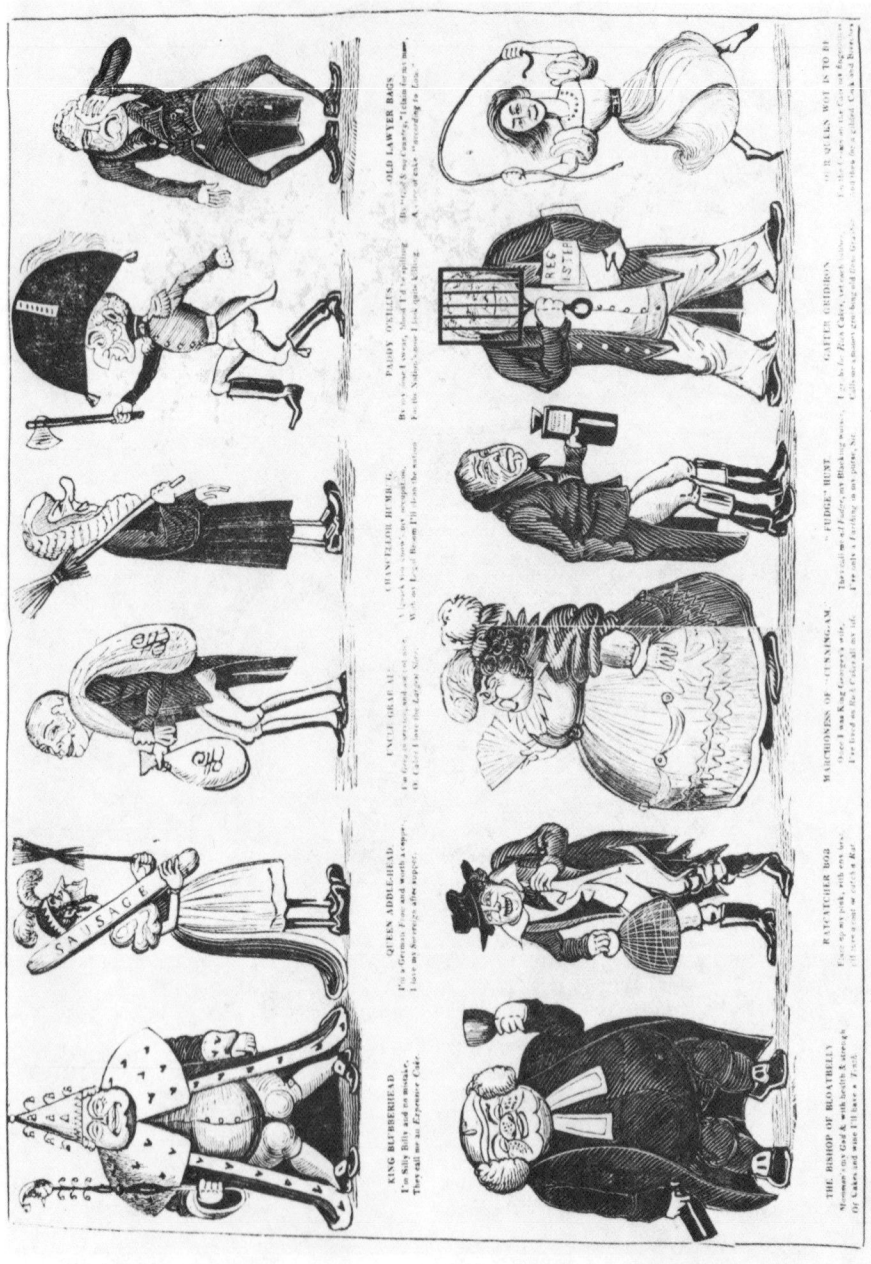

8. C.J. Grant 'TWELFTH NIGHT CHARACTERS,' Political Drama

9. Seymour 'GUY FAUX,' Figaro in London

10. Grant 'The Devil's Menagerie of State Paupers,'
John Bull's Picture Gallery

11. Seymour   'THE REFORM MILL FOR GRINDING THE OLD CONSTITUTION YOUNG,'
Figaro in London

12. Grant 'GRINDING THE OLD CORPORATORS YOUNG,' *Political Drama*

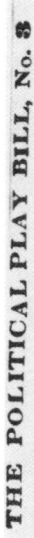

13. 'The Reform Boat, in Full Sail,' Political Play Bill

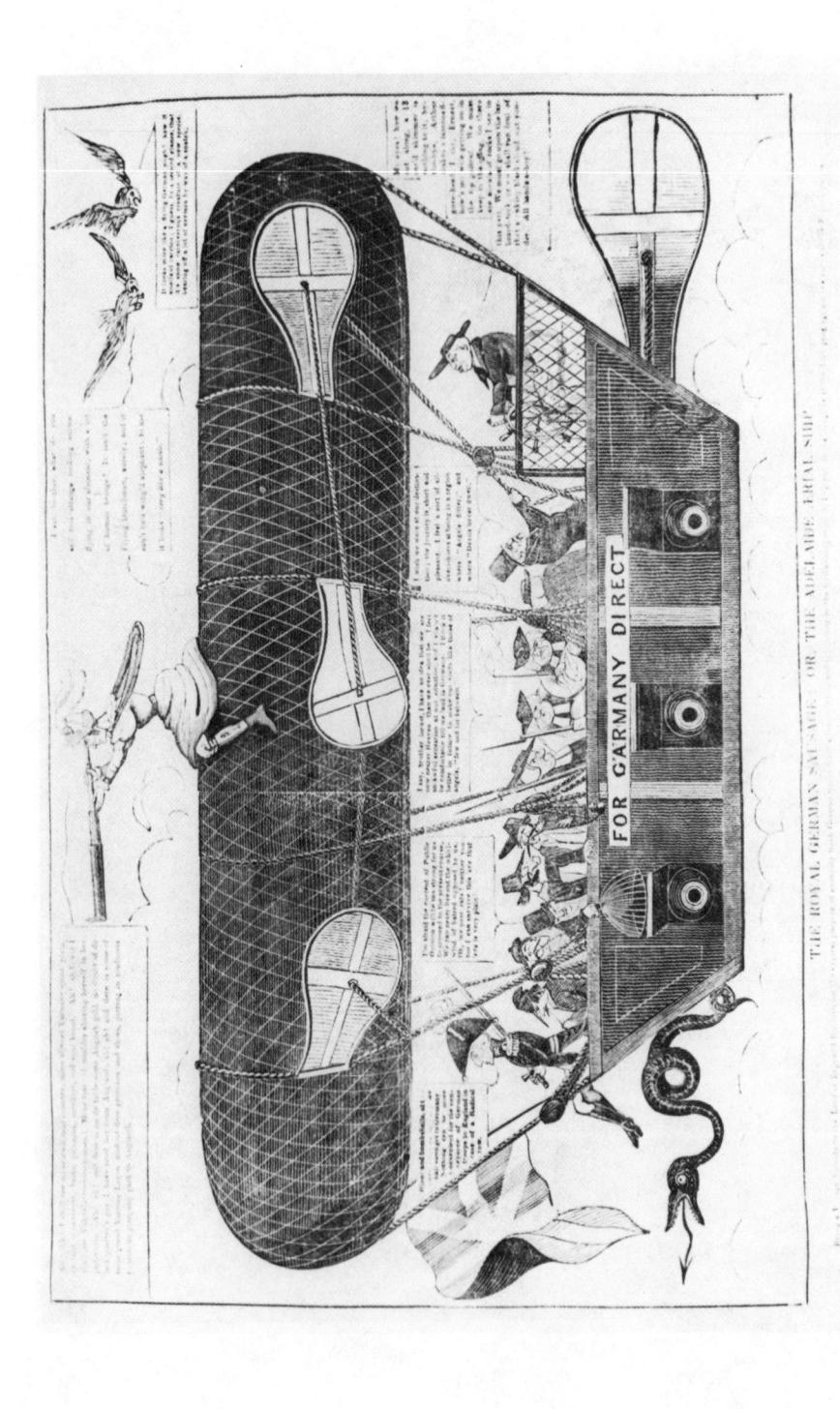

14. Grant 'THE ROYAL GERMAN SAUSAGE; OR, THE ADELAIDE AERIAL SHIP,' Political Drama

15. Grant　　　'THE GREAT BALLOON,' Lloyd's Political Jokes

16. Seymour   'THE BALANCE OF JUSTICE,' Figaro in London

17. Seymour 'TIMES REVOLUTIONS,' Figaro in London

18. Grant 'THE OLD TORY HACK COME TO A STAND,' Political Drama

19. J. Doyle   'DAME PARTINGTON and the OCEAN (OF REFORM),'
                                                           H.B. Political Sketches

20. Doyle 'FANCY BALL—JIM CROW DANCE & CHORUS,' H.B. Political Sketches

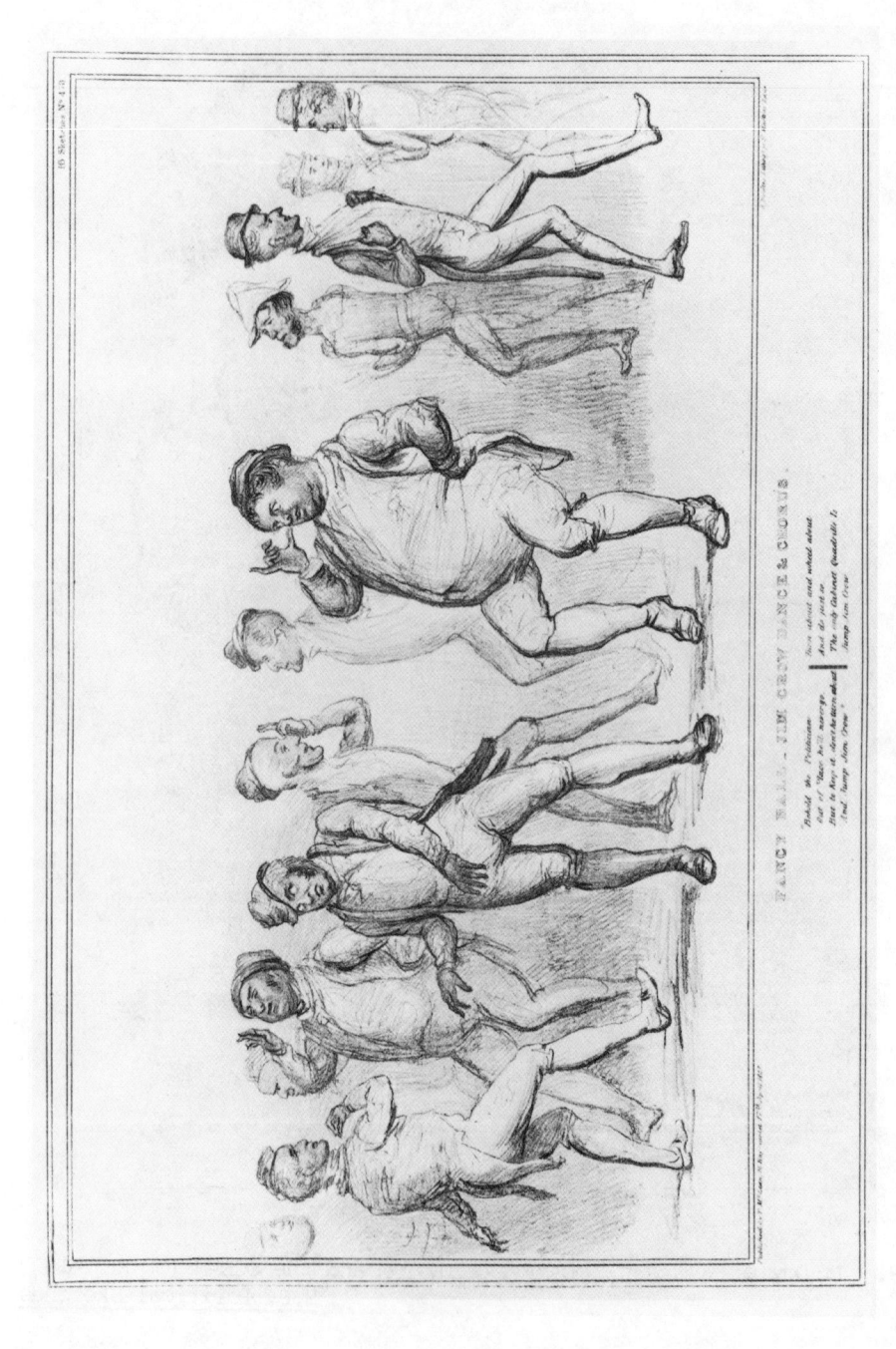

21. Grant 'THE INFERNAL MACHING; OR, BLOWING ALL THE RUBBISH TO HELL AT AN ANGLE OF FORTY-FIVE,' Political Drama

22. Grant   'OLD NICK'S GATHERINGS,' John Bull's Picture Gallery

THE POLITICAL DRAMA. No. 19.

| I govern the people. | I pray for the people. | I legislate for the people. | I fought for the people. | I preserve the peace for all four. | And I'll have all five. |

THE FIVE PLAGUES OF THE COUNTRY.

23. Grant   'THE FIVE PLAGUES OF THE COUNTRY,' Political Drama

No. 7.

John Bull's Picture Gallery.

Political, Satirical, and Humourous.

PRICE ONE PENNY

THE RAT HUNT.

Reform Yourselves, or my method may not suit You.

Chubb's Edition of the Reform Bill is just Printed, price 3d., containing every Clause and Schedule as in the Original Edition, published by the King's Printers at 2s. 6d.

This is undoubtedly the best and cheapest Edition of this important Measure yet out.--TIMES.

24. Grant   'THE RAT HUNT,' John Bull's Picture Gallery

25. Grant — 'Present State of John Bull,' John Bull's Picture Gallery

THE STEPPING STONE; OR, JOHN BULL PEEPING INTO FUTURITY.

26. ? 'THE STEPPING STONE; OR, JOHN BULL PEEPING INTO FUTURITY,' Weekly Show-Up

John Bull's Picture Gallery. No. 17.

THE POLITICAL CHEAT.

Open your mouth and shut your eyes, and see what I will give you.

John Bull in the Character of Diogenes on the look out.

BROUGHAM. Johnny, are you looking for the Reform Bill?
JOHN BULL. Na, mester, I ha gotten that, but I be looking for its benefits!

Just Published, No. 4, Price One Penny, of **THE DEVIL'S MENAGERIE OF STATE PAUPERS**

The Devil's Menagerie gives a Correct Statement of the Sums of Money received in Places, Pensions, or Sinecures, of every Pauper on the State List, from the King to the meanest Pensioner, and their Town and Country Residences are annexed, that the Public may know, not only who receives, but where the receivers reside.

Printed and Published by W. Chubb, 48, Holywell-street, Strand, London, and Sold by all Booksellers

27. Grant   'THE POLITICAL CHEAT. John Bull in the Character of Diogenes on the look out'

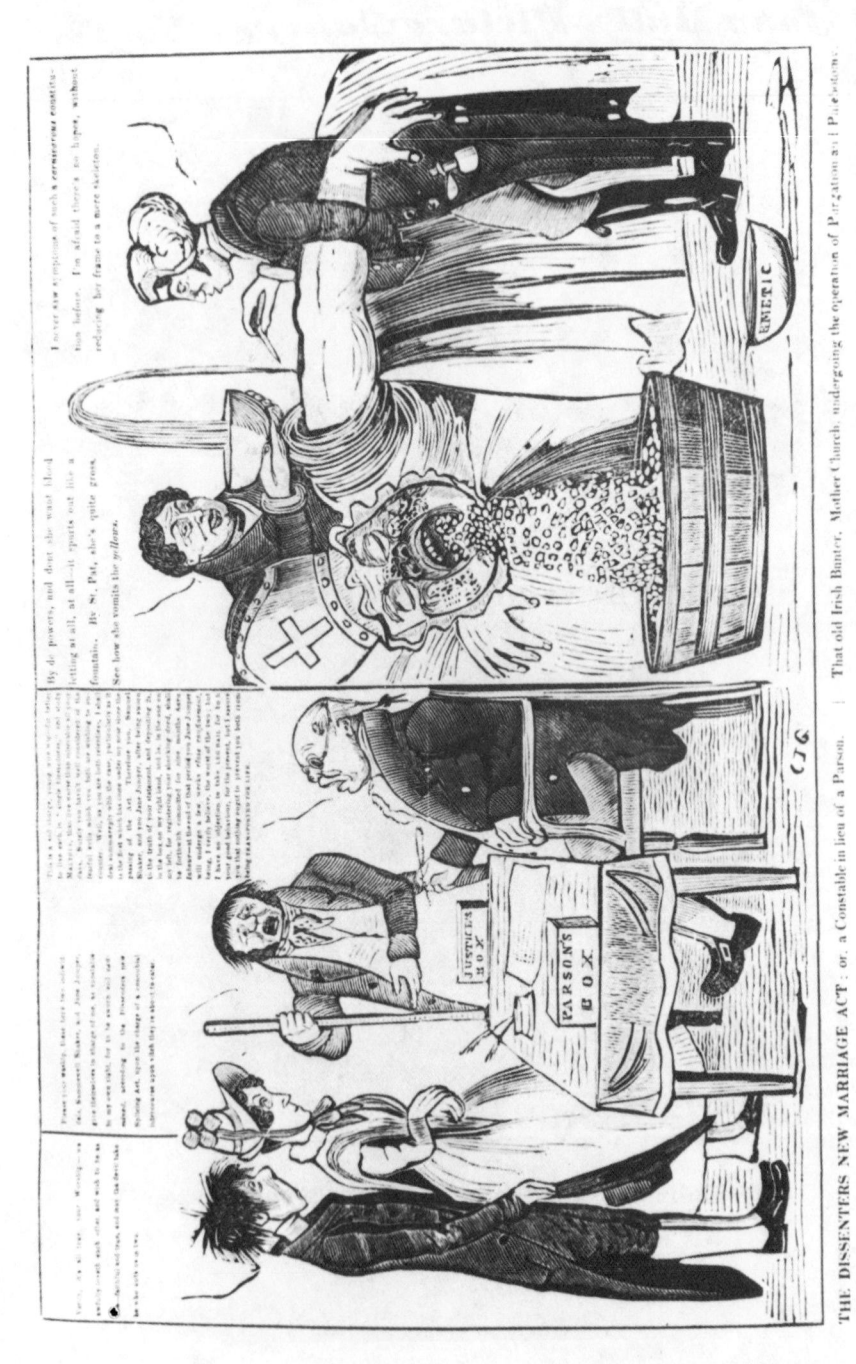

28. Grant, 'That old Irish Bunter, Mother Church, undergoing the operation of Purgation and Phlebotamy,' *Political Drama*

THE PROMOTION OF PRIESTIANITY.

"You know that by this craft we have our wealth."—THE MAKER OF DIANA'S SHRINES.

Thus they plunder and bleed in the name of believing,
While they practice, BY LAW, equal modes of deceiving;
And yet with assurance as bald as their pate,
Cry 'Heaven in mercy will soon mend the state';
Like Saints, with a look of serene admiration,
They recommend poverty, curse peculation,
While they laugh when they think of the wealth they procure—
The portion of orphans—the blood of the poor—

And finally, strut off in royal parade,
Deriding the fools and the dupes they have made.
And this is religion ! and this is benign !
And this is the practice of theory divine !
And this is the manner in which it is given
To ride in a JUGGERNAUT CHARIOT to Heaven,
And present, as an off'ring on God's holy fame,
The life of the spoil'd, by their avarice slain!

29. G. Dorrington? 'THE PROMOTION OF PRIESTIANITY,' A Slap at the Church

30. Grant, 'THE BENCH OF BISHOPS IN THE HOUSE OF LORDS DURING A DEBATE CONCERNING THE CHURCH,' Political Drama

31. Seymour   'CASE OF SURFEIT IN A BISHOP,' Figaro in London

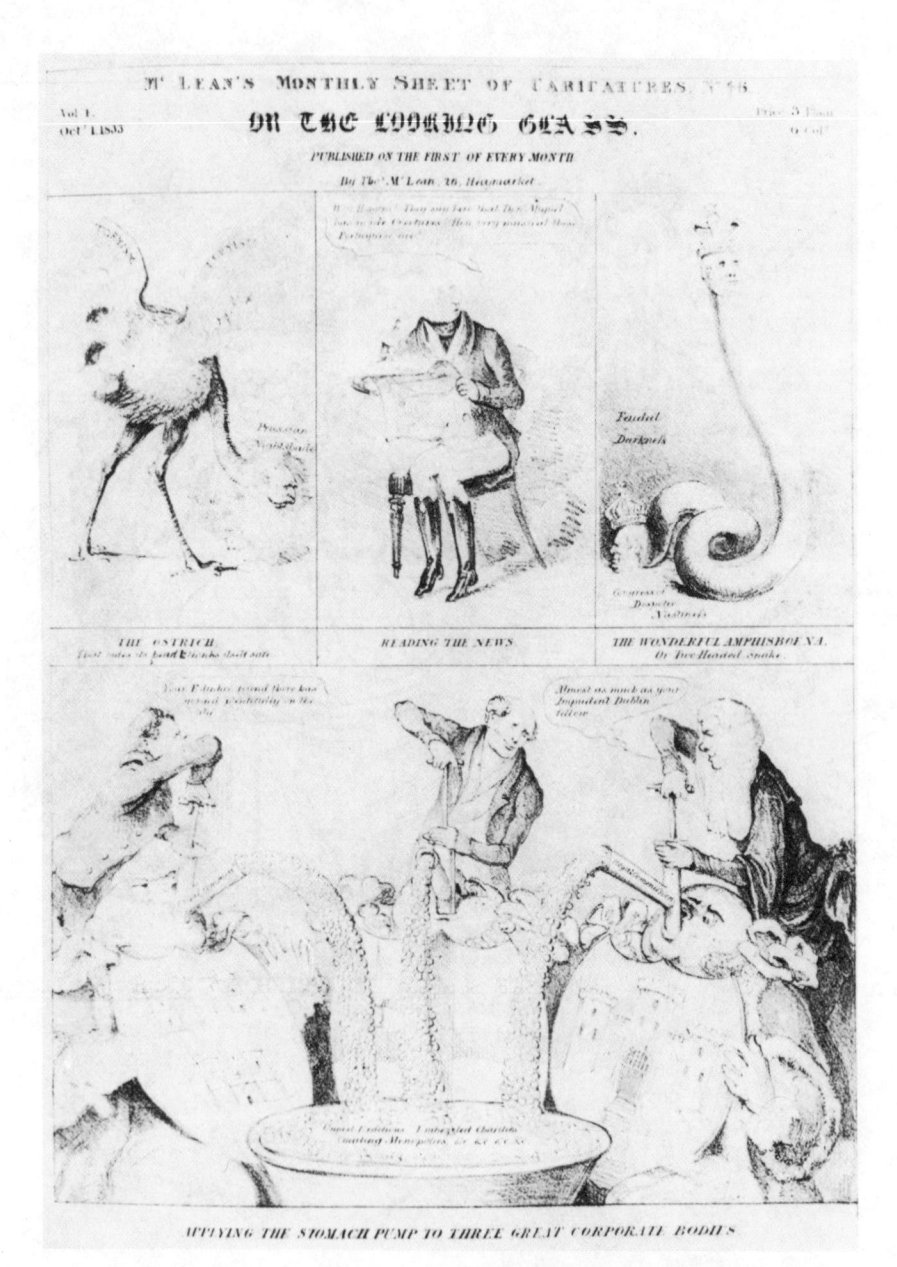

32. Seymour 'APPLYING THE STOMACH PUMP TO THREE GREAT CORPORATE BODIES,' McLean's Monthly Sheet of Caricatures

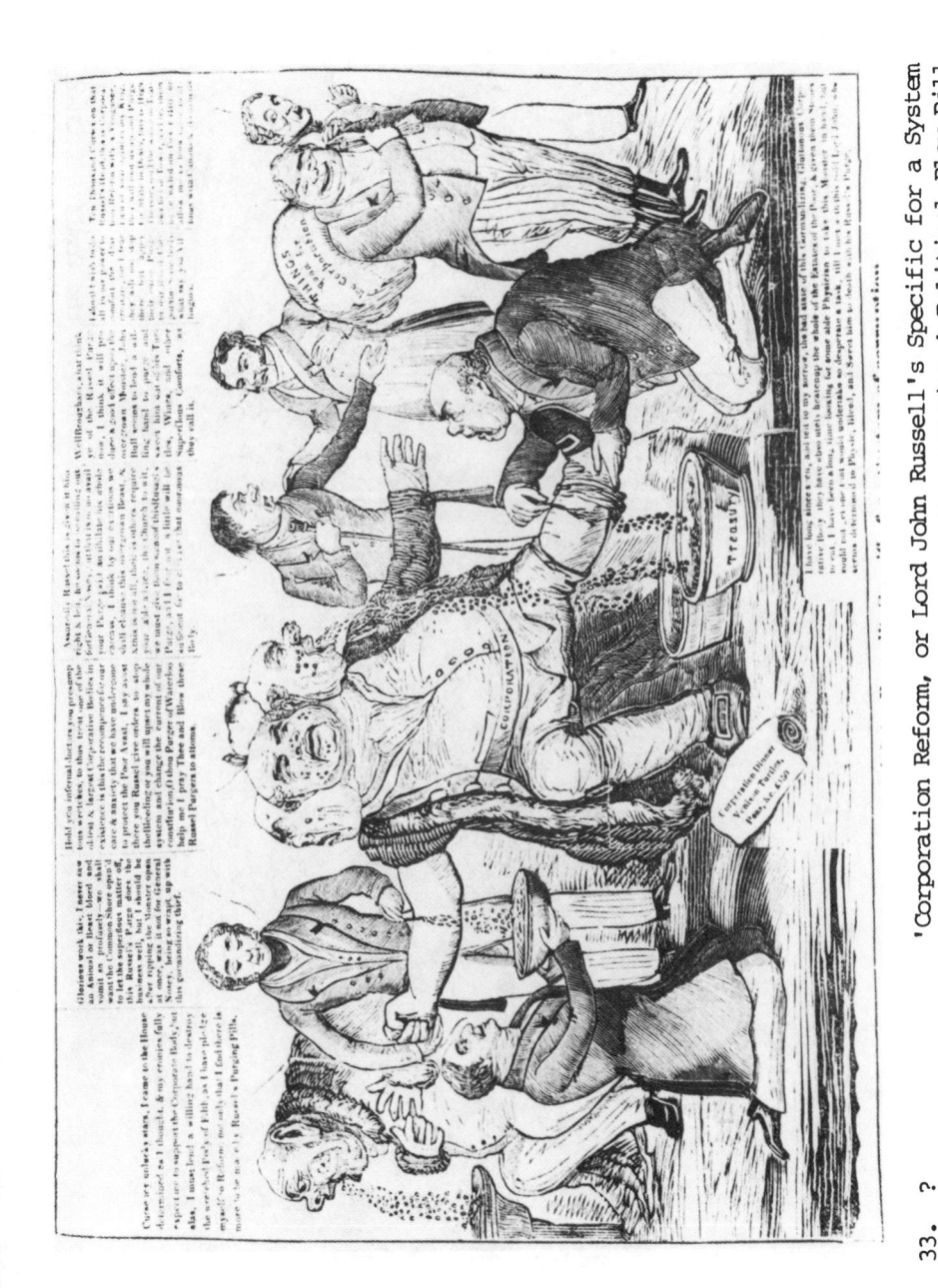

33. 'Corporation Reform, or Lord John Russell's Specific for a System of corruption,' Political Play Play Bill

34. ? 'Corporation Fed Witnesses being Examined by the Comic Sir Charles Wither-H-ell, before the Seraglio of Torys', *Political Play Bill*

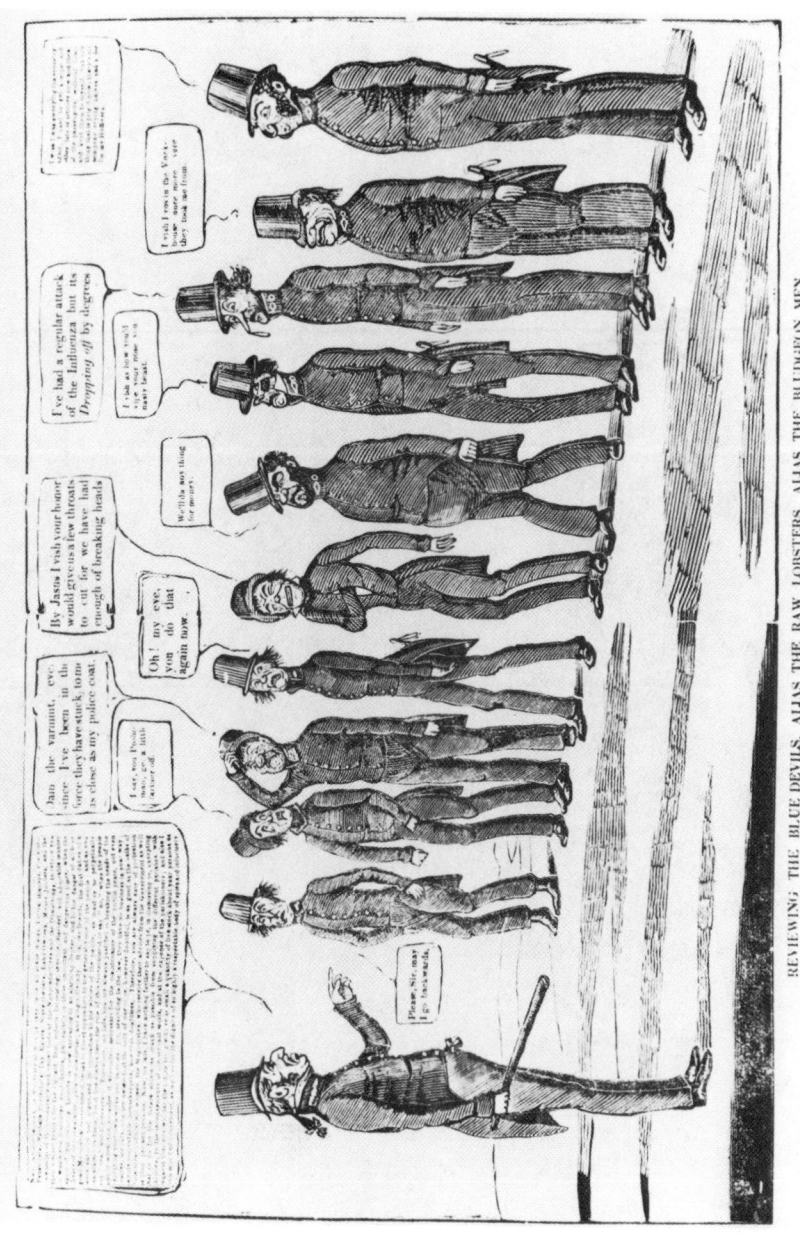

35. Grant, 'REVIEWING THE BLUE DEVILS, ALIAS THE RAW LOBSTERS, ALIAS THE BLUDGEON MEN,' Political Drama

36. Seymour   'THE KING'S SPEECH,' Figaro in London

37. Grant, 'THE ROYAL MOPSTICK PRO-ROGUE-ING THE HUMBUG PARLIAMENT; OR, CROSS READING THE SPEECH,' Political Drama

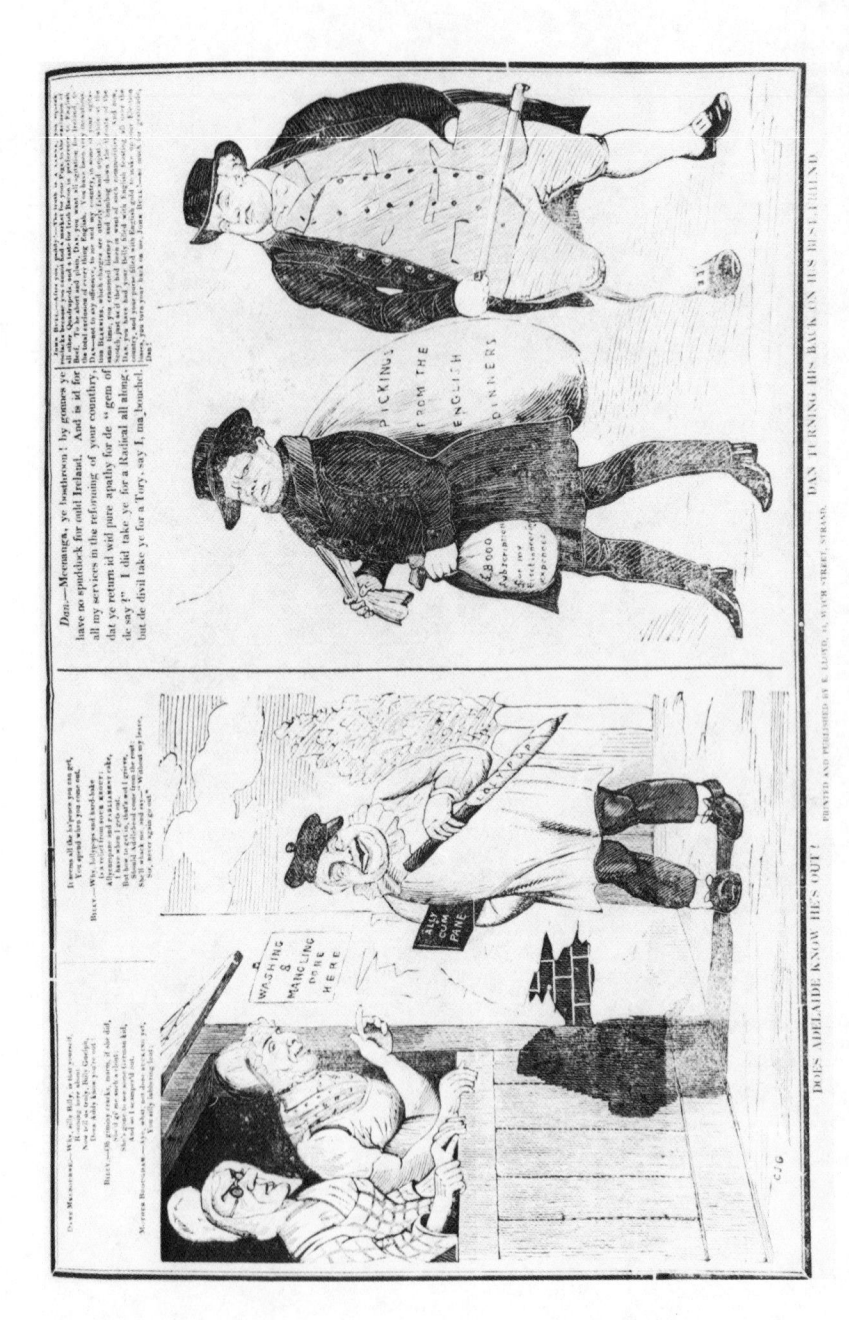

38. Grant 'DOES ADELAIDE KNOW HE'S OUT?,' Lloyd's Political Jokes

39. Grant 'GETTING READY FOR OPENING PARLIAMENT,' Lloyd's Political Jokes

40. Grant   'BILLY'S BIRTH DAY!,' Political Drama

'SILLY BILLY'S BIRTH-DAY,' Political Play Bill

42. Grant, 'MEN AND MEASURES,' Political Drama

43. 'The Royal Review at Woolwich, or Addle-head as General a-la-German, Political Play Bill

44. Grant 'Patience on a Monument Smiling at Grief'

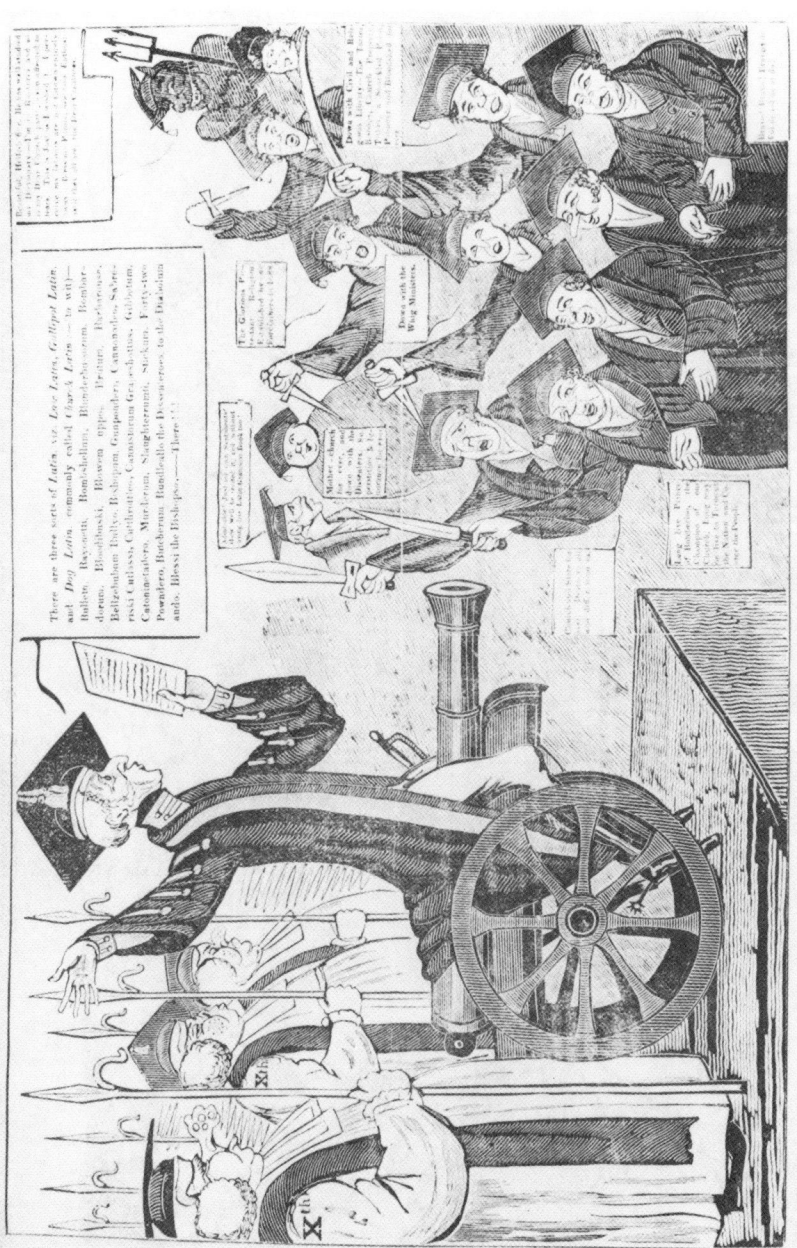

45. Grant 'THE OXFORD INSTALLATION! OLD SLAUGHTER ALIAS PADDY O'KILLUS, ALIAS NOSEY, ALIAS THE DUKE OF BUTCHERLOO AS CHANCELLOR!! READING HIS LATIN! SPEECH,' Political Drama

46. Grant 'THE MODERN SAINT PATRICK; OR, THE IRISH TUTELAR SAINT DRIVING THE VERMIN OUT OF IRELAND,' Political Drama

47. Grant   'DANIEL IN THE LION'S DEN,' Political Drama

48. Doyle 'THE CHANCELLOR OF THE UNIVERSITY OF OXFORD ATTENDED BY DOCTORS OF CIVIL LAW,' H.B. Political Sketches

49. Doyle 'A CHRISTMAS FIRE-SIDE,' H.B. Political Sketches

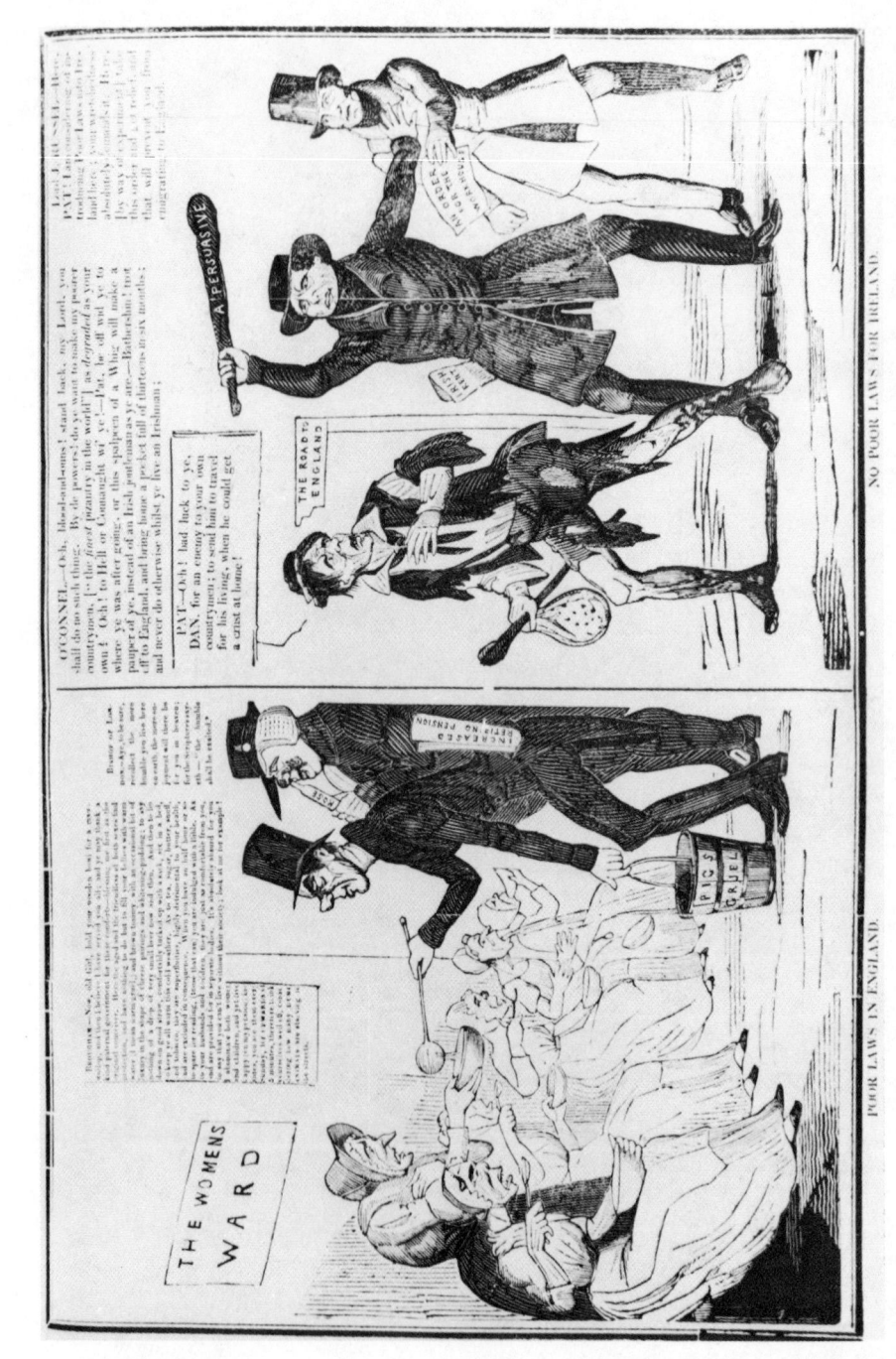

50. Grant 'POOR LAWS IN ENGLAND,' Lloyd's Political Jokes

51. Doyle 'SLEEPING PARTNERS IN A DOUBTFUL CONCERN,' H.B. Political Sketches

52. Seymour 'THE FACTORY FEROCITIES,' Figaro in London

53. Seymour   'A FEMALE PHILOSOPHER,' Figaro in London

54. Grant, 'INTERIOR OF AN ENGLISH WORKHOUSE UNDER THE NEW POOR LAW ACT,' *Political Drama*

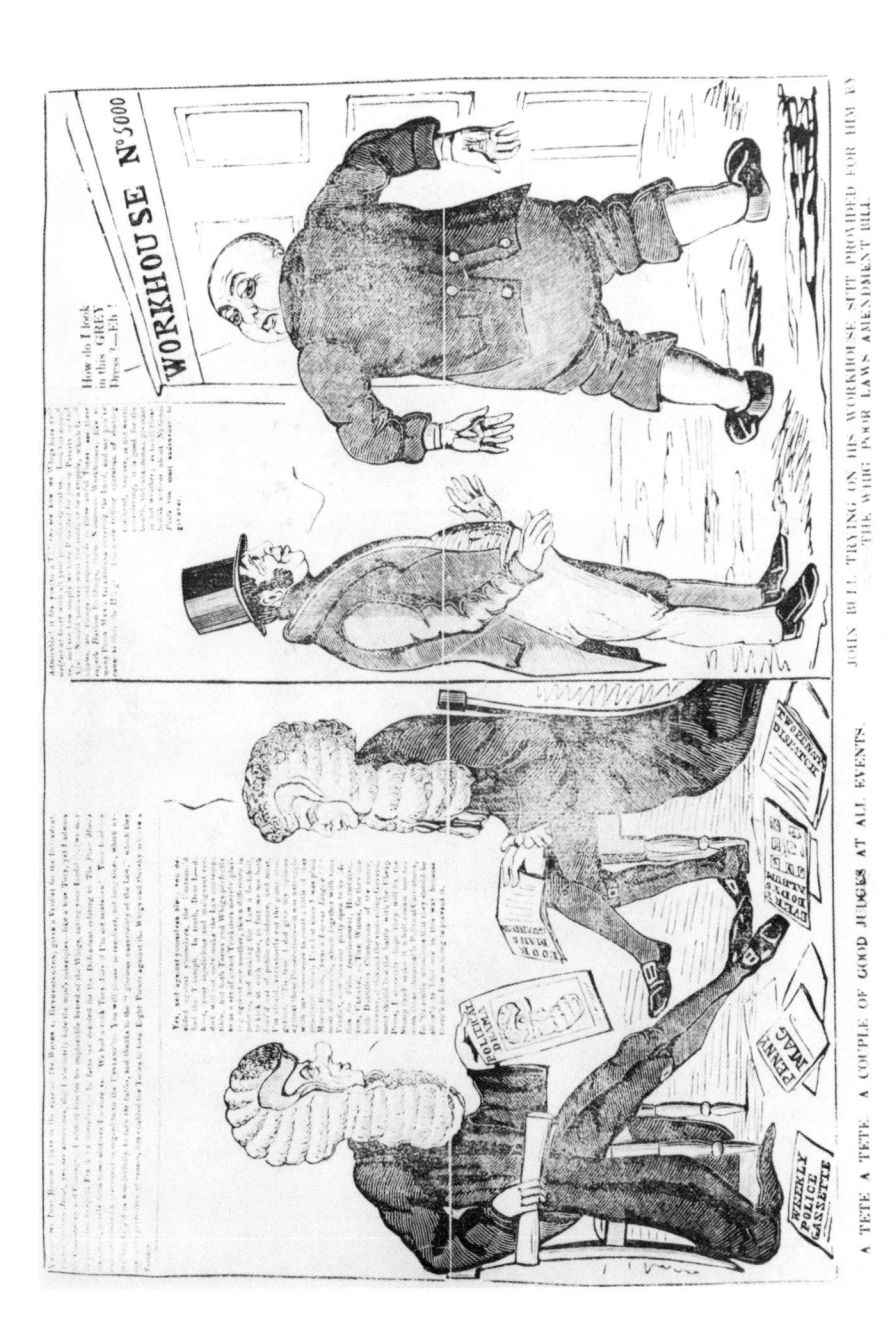

'A TETE A TETE. A COUPLE OF GOOD JUDGES AT ALL EVENTS.' JOHN BULL TRYING ON HIS WORKHOUSE SUIT PROVIDED FOR HIM BY THE WHIG POOR LAWS AMENDMENT BILL,' Political Drama

55. Grant

56. 'THE FRUITS OF THE NEW POOR LAW BILL,' Figaro in London

Awful fecundity—surely nothing is wanting to evince the march of *knowledge* among the young folks of the present day, than this.—Oh! Martineau and Malthus, what say you to this! O Tempore! O Mores!

I say, Sir John, there are a few spe- cimens of *good breeding* at all events, exercised under the new Law.

Ha! ha! I suppose you would call this the *fruits* of the new Bastardy Law.

Delightful plea. The sensualist can now enjoy himself without the fear of *corroborative testimony*.

I say, Bloom——t, 'tis pleasant to *work* in a good cause. I suppose you often "Rear the tender thought!"

Don't mention it Al——orps. There appears to be no lack of reading the Scriptures, now a days, for since the new Laws came in *operation,* "*Increase & Multiply,*" seems now all the go.

EFFECTS OF THE NEW BASTARDY LAW.

'EFFECTS OF THE NEW BASTARDY LAW,' Political Drama

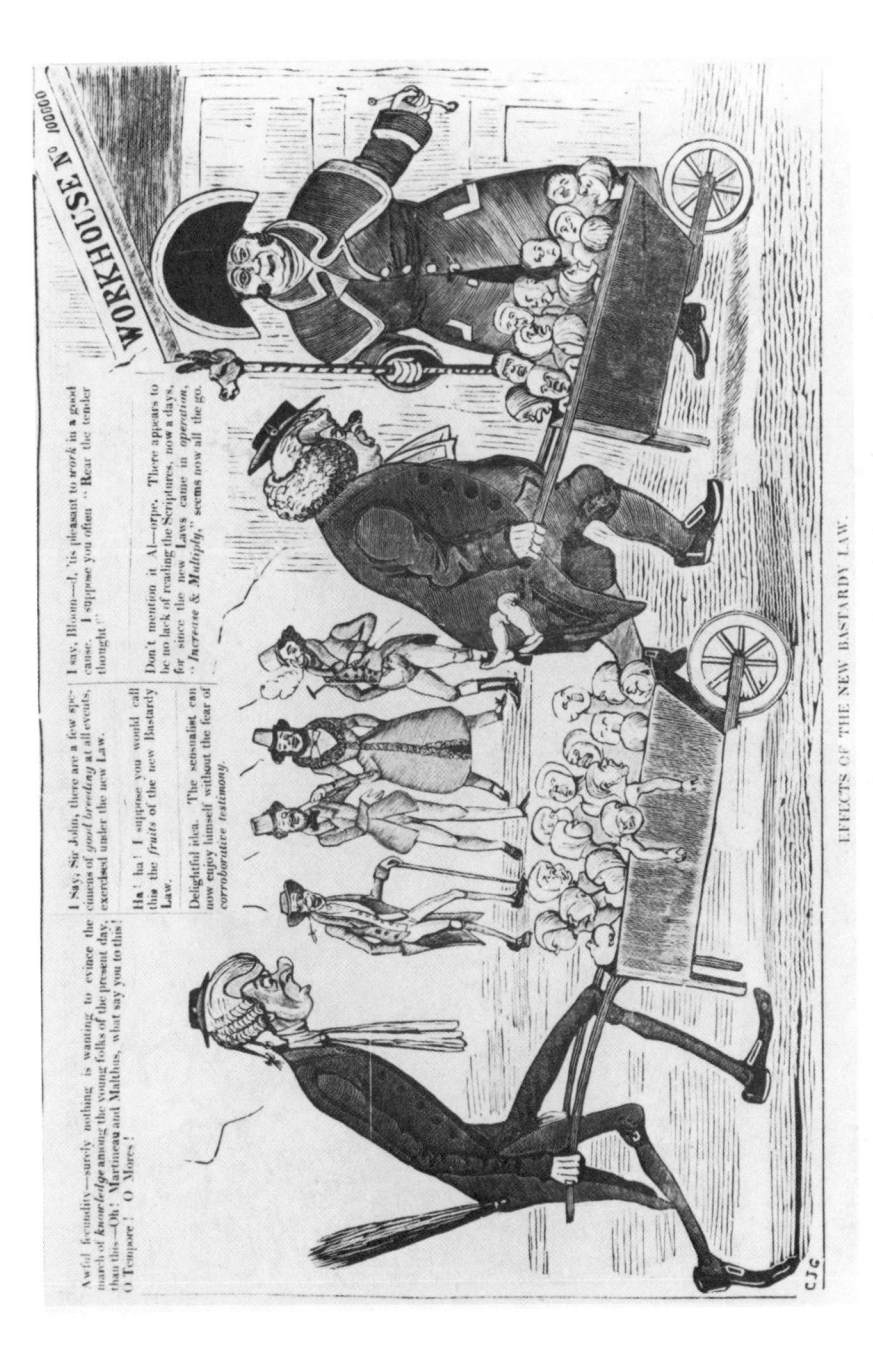

57. Grant

58. 'Innocent Pastime; or, the Blue Devils in their Glory,' *Satirical Puppet Show*

59. Grant 'THE GLORIOUS VERDICT OF COLD BATH FIELDS; OR, A HARD PULL FOR JUSTICE,' Political Drama

60. Seymour   'THE WOLVES LET LOOSE AT WOLVERHAMPTON,' Figaro in London

61. Grant 'THE FREEDOM OF AN ENGLISH ELECTION; OR, THE DRUNKEN DRAGOONS SHOOTING OLD WOMEN AND CHILDREN AT WOLVERHAMPTON BY WAY OF KEEPING THEIR HAND IN,' *Political Drama*

62. ? 'MILITARY PASTIME; OR, THE BASTARDS IN THEIR GLORY,' Weekly Show-Up

63. Grant 'THE LATE BLOODY AND BRUTAL EXHIBITION OF HORRID MILITARY TORTURE; OR, ARISTOCRATIC BASTARDS IN THEIR GLORY!!!,' Political Drama

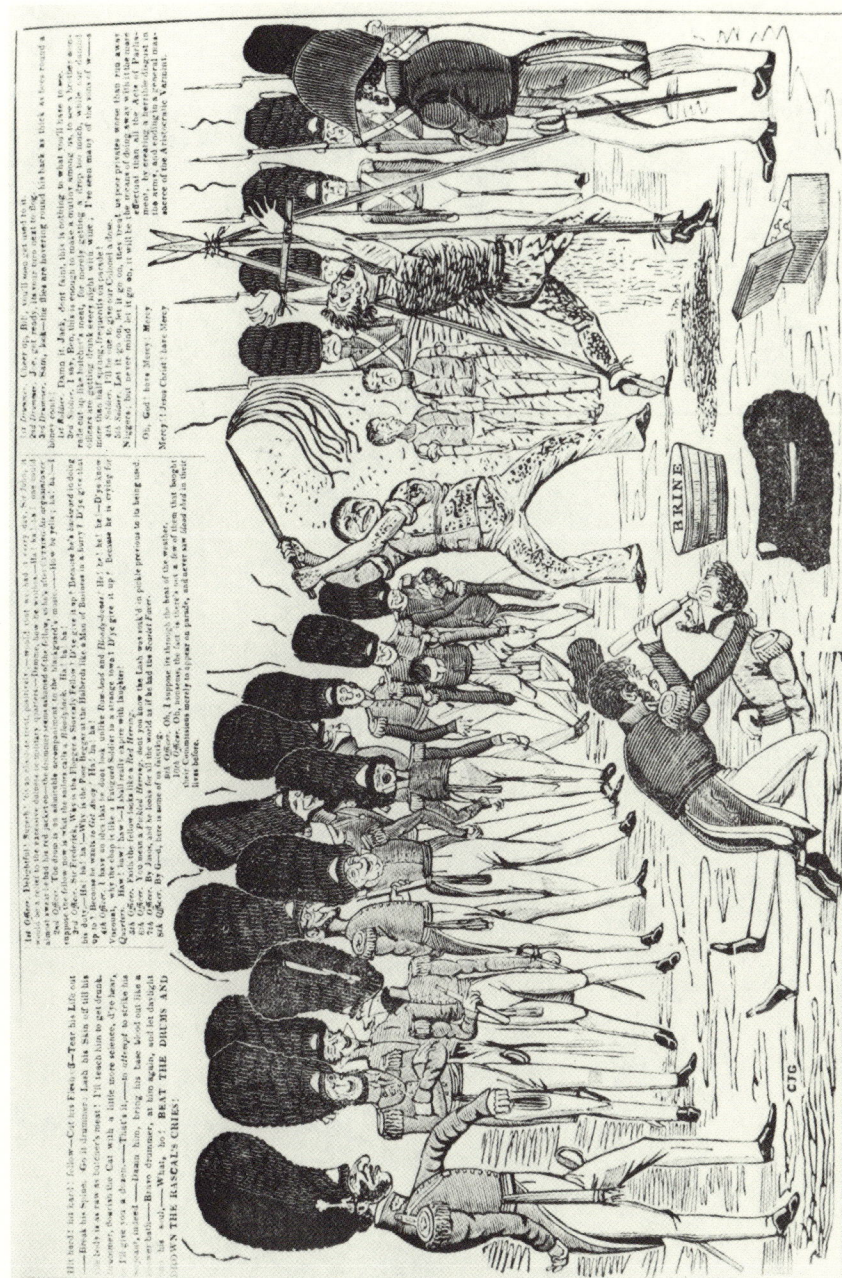

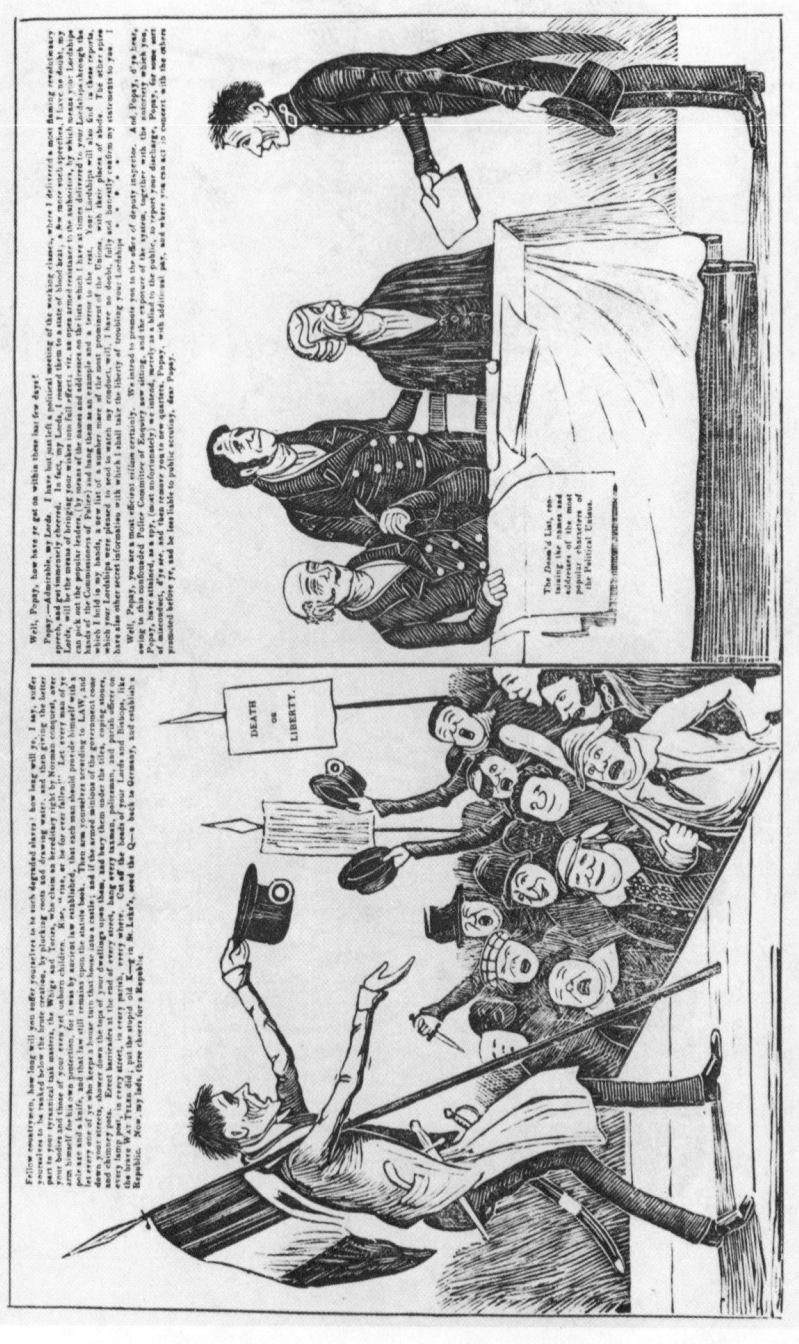

64. Grant 'POPAY THE SPY, addressing a Political Meeting in the garb of a brother Mechanic. POPAY GIVING IN HIS REPORTS TO HIS EMPLOYERS'

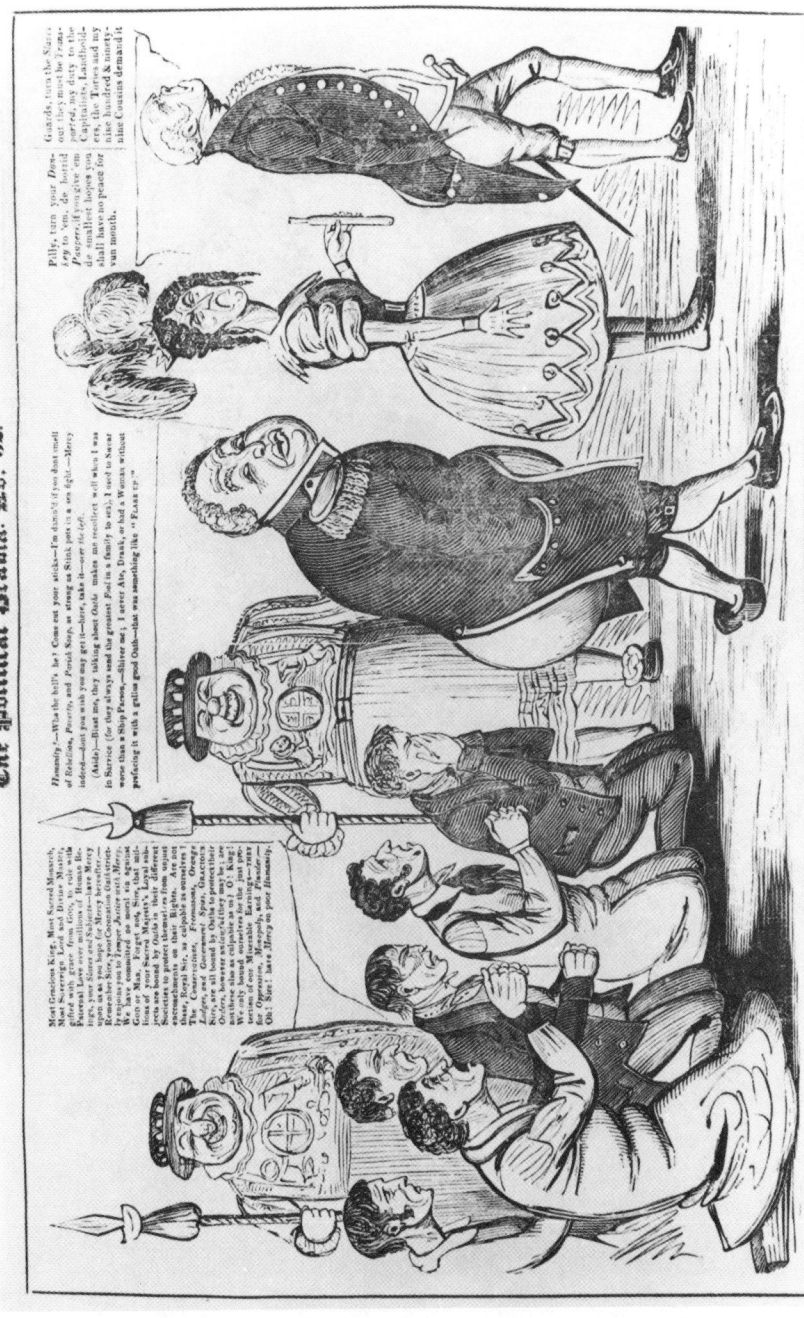

65. Grant 'THE DORCHESTER UNIONISTS IMPLORING MERCY!!! OF THEIR KING,' Political Drama.

66. Seymour: 'THE DAEMON OF MONOPOLY,' Figaro in London

67. Seymour   'COMBINATIONS,' McLean's Monthly Sheet of Caricatures

68. Seymour   'A MEETING OF THE TRADES' UNIONS. A SUNDAY "TURN OUT" OF THE TRADES' UNIONS,' McLean's Monthly Sheet of Caricatures

69. Seymour 'A TRADES' UNION COMMITTEE. PUTTING DOWN THE TRADES' UNIONS,' McLean's Monthly Sheet of Caricatures

70. Seymour 'A DEDICATION TO THE TEMPERANCE SOCIETY–O'ER ALL THE ILLS OF LIFE VICTORIOUS,' McLean's Monthly Sheet of Caricatures

71. Seymour   'THE TWO FISHERMEN. A DEDICATION TO THE TEMPERANCE SOCIETY,'
McLean's Monthly Sheet of Caricatures

72. Grant 'THE DRUNKEN PARLIAMENT DISCUSSING THE PREVENTION OF DRUNKENNESS BILL,' Political Drama

73. Grant   'JOHN BULL; or, an Englishman's Fireside!,'
                                                      Political Drama

THE SINNERS BEFORE SAINT ANDREW.

74. Grant 'THE SINNERS BEFORE SAINT ANDREW,' Political Drama

75. ? 'Church Fanaticism and the Gentlemen in Black,' Satirical Puppet Show

76. Grant   'THE FOUR FACTIONS, WHICH DISTRACT THE COUNTRY,'
Political Drama

77. George Cruikshank 'LIBERTY SUSPENDED! with the Bulwark of the Constitution!,'

78. Cruikshank 'A FREE BORN ENGLISHMAN!,'

79. Cruikshank 'Poor BULL & his Burden—or the Political MURRAION!!!,'

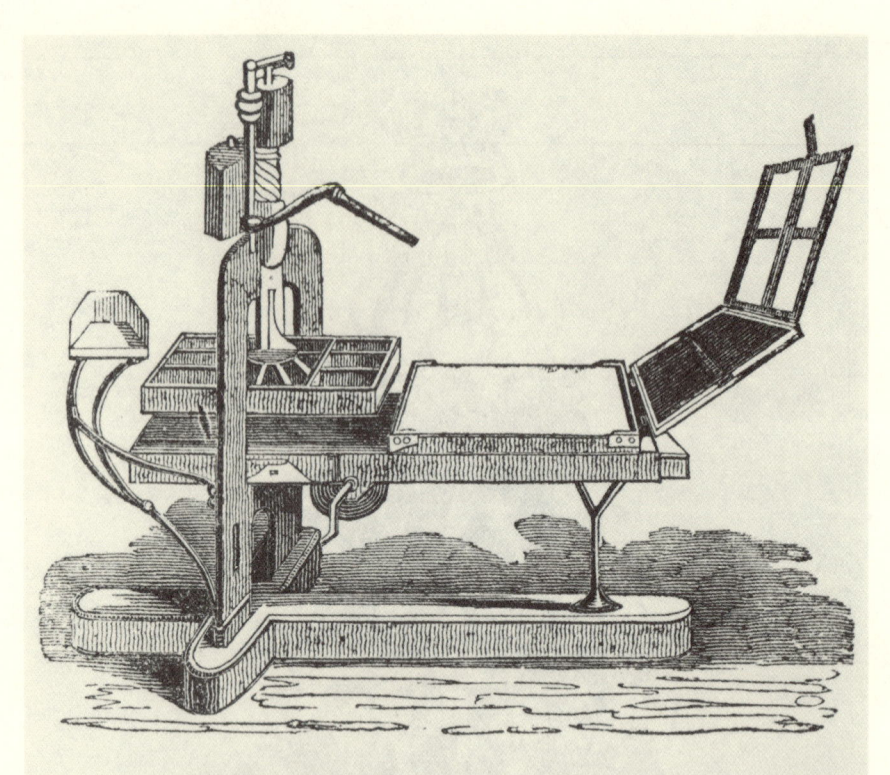

"Once enslaved, farewell!
* * * *
Do I forebode impossible events,
And tremble at vain dreams? Heav'n grant I may!"

THIS IS

THE THING,

that, in spite of new Acts,
And attempts to restrain it,
by Soldiers or Tax,
Will *poison* the Vermin,
That plunder the Wealth,
That lay in the House,
That Jack built.

80. Cruikshank   'THE THING,' Political House that Jack Built

THE PRESS, invented much about the same time with the *Reformation,* hath done more mischief to the discipline of our Church, than all the doctrine can make amends for. 'Twas an happy time, when all learning was in manuscript, and some little officer did keep the keys of the library! Now, since PRINTING came into the world, such is the mischief, that *a man cannot write a book but presently he is answered!* There have been ways found out to *fine* not the people, but even the *grounds and fields where they assembled:* but no art yet could prevent these SEDITIOUS MEETINGS OF LETTERS! Two or three brawny fellows in a corner, with meer ink and elbow-grease, do more harm than an *hundred systematic divines.* Their ugly printing *letters,* that look but like so many rotten teeth, how oft have they been pulled out by the public tooth-drawers! And yet these rascally operators of the press have got a trick to fasten them again in a few minutes, that they grow as firm a set, and as biting and talkative as ever! O PRINTING! how hast thou " *disturbed the peace!*" Lead, when moulded into bullets, is not so mortal as when founded into *letters!* There was a mistake sure in the story of Cadmus; and the *serpent's teeth* which he sowed, were nothing else but the *letters* which he invented.

Marvell's Rehearsal transprosed, 4to, 1672.

Being marked only with *four and twenty letters,—variously transposed* by the help of a PRINTING PRESS,—PAPER works miracles. The Devil dares no more come near a *Stationer's* heap, or a *Printer's Office,* than *Rats* dare put their noses into a Cheesemonger's Shop. *A Whip for the Devil,* 1669. p. 92.

THE SHOWMAN.

81. Cruikshank   'THE SHOWMAN,' Political Showman – At Home!

THE TRANSPARENCY, of which this is a copy, was exhibited by WILLIAM HONE during the ILLUMINATION commencing on the 11th, and ending on the 15th of November, 1820, in celebration of the VICTORY obtained by THE PRESS for the LIBERTIES OF THE PEOPLE, which had been assailed in the Person of *The Queen*; the words "TRIUMPH OF THE PRESS," being displayed in variegated lamps as a motto above it. On the 29th, when *The Queen* went to St. Paul's, it was again exhibited, with Lord Bacon's immortal words, "KNOWLEDGE IS POWER," displayed in like manner.—The Transparency was painted by Mr. GEORGE CRUIKSHANK.

'THE TRANSPARENCY,' Political Showman - At Home!

82. Cruikshank

83. Cruikshank 'THE "DAMNABLE ASSOCIATION," OR THE INFERNAL INQUISITION OF BLACK FRIARS,' A Slap at Slop and the Bridge Street Gang

84. William Heath 'THE MAN WOTS GOT THE WHIP HAND OF 'EM ALL'

MAGISTERIAL JUSTICE—A FACT.

85. Grant   'MAGISTERIAL JUSTICE – A FACT,' Political Drama

Have you read the Leader in this paper, Mr. Brisket?
No, I never touch a newspaper, they are all so wery wenal and mud of sentiment.

86. <u>Sketches by Seymour</u>

87. Doyle   "A TALE of a TUB" and the MORAL of the TAIL!," H.B. Political Sketches

88. Grant   'THE HEAD SCHOOLMASTER THREATENED,'

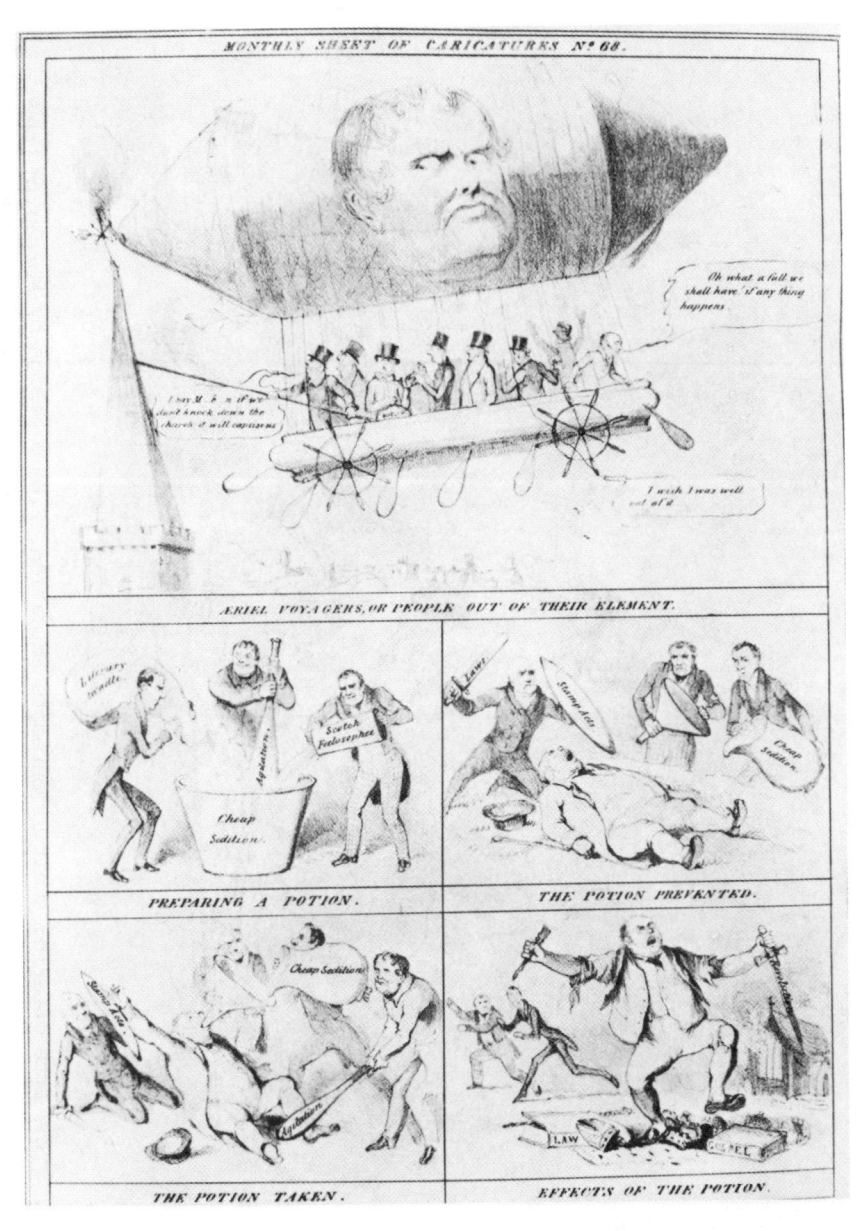

89. Seymour   'THE POTION,' McLean's Monthly Sheet of Caricatures

90. 'The arts offering their Tributes to Education. From a Design by Moreau in the Musee Francais,' Penny Magazine

91. 'Workhouse of the Windsor Union,' Penny Magazine ?

92. 'Power-looms. - Cotton Manufacture,' Penny Magazine

93. ? 'South Hetton Colliery,' Penny Magazine

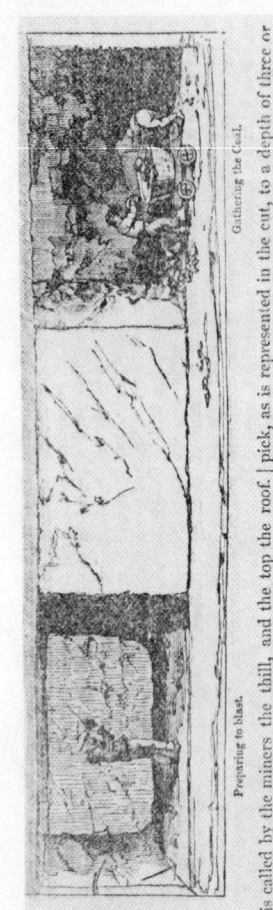

Preparing to blast.   *Gathering the Coal.*   *Pitmen forming a "bord."*

is called by the miners the thill, and the top the roof. Here and there along the walls of this passage a safety-lamp is suspended; and when the intense darkness of the place is occasionally illuminated by the slight ignition of the fire-damp, the whole scene presents an extraordinary appearance. The generation of inflammable air is frequently so great from the solid coal that the miners dare not proceed onward above a few feet from the current of fresh air. The light afforded by the safety-lamps seems to possess an unusual illuminating power; but though the visitor can see perfectly well, he still feels encompassed by pitchy and midnight darkness. In these galleries the miners or hewers, as they are called, carry on their work in pairs, each taking about twelve feet of the side wall to excavate, and leaving between each space an interval of the same width on which the roof may securely rest. The first process is to form what is denominated a "bord," which is done by digging out the coal from the bottom with a pick, as is represented in the cut, to a depth of three or four feet. The "bord" being completed has next to be formed into a "judd;" this is effected by picking away the sides, as had previously been done with the thill; and when finished, it forms a projecting mass of coal measuring on its surface about eleven feet by six. Into this judd a deep sloping hole is then bored, which is filled with gunpowder and fired by a train, when the judd is shivered into large fragments and scattered over the floor. In this way much labour is saved, and a larger and more profitable-sized coal is secured for the market.

The coal seams of Yorkshire average from one and a half to nine feet in thickness, while in the more northern coal-fields they run from two and a half to seven feet. Near Dudley, in Staffordshire, is a seam of coal known by the name of the ten-yard coal, from its extraordinary thickness. This remarkable bed is about seven miles long and four broad. Seams of coal have been worked as thin as eighteen inches, and instances have occurred

Dragsman and Foal.   *Forming a "judd."*

95. 'Rag Fair,' Penny Magazine

96. ? 'Hyde Park – Entrance from Piccadilly,' Penny Magazine

97. Seymour   'PATENT PENNY KNOWLEDGE MILL,' McLean's Monthly Sheet of Caricatures

98. W.C. Walker wood engraving after a plate in Colonel Macerone's *Defensive Instructions to the People*. *Poor Man's Guardian*

99. ? 'The Busy Busy B--,' The Caricaturist

100. Grant   'FRONTISPIECE FOR THE PENNY MAGAZINE '

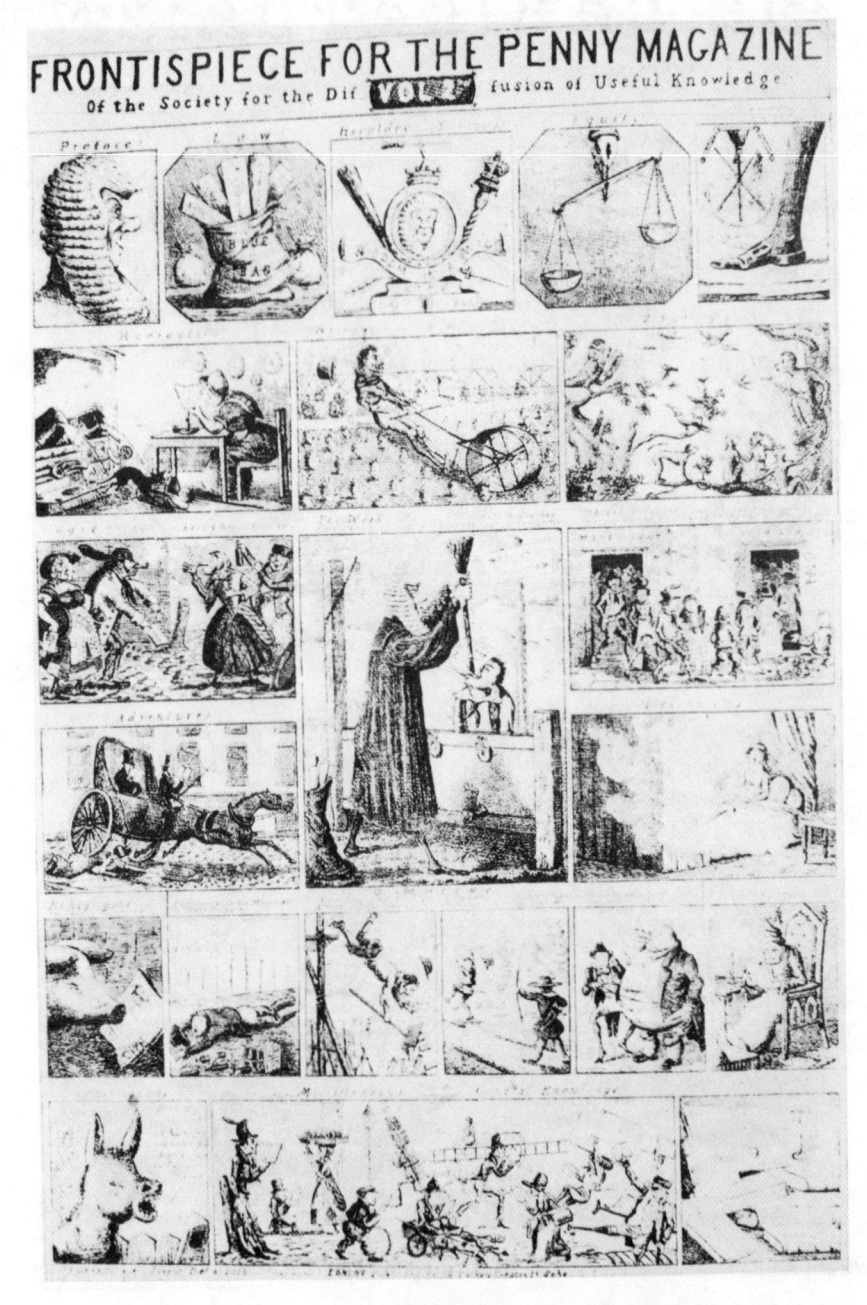

101. Grant   'THE LITERARY DUSTMAN, or L—d BROOM in Character,' Lloyd's Political Jokes

102. Grant 'POLITICAL SPORTSMEN; OR, PRACTISING AGAINST THE NEXT SESSION,' Political Drama

103. Grant 'FISHING FOR GUDGEONS AND FLATS,' Political Drama

THE CHANCELLOR'S DREAM; OR, KING RICHARD III. TRAVESTIE.

104. Grant 'THE CHANCELLOR'S DREAM; OR, KING RICHARD III. TRAVESTIE,' Political Drama

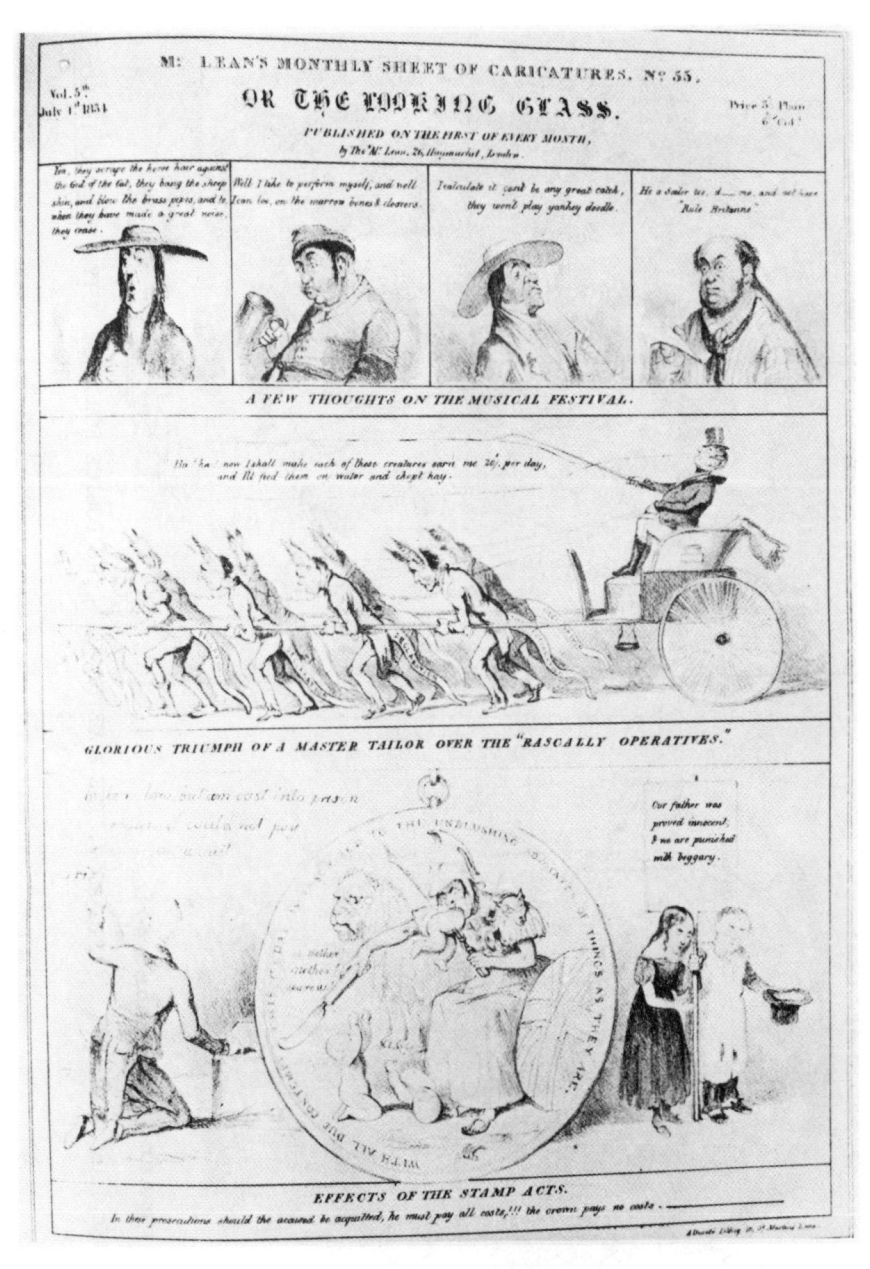

105. Seymour   'EFFECTS OF THE STAMP ACTS,'
McLean's Monthly Sheet of Caricatures

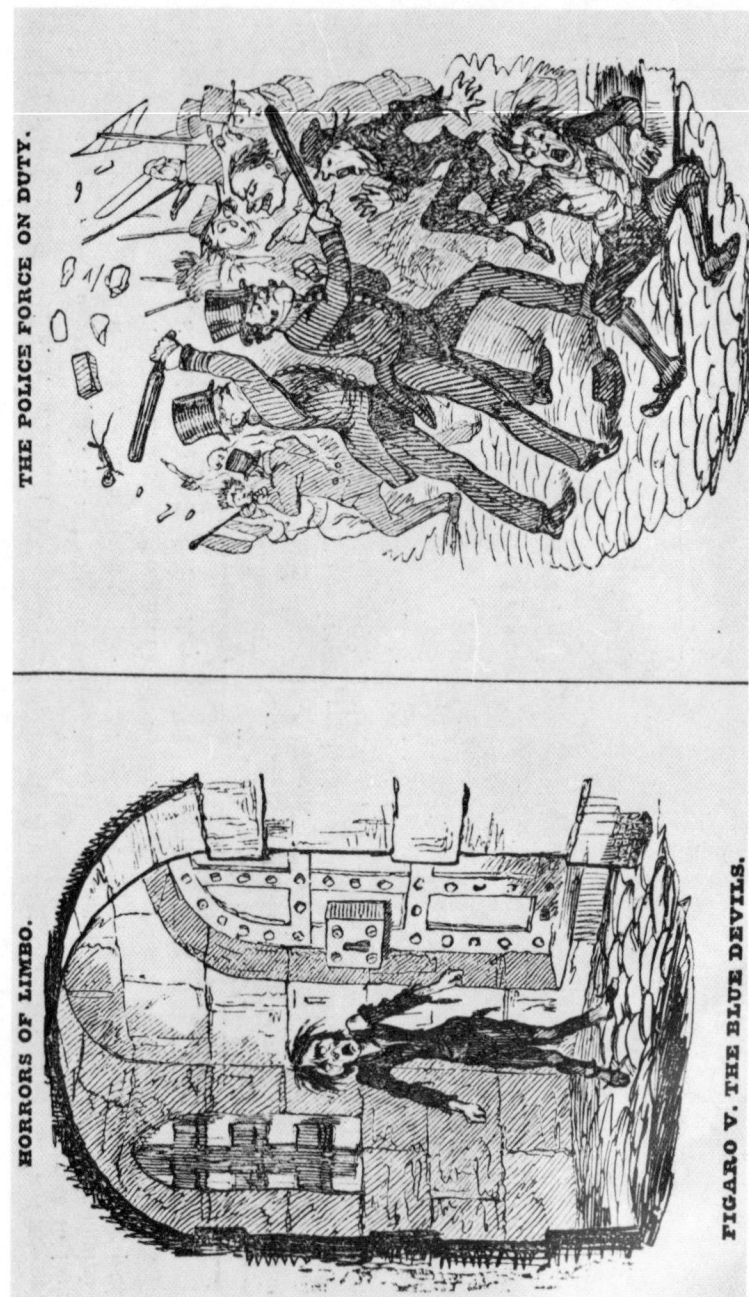

106. Seymour 'FIGARO V. THE BLUE DEVILS. THE POLICE FORCE ON DUTY,' Figaro in London

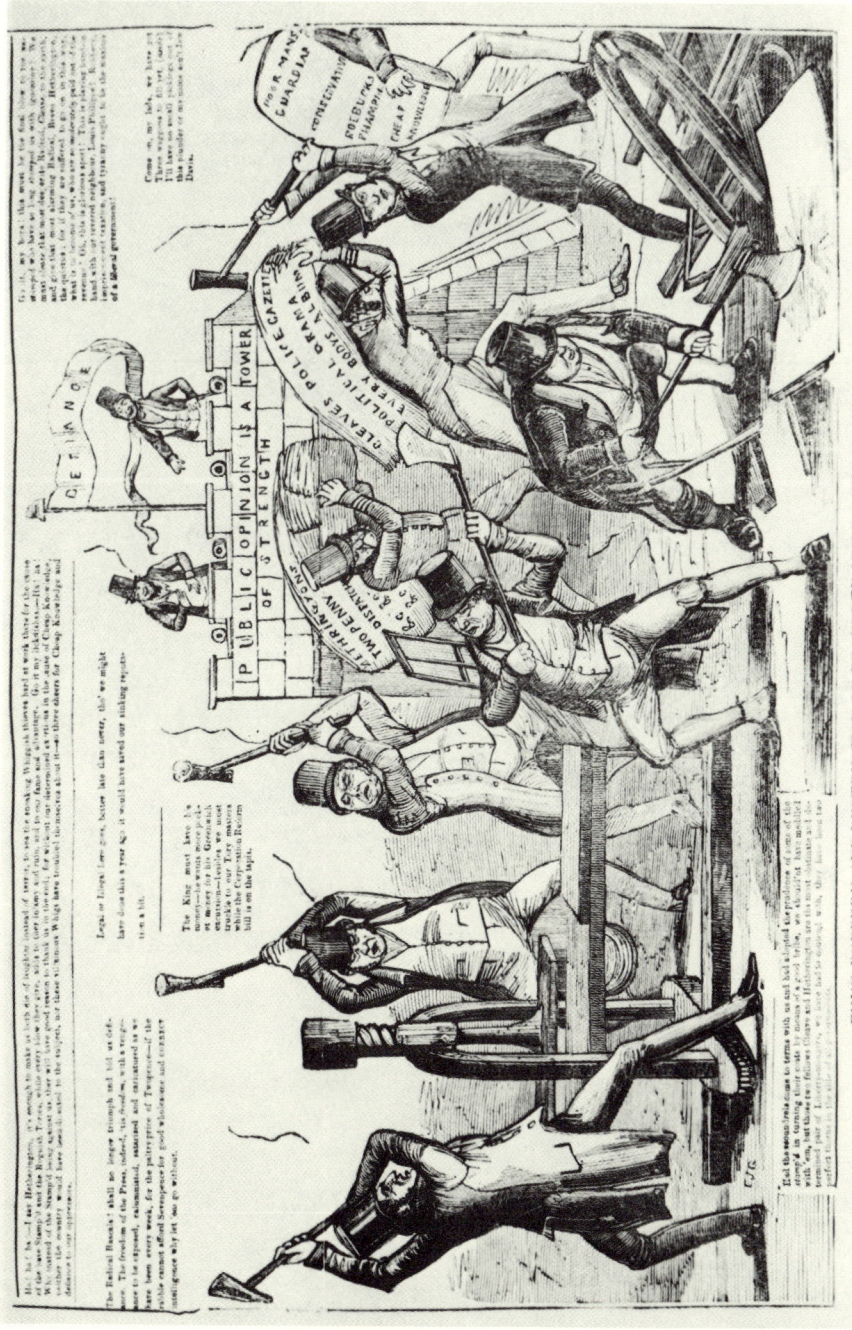

107. Grant   'WHIG ROBBERY AND DESTRUCTION OF PROPERTY UNDER THE NAME OF LAW,' *Political Drama*

THE NEW STAMP ACT.

108. Seymour   'THE NEW STAMP ACT,' <u>Figaro in London</u>

USEFUL SUNDAY LITERATURE FOR THE MASSES;
OR, MURDER MADE FAMILIAR.

Father of a Family (reads). "The wretched Murderer is supposed to have cut the throats of his three eldest Children, and then to have killed the Baby by beating it repeatedly with a Poker. * * * * * In person he is of a rather bloated appearance, with a bull neck, small eyes, broad large nose, and coarse vulgar mouth. His dress was a light blue coat, with brass buttons, elegant yellow summer vest, and pepper-and-salt trowsers. When at the Station House he expressed himself as being rather 'peckish,' and said he should like a Black Pudding, which, with a Cup of Coffee, was immediately procured for him."

109. J. Leech   'USEFUL SUNDAY LITERATURE FOR THE MASSES; OR, MURDER MADE FAMILIAR,' <u>Punch</u>

THE MORNING AFTER THE CORONATION.

THE NIGHT OF THE CORONATION.

Melbourne.—Twg hnn—he with the Pockets to let unfurnished, and the Lng ear. Ha, ha, ha.

Russell.—He's taking a walk while his nurse is drying his cloute. Ha, ha.

Rice.—He's a right good fellow tho' after all. Spends like a trump, and no gammon—he's out of luck this morning. "Very," that's all.

Bull.—This is the way I'm used, but it serves me right for being an ass—my fondness for raree shows, and my easy nature, makes these Scamps impose upon me, and then they turn round and jeer me; but I deserve to be laugh'd at

Who, in excessive trepidation,
From the fatigues of my Coronation,
Soothed me in my agitation?
               My Mother.

Who, after the sigbt cold I got,
So gently laid me in my cot,
And gave a basin of something hot?
               My Mother.

Who, watch'd me with an anxious eye,
Tuck'd in the clothes, and sitting nigh,
Sang me to sleep—with "Lullaby?"
               My Mother.

110. Grant   'THE MORNING AFTER THE CORONATION. THE NIGHT OF THE CORONATION,' Gleave's Penny Gazette of Variety

COAXING.

' Now, my dear Mr. Bull, you know you can't refuse me such a trifle!'

' Why, you wilful young puss; it is not the money I begrudge you, but I don't like these foreign chaps. I had a much better husband for you in my eye;—besides, I suspect the result will be that I shall have a swarm of young **Dukes** and **Duchesses**, and a bevy of German hangers-on to provide for; and the times are wretched bad—thousands on the verge of starvation!'

111.   ?   'COAXING,' Odd Fellow

THE MARCH OF COMMON SENSE.

THE DISTILLER AS HE WAS.

THE DISTILLER AS HE IS.

112. Grant 'THE MARCH OF COMMON SENSE,' <u>Cleave's Gazette</u>

POOR LAW SKETCHES.—"A DOG IN OFFICE."

113.   ?   'POOR LAW SKETCHES. - "A DOG IN OFFICE.",' <u>Odd Fellow</u>

THE POOR LAWS IN BRADFORD.

First Soldier. What d'ye say ye wont swallow 'em? How dare you presume to think that the Whigs don't know what is good for the welfare of the Bradford Paupers.

Second Soldier. It's plain we must *force* it down their throats with *Steel Lozenges*, and *Lead* Pills.

Third Soldier. The ignorant Boor has no idea of an independence of " Parochial Relief," or he'd never offer such resistance.

114. Grant 'THE POOR LAWS IN BRADFORD,' Cleave's Gazette

THE PENTONVILLE BASTILLE

Two victims to solitary confinement were removed in a state of madness from their cells to the asylum.—*The Newspapers.*

> ———His heart a prey to black despair,
> He eats not, drinks not, sleeps not, has no use
> Of anything but thought ; or, if he talks,
> 'Tis to himself, and then 'tis perfect raving.
> Then he defies the world, and bids it pass.
> Sometimes he gnaws his lips, then draws his mouth
> Into a scornful smile. *Dryden.*

MELBOURNE.—You are gaoler now ; therefore, are responsible for the misfortune.
GRAHAM.—You and the rest of the Whigs built the Bastille.
RUSSELL.—Brougham started the silent system, 'tis true ; and you Tories seem to have added new torments to it.
BROUGHAM.—Ah, there is six of one and half a dozen of the other !

115. Grant 'THE PENTONVILLE BASTILLE,' Cleave's Gazette

116. Grant 'THE WHIG NEW POLICE ACT IN FULL OPERATION,' Cleave's Illustrated Metropolitan Police Act

THE PHŒNIX OF CHARTISM.

AN ALLEGORICAL DRAMA.

TORIES.—Ah! see, see! we thought to have destroyed the Charter for ever, with its Six Points; but see, it rises again, in the form of a *Phœnix*, from its own ashes. D——ion, it is not to be annihilated. The torment *will* hover about us, despite of all victimizing and prosecutions.

117. Grant   'THE PHOENIX OF CHARTISM,' Cleave's Gazette

118. W. Newman 'LAW MAKING A MEAL IN THE MANUFACTURING DISTRICTS,' Odd Fellow

THE ANTI-CORN LAW GIANT, AND THE DWARFS OF MONOPOLY.

POLICEMAN PEEL.—You can't pass this way.

DWARFS.—Stop his progress, lug as he is, or he'll infect the whole nation with his sedition, and them it will end our beloved Class Legislation in Dear Bread, High Rents, Low Wages, Universal Starvation and Screwing Taxation, which is the life and strength of us Lords of the Land.

PEEL.—Go back; for see, we are the strongest in PHYSICAL FORCE.

THE GIANT COBDEN.—True, but I am stronger in MORAL FORCE; behold! (holding up the League packet of pamphlets and a placard): These are MY WEAPONS—TRUTH AND REASON, and they will soon prevail over your deadly ones. It is true, your name is Legion—but mine is LEAGUE—a LEAGUE of the nation: a LEAGUE of holiness, (strengthened by Providence) pleading the cause of the famishing millions: a LEAGUE of humanity against avarice and ambition.—Yes, we League against the enemies of this great Nation, and wish to save it from destruction; consequently, we are your Friends. Give us your Foreign Corn, and we promise you in return, that your Bread Acres shall be more valuable to you than they are now. Refuse us a little longer, deny us the right of giving our labour in exchange for Bread at the cheapest market—we fear—we dread the awful consequences!!

119. Grant   'THE ANTI-CORN LAW GIANT, AND THE DWARFS OF MONOPOLY,' <u>Penny Satirist</u>

120-1. W.M. Thackeray   'ILLUSTRATIONS OF THE RENT LAWS,'
Anti-Corn Law Circular

CHARACTERISTIC SKETCHES.—Nº LXXIII.

Lady of beauty, frail yet fair,
  Devoted to the shrine of folly,
Though decked in jewels rich and rare,
  Thy life will close in melancholy.

"Good Mr. *Town*, pray hold your tongue,
  And never mind my latter end;
I'm now both beautiful and young,
  And just the girl to get a friend."

Man of the phiz so dissipated,
  'Tis such as you who are to blame;
That woman, when by wine elated,
  Will on her sex bring scorn and shame.

"Hold, *Town*, your moral bantering cease,
  And turn your eagle eye so knowing,
To other *breeches* of the *peace*
  Committed by the acting *blowen*."

122. A. Henning   'The Saloon Lady,' <u>Town</u>

123. Grant wood engraving for the Penny Pickwick

HUMFRIES' CLOCK.

"Bos," Maker.

CHAPTER I.

THE VERY COMMENCEMENT OF THE BEGINNING.—THE READER'S FIRST INTRODUCTION TO MISTER HUMFRIES AND HIS REMARKABLE CLOCK.—AN EXTRAORDINARY SCENE AND STILL MORE EXTRAORDINARY INTERRUPTION.

125. G. Stiff   illustration for G.W.M. Reynolds,
                              The Mysteries of London

126. H. Anelay   The Mysteries of London

127. W. Gorway   The Mysteries of London

128. Leech 'FOREIGN AFFAIRS,' Punch

PUNCH'S PENCILLINGS.——N.º LXVI.

THE CHARITY BALL.

Having purchased a ticket for a Charity Ball, you are deluded by the promise of a pretty Partner to waltz, and are victimized as above.

129. Leech   'THE CHARITY BALL,' Punch

PUNCH'S LIFE BUOY.

(DEDICATED WITHOUT PERMISSION TO MR. JOHN LEECH.)

130. ? 'PUNCH'S LIFE BUOY,' <u>Man in the Moon</u>

A DROP OF LONDON WATER.

131. Kenny Meadows   'A DROP OF LONDON WATER,' Punch

AUTHORS' MISERIES. No. VI.

Old Gentleman. Miss Wiggets. Two Authors.

THE ARTFUL DODGER.

"Oh, how jolly green you must be to think you could form a Ministry!"

133. Leech 'THE ARTFUL DODGER,' Punch

134. R. Doyle, 'HIGH ART AND THE ROYAL ACADEMY,' Punch

SUBSTANCE AND SHADOW.

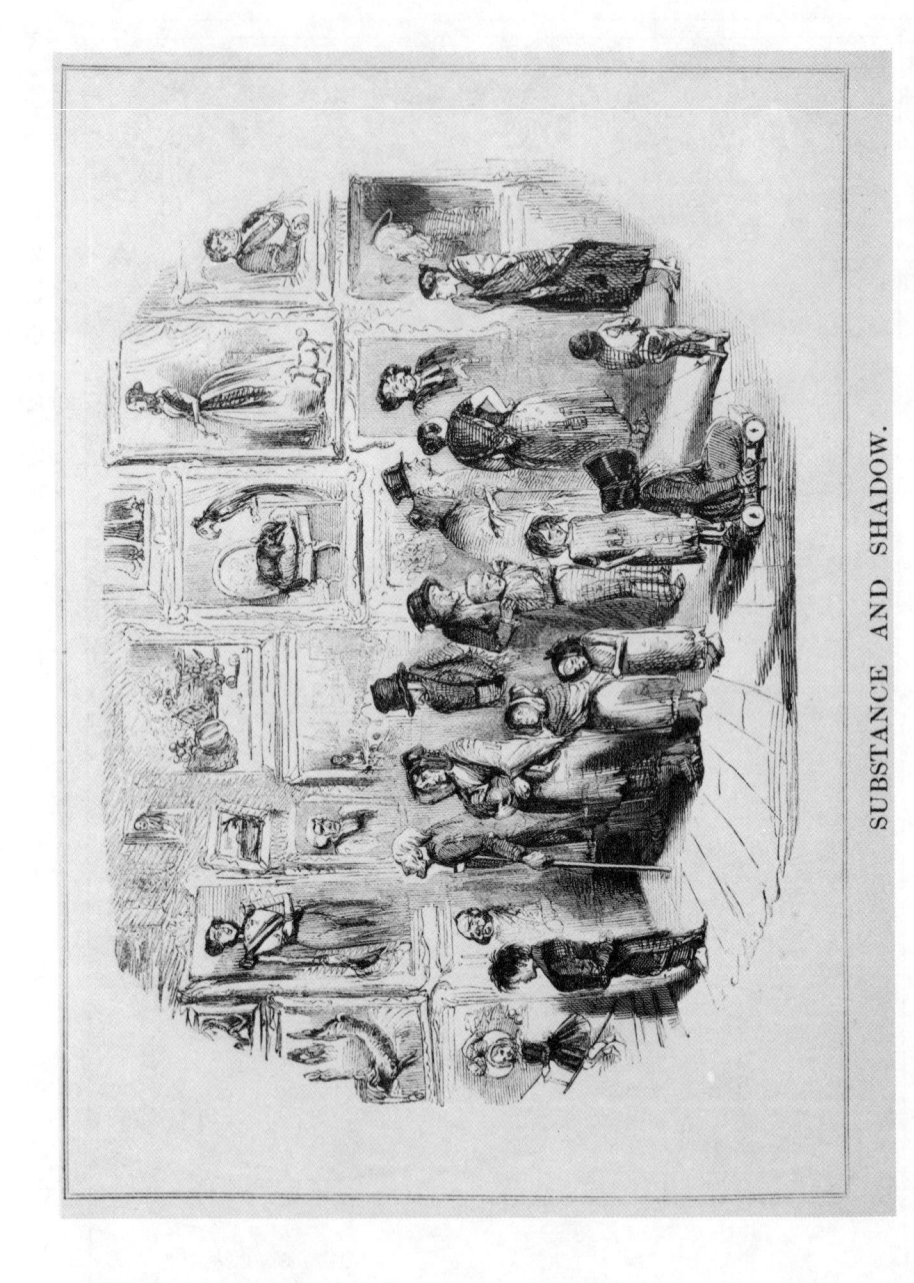

135. Leech 'SUBSTANCE AND SHADOW,' *Punch*

CAPITAL AND LABOUR.

136. 'CAPITAL AND LABOUR,' Punch

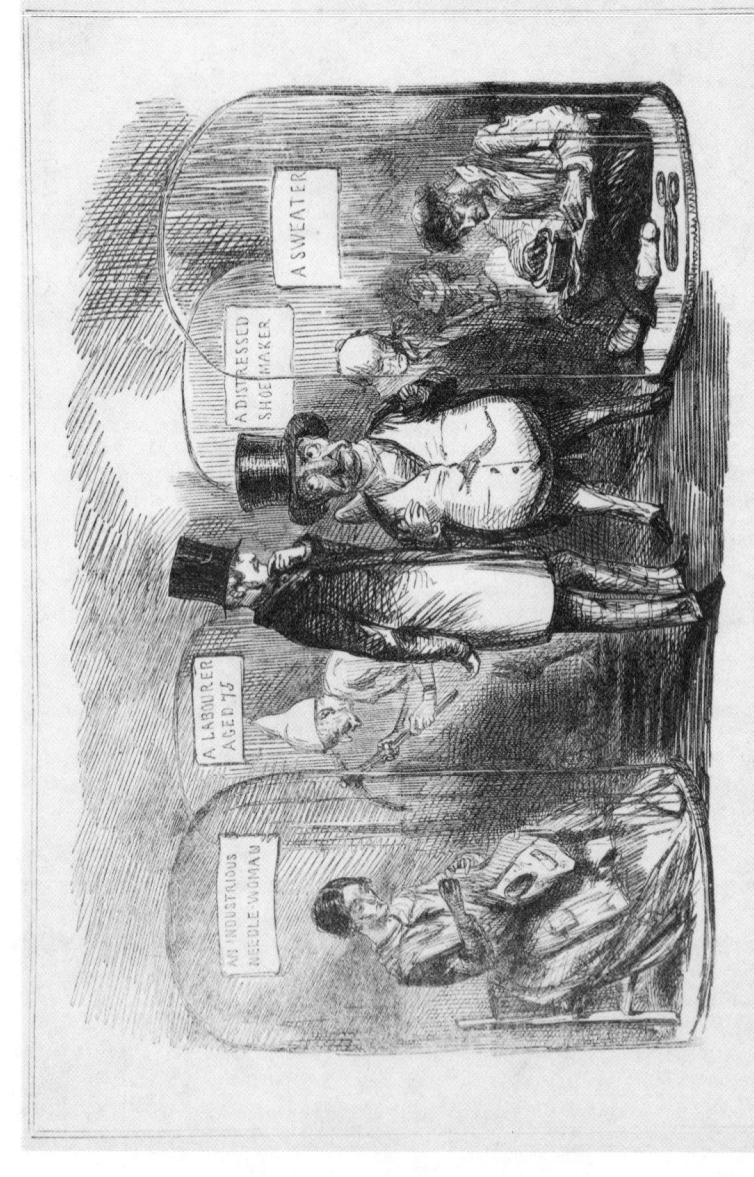

137. Leech 'SPECIMENS FROM MR. PUNCH'S INDUSTRIAL EXHIBITION OF 1850,' Punch

FLY LEAVES, No. 3.

A TRIO OF PUNCHITES.

1st "*Eminent Writer.*" I say, Douglas, what do you think of this PUPPET-SHOW?

2nd "*Eminent Writer.*" Why, I think we ought to put down all rival publications.

3rd "*Eminent Writer.*" Otherwise we shall be sold at the butter shops free, gratis, and for nothing.

138. ? 'A TRIO OF PUNCHITES,' Puppet Show

THE MAN IN THE MOON.

A REAL CASE OF DISTRESS.

139.   ?   'A REAL CASE OF DISTRESS,' <u>Man in the Moon</u>

THE RECONCILIATION;

OR, AS IT OUGHT TO BE.

140. Leech 'THE RECONCILIATION; OR, AS IT OUGHT TO BE,' Punch

A PHYSICAL FORCE CHARTIST ARMING FOR THE FIGHT.

141. Leech   'A PHYSICAL FORCE CHARTIST ARMING FOR THE FIGHT,'
                                                            Punch

142. ? 'THE CHARTIST "ORANGE TREE",' Puppet Show

126 THE PUPPET-SHOW.

SOCIAL SKETCHES BY GAVARNI—NO. I.

LONDON POLITENESS.

Obliging Londoner—Take the first Turning to your Right, then the Third to your Left, and you can't miss it.

Grateful Provincial—Oh!—I thank you, Sir.

143. P. Gavarni   'LONDON POLITENESS,' Puppet Show

HOW GAVARNI IDEALISES.

A LONDON CABMAN AS GAVARNI MAKES HIM.

144. ?   'HOW GAVARNI IDEALISES,' Man in the Moon

145. ?   'HOW GAVARNI IDEALISES,' Man in the Moon

LABOUR AND THE POOR.
No. 1.—A SCENE IN THE MINORIES.

"Vat! you vant more than two-pence a-piece for making the shirts, ven, if you vorks from six in the morning till twelve at night, you can make three, and only has to find your own thread! S'help my Abrahams, do yer vish to ruin me?"

146.   ?   'A SCENE IN THE MINORIES,' Penny Punch

LABOUR AND THE POOR.
No. IV.—THE TRUCK SYSTEM.

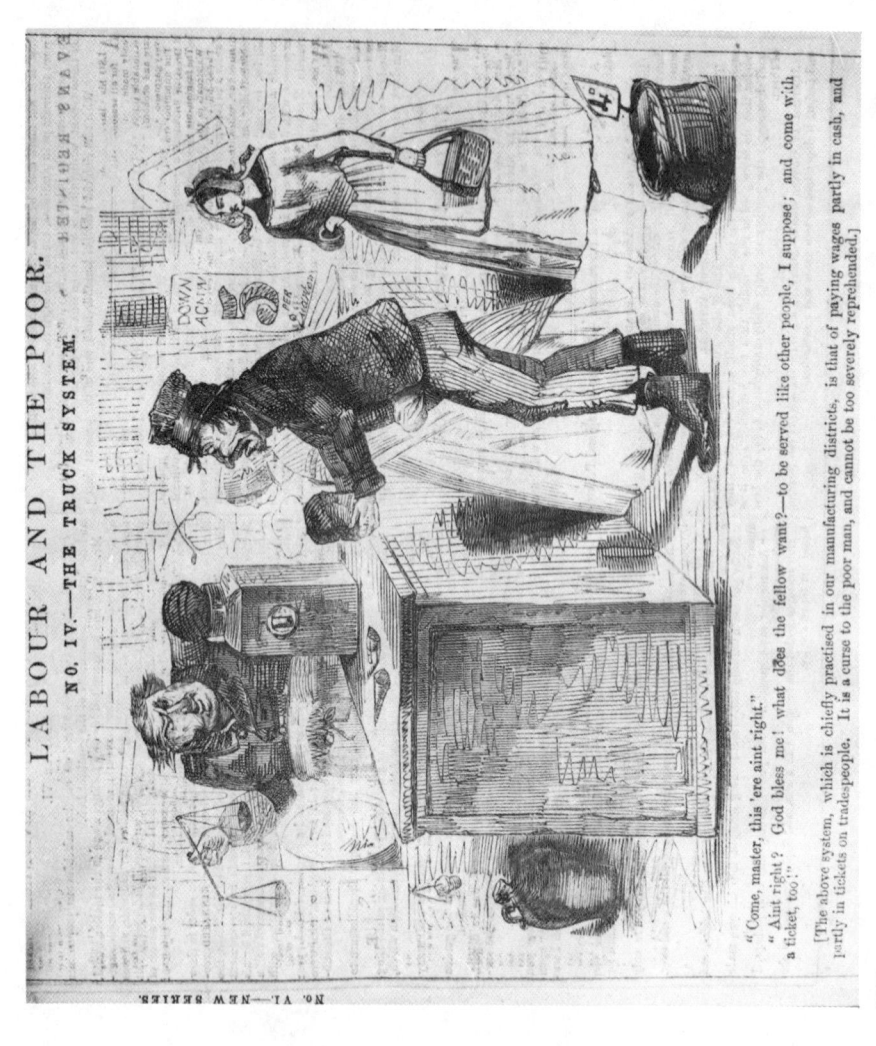

"Come, master, this 'ere aint right."
"Aint right? God bless me! what does the fellow want?—to be served like other people, I suppose; and come with a ticket, too!"

[The above system, which is chiefly practised in our manufacturing districts, is that of paying wages partly in cash, and partly in tickets on tradespeople. It is a curse to the poor man, and cannot be too severely reprehended.]

147. ? 'THE TRUCK SYSTEM,' Penny Punch

OUR FAMILY PICTURES. THE POOR GENTLEMAN'S FAMILY.—THE GOVERNESS.

148. 'THE GOVERNESS,' Life

View of the Conflagration of the City of Hamburgh.

149. ? 'View of the Conflagration of the City of Hamburgh,' Illustrated London News

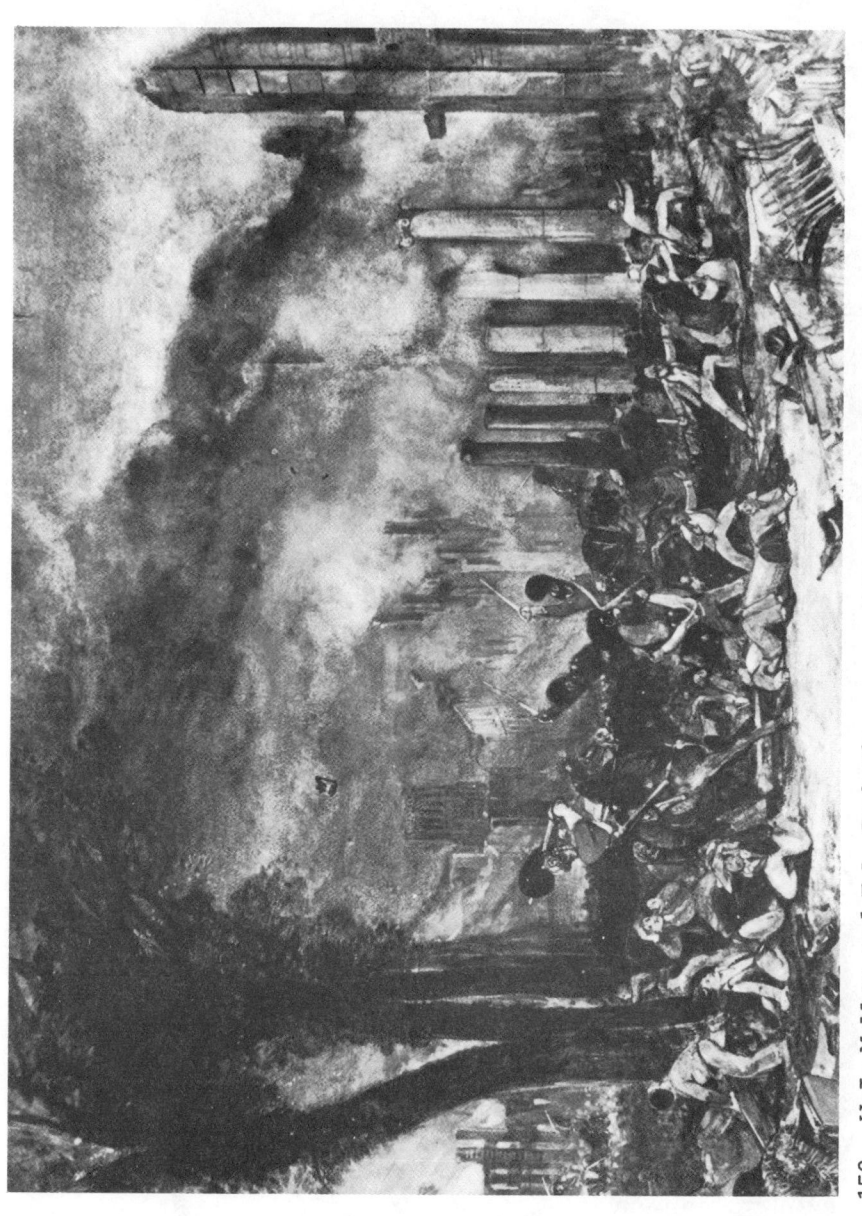

150. W.J. Muller and T.L. Rowbotham   'THE CHARGE OF THE DRAGOONS IN QUEEN-SQUARE DURING THE RIOTS OF 1831,'

151. ? Full Particulars of the Dreadful and Tremendous Riots at Bristol

EXPLOSION OF A FIREWORK MANUFACTORY, IN PRINCES ST. LAMBETH,
AT TWELVE O'CLOCK ON MONDAY MORNING, FEB. 28

152. ? 'EXPLOSION OF A FIREWORK MANUFACTORY, IN PRINCES ST. LAMBETH,'
Cleave's Gazette

153. ? 'TERRIBLE EXPLOSION OF D'ERNEST'S FIRE-WORK MANUFACTORY,' Bell's Penny Dispatch

DREADFUL EXPLOSION OF THE FIRE-WORK MANUFACTORY OF MONS. D'ERNST, IN DOUGHTY STREET, LAMBETH WALK, AND LOSS OF FOUR LIVES!

154. ? 'DREADFUL EXPLOSION OF THE FIRE-WORK MANUFACTORY OF MONS. D'ERNST, IN DOUGHTY STREET, LAMBETH WALK, AND LOSS OF FOUR LIVES!,' Lloyd's Companion to a Newspaper

COBURG.— FROM HIS ROYAL HIGHNESS PRINCE ALBERT'S DRAWING.

the observatory of Gotha, situated on a hill called Seebergen, at a short distance out of the town, and a little to the right of the road that leads to Erfurt. It forms a very prominent object in the surrounding landscape, being at an elevation of 1189 feet above the level of the sea. Since the departure of the Baron, the observations have been continued by his successor, Professor Lindenau, a name well known to astronomers. Literature has always flourished at Gotha; some of the most celebrated German writers in our days are either natives or residents in this town.

Coburg, the other residence-town of the Duke of Saxe-Coburg-Gotha, contains about 9500 inhabitants: it is built in the middle of a beautiful valley, on the banks of the Itz, and affords many attractions to visitors. As Gotha is devoted to learning and literature, so Coburg seems to be made the scene of pleasure: it has a theatre, several concert-rooms, and a number of casinos. The Palace, called Ehrenburgh, built in 1549, contains some handsome apartments, and some fine specimens of marqueterie in the doors; indeed, Coburg is, to this day, celebrated for that manufacture. The theatre belongs to the Duke, and is extremely well conducted. In the Arsenal there are some fine armour, and arms of all ages; and some trophies won by the Prince of Coburg, Austrian Field Marshal. The ancient castle of the Dukes of Coburg is situated on a commanding eminence overhanging the town. Some of the chambers are in their original condition: the rooms occupied by Luther, the bedstead he slept upon during his concealment here, and the pulpit in which he preached in the curious old Chapel, are shown. The Castle was besieged by Wallenstein in the Thirty Years' War; and he made the town of Coburg his head-quarters for some time.

KALENBERG, the subject of the third Illustration, is one of the many ducal country-houses: it is beautifully situated in a park and forest abounding with game of every description: its turreted angles, its bell-tower, and indented gables, render it a very picturesque pile. The interior is most elegantly fitted up.

155. ? 'COBURG. SCHLOSS KALENBERG,' Illustrated London News

156. ? 'LOUIS PHILIPPE INTRODUCING QUEEN VICTORIA TO THE QUEEN OF THE FRENCH,' Pictorial Times

'ARRIVAL AT TRERORT – THE ROYAL GREETING,' Pictorial Times

157. A.C.H. de Noe

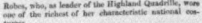

158. J. Gilbert   'Costume Ball,' Illustrated London News

Fig. 8.

159. Parl. Papers 1842

[No. 2.]

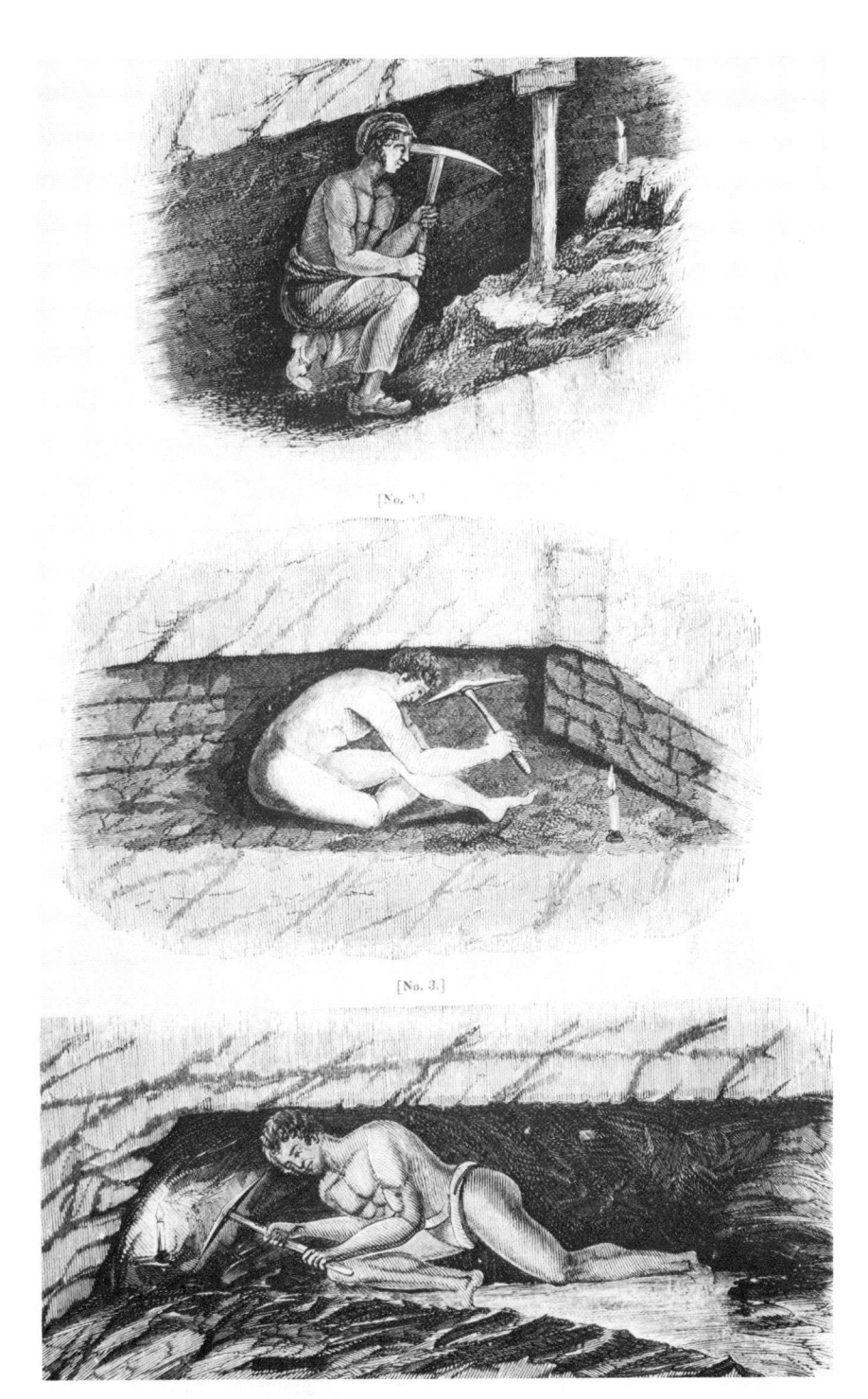

[No. 3.]

160. *Parl. Papers 1842*

161. Parl. Papers 1842

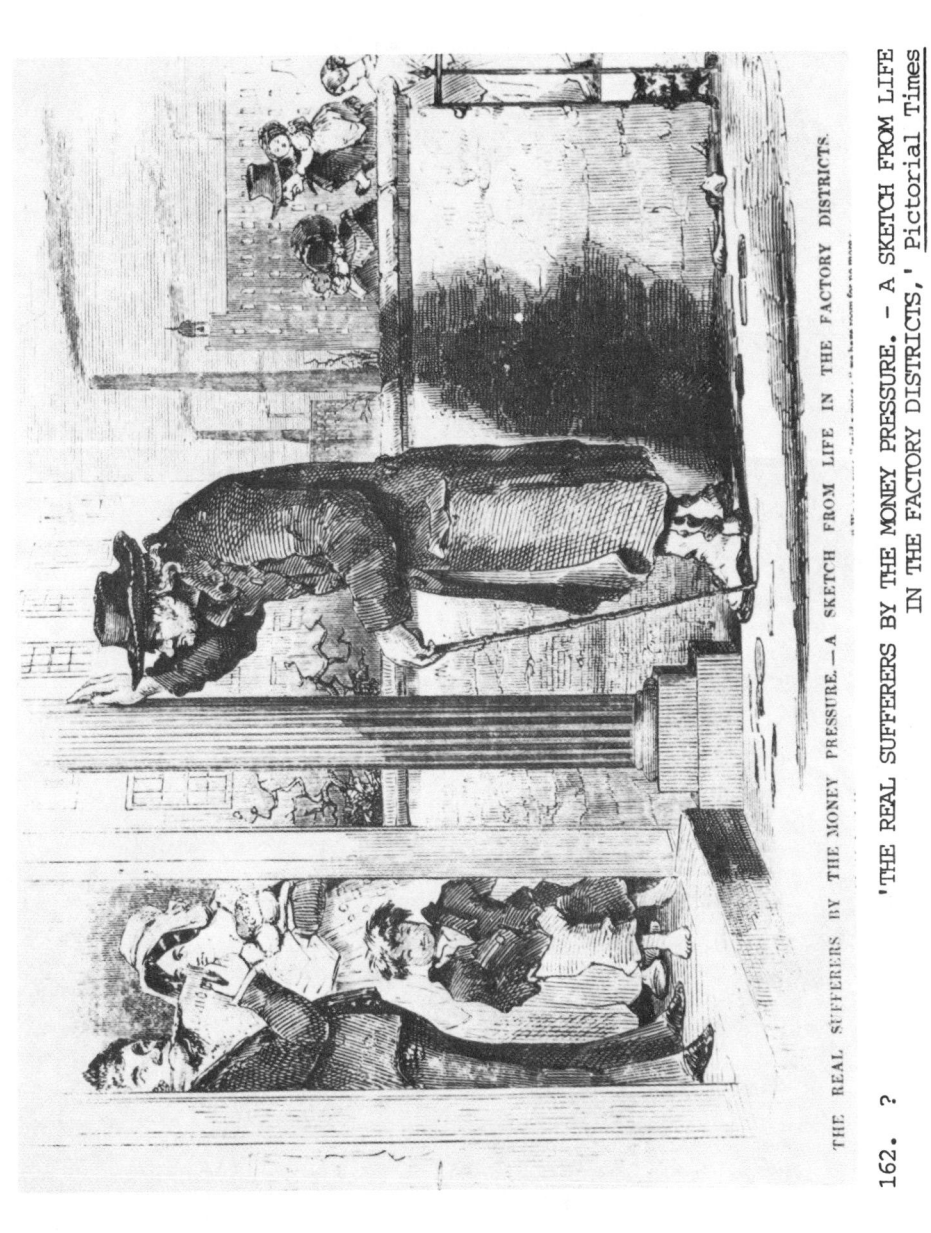

162. ? 'THE REAL SUFFERERS BY THE MONEY PRESSURE. — A SKETCH FROM LIFE IN THE FACTORY DISTRICTS,' Pictorial Times

VIEWS OF THE O'CONNELL PROPERTY IN IRELAND.

father's property in the more immediate neighbourhood of Derrynane Abbey. Before we left Waterville, Mr. O'Connell, addressing two or three persons in the crowd which were about his carriage, asked them several questions, the result of which was, the persons addressed declared that Mr. O'Connell was a good easy landlord, and had reduced their rents in the lands of Basilkaun and Inchies."

CLUVANE'S HOUSE.

Here is the Commissioner's report of the drive to Derrynane:—"At one townland (Ardeara), the wretchedness of which on my former visit had struck me, at my request we stopped and entered the cottages. This townland Mr. O'Connell holds on a lease for his own life under Mr. Bland, and sublets it as a middleman. The condition of the huts was perfectly horrible. In one of them, into which we all entered, in the presence of Mr. Maurice O'Connell, I requested your reporter to note down that a broken iron pot was the only furniture of any description in it. The cottage was full of stifling peat smoke, and a woman, clad

WATERVILLE.

Next is a fine View of Derrynane from the road. We must, however, quote "the Commissioner" in the locality:—

"I entered several of the cottages at a place called Derrynane Beg, within a mile from Derrynane. The distress of the people was horrible. There is not a pane of glass in the parish, nor a window of any kind in half the cottages. Some have got a hole in the wall for light, with a board to stop it up. In not one in a dozen is there a chair to sit upon, or anything whatever in the cottages beyond an iron pot and a rude bedstead with some straw on it; and not always that. In many of them the smoke is coming out of the doorway, for they have no chimneys. In one that I entered the fire was taken off the hinges and made a table of, by placing it on two turf-baskets. Unaided, and unguided, the poor creatures are in the lowest degree of squalid poverty have yet seen, and this within sight of Derrynane House. As one of the tenants told me 'they were eating one another's heads off, and if they did not get some assistance they would starve and the goods would be full.' Wretched as are the tenants of the Marquis of Conyngham's property in Donegal, their condition is fully equalled by the condition of the tenantry of Derrynane."

Again:—"We drove on to Derrynane Beg. We entered it by a bridle path for horses. Down this path a mountain stream was running ankle deep, and by this road we made our way, jumping from stone to stone, and sometimes compelled to wade to the much reputed Derrynane Beg. The cottages are built in clusters of two and three together —a dung-heap always beside each, over which we had generally to scramble to get into the door. We entered several of these cabins, some inhabited by tenants, and others by labourers. The general description the cabins are thatched with potato tops, with flat stones and sods piled on the thatches to mend them and keep them down; the doorways are narrow and about four feet and a half high; the windows of such cottages as had them are about eight inches by ten, without glass, and stopped up by boards; many are without any hole for a window at all; a cow, or a pig, was usually inside, and half a dozen children; the cot-

VALENTIA HOTEL.

in rags, with four or five half-naked children about her, was squatted on the mud floor near some smouldering turf. The excuse here was, that she was a pauper, and paid no rent. We entered six or seven cottages here all nearly the same; in some there was a turf-basket or two, in some a table. This constituted the only difference among them."

tages inside were almost invariably quite dark and filled with smoke, which found its way out of the doorways; and our inspection was carried on by means of lighted splints of bog timber, lighted at the turf fire on the mud floor, the dull red glare of which through the thick smoke on half-naked children, pigs, cows, filth, and mud, was such a picture as I cannot draw. This is the condition of the tenantry of Derrynane Beg."

Our Illustrations close with the exterior of Cluvane's Hut, on Mr. Hartop's property. This is but an average specimen of the Kerryman's cottage. "I have written to you," says the *Times*' Commissioner, "in former letters, much about miserable hovels in other parts of Ireland; they are more than equalled in Kerry. I have described the half-naked and potato-fed people I have met with elsewhere; here their nakedness is not less, and they know no other food. In filthiness and squalid poverty, starving on a rood of land with miles of waste land around him, which the application of knowledge and industry would make teem with plenty, the poor Kerryman exists in contented wretchedness. In a hovel like a pigstye, without chimney and without window, with but one room, an iron pot, and a rude bedstead, with some straw litter, as the only furniture, lied, or bed-clothes, the labourer, in the midst of half a dozen nearly naked children, with his barefooted wife, sits squatted on the mud floor round the peat fire. A garden plot of potatoes are their whole subsistence; and for this patch of land, and the hovel which shelters him and his family, his labour is sold to some farmer, who lets him his land for a year."

As a corroborative summary, the reporter says of the condition of the Derrynane tenantry:—

"There are no glass windows, and the people seem to be in much distress. There is no mangold-wurzel grown there. There are no green crops visible; there are no agricultural schools, nor instructors. With the exception of the free school at the Abbey, and one at Cahirciveen, I could not discover that there were any means of educating the children on the estates of Mr. O'Connell that I visited. The only plantations I saw were the trees round Derrynane. The people in general seem quite ignorant of the merest rudiments of agriculture; draining is quite neglected, and subsoiling a thing unknown. The cattle I saw were of a very bad description. To use the words of Lord Devon's report, 'the agricultural labourer on Mr. O'Connell's estate is 'badly housed, badly fed, badly clothed, and badly paid,'—and the only food of his tenantry is the potato. Their cabins are seldom a protection against the weather; a bed or a blanket is a rare luxury, and nearly in all their pig and manure-heap constitute their only property."

It it be asked how much a state of things has so long existed without being exposed, we may reply in the words of "the Commissioner:"—

"The county of Kerry, westward of Killarney. To Killarney the tide of English tourists sets in, to visit its far-famed lakes. The continual want of decencies and comforts has, at length, secured them; and but little is to be observed amongst the people there to distinguish them from the inhabitants of every other tourist's resort. There is the same eager pouncing on a stranger as a prize whom it is fair game to pluck; the same excess of civility and not a whit less of extortionate exaction. These are the excrescences which luxury and the careless spending of wealth usually create. Westward, however, of Killarney, but few visitors journey. There is no commerce, as infinitely subdivided and pauper tenantry, who (excepting a little butter, which they manufacture to pay their rents,) create nothing beyond their consumption. The planting of potatoes and the churning of butter, bounds their knowledge; the selling of a firkin of butter a-year to some Cork merchant is the extent of their intercourse with the rest of the world. Here, then, we may expect to find all the peculiarities of the Irish character strongly marked, and their habits still after their own hearts; and we do find them."

DERRYNANE ABBEY.

THE LATE FIRE IN CRIPPLEGATE.—On Thursday, *George John Ford*, a printer, was indicted for feloniously setting fire to certain premises in his occupation in Beaufort-buildings, Beech-street, Cripplegate, with intent to defraud the Imperial Insurance Company. The fire, which took place on the 7th of December, excited some interest at the time, and led to an inquiry. The Jury acquitted the prisoner; and Mr. Clarkson abandoned another indictment against him.

BRITISH MUSEUM.—This National Institution reopened yesterday, the 9th inst., having been closed some days, as usual, after the Christmas holidays. The models of the Parthenon, purchased of Mr. Lucas, were then for the first time, exhibited to the public. One of them represents that noble structure in its present ruined condition; and the other the sculptor's idea of its appearance in the days of its pristine splendour. Models of this description have long been wanting in the collection to illustrate the position those marchless prints, known as the Elgin Marbles, occupied in their original glorious resting-place. The indent of the casual or uninformed spectator in these wonderful works of art will be greatly increased by the admirable keys thus afforded him; which are of no contemptible size, being 12ft. by 6. In our next week's Number, we shall engrave this classical restoration.

PROMOTION FROM THE RANKS AND REWARDS FOR GOOD SERVICE.—A warrant has been promulgated by command of her Majesty, for the purpose of affording "a greater encouragement to the non-commissioned officers and soldiers of the army who may have distinguished themselves, or who may have given good, faithful, and efficient service." It is dated Windsor, Dec. 18, and is imprinted in 44 articles; by the first of which it is provided that whenever her Majesty shall see fit the grant of a commission without purchase to a non-commissioned officer, selected and recommended for this distinction by the Commander-in-chief, there shall be granted to such officer, in aid of an outfit as a commissioned officer, a sum of £100 if appointed to a cavalry regiment, and £100 if to an infantry regiment. Subsequent articles provide that a sum not exceeding £2,000 per annum is distributed in annuities of not above £20 each, to sergeants who may be thus completed for meritorious conduct, on the recommendation of the Commander-in-chief.—Under the denomination of " good conduct pay," a progressive increase of one penny per day, to to sixpence, and certain honourable distinctions, are also appointed to be given, under specified regulations, to soldiers who shall have completed ten, fifteen, twenty, twenty-five, or thirty years of actual service.—The remaining articles are occupied in detailing the regulations under which these gratuities, good conduct pay, &c., shall be forfeited or restored.

163. ? 'VIEWS OF THE O'CONNELL PROPERTY IN IRELAND,'
Illustrated London News

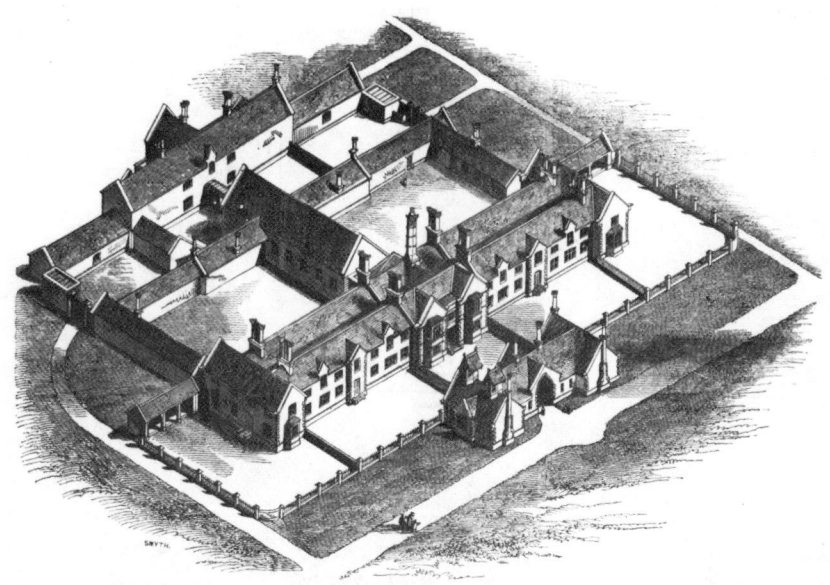

THE UNION WORKHOUSE TO BE ERECTED AT CANTERBURY.

plans to a purpose for which they were never intended, was not, it may be supposed, overmuch startled when Cobbett denounced the new buildings as "Bastiles."

Mr. P. Lewis, one of the Commissioners, when a member of the House of Commons, asserted that the statute of Elizabeth meant "to inflict compulsory labour by way of punishment, not to afford labour for the mere purpose of maintenance." The man who put such an odious interpretation on that Act, who regarded poverty as a crime, was not likely to approve of plans for Workhouses which did not bear all the external appearances of Bastiles.

The Andover Union Workhouse is constructed after the design which we have copied from the second Annual Report of the Commissioners. It was erected under the immediate superintendence of the Commissioners' own architect, and, when completed, was estimated to be capable of accommodating a greater number of inmates by one-third than the medical attendant ventured to recommend the Guardians to admit into it. It will be perceived that there are only four yards: these yards mark the number of classes into which the inmates are to be formed. The space allotted to each boy or girl in the dormitories was 77 cubic feet, and it was proposed by the Commissioners that the beds should be arranged in tiers, like berths in a ship. The Chapel and Dining Hall was the only day-room for the women, young and old; and there was only one day-room for the boys and girls, which was intended to be Day-Room, School-Room, and Dining-Room. The Guardians soon discovered that the space allotted to each inmate was insufficient, and, having dispensed with the services of the Commissioners' architect, they erected new School-Rooms for the boys and girls, and provided new wards for the sick by the addition of another story to one part of the building. The windows in the front of the building are thrown a slanting glance at the sky! The windows in the front of the building are thrown to the inmates a view of all external objects, excepting a slanting glance at the sky! The windows in the front of the building are those of the Guardians' Board-Room and Porter's Offices, and must not be confounded with the prison-like windows of the poor inmates' wards.

The work to which the male inmates were set was "compulsory labour by way of punishment." They were employed to pound bones charged with animal matter, the effluvium from which is described as having been intolerable. This kind of labour was very generally resorted to in the Workhouses in that part of England. Mr. Parker, the Ex-Assistant Commissioner, not only constantly verbally objected to it, but, in several instances, stated his objections in writing, whilst Mr. Chadwick wrote an unanswerable paper recommending its discontinuance. Mr. George Lewis, who succeeded his father as Commissioner, paid as little heed to the one as to the other until public opinion declared itself, and was about to hurl destruction on the supporters of this bone-crushing; then, and not till then, did he and his colleagues forbid this description of labour. Having been called to account for their tardiness in forbidding the poor to be employed at such disgusting and unhealthy work, the Commissioners endeavoured to shift the responsibility on their subordinate, who repelled the accusation, and brought home the delinquency to the Commissioners themselves.

The Ex-Assistant Commissioner offended the triumvirate on the subject of Workhouses. He objected to the prison-like appearance of the Commissioners' plans, and designed four or five Workhouse plans, which possess some claims to architectural taste. We have taken one of his designs by way of contrast to that of the Commissioners. It is an isometrical view of the Workhouse which is about to be erected at Canterbury. A building after the same design is erected at Aylesbury, and, with the exception of the range of buildings at the back and the group in front, which are not yet erected, one also at Rye, in Sussex.

It would appear that Mr. Parker did not propose to "test" within four walls the youthful and the aged poor; instead of walls their playgrounds and airing-yards are enclosed by an open fence. At Aylesbury, the aged inmates have converted their airing-yard into a pleasant garden, where they may be seen tending shrubs and flowers with as much care as they would bestow on the culture of similar plants in their cottage gardens. At either end of the main building are colonnades where

the children can take recreation in wet weather. The windows throughout the building are arranged in such a manner as to enable the inmates to enjoy the prospect from them. From the windows of the Aylesbury Workhouse there is a delightful view of the Chiltern Hills, and from the Rye Workhouse the coast of France is discernible in a clear day.

The range of buildings at the back is the Infirmary. It contains spacious dormitories and wards for various diseases, which require separate treatment. It is also provided with a surgery, nurses' rooms, and baths. The group of buildings in front is the Guardians' Offices and the Porter's Lodge.

The yards at the back of the main building, separated by the Chapel, are appropriated to the able-bodied male and female inmates. The sitting-room of the Master and Matron commands these yards.

The Schoolmaster and Matron, from their respective oriel windows in the wings of the principal building, view their pupils in the hours of recreation. The nurses, in like manner, can see the sick patients in the garden where the infirmary patients take air and exercise, whilst the porter and his wife can overlook the aged people.

The Kitchen department is at the distant end of the Chapel. The cooking is conducted by means of a steam apparatus, which not only performs all the duties required of a steam-kitchen, but also boils the linen in the wash-house, and supplies hot water to the washing-tubs in the laundry, and baths in the Infirmary and receiving wards.

The Chapel is a handsome hall 58 feet by 23 feet. The roof is included in the area of the section, and its timbers are so arranged as to give the hall the appearance of a place of worship. The service in a Workhouse is in the nature of domestic prayer, and therefore the Chapel is not inappropriately the Dining Hall as well as the hall where the family assemble for their orisons.

The Turret in the centre of the principal building is a shaft, which, by a simple contrivance that has received the approbation of Dr. Arnott, efficiently ventilates the day rooms and dormitories. The necessity for ventilation in such establishments as Workhouses is too obvious to require remark. The means which have been employed to effect this desideratum in public buildings have generally been so imperfect as to make it doubtful whether the prospect of fever and the ills of an unwholesome atmosphere were not equivalent to the chance of colds, catarrhs, and other ailments, which are brought about by exposure to currents of chilling air. According to Mr. Parker's system, the apartments are heated by hot water, and the warmth evolved by it attracts fresh air, which, tempered by contact with the heated water-pipes, flows into the apartments in small jets, whilst the vitiated air escapes through the ventilators, and passes off through the central shaft. The Commissioners, in their plans, deemed 150 cubic feet sufficient space for a full grown person, and 77 for a child. Mr. Parker, with efficient ventilation, assigns to each adult in health 266 cubic feet, being the average volume of air drawn into the lungs of a full grown man in twenty-four hours, and in sickness 300; whilst to each child he allows 160 cubic feet.

The bitter feeling which the Commissioners evinced before the Andover Committee on the subject of Workhouse Plans was remarkable; they insinuated that Mr. Parker had no authority to visit the Aylesbury Union for the purpose of introducing his improved plans. Dysentery, diarrhœa, and fever, had made sad havoc there, amongst the inmates of the old Workhouse; yet, with the knowledge that such diseases were endemic, they insinuated that he committed an official irregularity in going there to remedy the evil. In conveying this insinuation they violently objected to the production of notes marked "private," as if they expected Mr. Parker to sit quietly under an insinuation, and keep his defence in his pocket. The production of a note marked "private," overturned the much-abused doctrine of confidentiality and the tables on these high public functionaries.

Under the administration of the present Poor-Law Commissioners, the Poor-Law expenditure has increased about one million in the last eight years. In 1837, says the *Edinburgh Review*, it was four millions; in 1845 it was five millions. In 1843, one-tenth of the population was in a state of pauperism; whilst in 1844, say the Commissioners in their Eleventh Annual Report, the number of persons relieved may be taken at nearly one-eighth part of the population.

The *Westminster Review*, which has taken alarm at this state of things, says:—"There is to us a solemnity in this announcement like that of a funeral knell—the knell of a nation. One-eighth part of the population of England and Wales paupers in a year of railroad activity, and with wheat at 51s. and 5d."

The Commissioners' days are numbered, and, in the meantime, public opinion forbids the erection of "Bastiles."

THE ANDOVER UNION WORKHOUSE.

London: Printed and Published at the Office, 198, Strand, in the Parish of St. Clement Danes, in the County of Middlesex, by WILLIAM LITTLE, 198, Strand, aforesaid.—SATURDAY, NOVEMBER 7, 1846.

164. ? 'THE UNION WORKHOUSE TO BE ERECTED AT CANTERBURY. THE ANDOVER UNION WORKHOUSE,' Illustrated London News

165. ? 'POOR LAW DIVORCE,' Pictorial Times

TRANSPORTATION OF THE CASUAL POOR.—THE HALT, THE LAME, THE BLIND, IN SEARCH OF A SUBURBAN FAMISH HOUSE
(Punishment of the Travelling Pauper.)

166. ? 'TRANSPORTATION OF THE CASUAL POOR,' *Pictorial Times*

POOR LAW IMPRISONMENT.—THE UNION WINDOWS ALWAYS LOOKING INWARDS, COUNTRY PROSPECTS ARE EXCHANGED FOR EXPANSIVE VIEWS OF THE WALL.

167. ? 'POOR LAW IMPRISONMENT,' Pictorial Times

168. 'POOR LAW EXERCISE,' Pictorial Times ?

169. W.G. Mason 'FIELD-LANE LODGING-HOUSE,' Poor Man's Guardian

ENON CHAPEL CEMETERY AND DANCING SALOON.

170. Mason 'ENON CHAPEL CEMETERY AND DANCING SALOON,' Poor Man's Guardian

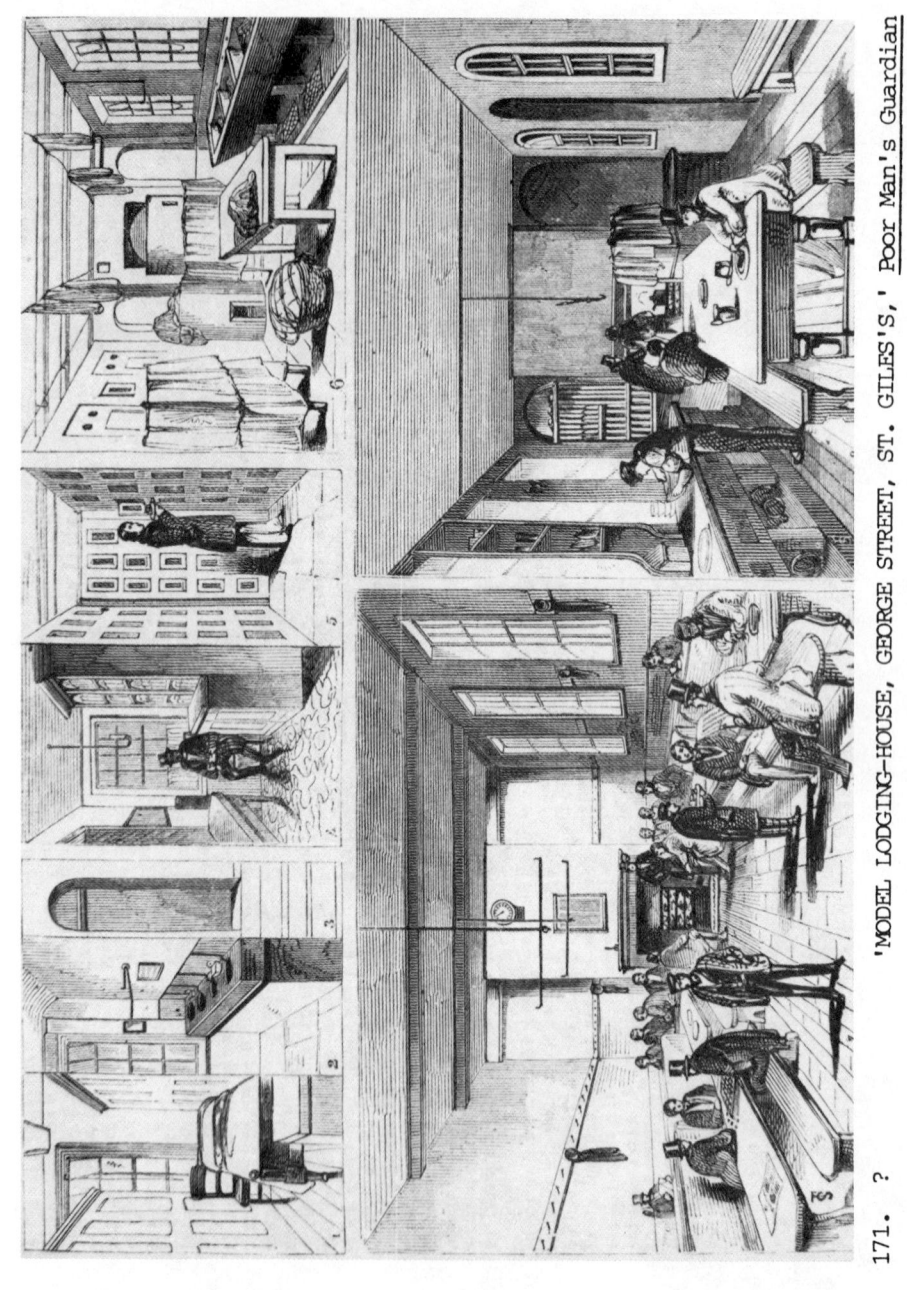

171. ? 'MODEL LODGING-HOUSE, GEORGE STREET, ST. GILES'S,' Poor Man's Guardian

172. Mason 'SOUP KITCHEN IN LEICESTER SQUARE,'
Poor Man's Guardian

VISIT OF HIS ROYAL HIGHNESS PRINCE ALBERT TO THE SOUP KITCHEN, LEICESTER-SQUARE.

173. ? 'VISIT OF HIS ROYAL HIGHNESS PRINCE ALBERT TO THE SOUP KITCHEN, LEICESTER SQUARE,' Illustrated London News

174. ? 'CONDITION OF THE POOR,' Pictorial Times

175. 'LONDON IN 1842,' (Northern prospect), *Illustrated London News*

176. 'ST. PANCRAS' BATHS AND WASHHOUSES,'
Illustrated London News

177. ? 'THE PHILANTHROPIC SOCIETY'S FARM, AT RED HILL,' Illustrated London News

FIG. 3.—PARADISE-ROW, AGAR-TOWN.

178. ? 'THE HOUSES OF THE LONDON POOR,' Builder

DUKE-STREET, SOUTHWARK.

MINT-STREET, LOOKING TOWARDS HIGH-STREET.

AT THE BACK OF EWER-STREET, GRAVEL-LANE.

179. ?   'SOUTHWARK,' Builder

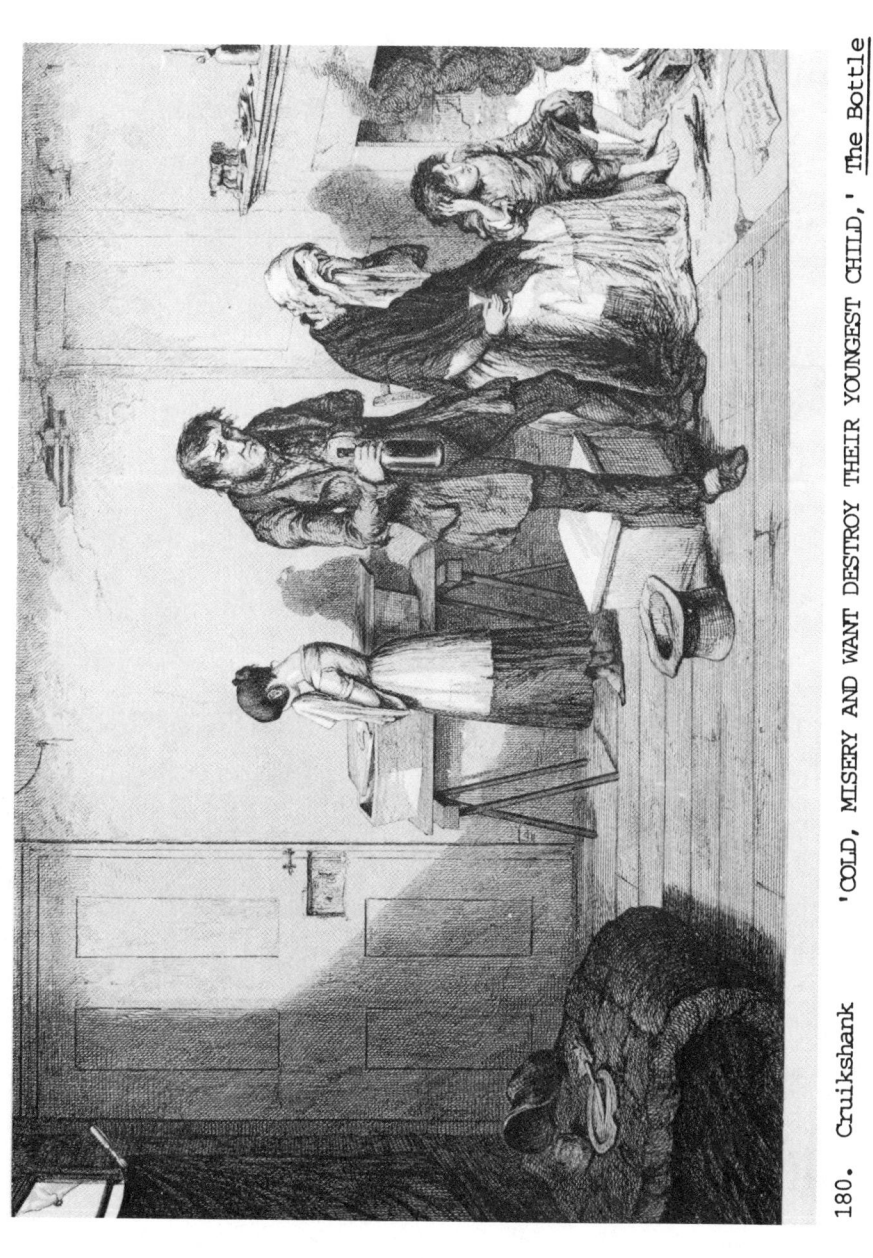

180. Cruikshank 'COLD, MISERY AND WANT DESTROY THEIR YOUNGEST CHILD,' The Bottle

181. Cruikshank 'FEARFUL QUARRELS AND BRUTAL VIOLENCE ARE THE NATURAL CONSEQUENCES OF THE FREQUENT USE OF THE BOTTLE,' The Bottle

182. Cruikshank 'NEGLECTED BY THEIR PARENTS, EDUCATED ONLY IN THE STREETS AND FALLING INTO THE HANDS OF WRETCHES WHO LIVE UPON THE VICES OF OTHERS THEY ARE LED TO THE GIN-SHOP TO DRINK AT THAT FOUNTAIN WHICH NOURISHES EVERY SPECIMEN OF CRIME,' The Drunkard's Children

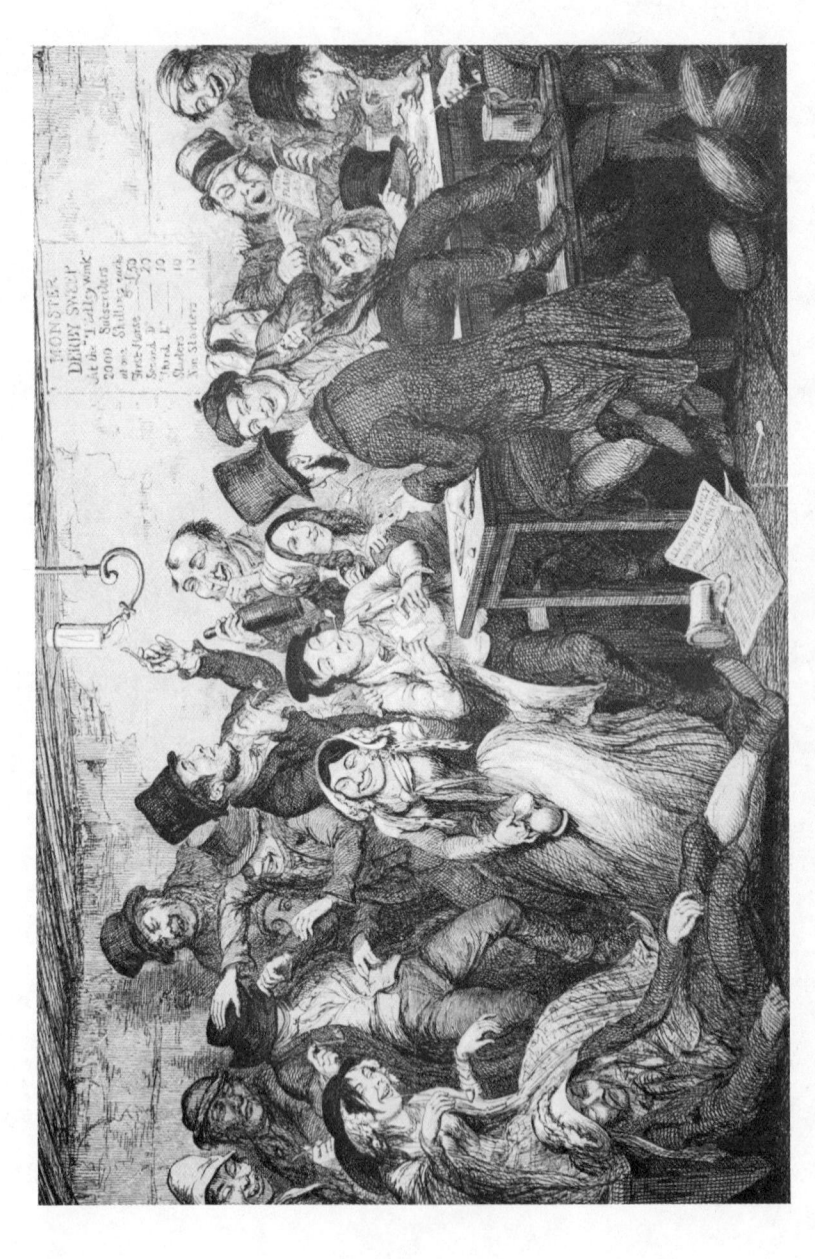

183. Cruikshank 'BETWEEN THE FINE FLARING GIN PALACE AND THE LOW DIRTY BEER SHOP, THE BOY THIEF SQUANDERS AND GAMBLES AWAY HIS ILL-GOTTEN GAINS,'
The Drunkard's Children

184. Cruikshank 'THE MANIAC FATHER AND CONVICT BROTHER ARE GONE. – THE POOR GIRL, HOMELESS, FRIENDLESS, DESERTED AND GIN-MAD, COMMITS SELF-MURDER,' The Drunkard's Children

SCENES IN THE HISTORY OF A RAGGED BOY.—No. II.—THE FIRST THEFT.

185. ? 'THE FIRST THEFT,' Ragged School Union Magazine

SCENES IN THE HISTORY OF A RAGGED BOY.—No. V.—LIFE IN THE BUSH.

'LIFE IN THE BUSH,' Ragged School Union Magazine

SCENES IN THE HISTORY OF A RAGGED BOY.—No. VI.—THE HOME IN AUSTRALIA.

187. ? 'THE HOME IN AUSTRALIA,' Ragged School Union Magazine

188. G. Measom 'INTERIOR OF A GIN PALACE,' True Briton

No. II.—THE HOME OF THE DRUNKARD.

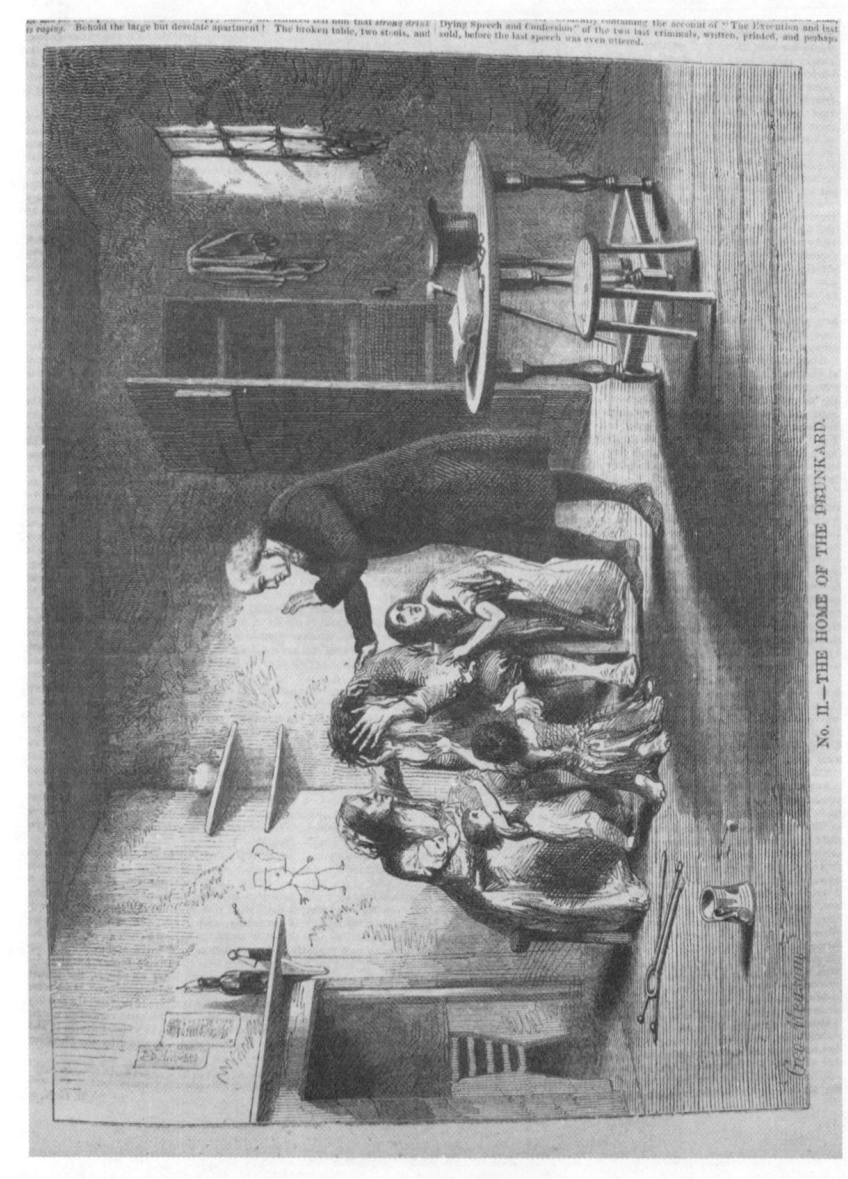

189. Meason 'THE HOME OF THE DRUNKARD,' *True Briton*

190. Meason 'THE DEATH-BED OF THE HOLY,' True Briton

THE SCENE AT NEW CROSS.

THE DISTURBANCES IN THE MANUFACTURING DISTRICTS.

A supplement to the *London Gazette* of Friday last, offering a reward of fifty pounds for the authors, abettors, or perpetrators of the outrages at Manchester, was published on Saturday.

DEPARTURE OF TROOPS FOR THE MANUFACTURING DISTRICTS.

Throughout Saturday the greatest bustle and activity was displayed at the Home Office, at the Horse Guards, &c., in consequence of the arrival at the former place of an express from Manchester as early as seven o'clock, which, from its important nature, was immediately forwarded to the residence of Sir James Graham, who shortly after, with Mr. Manners Sutton, the under-secretary was in attendance at the Home Office. About nine o'clock three of the magistrates of Manchester, who had left that town late on Friday night, and had come express to London for the purpose of laying before her Majesty's Government the latest information as to the state of the disturbed districts, and to impress upon them the necessity of the most energetic measures being immediately adopted for the suppression of the disturbances, were admitted to an interview with Sir J. Graham, which was of considerable length. Whatever was the extent of the communication made by the deputation to the right hon. baronet has not been permitted to transpire, but their importance may be conjectured from the fact, that summonses were immediately afterwards issued for holding a Cabinet Council at the Foreign Office, in Downing-street, at twelve o'clock, which was attended by Sir Robert Peel, and the whole of the Cabinet ministers in town. Previous to the assembling of the Council, Sir Robert Peel visited Sir James Graham at the Home Office, and in the course of the morning two gentlemen, forming a deputation from Macclesfield, had an interview with the right hon. secretary. Immediately after the conclusion of the deliberations of the Cabinet Council, which occupied upwards of two hours, orders were forwarded from the Horse Guards to Woolwich, for a party of the Royal Artillery to hold themselves in instant readiness to depart for Manchester; and a similar order was despatched to St. George's Barracks, Charing-cross, for the departure of the third battalion of the Grenadier Guards, stationed at that barracks, for the same destination, *viâ* the London and Birmingham Railway.

The fact that troops had been ordered off to the disturbed districts soon became publicly known both at Woolwich and in the metropolis, and produced an intense feeling of alarm and excitement in the minds of individuals generally. Large crowds of persons shortly began to assemble in the neighbourhood of the barracks at Charing-cross, for the purpose of witnessing the departure of the troops, who congregated themselves together in detached groups, and appeared to be canvassing the objects and views of the "turn-outs," and the probable ultimate result of their proceeding. About six o'clock a detachment of 150 of the Royal Artillery left Woolwich, having in charge four heavy pieces of ordnance, each drawn by four horses, and accompanied by numerous waggons, containing ammunition, baggage, stores, and accoutrements, under the command of Lieutenant-Colonel Smith, and proceeded to the terminus of the London and Birmingham Railway. At eight the third battalion of the Grenadier Guards marched out of St. George's Barracks, numbering between six and seven hundred strong, under the command of Colonel Sir Ord Honeyman, Bart., headed by the band playing, through the front gates in Trafalgar-square, and proceeded along Pall-mall East, Pall-mall, and Regent-street, into the New-road, on their way to Euston-square. They were followed by a large crowd of persons, which continued during their progress to increase, by accumulations of working men and boys, until their arrival at the railway station. By the time they reached the Quadrant, murmurs of groans and hisses burst from the crowd, which continued to increase as they advanced up Regent-street, mingled with exclamations of "Remember, you are brothers." About the middle of Regent-street, the crowd pressing closely on the band, the officer in command directed the band to strike playing, and at the same time ordered the soldiers to "fix bayonets," which order was immediately obeyed. This, however, did not silence the groans and hisses, which were uttered by the crowd until the battalion reached the terminus.

one or more quarters of the town. At 7 o'clock this morning, upwards of one hundred respectable inhabitants were sworn in as special constables. Although the apprehended attack on the carts coming with supplies to market did not take place, the markets and shambles have been very scantily supplied. At 8 o'clock information was early received of the Town-hall, that a large mob had gone to turn out the hands at the engine manufactory of the Leeds Railway. On receipt of this intelligence, a large body of police and special constables were despatched, who succeeded in preventing any further outrage, although the hands did not return to work. About noon a strong force of mounted police, with one hundred police constables on foot, and about an equal number of special constables, were despatched to Little Ireland, in the township of Chorlton-on-Medlock, where they succeeded in dispersing a large crowd, and seizing large accumulations of stones and brickbats. No less than ten cart loads were removed under the protection of this body, who entered many houses, where they found large accumulated loads. The police were attacked with showers of stones, and amongst others, Superintendent Sawley was severely injured by a blow from a brickbat. At this time, and until four o'clock, the Town-hall was under the protection of the special constables, of whom there were large bodies, numbers arriving constantly to be sworn in. The Riot Act was read at an early period of the day by D. Maude, Esq. It was subsequently read at other parts of the town, and the following notice, in large letters, was extensively posted:—"Public Notice.—The Riot Act has been read, and all persons are desired to go peaceably to their respective homes, on pain of being apprehended and punished as rioters and disturbers of the public peace. William Neild, Mayor. Town Hall, August 10, 1812." At this hour the streets were being secured by large detachments of foot and horse police in every direction. About noon a messenger arrived at the Town-hall, by an express train from Preston, from the magistrates, requesting military aid. Expectations of a general turn-out were entertained as early as Thursday, on account of which many special constables were sworn in, and the sergeants of militia, as well as the pensioners, were called to active service, and took up their quarters at the prison. It was understood at the Town-hall, that three troops of the Lancashire Yeomanry had been called out for active service. Three persons have been killed; and although this town is but a poor condition to spare any troops, 150 Rifles have been sent down by the three o'clock train. This morning none of the mills, except those of Messrs. Birley, in Oxford-street, and Messrs. Kennedy, in the same street, have commenced work. The suburbs of the town have been crowded with gangs of marauders, on the pretence of seeking alms. About noon a very daring and riotous attack was made on a mill at Quarry-bank, near Willaslow, belonging to Mr. Greg, the late member for Manchester, by about 500 men; who,

DEPARTURE OF TROOPS BY THE LONDON AND BIRMINGHAM RAILWAY.

LONDON AND BIRMINGHAM RAILWAY, SUNDAY.—This morning, as early as 9 o'clock, another troop of Royal Horse Artillery arrived at Woolwich at the Euston Station of the London and Birmingham Railway, with three field-pieces and ammunition. About 4 o'clock, the Quartermaster of the 34th Foot, from Portsmouth, attended by an orderly, arrived, and ordered refreshment to be procured from the various public-houses for that regiment, which was *en route* by the South Western Railway from Portsmouth. The greatest excitement at this time prevailed, the Quartermaster being obliged to be escorted from the various public-houses by the police. In an hour after, two waggons, laden with ammunition and guarded by several soldiers of the 34th, came up, and was shortly after followed by the regiment, under the command of Colonel Airey, consisting of 600 men. On their arrival they were greeted with much discordant yelling by the mob, and it was as much as the police could do to prevent them from forcing an entry into the railway yard.

MANCHESTER, SATURDAY EVENING.

Captain Sleigh, the active assistant-commissioner of police, was on duty all last night, and in constant hourly communication with Colonel Wemyss, as from information obtained from authentic quarters, it was feared that incendiary attempts would be made upon

MANCHESTER OPERATIVE.

CHARTIST EXCITEMENT.—THE POLICE FORCE IN BONNER'S-FIELDS, ON MONDAY LAST.

192. ? 'CHARTIST EXCITEMENT. – THE POLICE FORCE IN BONNER'S FIELDS, ON MONDAY LAST,' *Illustrated London News*

'OUR TROOPS RECOVERING THEIR CANNON,' Illustrated London News

193. ?

THE POLISH INSURRECTION.

POLISH VOLUNTEER.—(FROM A PAINTING IN THE POSSESSION OF THE LITERARY ASSOCIATION OF THE FRIENDS OF POLAND.)

"And Freedom shriek'd when Kosciusko fell."—CAMPBELL.

Eternal Pow'r! whose Word Divine,
   Hath said "that where thy Spirit dwells
There also Freedom builds her shrine!"
   And there the human bosom swells
With thoughts above the sordid earth,
   With aspirations raised to THEE,
Till rapt with love of deathless worth,
   Man becomes what he ought to be.
Wilt Thou at last dash down the chain
   Close riveted to Poland's neck?
Wilt Thou at last destroy the reign
   Of ruthless tyranny, and check
The Calmuc vulture's shriek for blood,
   The bloood of beauty and the brave,
Who for the Christian cause oft stood,
   Or, falling, found a glorious grave?
'Twere blasphemy to doubt Thou art
Where Freedom fires the human heart!

Who thunders at Vienna's gate?
   Why skulks the Hun behind his walls?

Why not come forth and brave her fate
   Which never valiant heart appals?
The Austrian cowers before the Turk—
   The Cross before the Crescent flies;
The scimitar hews out its work,
   Amidst a Nation's agonies!
On!—on!—the thundering Spahis come,
   Like wolf-packs o'er the snow-clad plain;
And Europe shudders at her doom,
   And quail the crests of France and Spain.
Where are the Champions of the Cross?—
   Have they forgotten Ascalon?
Why rush not to retrieve the loss,
   And prop pale Austria's tottering Throne?
No! none come forward in that hour
   Of mortal peril, save One Pow'r.
Brave Poland's spear is gleaming high—
   Her pennons float the frowning sky;
John Sobieski comes—his swords
   Scatter like chaff, the Moslem hordes.
The Austrian breathes—his throne is saved—
   Dictates the peace he lately craved;

POLISH INSURGENTS.

195. H. Valentin   'SKETCHES FROM THE BARRICADES. BARRICADE ON THE BOULEVARD MONIMARTE,' Illustrated London News

BEHIND THE BARRICADE.—DRAWN BY GAVARNI.

196. Gavarni 'BEHIND THE BARRICADE,' Illustrated London News

SKETCHES FROM THE FRENCH REVOLUTION.—BY GAVARNI.

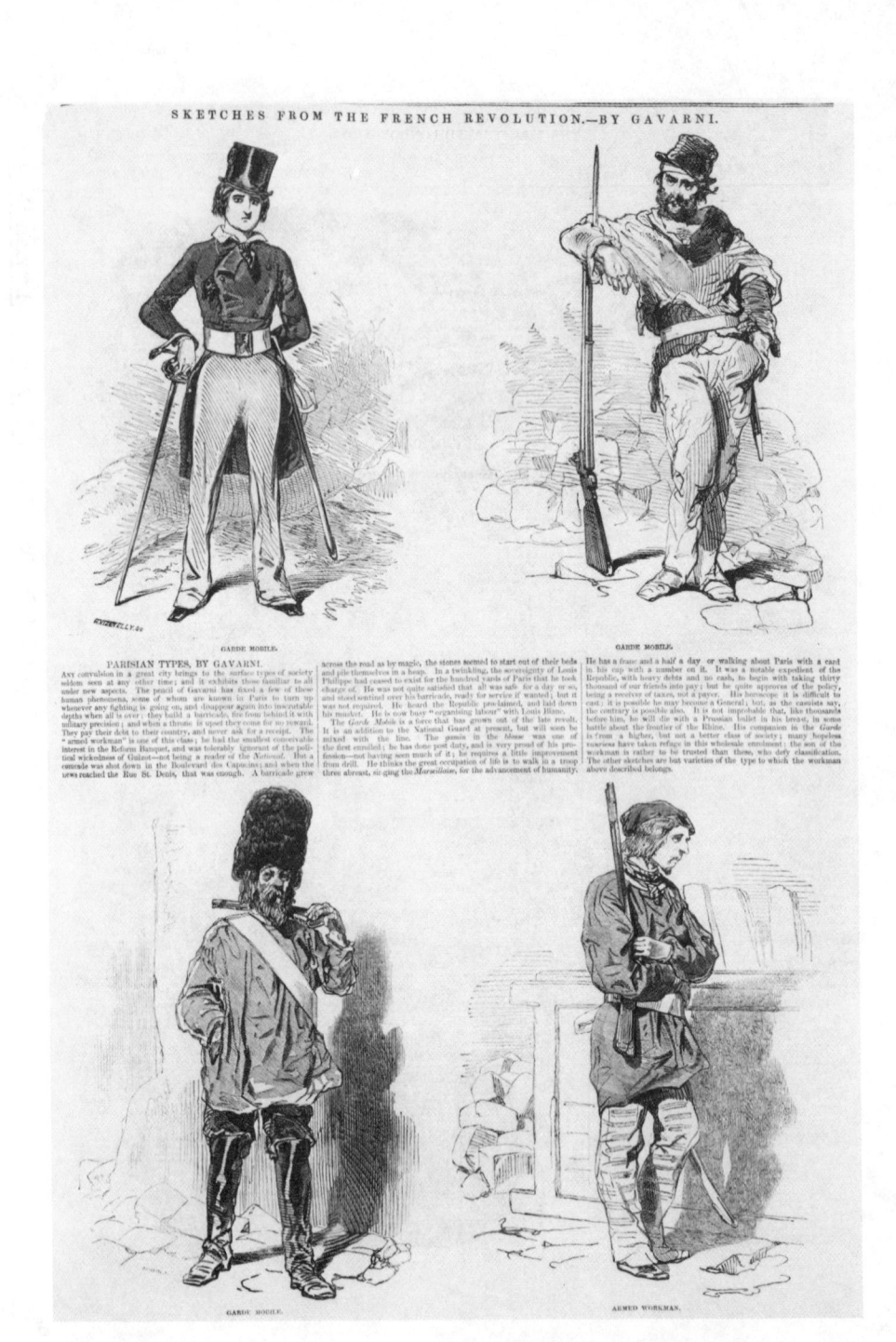

GARDE MOBILE.

GARDE MOBILE.

PARISIAN TYPES, BY GAVARNI.

Any convulsion in a great city brings to the surface types of society seldom seen at any other time; and it exhibits those familiar to all under new aspects. The pencil of Gavarni has fixed a few of these human phenomena, some of whom are known in Paris to turn up whenever any fighting is going on, and disappear again into inscrutable depths when all is over; they build a barricade, fire from behind it with unitary precision; and when a throne is upset they come for no reward. They pay their debt to their country, and never ask for a receipt. The "armed workman" is one of this class; he had the smallest conceivable interest in the Reform Banquet, and was tolerably ignorant of the political wickedness of Guizot—not being a reader of the *National*. But a comrade was shot down in the Boulevard des Capucines; and when the news reached the Rue St. Denis, that was enough. A barricade grew across the road as by magic, the stones seemed to start out of their beds and pile themselves in a heap. In a twinkling, the sovereignty of Louis Philippe had ceased to exist for the hundred yards of Paris that he took charge of. He was not quite satisfied that all was safe for a day or so, and stood sentinel over his barricade, ready for service if wanted; but it was not required. He heard the Republic proclaimed, and laid down his musket. He is now busy "organising labour" with Louis Blanc.

The *Garde Mobile* is a force that has grown out of the late result. It is an addition to the National Guard at present, but will soon be mixed with the line. The gamin in the blouse was one of the first enrolled; he has done post duty, and is very proud of his fusion—not having seen much of it; he requires a little improvement from drill. He thinks the great occupation of life is to walk in a troop three abreast, singing the *Marseillaise*, for the advancement of humanity.

He has a franc and a half a day or walking about Paris with a card in his cap with a number on it. It was a notable expedient of the Republic, with heavy debts and no cash, to begin with taking thirty thousand of our friends into pay; but he quite approves of the policy, being a receiver of taxes, not a payer. His horoscope it is difficult to cast: it is possible he may become a General, but, as the casuists say, the contrary is possible also. It is not improbable that, like thousands before him, he will die with a Prussian bullet in his breast, in some battle about the frontier of the Rhine. His companion in the *Garde* is from a higher, but not a better class of society; many hopeless uneasiness have taken refuge in this wholesale enrolment; the son of the workman is rather to be trusted than those, who defy classification. The other sketches are but varieties of the type to which the workman above described belongs.

GARDE MOBILE.

ARMED WORKMAN.

197. Gavarni — 'SKETCHES FROM THE FRENCH REVOLUTION,' *Illustrated London News*

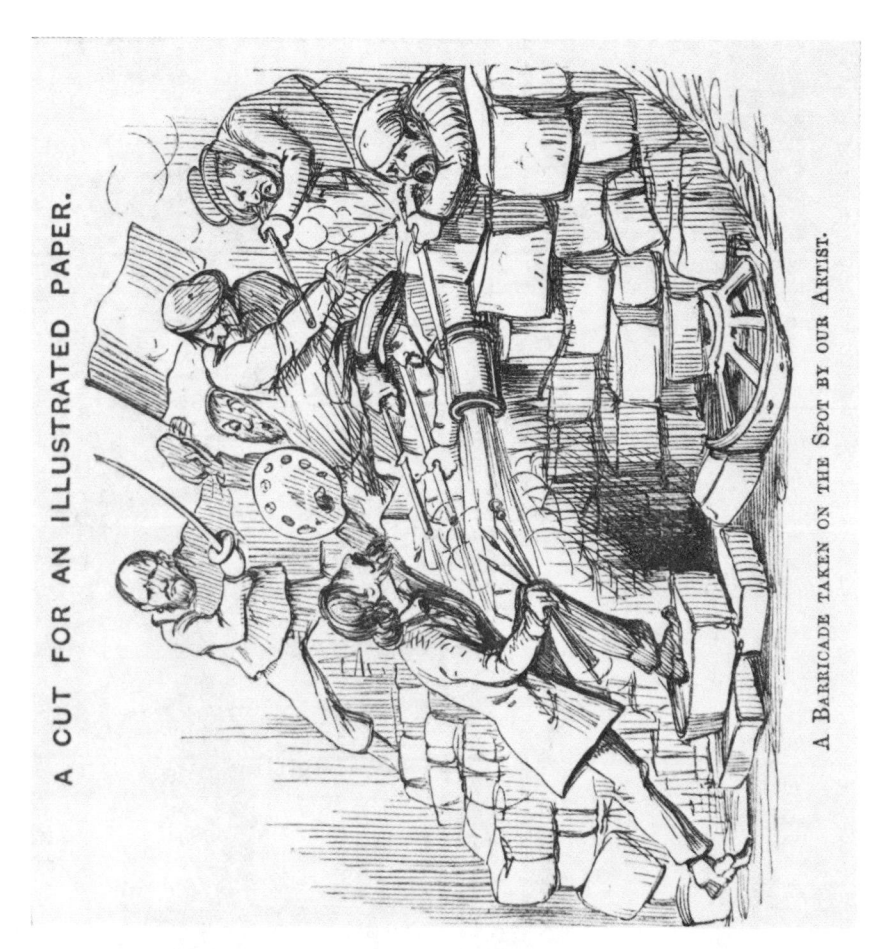

198. ? 'A CUT FOR AN ILLUSTRATED PAPER,' Punch

199. ? 'PATENT VERTICAL PRINTING MACHINE, IN THE GREAT EXHIBITION,' Illustrated London News